*Third Edition*

# TECHNICAL ASPECTS OF DATA COMMUNICATION

*John E. McNamara*

DIGITAL PRESS

9 8 7 6 5 4 3 2 1

Order number EY-8262E-DP

Printed in the United States of America.

Designed by David Ford. Production coordinated by Editorial Inc. Automatically typeset by DEKR Corporation.

AT&T and Dataphone are trademarks and Touch-Tone is a registered trademark of American Telephone and Telegraph Company.
Bell is a trademark of the Bell telephone companies.
PDP-8 and DDCMP are trademarks of Digital Equipment Corporation.
Smartmodem 1200 and Smartmodem 2400 are trademarks of Hayes Microcomputer Products, Inc.
IBM is a registered trademark of International Business Machines Corporation.
VADIC is a trademark of Racal-Vadic.
Teletype is a trademark of Teletype Corporation.
Zilog is a trademark of Zilog, Inc.

**Library of Congress Cataloging-in-Publication Data**

McNamara, John E.
　Technical aspects of data communication

　Includes index.
　1. Data transmission systems.　　I. Title.
TK5105.M33 1988　　　629.398'1　　88-3838
ISBN 1-55558-007-6

# Preface

This book is intended for those who are about to design a data communication system, are about to purchase or program data communication hardware, or are just interested in knowing more about data communication. It is intended to fit between the books that treat data communication solely on a system level, without reference to hardware and transmission features and problems, and those hardware manuals which specify in detail the function of each bit in each register. It presumes some technical inclination on the part of the reader, since some block diagrams are shown. It also presumes some software background, as some registers with bit functional assignments are also shown. However, all such material is presented only as an example of how some manufacturers have approached the problems being discussed. The reader need not accept those particular solutions, but he or she will be given the background necessary to know what to look for in various hardware and software systems that are used in data communication. Specific computer hardware offerings are not described because they change rapidly.

In the same fashion as the first two editions, this edition begins with a discussion of a simple asynchronous interface implemented with a specialized integrated circuit called a UART. The next chapters connect this device to communication lines and discuss interface standards ranging from the classic EIA-232-D to the just-announced EIA-530. Elsewhere in the book, modems and modem control are discussed, with new material on modern high-speed modems and error-correcting modems. In addition to the material on error-correcting modems, a chapter on error detection includes detailed information on hardware and software methods. The operation of an error detection system is often coupled with the operation of a communication protocol, so several chapters are devoted to protocols, including new material on the ISO layered model of protocols and an introduction to the Kermit file transfer protocol. Near the end of the book, digital transmission systems (such as T1 carrier) are discussed, and a new chapter gives an introduction to the Integrated Services Digital Network (ISDN). Finally, a revised chapter on local area networks (LANs) shows how data communication is the key to information and resources sharing in modern networks of personal computers and work stations.

Despite all the material just listed, this book will not teach anyone everything about data communication. Knowledge of data communication is acquired by a bootstrapping process in which one learns enough to read the next book or explore the next problem, from which one learns enough to go on further. This book is intended to fill a place in that process.

# Acknowledgments

The production of a book is the result of a great deal of work by a great many people. It is impossible to thank all of the people I should, but I would like to make an attempt, and apologize in advance to anyone I have overlooked.

The personnel of Digital Press, coordinated by Mike Meehan and Chase Duffy, and assisted by Beth French, have been extremely helpful. Much of the production work was done by Editorial Inc under the capable supervision of Jonathan Weinert. Design was by David Ford and art was by Carol Keller; their excellent work speaks for itself. Copy editor Barbara Jatkola did skillful editing for which I am thankful now and for which readers will be thankful in the future. Thanks also go to Marilyn Rowland for the indexing and to Kevin Krugh and the personnel at DEKR for their assistance.

I would also like to thank the reviewers, especially Frank da Cruz, Ralph Gorin, Brian Reid, and Henry Etlinger. In addition, David Mitton of Digital Equipment Corporation, Andrew Coppola, Paul Himottu, Charlie Davis, and Bob Wambach of Stratus Computer Incorporated, Matt Olenski of Microcom Incorporated, Anna Lacaze and D. J. Pollard AT&T, Pauline Roberts of Telecom Canada, Richard Wurtz, Jr. of Universal Data Systems, Sharon O'Brien of Hayes Microcomputer Products Incorporated, and Steve Norton of New England Telephone Company provided helpful suggestions and information.

Contributors to the previous editions, such as Larry Allen, Rick Allen, Dave Butler, Frank Fritsch, Allen Kent, and Mike Patton deserve repeated thanks. I especially want to thank Vince Bastiani and Marcia Kenah for getting the first edition started. Going further back, I would like to thank

Paul Magoon, Wayne Gray, Jesse Piper, and Norman Paquette of Stevens High School, and of course my parents, for their encouragement.

Many of the figures and charts in this book are reproduced from publications of the EIA, the CCITT, Hayes Microcomputer Products, and Zilog Incorporated. Their permission to reprint these items is gratefully acknowledged.

John McNamara

January 1988

# Contents

### 6. A Single Line Asynchronous UART with Private Line Modem Control 59

Expansion of the Chapter 2 block diagram, adding modem control and modem status bits to the registers described in Chapter 2.

### 7. Asynchronous Multiplexers 62

Single Line asynchronous interfaces, identification of parts that could be shared in a multiple line interface, additional features that could be added, FIFO, choice of line sizes for multiplexers, pros and cons of multiplexers.

### 8. Telephone Switching Systems 68

Historical development of the need for telephone switching systems, magneto switchboards, terminology, common battery systems, Strowger, detection of service request, dialing, tone signaling, speed of connection, CCIS, traffic capacity, hunt groups, noise, switched network structure, VNL and SDN design, echo suppressors, network management.

### 9. Modem Control for Switched Network Use 80

Control leads previously discussed in Chapter 5, definitions of additional leads for switched network use, reason for those leads being required, control of half-duplex modems, reverse channels, split speed modems.

### 10. Asynchronous Modems for Switched Network Use 94

Available frequency spectrum, details of the 300 bps ("103-type") modem, originate mode and answer mode, eye patterns, carrier loss clamps, a comparison of spectrum utilization by 300 bps and 1200 bps FSK modems.

### 11. Automatic Calling Units 101

Applications, condensed versions of EIA-366 and CCITT V.25 references for parallel interface autodiallers, condensed versions of CCITT V.25 bis, AT Command Set, Vadic VA831, and Digital Equipment DF03-AC references for serial interface autodiallers.

### 12. Asynchronous Multiplexers with Modem Control 113

Programmable formats and speeds, common terminal operating speeds, direct memory transfers, current addresses and byte counts, monitoring and controlling modems on 16 lines, transition detection systems, scanners, secondary registers.

## 28. Local Area Networks  265

Large computers versus personal computers, sharing file and printer services, definition of Local Area Network (LAN); star, ring, and bus topologies; access control via polling, tokens, ALOHA, and CSMA/CD.

## Appendixes

### A. How Far—How Fast?  275
Speed versus distance tables for various types of interface circuits.

### B. Modem Options  287
A list of modem options and their functions.

### C. Codes  299
Tables of Baudot, ASCII, and other communication codes.

### D. Universal Synchronous Asynchronous Receiver Transmitter (USART)  307
Explanation of the USART, bit assignments and signal functions.

### E. Format and Speed Table for Asynchronous Communication  316
A list of character formats, character rates, and baud rates for various terminals.

### F. Channel Conditioning  320
Parameters for private line conditioning offered by AT&T.

### G. Interface Connector Pinning  325
Pinning assignment for the 25-pin D-subminiature connector as used in EIA-232-D and EIA-530.

### H. Hayes Smartmodem 1200™ and Hayes Smartmodem 2400™ Dialling Commands and Responses  329
An excerpt from the quick reference cards for these products showing the flexibility and complexity of modern serial interface dialling.

### I. Where to Get More Information  336
A list of addresses and telephone numbers for obtaining EIA, CCITT, ISO, ANSI, and AT&T documents.

## Glossary  339

## Index  363

# 1

## Asynchronous Communications

Bits of binary data are commonly transferred between electronic devices by changes in current or voltage. Data may be transferred in "parallel" over several lines at once or in "serial" over a single line. The transfers may be "asynchronous," in which the data is transferred at nonuniform rates, or they may be "synchronous," in which case the exact departure or arrival time of each bit of information is predictable.

In parallel transmission, each bit of the set of bits that represents a character has its own wire. An additional wire called the "strobe" or "clock" lead notifies the receiver unit that all the bits are present on their respective wires so that the voltages on the wires can be sampled. Figure 1–1 schematically depicts the parallel transfer of the eight-bit character 11000001. In serial transmission, the bits that represent a character are sent down a single wire one after the other.

Computers and other high-speed digital systems generally operate on parallel data, so data is transferred in parallel between these devices wherever they are in close physical proximity. As the distance between these devices increases, however, the multiple wires not only become more costly, but the complexity of the line drivers and receivers also increases, due to the increased difficulty of properly driving and receiving signals on long wires.

Serial transmission is generally used where the cost of the communication medium is high enough to justify a transmitter and receiver system that will serialize the bits that represent the character, send them over a single line, and reassemble them in parallel form at the reception end. Conversion from parallel to serial and from serial to parallel is typically

1

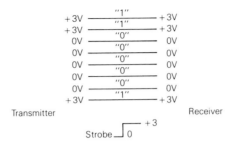

Figure 1–1   Parallel Data Transfer

done with shift registers. In most data communication applications, serial transmission is preferable to parallel transmission.

Asynchronous operation is typically used where efficient use of the transmission facility is not important and where error checking is done by a human operator. Examples include simple terminal-to-computer applications, including the connection of a keyboard to a personal computer. Synchronous operation is typically used when transmission efficiency is important and when error checking is required. Examples include most computer-to-computer transmission.

Like many things in data communication, however, the use of asynchronous versus synchronous is influenced by economy and tradition as well as technology. Since asynchronous operation is the simpler of the two methods, it will be discussed first, with synchronous operation postponed until a later chapter.

Asynchronous data transmission was first used by mechanical teleprinters, so many of the conventions and much of the terminology originated from that use. Because of the mechanism design in early teleprinters, and to facilitate fail-safe operation, serial teleprinter systems adopted the convention that an idle line (no data being sent) was one in which current was flowing. Data transmission occurred when the current in the line was interrupted in a specified fashion. By convention, the idle (current flowing) state was called the "1" state or "MARK" condition, and the lack-of-current state was called the "0" state or "SPACE" condition. To start the mechanism of the receiving teleprinter, the line was brought to the "0" state for one bit time; this was (and is) called the "START" bit. For the next eight successive bit times (see Figure 1–2 in the case of eight-bit code), the line was conditioned to a "1" state or "0" state as required to represent the character being sent. To allow the mechanism of the receiving teleprinter to coast back to a known position in time for the beginning (START bit) of the next character, one or more bit times of "1" state (idle) were sent. This period was (and is) called the "STOP" bit interval. In modern systems, the only function of the STOP bit is to ensure that there will be a "1" state to "0" state transition to identify the beginning of the START bit.

Except for the requirement that the line be idle for at least the STOP bit interval, the transmission of the next character could begin at any time. The lack of a continuous synchronous agreement between the transmitter and the receiver—specifically, the lack of a clocking signal within or accompanying the data channel—causes this type of transmission to be called "asynchronous," literally "without synchronization." The asynchronous character format is shown in Figure 1–2.

Before discussing the details of sending and receiving asynchronous serial data, a brief discussion of codes is in order. Asynchronous data transmission between electronic devices uses eight-bit codes to represent characters, but this was not always the case. The following paragraphs give a brief review of the use of shorter codes when asynchronous transmission was accomplished with mechanical teleprinters.

While it is true that precise synchronization between transmitting station and receiving station is not necessary in asynchronous transmission, the receiving station must have a fairly good idea of what rate the transmitting station is using to transmit the bits in order to sample the received bits at the proper times. This used to be a problem when teleprinters used electric motors to determine their operating speed, rather than using quartz crystals as they do today. In countries where power grid networks did not keep the voltages and frequencies of the power lines in various communities in relative agreement, even the use of synchronous motors could not ensure

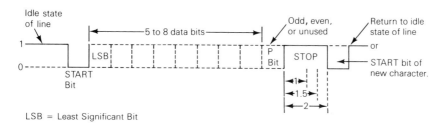

LSB = Least Significant Bit

Figure 1–2   Asynchronous Data Character Format

that teleprinters in diverse locations were operating at exactly the same speed. This problem was partially solved by retiming the reception of each character from the edge of the START bit, but the sampling of the last received data bit in the character still could take place off-center if the difference in motor speeds was too great. For this reason, the number of bits representing each character was usually five under those circumstances. Five-bit code, also called five-level code, was named "Baudot code" after Emil Baudot, who invented the first constant length teleprinter code in 1874. In theory, five bits could be used to represent 32 different characters. Since that was not enough to represent all alphabetic characters and the numerals 0–9, a shifting character called "Figures Shift" was used to place the reception station in figures mode, after which all subsequent code combinations would be interpreted as numbers. The station could be returned to letters mode by sending "Letters Shift." Appendix C lists some versions of the Baudot code.

While ordinary message text could be transmitted and received quite well with five-level code, the newspaper industry found the lack of differentiation between upper- and lower-case letters to be a problem. A six-level code, which was similar to the five-level code, used the shift feature to designate the difference between upper- and lower-case letters and used a sixth bit to increase the number of available symbols. Appendix C also lists a version of this code.

The most widely used code today is the ASCII code, also listed in Appendix C, which is essentially a seven-level code. It is almost always transmitted with a parity bit (see Chapter 13), which makes a total of eight bits per character. Transmission and reception of asynchronous data is now done with integrated circuits referred to as "UARTs" (Universal Asynchronous Receiver Transmitters). The remainder of this chapter offers a simplified view of the circuitry used within UART chips. This gives some insight into the design issues involved, the terminology used, and the error flags that a programmer might see. To simplify the discussion, only eight-bit codes will be mentioned, although almost all UARTs will accommodate five-, six-, seven-, and eight-bit codes.

A simplified circuit for receiving asynchronous serial data is shown in Figure 1–3. The circuit contains a "16 × clock," which samples the incoming data line at 16 times the anticipated bit rate. The line is sampled at such a rapid rate in order to detect the 1-to-0 transition (when the START

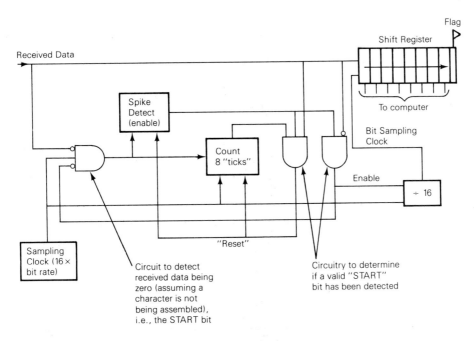

Figure 1–3   Asynchronous Serial Data Receiver

bit begins) as soon as possible after it occurs. The circuit that detects the 1-to-0 transition enables a "spike detection" circuit, which counts eight ticks of the 16 × clock (half a bit time) and checks the line to see whether it is still in the "0" state. If it is, a valid START bit has presumably arrived; if the line has returned to the "1" state, it is assumed that the initial 1-to-0 transition was due to noise on the line, and no further action is taken. If the "spike detector" circuit determines that a valid START signal has arrived, it enables a counter that divides the 16 × clock by 16 to produce a sampling clock that ticks once per bit time. This "tick" occurs roughly at the center of the bit being sampled; the circuitry just described does not detect the initial 1-to-0 transition exactly when it occurs. This error can be made smaller by sampling at 32 times the bit rate and even further minimized by sampling at 64 times the bit rate. When higher sampling rates are used, the counter in the spike detect circuit and the counter in the bit sampler circuit must both be made larger.

The bit sampler circuit strobes the state of the line eight times (in the case of eight-bit characters), then generates a signal to the computer or controller with which it is associated. This signal is called a "flag" and announces that a character has been received. The computer can then parallel transfer the character from the register into which it was shifted by the receiver.

In the example cited above, a single register has the received data shifted into it from the line, and that register is also used to store the character until the computer is ready to read it. The problem with this "single-buffered" interface is that the computer has only the length of time during the STOP bit to read the character before another arrives. A simple but powerful alteration to the circuit provides a second register into which the received character can be parallel transferred as soon as the eighth bit has been sampled (see Figure 1–4). The flag is generated when the parallel transfer occurs and the buffer used for assembling the characters by shifting bits in off the line becomes immediately available for the next character. The computer thus has the entire time of the assembly of the second character to read the first one. This provision of a "holding buffer" characterizes a "double-buffered" receiver. The only possible congestion occurs when a character has been assembled and transferred to the holding buffer and a second character also gets completely assembled. (It is possible to carry this idea a few steps further and build "triple-buffered" or "quadruple-buffered" receivers.)

Regardless of the number of buffers used, the arrival of a character that cannot be handled because the previous characters have not been read is called a "Data Overrun." In the case of an overrun, most asynchronous receiver circuits use the newly arriving character to overwrite a stored

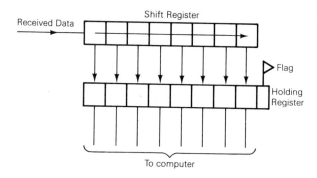

Figure 1–4  Double Buffered Asynchronous Receiver

character and provide an error status bit when the character that overwrote another is read out, indicating that a character has been lost.

Because the STOP bit arrival time is no longer the sole time available to the computer for reading the character in multiple-buffered interfaces, there is time for circuitry to check the "ninth bit"—i.e., the STOP bit—to confirm that it is a one. If it is not a one, one of the following conditions exists: The communications line continuity is broken, the receiver timing is confused, or the transmitting station is sending a special signal of some sort. The existence of one of these conditions typically provides an error lead in the asynchronous receiver in addition to the Overrun lead just described. This error generally results when the receiver has lost track of which zeros in the transmission are the START bits and which are just zeros in the data. If, for some reason, the receiver treats a data bit as a START bit, it will assemble the next eight bits as a character. Since these eight bits are really parts of two characters (the end of one and the beginning of another), the ninth bit to arrive will not be the STOP bit but rather a data bit from the second character. If it is a zero, the error-checking circuit will detect an error. "Framing" is the process of deciding which groups of eight bits constitute characters; since this error is due to a failure in that process, it is known as a "Framing Error."

Failures in the framing process can generally be avoided. The idle line condition is a MARK (ones) condition for both current loop transmission and transmission involving modems, and any amount of idle time more than a character time in length will correct this condition. Also, for randomly received characters, the receiver will eventually become realigned and use the correct zeros as START elements. You can check this by writing down a few dozen characters and prefixing the START bits and suffixing the STOP bits. Then choose a zero in the first character as a START bit, count out eight bits, call the next bit STOP (even if it is a zero), look for the next zero, and call that the START of the next character. Since some ones will intervene before you find that zero, you will have moved the starting point of the framing process. Eventually you will repeat these steps and choose an actual START bit. From there on, you are back in proper framing. Loss of framing is not a common problem, but gibberish can occur, and it is important that modems are arranged for "MARK HOLD"—i.e., the presentation of MARK on the received data lead when the line has not yet been established.

Asynchronous transmitters are also implemented with shift registers. A simplified circuit is shown in Figure 1–5. The computer parallel loads a character for transmission into the shift register. The circuitry can easily be arranged so that the parallel load automatically loads a zero at one end of the character to serve as a START bit and a one at the other end to serve as a STOP bit. The parallel loading of the character starts the shifting circuitry, which successively shifts out the START bit, the eight data bits, and the STOP bit to a flip-flop called "Line," while shifting zeros into the shift register. The Line flip-flop is connected to the communications line. When all the shift register bits are zeros, the STOP bit is being applied to the communications line by the Line flip-flop, the shifting process is stopped, and a zero-detector circuit signals the computer that another character may be parallel loaded. If the computer has another character available, it parallel loads that character into the shift register, a timer ensures that the Line flip-flop has been asserting the STOP bit for at least a bit time, and the shifting process begins again. If the computer does not have a character available, the Line flip-flop merely applies the STOP bit (MARK or "1") to the line for a while until the computer does have another character available. As in the receiver case, the computer has one bit time, the STOP bit time, to respond to the flag. In contrast, however, the unavail-

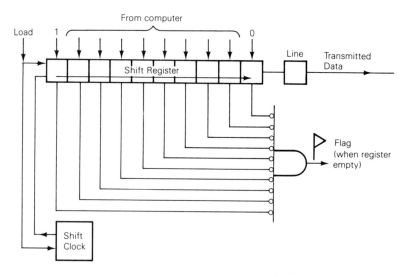

Figure 1–5   Asynchronous Serial Data Transmitter

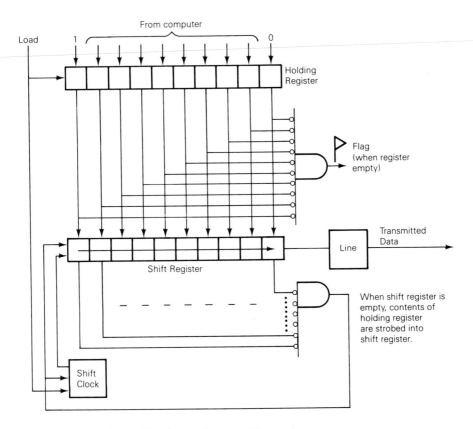

Figure 1–6   Double Buffered Asynchronous Transmitter

ability of the computer in time does not have fatal consequences; only efficient use of the line is lost, not any data.

Because it is desirable to keep the communications line running at full speed and because the computer may have crests and valleys of activity, double buffering may also be used in transmitters. (Triple or quadruple buffering is far less common in transmitters than in receivers.) The simplified circuit is shown in Figure 1–6. Here, the computer loads a transmitter holding buffer whenever the flag signal indicates that the buffer is available. The transmitter circuitry automatically loads the shift register from the holding register whenever the shift register is available and there is a character in the holding buffer. In this way, the computer has an entire character time (during the shifting out of a character) to refresh the transmitter holding buffer without the line going idle unnecessarily.

One interesting consequence of double-buffered transmitters is that while they smooth the load on the computer, they can pose a problem when the communications line has control signals associated with it. If a line is equipped with modems whose transmitter units are turned off and on by means of a "Request to Send" lead, the program that controls that lead must not turn it off immediately upon loading the holding register of the transmitter, as the character loaded into the holding buffer has not yet been transmitted. In fact, the program controlling the Request to Send lead must not turn it off until *two* character times have elapsed—one for the character being shifted out when the holding register was loaded, and one for the character just loaded into the holding register. Some UARTs have a "Transmitter Empty" bit to indicate that both the holding and shifting registers are empty and thus facilitate proper control of the Request to Send lead.

In Chapter 2, a simple version of a single line asynchronous interface utilizing a UART is discussed in detail, including programming information.

# A Single-Line Asynchronous UART

It is possible to buy an integrated circuit that does all the reception and transmission tasks described in Chapter 1. This device, the Universal Asynchronous Receiver/Transmitter (UART), converts a serial stream of bits arriving over a single wire into a character that can be read in parallel form by a microprocessor connected to the UART by a parallel bus. In a symmetrical fashion, the microprocessor can load characters in parallel form into the UART and have those characters converted into a serial bit stream.

The parallel bus connections also allow the microprocessor to access additional registers within the UART besides those that contain characters involved in the reception/transmission process. The additional registers contain bits that provide status information and bits that control various operating characteristics of the UART. For example, there are status bits that indicate that a received character is available for reading and status bits that indicate that the transmitter is available for the microprocessor to load a character for transmission. Additional status bits provide Overrun and Framing Error indications (see Chapter 1) and Parity Error indication (see Chapter 13). Control bits permit the selection of various character lengths (five, six, seven, or eight bits per character), various types of parity (odd, even, none), and various STOP bit arrangements (1 bit time, 1.5 bit times, or 2 bit times). Appendix D contains a detailed description of a commercially available UART, but this chapter describes a simplified UART, and future chapters embellish this hypothetical device.

Figure 2–1 shows a block diagram of a single line asynchronous UART. At the left of the drawing is a microprocessor input/output bus, typically a structure of several dozen conductors. Some of the conductors in that bus are "address leads." Circuitry connected to the UART, but not shown in the drawing, monitors those leads and enables the "bus transceivers" whenever the address assigned to the UART chip appears. In a typical installation, a few address leads are also brought into the UART chip to allow the microprocessor to select which register will be read or written. When a register is to be read, the address leads within the UART gate the contents of the receiver buffer, the receiver status register, or the transmitter status register onto the leads labeled "Internal Data Bus." This permits the bus transceivers to place the data that has been read onto the microprocessor bus. When a register is to be written, data on the microprocessor bus is received by the bus transceivers and is presented to the receiver status register, the transmitter status register, or the transmitter buffer register via the internal data bus. One of the leads in the microprocessor bus is typically a strobe signal that is passed through the bus transceivers and used to record the data into the register selected by the address leads.

Three blocks in the diagram remain to be explained: baud* rate generators, interrupt control logic, and level conversion. The baud rate generator produces the clock signals that are used to shift out characters being transmitted and to sample the line for signals being received. For reasons that should be evident from Chapter 1, the clock rate used for transmission must be the same as that used by the distant station for reception, and vice versa. Since there are a number of choices for transmission and reception speeds, UARTs provide a programmable selection of popular baud rates.

The interrupt control logic is provided to obviate the need for the microprocessor to continually examine the receiver and transmitter status registers to see whether there are characters to be handled. Instead, the interrupt logic (if enabled) will alert the microprocessor whenever the receiver has assembled a character or the transmitter is ready to accept a character for transmission. Some UARTs provide separate interrupt leads for the receiver and transmitter; this allows the microprocessor to assign different

---

*The serial transfer of data within a terminal or computer interface is described in terms of bits per second (bps). The signaling rate of transmission facilities is described in baud (see Glossary). Bits per second and baud are equivalent if each signaling element on the transmission facility conveys one bit of information. Since this is often the case, many advertisements and some data communication literature use the two terms interchangeably. In this book, an effort has been made to use the two terms correctly, except where the application is unclear; in the latter case, baud has been used.

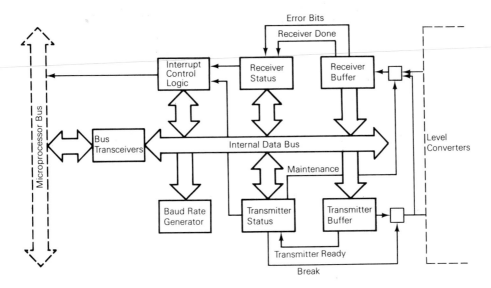

Figure 2–1   Block Diagram of a Single Line UART

levels of priority to the two kinds of interrupt. In asynchronous transmission, it is more important to service receivers than to service transmitters. This is because late service of a receiver may result in lost characters, while late service of a transmitter will result only in longer stop element times.

The one remaining block to be explained is that labeled "Level Converters." Data communication is seldom done at the same voltage and current levels as those used within a computer, since the computer's transistor–transistor logic (TTL) levels are too sensitive to things such as noise, ground potential differences, and damage from short circuits to lines carrying higher voltages to be practical for transmissions over distances greater than a few feet. Thus, UARTs are typically connected to level converter circuits, which convert the TTL logic levels to EIA-232-D, EIA-422-A, or EIA-423-A voltage levels. Since the level conversion circuitry is not contained within the UART, it has been shown by dashed lines in Figure 2–1. EIA voltage level interfaces are explained in Chapters 3 and 4.

Figure 2–2 shows sample bit assignments for registers in a UART. Several of the registers have very few bits used, but as future chapters discuss additional features, these bit positions will be filled in.

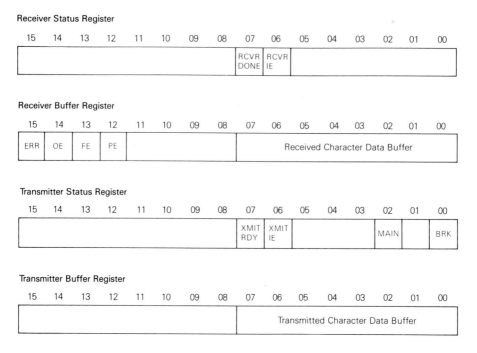

Figure 2–2   Sample Bit Assignments for a Single Line UART

The receiver status register need consist only of two bits: a received character available bit (RCVR DONE) and a bit that will allow the setting of the Done bit to generate an interrupt. (On some occasions, the computer program will not want to be interrupted by arriving characters; in these cases, the interrupt enable bit, RCVR IE, is cleared by the program to ensure that no interrupts occur.)

The receiver buffer register has eight bits (07–00) for presenting the received characters for the microprocessor to read, and three bits to report the Overrun Error (OE) and Framing Error (FE) described in Chapter 1 and the Parity Error (PE) described in Chapter 13. For the convenience of the program, these error bits can be logically combined to produce a single ERRor (ERR) bit that will be set whenever one or more of the error bits are set. In this way, the microprocessor program can check for errors by testing a single bit, which in most cases will be clear. In the unlikely case where it is set, the program can then test all three error bits to determine the type of error.

Like the receiver status register, the transmitter status register needs only two bits: one to say that the transmitter is available for loading (XMIT RDY), and one to enable and disable the ability of the Ready bit to generate interrupts. The Transmitter Interrupt Enable bit is abbreviated XMIT IE. The other two bits shown are MAIN and BRK. The Maintenance bit loops the transmitter's output, which is a serial communications line, to the receiver's input, also a serial communications line. This permits the transmitter to send to the receiver, a feature handy in trouble situations when it is desirable to determine whether the various elements of the data communication system are functioning correctly. When set, the BRK bit brings the transmitted data line to the SPACE ("0") state for as long as the bit is set. This permits the sending of a special signal, called "Break." The Break signal is used by some terminals as a special control character.

The transmitter buffer register provides eight bit positions (07–00), which can be loaded by the microprocessor with the character to be transmitted.

A microprocessor program typically operates the UART with bit 06 of the receiver status register (Receiver Interrupt Enable) set and with bit 06 of the transmitter status register (Transmitter Interrupt Enable) set. When a character has been received, the UART sets bit 07 of the receiver status register (Receiver Done), and this generates an interrupt. The program then responds to the interrupt and reads the receiver buffer register. Logic within the UART detects that the receiver buffer has been read and prepares to replace the data in the receiver buffer with new data. Should the UART need to use its receiver buffer for new characters without having first noted a read of that register, it would detect that an overrun condition was occurring and would assert the Overrun Error bit (see Chapter 1). Many UARTs reduce the probability of this occurring by placing received characters in a first-in first-out (FIFO) buffer that enables some number of characters (typically four) to be received without the buffer having been read. After reading the characters from the receiver buffer, the microprocessor program checks for errors, then stores the characters in memory.

Similarly, when a line's transmitter is available for transmitting a character, bit 07 (Transmitter Ready) of the transmitter status register sets. The setting of this bit causes an interrupt to the program, which checks to see whether it has anything to send on this line. If so, it loads that character into the transmitter buffer, and this automatically clears the Transmitter Ready bit.

Additional control and status bits for single line asynchronous UARTs provide for variable character formats and operating speeds. In addition, control leads for use with modulator-demodulators (modems)* may be required. For single line asynchronous UARTs with more features, refer to Chapter 6. For multiple line asynchronous interfaces, refer to Chapter 7.

---

*Some AT&T and Bell System operating company literature refers to modems as "data sets," a term used in this book only in conjunction with signal names such as "Data Set Ready."

# 3

## Interface Standards

In the early days of data communication in the United States, the associated operating companies of AT&T were, for all practical purposes, the only providers of data communication service. Therefore, the modems developed by the engineers at Bell Laboratories and manufactured by Western Electric were the standards of the industry. There were, however, a large number of computer and data terminal manufacturers that needed to know the electrical characteristics of the Bell modem interfaces. In addition, independent modem manufacturers offered a few high-speed synchronous modems for private line use, and these manufacturers needed to know the electrical characteristics of the computer and terminal manufacturers' interfaces.

To solve these problems, the Electrical Industry Association (EIA), in cooperation with the Bell System, the independent modem manufacturers, and the computer manufacturers, developed a standard titled "Interface between Data Terminal Equipment and Data Circuit-Terminating Equipment Employing Serial Binary Data Interchange." This standard was called RS-232. The latest version of this standard is EIA-232-D, a designation that reflects both the latest revision level (D) and the present EIA practice of prefixing their standards with "EIA" rather than "RS." Copies of this standard may be purchased from the EIA Sales Order Department, Electronic Industries Association, 2001 Eye Street N.W., Washington, D.C. 20006. (Persons visiting the EIA headquarters may wish to know that Eye Street is I Street.) Newer standards, EIA-422-A and EIA-423-A, have been issued. Although these may in time supplant the EIA-232-D standard, 232 is still the standard to which modem interfaces are designed.

In countries other than the United States, telephone service is generally provided by government post, telegraph, and telephone (PTT) authorities. While each authority is in a position to determine interface standards for its own country, many of the modems, terminals, and computers used to provide data communication services in one country are manufactured in another. To permit the economic manufacture of these modems, terminals, and computers and to facilitate data communication between various countries, the PTTs of the United Nations countries, in conjunction with the Comite Consultatif International Telephonique et Telegraphique (CCITT), have promulgated standards for data communication interfaces and for other aspects of telecommunications.

The CCITT, a part of the International Telecommunications Union, which in turn is part of the United Nations, recognizes that varying national requirements, nationalism, and other factors preclude firm standards, so the working committees develop "recommendations" that are adopted and published by the CCITT as a whole. These recommendations cover all phases of telecommunications, from operator procedures to controlling electrical interference from trolley/tram lines into telecommunications cables. The recommendations are reviewed at plenary assemblies held at approximately four-year intervals and are then published in sets of books referred to by color. For example, the Second Plenary Assembly was held in New Delhi, India, in 1960 and resulted in the publication of the *Red Book*; the third was held in Geneva, Switzerland, in 1964 and resulted in the *Blue Book*; the fourth was held in Mar Del Plata, Argentina, in 1968 and resulted in the *White Book*; and the fifth, sixth, and seventh were held in Geneva in 1972, 1976, and 1980 and resulted in the *Green Book*, the *Orange Book*, and the *Yellow Book*. With the 1984 Plenary Assembly (Málaga–Torremolinos, Spain), the color cycle returned to the *Red Book*.

Each of these books consists of numbered volumes covering various phases of telecommunications. The present volume relating to data transmission is Volume VIII and contains recommendations prefixed with the letters V and X. These volumes are available from the United Nations Bookstore, Room 32B, United Nations General Assembly Building, New York, New York 10017, and also can be ordered from International Telecommunications Union, General Secretariat, Sales Service, Place de Nation, CH 1211, Geneva 20, Switzerland. A preliminary letter of inquiry is recommended, as prepayment is required. Some of the applicable recommendations for data communication interfaces are listed below. All are contained in Volume VIII.

V.10    Electrical Characteristics for Unbalanced Double-Current Interchange Circuits for General Use with Integrated Circuit Equipment in the Field of Data Communications

V.11    Electrical Characteristics for Balanced Double-Current Interchange Circuits for General Use with Integrated Circuit Equipment in the Field of Data Communications

V.24    List of Definitions for Interchange Circuits between Data Terminal Equipment and Data Circuit Terminating Equipment

V.28    Electrical Characteristics for Unbalanced Double-Current Interchange Circuits

V.35    Transmission of 48 Kilobits per Second Data Using 60- to 108-kH Group Band Circuits

Returning to the EIA-232-D standard, it is important to note exactly what this standard contains: (1) the electrical signal characteristics, (2) the interface mechanical characteristics, (3) a functional description of the interchange circuits, (4) a list of standard subsets of specific interchange circuits for specific groups of communications system applications, and (5) recommendations and explanatory notes.

Typical advertisements for computer/modem interfaces and terminals that say "EIA-232-D compatible" really mean that the electrical and mechanical characteristics do not violate EIA-232-D. There is little in the "EIA-232-D compatible" statement to guarantee that the function of the interchange circuits meets EIA-232-D or, more importantly, that the interchange circuits provided are sufficient to cover all systems applications. For example, a computer/modem interface that provides only level conversion for the transmitted data lead and the received data lead may have the proper electrical and mechanical characteristics to be EIA-232-D compatible, but due to the lack of control leads, it is virtually useless on switched network service. Thus, it is important when reviewing specifications for computer/modem interfaces and for terminals to understand what the various interface leads do. This information is summarized in Table 3–1.

Additional applications information is contained in both EIA-232-D and CCITT V.28. The purchase of EIA-232-D is especially recommended. A brief synopsis follows.

### Table 3–1   EIA Interchange Circuit for Various Types of Communications Channels

|  | *Interchange Circuit* | A | B | C | D | E | F | G | H | I | J | K | L | M | Z |
|---|---|---|---|---|---|---|---|---|---|---|---|---|---|---|---|
| AB | Signal Ground | x | x | x | x | x | x | x | x | x | x | x | x | x | x |
| BA | Transmitted Data | x | x |  | x | x | x |  | x |  | x |  | x | x | o |
| BB | Received Data |  |  | x | x | x |  | x |  | x |  | x | x | x | o |
| CA | Request to Send |  | x |  | x |  | x |  |  |  | x |  | x |  | o |
| CB | Clear to Send | x | x |  | x | x | x |  | x |  | x |  | x | x | o |
| CC | DCE Ready | x | x | x | x | x | x | x | x | x | x | x | x | x | o |
| CD | DTE Ready | s | s | s | s | s | s | s | s | s | s | s | s | s | o |
| CE | Ring Indicator | s | s | s | s | s | s | s | s | s | s | s | s | s | o |
| CF | Received Line Signal Detector |  |  | x | x | x |  | x |  | x |  | x | x | x | o |
| CG | Signal Quality Detector |  |  |  |  |  |  |  |  |  |  |  |  |  | o |
| CH/CI | Data Signaling Rate Selector (DTE) (DCE) |  |  |  |  |  |  |  |  |  |  |  |  |  | o |
| DA/DB | Transmitter Signal Element Timing (DTE) (DCE) | t | t |  | t | t | t |  | t |  | t | t | t | t | o |

*Key to Columns:*

A — Transmit Only
B — Transmit Only*
C — Receive Only
D — Duplex,* Half-Duplex
E — Duplex
F — Primary Channel Transmit Only*/Secondary Channel Receive Only
G — Primary Channel Receive Only/Secondary Channel Transmit Only*
H — Primary Channel Transmit Only/Secondary Channel Receive Only
I — Primary Channel Receive Only/Secondary Channel Transmit Only
J — Primary Channel Transmit Only*/Half-Duplex Secondary Channel
K — Primary Channel Receive Only/Half-Duplex Secondary Channel
L — Duplex Primary Channel*/Duplex Secondary Channel*
L — Half-Duplex Primary Channel/Half-Duplex Secondary Channel
M — Duplex Primary Channel/Duplex Secondary Channel
Z — Special (Circuits Specified by Supplier)

*Indicates the inclusion of Circuit CA (Request to Send) in One Way Only (Transmit) or Duplex configuration where it might ordinarily not be expected, but where it might be used to indicate a nontransmit mode to the DCE to permit it to remove a line signal or to send synchronizing or training signals as required.

NOTE. When data communications literature refers to an "EIA-232-D Type D or Type E Interface," it is referring to this chart.

| | *Interchange Circuit* | *A* | *B* | *C* | *D* | *E* | *F* | *G* | *H* | *I* | *J* | *K* | *L* | *M* | *Z* |
|---|---|---|---|---|---|---|---|---|---|---|---|---|---|---|---|
| DD | Receiver Signal Element Timing (DCE) | | | t | t | t | | t | | t | | t | t | t | o |
| SBA | Secondary Transmitted Data | | | | | | | x | | x | x | x | x | x | o |
| SBB | Secondary Received Data | | | | | | x | | x | | x | x | x | x | o |
| SCA | Secondary Request to Send | | | | | | | x | | x | x | x | | | o |
| SCB | Secondary Clear to Send | | | | | | | x | | x | x | x | x | x | o |
| SCF | Secondary Received Line Signal Detector | | | | | | x | | x | | x | x | x | x | o |
| LL | Local Loopback | | | — | — | | | | | | | | — | — | o |
| RL | Remote Loopback | | | — | — | | | | | | | | — | — | o |
| TM | Test Mode | — | — | — | — | — | — | — | — | — | — | — | — | — | o |

*Legend:*
 o: to be specified by the supplier
 —: optional
 s: additional interchange circuits required for switched service
 t: additional interchange circuits required for synchronous channel
 x: basic interchange circuits, all systems

The EIA specifications are keyed to the equivalent circuit for the interface leads shown in Figure 3–1. The following list is a condensation of the EIA standard EIA-232-D rules for this interface circuit. These rules are summarized in Table 3–2a. The CCITT V.28 specifications are reproduced in Table 3–2b, with permission of the CCITT.

1. The open circuit voltage $V_0$ shall not have a magnitude greater than 25 volts.

2. The driver circuit shall be able to sustain a short circuit to any other wire in the cable without damage to itself or to the other equipment, and the short circuit current shall not exceed 0.5 ampere.

3. Signals shall be considered to be in the MARK ("1") state when the voltage $V_1$ is more negative than $-3$ volts with respect to Circuit AB (Signal Ground). Signals shall be considered to be in the SPACE ("0") state when $V_1$ is more positive than $+3$ volts with respect to Signal Ground. The region between $-3$ and $+3$ volts is defined as the transition region, within which the signal state is not defined.

4. The load impedance ($R_L$ and $C_L$) shall have a DC resistance $R_L$, which is less than 7000 ohms when measured with an applied voltage of from 3 to 25 volts but more than 3000 ohms when measured with a voltage of less than 25 volts.

5. When the terminator load resistance $R_L$ meets the requirements of Rule 4 above and the terminator open circuit voltage ($E_L$) is zero, the voltage $V_1$ shall be between 5 volts and 15 volts in magnitude.

6. The driver shall assert a voltage between $-5$ and $-15$ volts relative to signal ground to represent a MARK signal condition. The driver shall assert a voltage between $+5$ and $+15$ volts relative to signal ground to represent a SPACE signal.

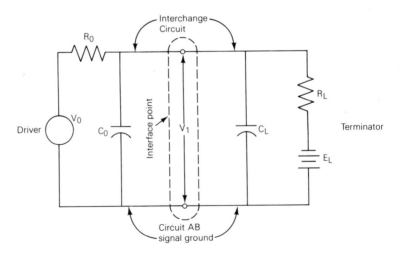

Figure 3–1   Interchange Equivalent Circuit

Table 3–2a   Condensed EIA-232-D Electrical Specifications

| | |
|---|---|
| Driver output logic levels with 3K to 7K load | $15\text{ V} >_{oh} > 5\text{ V}$ <br> $-5\text{ V} >_{ol} > -15\text{ V}$ |
| Driver output voltage with open circuit | $/V_o/ < 25\text{ V}$ |
| Driver output impedance with power off | $R_o > 300$ ohms |
| Output short circuit current | $/I_o/ < 0.5\text{ A}$ |
| Driver slew rate | $dv/dt < 30\text{ V}/\mu s$ |
| Receiver input impedance | $7\text{ k}\Omega > R_{in} > 3\text{ k}\Omega$ |
| Receiver input voltage | $\pm 15$ V compatible with driver |
| Receiver output with open circuit input | MARK |
| Receiver output with +3 V input | SPACE |
| Receiver output with −3 V input | MARK |
| $\left.\begin{array}{l}+15\\+5\end{array}\right\}$ | LOGIC "0" = SPACE = CONTROL ON |
| $\left.\begin{array}{l}+5\\+3\end{array}\right\}$ | Noise margin |
| $\left.\begin{array}{l}+3\\-3\end{array}\right\}$ | Transition region |
| $\left.\begin{array}{l}-3\\-5\end{array}\right\}$ | Noise margin |
| $\left.\begin{array}{l}-5\\-15\end{array}\right\}$ | LOGIC "1" = MARK = CONTROL OFF |

Note that this rule in conjunction with Rule 3 above allows 2 volts of noise margin. This is discussed more fully in Appendix A.

7. The driver shall change the output voltage at a rate not exceeding 30 volts per microsecond, but the time required for the signal to pass through the −3 to +3 transition region shall not exceed 1 millisecond when the nominal length of a bit is 25 milliseconds or less, 4 percent of a bit time when the length of a bit is between 25 milliseconds and 125 microseconds, and 5 microseconds when the length of a bit is less than 125 microseconds.

8. The shunt capacitance of the terminator ($C_L$) shall not exceed 2500 picofarads, including the capacitance of the cable.

9. The impedance of the driver circuit under power-off conditions shall be greater than 300 ohms.

Table 3–2b   CCITT V.28 Electrical Characteristics for Unbalanced Double-Current Interchange Circuits

---

*(Geneva, 1972; amended at Geneva, 1980, Málaga–Torremolinos, 1984)*

1.   *Scope*
The electrical characteristics specified in this Recommendation apply generally to interchange circuits operating with data signaling rates below the limit of 20,000 bits per second.

2.   *Interchange equivalent circuit*
Figure 1/V.28 shows the interchange equivalent circuit with the electrical parameters, which are defined below.

This equivalent circuit is independent of whether the generator is located in the data circuit-terminating equipment and the load in the data terminal equipment or vice versa.

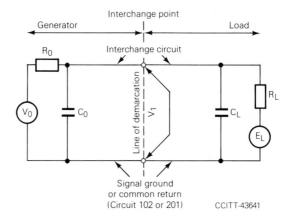

Figure 1/V.28   Interchange Equivalent Circuit

$V_0$   is the open-circuit generator voltage.

$R_0$   is the total effective d.c. resistance associated with the generator, measured at the interchange point.

$C_0$   is the total effective capacitance associated with the generator, measured at the interchange point.

$V_1$   is the voltage at the interchange point with respect to signal ground or common return.

$C_L$ is the total effective capacitance associated with the load, measured at the interchange point.

$R_L$ is the total effective d.c. resistance associated with the load, measured at the interchange point.

$E_L$ is the open-circuit load voltage (bias).

The impedance associated with the generator (load) includes any cable impedance on the generator (load) side of the interchange point.

The equipment at both sides of the interface may implement generators as well as receivers in any combination.

For data transmission applications, it is commonly accepted that the interface cabling is provided by the DTE. This introduces the line of demarcation between the DTE plus cable and the DCE. This line is also called the interchange point and is physically implemented in the form of a connector. The applications also require interchange circuits in both directions. This leads to an illustration as shown in Figure 2/V.28.

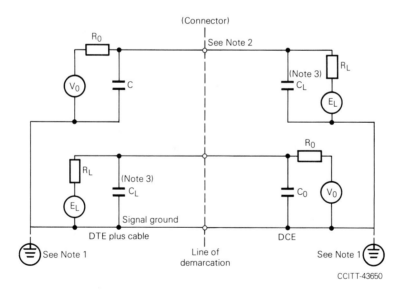

Figure 2/V.28  Practical Representation of the Interface

*Table 3–2b (Cont.)*

Note 1—Signal ground may be further connected to external protective ground if national regulations require.

Note 2—For data transmission over telephone-type facilities, ISO has specified a 25-pin connector and pin assignments in accordance with ISO 2110.

Note 3—Many existing interchange circuit generators do not provide for meeting the maximum rise time requirement of Recommendation V.28 paragraph 6 when driving a capacitance of greater than 2500 pf, the maximum permitted load capacitance $(C_L)$, which includes the capacitance of the DTE supplied interface cable.

3.   *Load*
The test conditions for measuring the load impedance are shown in Figure 3/V.28.

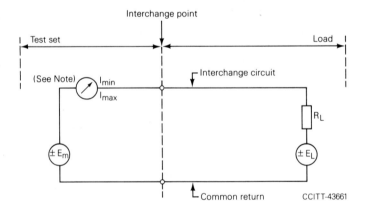

Figure 3/V.28   Equivalent Test Circuit

Note—The internal resistance of the ammeter shall be much less than the load resistance $(R_L)$.

The impedance on the load side of an interchange circuit shall have a d.c. resistance $(R_L)$ neither less than 3000 ohms nor more than 7000 ohms. With an applied voltage $(E_m)$, *3 to 15 volts in magnitude, the measured input current (I)* shall be within the following limits:

$$I_{min,max} - \left| \frac{E_m \pm E_{L\ max}}{R_{L-max,min}} \right|$$

The open-circuit load voltage $(E_L)$ shall not exceed two volts.

The effective shunt capacitance ($C_L$) of the load, measured at the interchange point, shall not exceed 2500 picofarads.

To avoid inducing voltage surges on interchange circuits the reactive component of the load impedance shall not be inductive.

Note—This is subject to further study.

The load on an interchange circuit shall not prejudice continuous operation with any input signals within the voltage limits specified in paragraph 4 below.

4.  *Generator*

    The generator on an interchange circuit shall withstand an open circuit and a short circuit between itself and any other interchange circuit (including generators and loads) without sustaining damage to itself or its associated equipment.

    The open circuit generator voltage ($V_0$) on any interchange circuit shall not exceed 25 volts in magnitude. The impedance ($R_0$ and $C_0$) on the generator side of an interchange circuit is not specified; however, the combination of $V_0$ and $R_0$ shall be selected so that a short circuit between any two interchange circuits shall not result in any case in a current in excess of one-half ampere.

    Additionally, when the load open-circuit voltage ($E_L$) is zero, the voltage ($V_1$) at the interchange point shall not be less than 5 volts and not more than 15 volts in magnitude (either positive or negative polarity), for any load resistance ($R_L$) in the range between 3000 ohms and 7000 ohms.

    The effective shunt capacitance ($C_0$) at the generator side of an interchange circuit is not specified. However, in addition to any load resistance ($R_L$) the generator shall be capable of driving all of the capacitance at the generator side ($C_0$), plus a load capacitance ($C_L$) of 2500 picofarads.

    Note—Relay or switch contacts may be used to generate signals on an interchange circuit, with appropriate measures to insure that signals so generated comply with the applicable clauses of paragraph 6 below.

5.  *Significant levels ($V_1$)*

    For data interchange circuits, the signal shall be considered into the binary "1" condition when the voltage ($V_1$) on the interchange circuit measured at the interchange point is more negative than minus 3 volts. The signal shall be considered in the binary "0" condition when the voltage ($V_1$) is more positive than plus 3 volts.

*Table 3–2b (Cont.)*

For control and timing interchange circuits, the circuit shall be considered ON when the voltage $(V_1)$ on the interchange circuit is more positive than plus 3 volts, and shall be considered OFF when the voltage $(V_1)$ is more negative than minus 3 volts (See Figure 4/V.28).

Note—In certain countries, in the case of direct connection to d.c. telegraph-type circuits only, the voltage polarities in Figure 4/V.28 may be reversed.

The region between plus 3 volts and minus 3 volts is defined as the transition region. For an exception to this, see paragraph 7 below.

| $V_1 < -3$ volts | $V_1 > +3$ volts |
|---|---|
| 1 | 0 |
| OFF | ON |

Figure 4/V.28    Correlation Table

6.    *Signal characteristics*
The following limitations to the characteristics of signals transmitted across the interchange point, exclusive of external interference, shall be met at the interchange point when the interchange circuit is loaded with any receiving circuit which meets the characteristics specified in paragraph 3 above.

These limitations apply to all (data, control, and timing) interchange signals unless otherwise specified.

1) All interchange signals entering into the transition region shall proceed through this region to the opposite signal state and shall not re-enter this region until the next significant change of signal condition, except as indicated in 6) below.

2) There shall be no reversal of the direction of voltage change while the signal is in the transition region, except as indicated in 6) below.

3) For control interchange circuits, the time required for the signal to pass through the transition region during a change in state shall not exceed one millisecond.

4) For data and timing interchange circuits, the time required for the signal to pass through the transition region during a change in state shall not exceed one millisecond or 3 percent of the nominal element period on the interchange circuit, whichever is the less.

5) To reduce crosstalk between interchange circuits the maximum instantaneous rate of voltage change will be limited. A provisional limit will be 30 volts per microsecond.

6) When electromechanical devices are used on interchange circuits, points 1) and 2) above do not apply to data interchange circuits.

7. *Detection of generator power off or circuit failure*
Certain applications require detection of various fault conditions in the interchange circuits, e.g.:

1) generator power-off condition

2) receiver not connected with a generator

3) open-circuited interconnecting cable

4) short-circuited interconnecting cable

The power-off impedance of the generator side of these circuits shall not be less than 300 ohms when measured with an applied voltage (either positive or negative polarity) not greater than 2 volts in magnitude referenced to signal ground or common return.

The interpretation of a fault condition by a receiver (or load) is application dependent. Each application may use a combination of the following classification:

Type 0: No interpretation. A receiver or load does not have detection capability.

Type 1: Data circuits assume a binary 1 state. Control and timing circuits assume an OFF condition.

The association of the circuit failure detection to particular interchange circuits in accordance with the above types is a matter of the functional and procedural characteristics specification of the interface.

The interchange circuits monitoring circuit failure fault conditions in the general telephone network are indicated in Recommendation V.24.

Years ago each interface designer took a turn at trying to meet the electrical specifications in Table 3–2a, with varying degrees of success. Now integrated circuit manufacturers have come to the rescue and are providing circuits that meet these specifications in terms of voltages used, rate of change of voltages, impedances, and so on. Certain aspects of the electrical characteristics still pose problems, however. First, for the driver to assert voltages of +5 and −5, the hardware in which these circuits are located must contain power supply voltages that are more positive than +6 and more negative than −6, unless special chips that contain internal "charge-pump" circuitry are used. The reason for this is that the drivers use transistors to control the voltages on the line being driven; these transistors are in series with the power provided to the integrated circuit, and a voltage drop of about a volt occurs across the transistors. Typically, voltages of +12 and −12 are used to power the driver integrated circuits.

The second electrical problem is that of cable capacitance. The EIA standard specifies that the capacitance of the circuit being driven (the terminator) shall be less than 2500 picofarads, including the cable to it. Since 40 to 50 picofarads per foot is a fairly common capacitance of multiconductor cable, a cable length of 50 feet is the maximum possible before the capacitance specification is violated.

The most obvious consequence of violating the capacitance specification is that the amount of time needed to accomplish a transition from the MARK state to the SPACE state, and vice versa, will be increased from the maximums allowed by the EIA-232-D standard. Since it is also likely that the resistance of the driver and receiver circuitry is different for the MARK–SPACE transition than for the SPACE–MARK transition, there will always be a different amount of time required to charge the cable capacitance in the two transitions. The increased capacitance caused by going beyond 50 feet will compound that difference, with the result that the receiver circuits will produce MARK bits that are longer than the SPACE bits ("marking distortion") or SPACE bits that are longer than the MARK bits ("spacing distortion"). This type of distortion, called "bias distortion," can cause characters to be received incorrectly, especially if clock speed distortion is present or if there is noise associated with the transitions between the signal states. Examples of these effects are shown in Figure 3–2. In the speed versus distance charts shown in Appendix A, a bias distortion limit

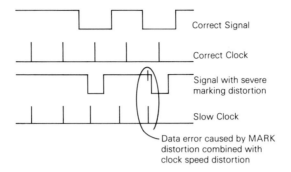

Correct Signal

Correct Clock

Signal with severe
marking distortion

Slow Clock

Data error caused by MARK
distortion combined with
clock speed distortion

Figure 3–2   Effect of Clock Distortion and Bias
Distortion

of 10 percent was arbitrarily chosen as a maximum to allow for the existence of other types of distortion. As the speed versus distance charts
indicate, it is possible to use EIA interfaces over cable distances in excess
of 50 feet, but doing so violates the standard.

In addition to the capacitance problems posed by distances over 50 feet,
further difficulty may be produced by crosstalk, especially when synchronous interfaces containing clock leads are used. Shielded clock leads are
recommended, but a discussion of synchronous interfaces will be deferred
until Chapter 14.

The third and final problem of electrical properties of the EIA interface
not solved by integrated circuits is that of ground reference. In the rules
listed above, the voltage $V_1$ is always measured relative to the Signal
Ground, Circuit AB. In order that $V_1$ not reach arbitrarily large values
relative to the logic ground at the receiver, it is customary to connect
Circuit AB to the logic ground of the device containing the receiver circuit.
Unfortunately, since logic ground at the transmitting station and logic
ground at the receiving station may differ, a ground current may flow
through the Signal Ground wire. Since that wire has nonzero resistance, a
voltage drop will exist across it. That voltage drop will cause the voltage
applied to the interchange circuit by the driver to appear differently to the
receiver than would be the case if no ground differential existed. For example, in Figure 3–3, the driver is asserting +5 volts, but the receiver sees
only +3 volts.

In Figure 3–4, the driver is asserting −5 volts, but the receiver sees −7

Figure 3–3   Effect of Ground Potential Difference on a +5 Volt Signal

Figure 3–4   Effect of Ground Potential Difference on a −5 Volt Signal

volts. The 2 volt drop in the "ground" wire remains the same regardless of the assertion of the driver because the 2 volt differential is due to a difference between logic ground at the transmitting and receiving stations, independent of the data being transmitted. The difference between the logic grounds is probably due to the difference between the electrical grounds at the transmitting and receiving stations, which in turn is due to the two stations being on different electrical feeders.

Comparing Figures 3–3 and 3–4 to the condensed set of EIA rules listed above shows that the data will be interpreted correctly despite the ground potential differences at the receiving and transmitting stations because the potential difference is absorbed in the "noise margin" provided in the EIA spec. Consider, however, the same examples with a ground potential difference of 9 volts; the receiver will see −4 volts and −14 volts, respectively, in the two figures. Each of these will be interpreted as a MARK. In fact, the potential difference does not have to be that big for loss to occur. A potential difference of 3 volts is sufficient for the receiver to see +2 volts in Figure 3–3, and +2 volts is in the undefined (transition) region.

Furthermore, since ground potential differences cause receivers to change their threshold points, the effects of the bias distortion caused by cable capacitance is increased. See Appendix A, Figures A–2 through A–7.

In summary, EIA-232-D was intended as an interface specification for connection of computer/modem interfaces and terminals to modems over distances of 50 feet or less. It will work moderately well over greater distances, as indicated in Appendix A, and in fact will work over distances far greater than those shown. However, cable capacitance, clock speed distortion, noise, and ground potential difference make successful operation in many cases increasingly unlikely at distances beyond those shown in Appendix A.

Realizing the unsuitability of a single specification for both local connection and longer distance transmission, the Electronic Industries Association came out with two newer specifications, EIA-422-A (Electrical Characteristics of Balanced Voltage Digital Interface Circuits) and EIA-423-A (Electrical Characteristics of Unbalanced Voltage Digital Interface Circuits). The companion CCITT Recommendations are V.11 and V.10, respectively.

Figure 3–5 shows a balanced digital interface circuit appropriate to EIA-422-A. Briefly stated, the rules are: 1) the A terminal of the generator shall be negative with respect to the B terminal for a binary "1" (MARK or OFF) state, and 2) the A terminal of the generator shall be positive with respect to the B terminal for a binary "0" (SPACE or ON). There are also various rules concerning open circuit voltages, short circuit currents, power-off characteristics, output signal waveform, receiver input current/voltage relationships, input sensitivity, and input balance. The most important part of this specification is that the receiver makes its determination of what is a MARK and what is a SPACE on the basis of the relationship of the A terminal to the B, not the relationship of the terminal to ground. EIA-422-A includes a speed versus distance table, which is reproduced in Appendix A.

EIA-423-A applies to unbalanced voltage interfaces. Figure 3–6 shows a generator and load arrangement appropriate to EIA-423-A. The rules here are: 1) the A terminal of the generator shall be negative with respect to the C terminal for a binary "1" (MARK or OFF) state, and 2) the A terminal of the generator shall be positive with respect to the C terminal for a binary "0" (SPACE or ON) state. As with EIA-422-A, there are also various rules concerning the open circuit voltages, the short circuit currents, and so on. The most important aspect of this specification is that the receiver determines the signal being transmitted on the basis of the voltage of lead A relative to the signal ground lead. Only a limited amount—4 volts—of $V_g$ (ground potential difference) can be accommodated. EIA-423-A also includes a speed versus distance table, which is reproduced in Appendix A.

To define the functional and mechanical characteristics of the EIA-422-A and EIA-423-A interfaces, the Electronic Industries Association created EIA-449. This standard divides the interchange circuits into two categories, Category I (two data, three timing, and five other circuits) and Category II (all other circuits). Below 20,000 bps, Category I circuits can be implemented with EIA-422-A or EIA-423-A drivers and receivers. Above 20,000 bps, EIA-422-A circuitry must be used. The Category II circuits, which are generally status and maintenance circuits, are always EIA-423-A. EIA-449 also specifies the mechanical characteristics of the connectors (a 37-pin connector) and specifies the circuit names, functions, and pin assignments.

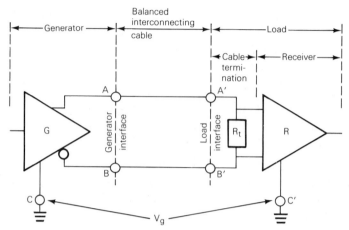

Legend

| | | |
|---|---|---|
| $R_t$ | = | Optional cable termination resistance |
| $V_g$ | = | Ground potential difference |
| A,B | = | Generator interface points |
| A',B' | = | Load interface points |
| C | = | Generator circuit ground |
| C' | = | Load circuit ground |

Figure 3–5  Balanced Digital Interface Circuit

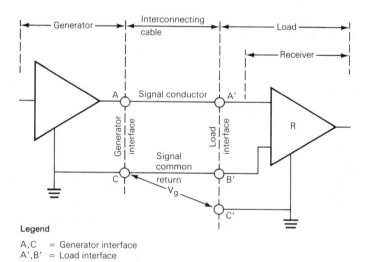

Legend

| | | |
|---|---|---|
| A,C | = | Generator interface |
| A',B' | = | Load interface |
| C' | = | Load circuit ground |
| C | = | Generator circuit ground |
| $V_g$ | = | Ground potential difference |

Figure 3–6  Unbalanced Digital Interface Circuit

Since EIA-449 permits the use of EIA-423-A drivers and receivers at speeds below 20,000 bps and EIA-423-A is an unbalanced interface, it is possible to interoperate an EIA-449 interface and an EIA-232-D interface at speeds below 20,000 bps if certain precautions are taken. EIA Industrial Electronics Bulletin Number 12, "Application Notes on Interconnection Between Interface Circuits Using RS-449 and RS-232-C," explains these precautions in detail. The precautions involve overvoltage protection, fail-safe circuitry, load resistance, and signal waveshaping, in addition to the mechanics of connecting 37-pin connectors to 25-pin connectors.

While an increasing number of products have adopted EIA-422-A and EIA-423-A over the past ten years, the EIA-449 functional and mechanical characteristics associated with these interfaces have not been widely adopted. Computers have become much smaller, and the price of gold has become much higher, since the 37-pin connector was first proposed. Many computer manufacturers have chosen their own connector for EIA-422-A and EIA-423-A; in many cases they have chosen the 25-pin connector normally used for EIA-232-D.

In response to the industry's lack of enthusiasm for the 37-pin connector, a new standard, EIA-530, has been adopted with the intent of gradually replacing EIA-449. The new standard is called "High Speed 25-Position Interface for Data Terminal Equipment [DTE] and Data Circuit Terminating Equipment [DCE]." It is intended for use at signaling rates from 20,000 bps to a nominal upper limit of 2 megabits per second. Like EIA-449, it divides the interchange circuits into two categories. The high-speed circuits (Category I) are always implemented with EIA-422-A and include Transmitted Data, Received Data, Transmit Signal Element Timing—DTE, Transmit Signal Element Timing—DCE, Receiver Signal Element Timing—DCE, Request to Send, Clear to Send, Received Line Signal Detector, DCE (Data Set) Ready, and DTE (Data Terminal) Ready. The low-speed circuits (Category II) are always implemented with EIA-423-A and include Local Loopback, Remote Loopback, and Test Mode.

There are several interesting differences between EIA-530 and other EIA interface standards:

1. The interchange circuit definitions are the same as those for EIA-232-D, but no mention is made of passing information between the DTE and the DCE for automatic calling or configuring the DCE (see Chapter 11).

2. Circuit TM, Test Mode, is mandatory for all except "Data and Timing Only"

interfaces. In other words, if Request to Send, Clear to Send, and so on are provided, Test Mode must also be provided. EIA-530 goes into considerable detail concerning testing.

3. An unusual feature of the implementation of EIA-423-A used for the Category II circuits is that only a single ground reference line is used across the interface and all receivers and transmitters are referenced to it. EIA-423-A normally requires that the transmitters of the DTE send their reference ground across the interface to the receivers of the DCE, and vice versa.

4. If any of the control signals is not implemented, it must be replaced with a dummy generator (see EIA-530 for details).

5. Circuit CE (CCITT 125), Calling Indicator, is not included.

6. A specific distance limit for EIA-422-A operation is chosen for "nontailored" applications. That distance is 60 meters (200 feet).

The pin assignments for EIA-530 are given in Appendix G. While the pinning is similar to EIA-232-D, interoperation is not possible without considerable effort. Further, attempted interoperation or accidental cross-plugging poses a danger because the voltages present on an EIA-232-D interface may damage 422/423 interface integrated circuits if those circuits were designed to operate only at 422/423 voltage limits of ±6 volts. Voltages used in EIA-232-D interfaces may be considerably higher; an open circuit voltage as high as 25 volts can occur. EIA-449 interfaces can interoperate with EIA-530 interfaces; this is discussed in EIA-530.

Despite the advances made in the speeds and distances possible with the EIA interfaces, occasions arise when these capabilities are insufficient. Achieving data communication beyond the limits of the EIA interfaces is discussed in the next chapter.

# 4

## Beyond Interface Standards

In Appendix A, the speed versus distance characteristics of EIA-232-D, EIA-423-A, and EIA-422-A are discussed in detail, but the information presented there can be summarized in the following table:

|            | EIA-232-D | EIA-423-A | EIA-422-A |
|------------|-----------|-----------|-----------|
| 300 baud   | 3000 ft   | 4000 ft   | 4000 ft   |
| 2400 baud  | 500 ft    | 1500 ft   | 4000 ft   |
| 9600 baud  | 250 ft    | 400 ft    | 4000 ft   |

As indicated in the preceding chapters and in Appendix A, the numbers in the table are only approximate, and other factors, such as ground potential differences between the transmitting and receiving stations, will influence the results obtained. ("Your mileage may vary.")

One of the external factors that may influence the ability to transmit data is noise. For example, consider a requirement to transmit telemetry and control information between switching stations of a power distribution network. Since the most direct and economical path is to run the data communication wiring along the same right of way as the power lines, data transmission must be accomplished in a very high noise environment. An excellent solution in this situation, and in many less dramatic noise environments, is the use of fiber optics.

In an optical fiber installation, a laser or a light emitting diode (LED) emits light into the end of a glass or plastic fiber. The behavior of the light within the fiber depends on the type of fiber being used. In some cases, the light bounces off the inside of the fiber surface; in other cases, the light is bent back toward the center if it deviates toward the edges of the fiber; and in yet other cases, all the light travels in a straight line down the center of the fiber. Regardless of the method used, the basic concept is that the light is trapped within the fiber until it reaches a photodetector at the distant end, at which point an electrical signal is recovered. There are several extremely important virtues of fiber-optic transmission:

1. Tremendous bandwidth is available. Transmission rates in excess of one trillion bps (1 gigabit) have been demonstrated.
2. The fibers are very small. A cable the size of a 25-pair wire cable can carry 25 fiber pairs, each carrying the tremendous bandwidths cited above.
3. There is no crosstalk. Fibers do not allow their signals to escape into other fibers. This also makes them very secure and difficult to tap.
4. While the receiver units are sensitive to noise and must be carefully constructed, the transmission medium is not sensitive to noise.
5. There is no electrical path between the transmitting point and the receiving point. Ground differences and lightning strikes have no effect.
6. Signal regeneration is required at intervals measured in dozens of miles, rather than at one-mile intervals common with other transmission methods.

As with other data transmission systems, there are a number of fiber-optic transmission methods available, and the high-capacity long-distance methods cited in items 1 and 6 of the above list are too expensive for use by other than telecommunications companies. However, less sophisticated products that have all the other virtues listed above are available at very reasonable prices. For example, a system consisting of two full-duplex "fiber-optic data drivers" and 200 feet of duplex plastic fiber to connect them can be purchased for less than $325. Each fiber-optic data driver plugs into, and is powered by, a standard EIA-232-D connector. Transmission is possible at rates up to 19,200 bps over the 200-foot distance. The distance can be increased to 3300 feet by using a slightly different data driver and glass fiber rather than plastic.

Anyone planning a data transmission system that will operate in a noisy environment, or a system that involves transmission between buildings, should seriously consider the use of fiber optics. As indicated above, a wide range of products from the simple to the sophisticated is available.

In many data communications applications, the user does not have the choice of using various EIA interfaces, line drivers, or fiber optics, but must use a line leased from the telephone company and equipped with modems.

The remainder of this chapter deals with simple modems for use on leased lines (also called private lines) and the interface leads used to control these modems.

At one time, the phrase "private line" meant a single party telephone line as opposed to a "party line," but now it refers to a circuit permanently in place between two end points. While the circuit may be accomplished by wires, it can also be accomplished by microwaves, light beams, satellite links, and so on.

The simplest case of a private line is one that a person or company owns and installs without the assistance of a common carrier, such as the telephone company. Generally speaking, such lines can easily be installed within the same building or on the same continuous property, where "continuous" usually includes property pieces directly across from each other on opposite sides of a public right of way. With appropriate licensing arrangements, it can also include microwave towers or satellite earth stations.

The more common case is one in which a person or company rents a line from the local common carrier. This is usually the telephone company but may be one of the specialized common carriers; in many countries, it is the government post and telegraph (PTT) authority.

When customer-owned wire is used, the electrical characteristics of the wire, the electrical interference presented to the wire by outside sources, and the possibility of the wire creating interference are the limiting factors on the speed and distance of transmission. For licensed, customer-owned facilities (such as microwave), maximum signal rates and signal powers are determined by the equipment and the licensing restrictions. For channels provided by common carriers, the common carrier tariffs specify the operating restrictions as well as the rental rates for various services.

While digital transmission (see Chapter 23) offers signaling rates of 1200 baud to 1.544 megabaud, and while the analog offerings of the telephone companies can be subdivided into chunks larger than those required for voice grade transmission, the most common size channel used for data communication is the "voice grade" channel. This facility has a frequency response of roughly 300 to 3000 Hz. The equipment used to construct voice grade private lines is somewhat different from that used to construct dialed network calls. Amplifiers are used to repeat or regenerate the audio signals on a telephone transmission medium. While some of these amplifiers have been designed to operate on a "two-wire" basis, most of them operate on a "four-wire" basis. The remainder of this book assumes that all transmission facilities containing amplifiers are four-wire transmission facilities.

A simple connection between two telephones is shown in Figure 4–1. Note that only two wires are required for the connection and that the signals from party A to party B and those from party B to party A are present on the line simultaneously. If a substantial distance separates the two parties, it may be necessary to add amplification (repeaters). Since amplifiers are essentially unidirectional devices (i.e., have an INPUT side and an OUTPUT side), it is necessary for the transmission facility to be divided in half. The east-west transmission facility contains an amplifier for party A to transmit more loudly to party B, and the west-east transmission facility contains an amplifier for party B to transmit more loudly to party A. Such an arrangement is shown in Figure 4–2. Note that in this case the telephone instruments do not contain circuitry to permit signals from the transmitter and the earpiece to be simultaneously present on a single wire pair. Rather, the transmitter of each telephone runs through the amplifier to the earpiece of the other telephone.

In a nationwide telephone network, amplifiers are also used, but the telephone switching systems used at the ends of the connection are those used for local calls. Since local calls have traditionally been switched on a two-wire basis, without amplifiers, the local switching equipment and the "local loops" (the wires to people's homes and businesses) are designed for

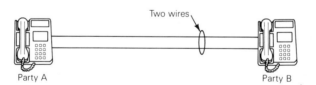

Figure 4–1   A Simple Connection between Two Telephones

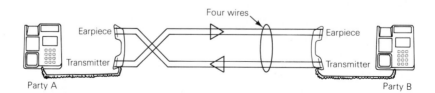

Figure 4–2   A Four-Wire Connection between Two Telephones

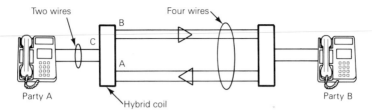

**Note**  For simplicity, power supplies have been left out of these figures.

Figure 4–3   A Connection between Two Two-Wire Telephones over a Four-Wire Transmission Facility

only two-wire operation. Thus, a conversion must be made between the two-wire circuits used locally and the four-wire circuits used for long-distance transmission. This is accomplished by a hybrid coil, which is shown as a simple rectangle in Figure 4–3. The "rules" of the hybrid coil are that signals entering at A go to C but not to B, while signals entering at C go to B but not to A. In some ways, the hybrid coil may be likened to a divider strip down the center of a highway at the point where a divided highway becomes an undivided highway. Figure 4–4a shows how hybrid coils fit into a typical long-distance call. Note that most of the switching equipment interspersed between the "local offices" is capable of switching all four wires simultaneously.

Figure 4–4b shows a two-wire private line as it is usually implemented over a substantial distance, and Figure 4–4c shows a four-wire private line. Note that the only difference between the two-wire and four-wire private lines is that the local loop in the latter case consists of two pairs rather than one. For this reason, the cost of a four-wire private line is usually only slightly more than that of a two-wire private line for the distance between local "rating points" (usually the local switching centers), plus the cost of an additional local loop pair at each end. Thus, for a small additional investment, the customer gets two complete circuits of voice grade quality—one from east to west and one from west to east. Essentially the only reasons one would ever want a two-wire private line for data transmission are that over shorter distances (sometimes within the same state) four-wire is exactly twice the price of two-wire, or that the application permanently calls for transmission in only one direction. Even half-duplex transmission can benefit from four-wire facilities because of the lack of turnaround delay. Usually, however, people with four-wire facilities make the most of them by using full duplex.

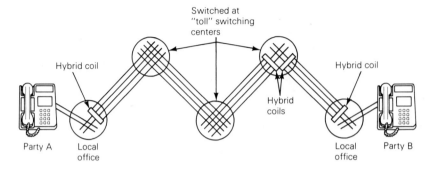

Figure 4–4a   Typical Telephone Call

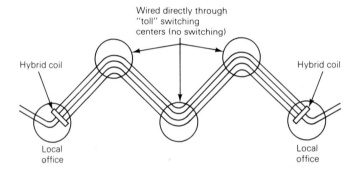

Figure 4–4b   Typical Two-Wire Circuit Implementation

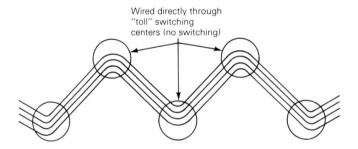

Figure 4–4c   Typical Four-Wire Circuit Implementation

In summary, private lines offer the benefit of obtaining four-wire service for only a modest increase in cost over two-wire service.

A second feature of private lines is that the same transmission facilities are used for the connection at all times. In Figure 4–4a it should be noted that the connections shown between switching centers could consist of different transmission facilities on various calls. The common carriers do their best to keep the electrical characteristics of the transmission facilities consistent. It is possible, however, for calls from one point to another to go through entirely different cities at different times of day, so there is considerable variation. On private lines, the facilities are fixed, with the exception of microwave protection switching, which uses different routes due to atmospheric problems. As a result, the electrical characteristics of the circuit are less variable with time. Additional circuitry can be added to correct for the various degradations that do exist. This process is called "conditioning." When done by the common carriers, there is usually a one-time charge and a monthly charge for conditioning. The cost of conditioning rapidly becomes a minor part of the line cost as the distance increases. Many synchronous modems will operate on unconditioned lines and thus eliminate conditioning costs altogether.

The third and most important feature of private lines is that they can offer cost savings if there is sufficient traffic between the two points involved. The cost justification for a private line is a rather complex process and depends on the application. First of all, private lines are generally unsuitable for applications where the end points of calls vary. In addition, private lines are usually unsuitable for applications where calls are infrequent, such as inventory control systems where each plant calls the central computer once a day for five minutes or where the central computer calls each plant for a similar length of time. When data traffic is heavy or when the calls are so frequent that call setup time would be annoying, however, private lines are ideal. Reservation systems, process control networks, and similar computer-to-computer communications networks are examples. The basic questions to be answered are:

1. Is the application suited to private lines?
2. How does the cost of separate telephone calls compare to the cost of a private line?
3. Does a private line offer a necessary feature, such as four-wire operation?
4. Can a back-up system be installed?

If a private line is desirable, it becomes necessary to consider the various modems that could be used. Both asynchronous and synchronous modems are available, and most users of private lines use synchronous modems because they offer higher speeds. However, since synchronous transmission will not be discussed until Chapter 14 and asynchronous modems offer a good introduction to modem control requirements, this chapter concentrates on asynchronous modems.

The simplest modems available for private line use are those that are "Bell 103 compatible." This type of modem, when arranged for "originate" frequencies, converts the data presented to it on the Transmit Data lead to tones of 1070 Hz for a binary "0" (SPACE) and 1270 Hz for a binary "1" (MARK). When this modem receives a tone of 2025 Hz, it applies a SPACE signal to the Received Data lead, and when it receives a tone of 2225 Hz, it applies a MARK signal to the Received Data lead. The 1070/1270 Hz signals are being sent to, and the 2025/2225 Hz signals are being received from, a similar 103 that is equipped for "answer" frequencies. A 103 equipped for answer frequencies transmits a SPACE as 2025 Hz and a MARK as 2225 Hz. It interprets a received signal of 1070 Hz as a SPACE and a received signal of 1270 Hz as a MARK.

When configuring a private line with these modems, one of the questions to be answered for each modem is whether the tones should be "Answer Mode" or "Originate Mode." In a two-point private line, one of the stations will be in Answer Mode and one will be in Originate Mode. If the modems are being used on a multipoint private line, the choice of Answer Mode or Originate Mode must be programmably changed as various combinations of stations communicate with each other. (Before modern programmable-option modems, the Answer/Originate choice was done via jumpers or an interface lead called "CY.")

While one of the benefits of private wire configurations is that four-wire service is available for a marginal increase in cost, it should be noted that 103-type modems can operate in full-duplex mode on two-wire facilities. They accomplish this essentially by dividing the two-wire transmission path into two channels on the basis of the frequencies used. One channel is the band of frequencies from 300 to 1700 Hz and the other from 1700 to 3000 Hz. This separation is accomplished with filters, as shown in Figure 4–5.

The transmitter section of the modem that uses originate frequencies has a filter that allows the 300 to 1700 Hz frequencies to reach the line. This filter is provided to prevent various extraneous frequencies generated by the modulation process from reaching the line. The receiver section of that same modem has a filter that allows only the 1700 to 3000 Hz frequencies through. This filter prevents the receiver from "hearing" the transmitter

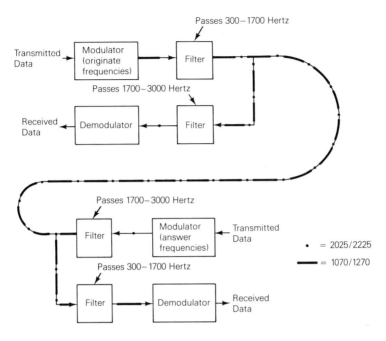

Figure 4–5   300 Baud Full-Duplex Modem Frequency Assignment and Operation

in the same modem. The modem at the other end of the line has exactly the opposite set of filters. A filter on the transmitter allows 1700 to 3000 Hz to be transmitted to the line, and a filter in front of the receiver blocks these same frequencies from reaching the receiver. Note, however, that each receiver's filter does allow the frequencies from the other modem's transmitter to pass through.

The 103-type modem has a relatively small number of control leads. The "Request to Send" lead turns on the modem's transmitter section; the purpose of this lead varies with the application. In multipoint systems, where a master station transmits to a number of slave stations, the master station would have its Request to Send lead asserted, while the slave stations, with the exception of the slave responding to the poll from the master station, would have their Request to Send leads negated.

An additional lead called "Data Channel Received Line Signal Detector" or "Carrier Detect" has the following function in 103-type modems: When asserted, it indicates that the receiver section of the modem is receiving tones from the distant modem.

The 103 uses the frequency spectrum available on a voice grade line to

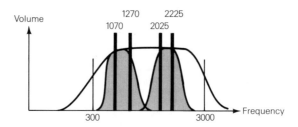

Figure 4–6   Frequency Utilization for 300 Baud
Full-Duplex Modem

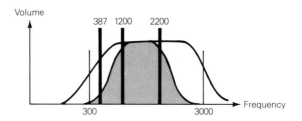

Figure 4–7   Frequency Utilization for 1200 Baud
Half-Duplex Modem with Reverse Channel

transmit data in both directions simultaneously as shown in Figure 4–6. It is also possible to use the frequency spectrum shown in Figure 4–7. Here a SPACE is represented by 2200 Hz and a MARK by 1200 Hz, and data is transmitted at 1200 bps in only one direction at a time. If four-wire facilities are used, two frequency spectra are available: one for data transmitted from west to east and one for data transmitted from east to west. In diagram form, this would be represented as two copies of Figure 4–7. The rarely used Bell System 202-series modems and their equivalents are examples of this type of modem.

The 103-type and 202-type modems discussed here also can be used on the public switched telephone network (PSTN). In a symmetrical fashion, the more sophisticated PSTN modems discussed later in the book also can be used on private lines. The reason for discussing the 103-type and 202-type here is that they are the simplest modems, and their use on private lines introduces the need for control leads by which a computer/modem interface controls the actions of a modem and by which a modem reports its status to the computer/modem interface. The control and status leads for private line modems are discussed in Chapter 5.

# 5

## Private Line Modem Control

The interface circuits defined here are those required for interfacing the private line modems discussed at the end of Chapter 4. In Chapter 9, this list is expanded to include the interface leads required for controlling modems on switched network connections. These definitions are taken from EIA-232-D and are reproduced here by permission of EIA. The CCITT definitions are taken from Recommendation V.24 and are reproduced here by permission of the CCITT. To make these definitions more readable, two slight changes have been made:

1. CCITT circuits are identified by name as well as number. For example, reference to "Circuit 103" has been changed to "Circuit 103 (Transmitted Data)."

2. Additional comments or references to other portions of the book have been added in square brackets [ ].

A comparison between these definitions and earlier versions will reveal that Protective Ground (EIA AA/CCITT 101) is no longer included, the definition of Signal Ground (EIA AB/CCITT 102) has been changed, and several circuit definitions now contain references to serial automatic calling units. Serial automatic calling units are discussed in Chapter 11, so readers are advised to skim any references to them in the paragraphs below and to return for a more careful reading of those references after reading Chapter 11.

| EIA-232-D Definitions | CCITT V.24 Definitions |
|---|---|
| *Circuit AB*—Signal Ground or Common Return (CCITT 102) <br> Direction: Not applicable | *Circuit 102*—Signal Ground or Common Return |

**EIA-232-D**
**Definitions**

*Circuit AB (Cont.)*

This conductor establishes the common ground reference potential for all interchange circuits. Within the DCE, this circuit shall be brought to one point, and it shall be possible to connect this point to Protective Ground by means of a wire strap inside the equipment. This wire strap can be connected or removed at installation, as may be required to meet applicable regulations or to minimize the introduction of noise into electronic circuitry. The strap may be paralleled by an impedance (high at low frequencies) to provide, when the strap is removed, for immunity to static discharges or for other purposes. (The requirement for a removable strap is not intended to change the satisfactory status of existing DCEs which provide, in accordance with EIA-422-A, a connection of circuit AB to Protective Ground with a 100-ohm resistor.)

*Circuit BA*—Transmitted Data (CCITT 103)
Direction: To DCE

Signals on this circuit are generated by the DTE and are transferred to the local transmitting signal converter for transmission of data to remote DTEs or for maintenance or control of the local transmitting signal converter.

The DTE holds Circuit BA (Transmitted Data) in marking condition at all times when no data are being transmitted.

In all systems, the DTE shall not transmit data unless an ON condition is present on all of the following four circuits, where implemented.

1. Circuit CA (Request to Send)

**CCITT V.24**
**Definitions**

*Circuit 102 (Cont.)*

This conductor establishes the signal common return for unbalanced interchange circuits with electrical characteristics according to Recommendation V.28 and the d.c. reference potential for interchange circuits according to Recommendations V.10, V.11 and V.35.

Within the DCE, this circuit shall be brought to one point, and it shall be possible to connect this point to protective ground or earth by means of a metallic strap within the equipment. This metallic strap can be connected or removed at installation, as may be required to meet applicable regulations or to minimize the introduction of noise into electronic circuitry. Caution should be exercised to prevent the establishment of ground loops carrying high currents.

*Circuit 103*—Transmitted Data
Direction: To DCE

The data signals originated by the DTE:

1. to be transmitted via the data channel to one or more remote data stations,

2. to be passed to the DCE for maintenance test purposes under control of the DTE, or

3. for the programming or control of serial automatic calling DCEs,

are transferred on this circuit to the DCE.

| EIA-232-D Definitions | CCITT V.24 Definitions |
|---|---|

2. Circuit CB (Clear to Send)

3. Circuit CC (DCE Ready)

4. Circuit CD (DTE Ready)

*Circuit BB*—Received Data (CCITT 104)
Direction: From DCE

Signals on this circuit are generated by the receiving signal converter in response to data signals received from remote DTE via the remote transmitting signal converter, or by the receiving signal converter in response to maintenance or control data signals from the local DTE. Circuit BB (Received Data) shall be held in the binary ONE (Marking) condition at all times when Circuit CF (Received Line Signal Detector) is in the OFF condition.

On a half-duplex channel, Circuit BB shall be held in the binary ONE (Marking) condition when Circuit CA (Request to Send) is in the ON condition and for a brief interval following the ON to OFF transition of Circuit CA to allow for the completion of transmission (see Circuit BA—Transmitted Data) and the decay of line reflections.

*Circuit CA*—Request to Send (CCITT 105)
Direction: To DCE

This circuit is used to condition the local DCE for data transmission and, on a half-duplex channel, to control the direction of data transmission of the local DCE.

On one way only channels or duplex channels, the ON condition maintains the data communication equipment in the transmit mode. The OFF condition

*Circuit 104*—Received Data
Direction: From DCE

The data signals generated by the DCE:

1. in response to data channel line signals received from a remote data station,

2. in response to the DTE maintenance test signals, or

3. data signals generated by a serial automatic calling DCE, in response to programming or control signals from the DTE, are transferred on this circuit to the DTE.

NOTE—The reception conditions for maintenance test signals are specified with circuit 107.

*Circuit 105*—Request to Send
Direction: To DCE

Signals on this circuit control the data channel transmit function of the DCE.

The ON condition causes the DCE to assume the data channel transmit mode.

The OFF condition causes the DCE to assume the data channel non-transmit mode, when all data transferred on circuit 103 (Transmitted Data) have been transmitted.

**EIA-232-D**
**Definitions**

*Circuit CA (Cont.)*

maintains the DCE in a non-transmit mode.

On a half-duplex channel, the ON condition maintains the DCE in the transmit mode and inhibits the receive mode. The OFF condition maintains the DCE in the receive mode.

A transition from OFF to ON instructs the DCE to enter the transmit mode. The DCE responds by taking such action as may be necessary and indicates completion of such actions by turning ON Circuit CB (Clear to Send), thereby indicating to the DTE that data may be transferred across the interface point on interchange Circuit BA (Transmitted Data).

A transition from ON to OFF instructs the DCE to complete the transmission of all data which was previously transferred across the interface point on interchange Circuit BA and then assume a non-transmit mode or a receive mode as appropriate. The DCE responds to this instruction by turning OFF Circuit CB (Clear to Send) when it is prepared to again respond to a subsequent ON condition of Circuit CA.

NOTE—A non-transmit mode does not imply that all line signals have been removed from the communication channel.

When Circuit CA is turned OFF, it shall not be turned ON again until Circuit CB has been turned OFF by the data communication equipment.

**CCITT V.24**
**Definitions**

*Interrelationship of Circuits 103, 105, and 106*

The DTE signals its intent to transmit data by turning ON Circuit 105 (Request to Send). It is then the responsibility of the DCE to enter the transmit mode, i.e., be prepared to transmit data, and also to alert the remote DCE and condition it to receive data. The means by which a DCE enters the transmit mode and alerts and conditions the remote modem are described in the appropriate DCE Recommendation.

When the transmitting DCE turns Circuit 106 (Ready for Sending) ON with circuit 107 (Data Set Ready) in the ON condition, the DTE is permitted to transfer data across the interface on Circuit 103 (Transmitted Data). By turning ON Circuit 106 with circuit 107 ON, it is implied that all data transferred across the interface prior to the time that any one of the four circuits (105, 106, 107, and 108/1 or 108/2) is again turned OFF, will be transferred to the line; however, the ON condition of Circuit 106 is not necessarily a guarantee that the remote DCE is in the receive mode. (Depending on the complexity and sophistication of the transmitting signal converter, there may be a delay ranging from less than a millisecond up to several seconds between the time a bit is transferred across the interface until the time a signal element representing this bit is transmitted on the line.)

When the transmitting DCE turns circuit 106 (Ready for Sending) ON, with circuit 107 (Data Set Ready) in the OFF condition, the DTE is permitted to

**EIA-232-D**
**Definitions**

It is permissible to turn Circuit CA ON at any time when Circuit CB is OFF regardless of the condition of any other interchange circuit.

**CCITT V.24**
**Definitions**

transfer programming or control signals to a serial automatic calling DCE across the interface on circuit 103 (Transmitted Data).

During data transfer, the DTE shall not turn Circuit 105 (Request to Send) OFF before the end of the last bit (data bit or stop element) transferred across the interface on Circuit 103. Similarly, in certain full-duplex switched network applications where Circuit 105 is not implemented (see specific DCE Recommendations), this requirement applies equally when Circuit 108/1–108/2 is turned OFF to terminate a switched network call.

Where Circuit 105 is provided, the ON and OFF conditions on Circuit 106 during the data transfer phase (i.e. circuit 107 ON) shall be responses to the ON and OFF conditions on Circuit 105. For the appropriate response times of Circuit 106, and for the operation of Circuit 106 when Circuit 105 is not provided, refer to the relevant Recommendation for DCE.

For serial automatic calling DCEs, the ON and OFF conditions on circuit 106 (Ready for Sending) outside the data transfer phase (i.e. circuit 107 [Data Set Ready] OFF) shall be dependent on the interface state during automatic call set-up and associated procedures. The transitions on circuit 106 for this application shall be as detailed in Recommendation V.25 *bis*.

When Circuit 105 (Request to Send) and Circuit 106 (Ready for Sending) are both OFF, the DTE shall maintain a binary 1 condition on Circuit 103 (Transmitted

**EIA-232-D**
**Definitions**

**CCITT V.24**
**Definitions**

*Interrelationship (Cont.)*

Data). When Circuit 105 is turned OFF it shall not be turned ON again until Circuit 106 is turned OFF by the DCE.

*Circuit CB*—Clear to Send (CCITT 106—Ready for Sending)
Direction: From DCE

Signals on this circuit are generated by the DCE to indicate whether or not the DCE is ready to transmit data.

The ON condition together with the ON condition on interchange circuits CA, CC and, where implemented, CD, is an indication to the DTE that signals presented on Circuit BA (Transmitted Data) will be transmitted to the communication channel.

The OFF condition is an indication to the DTE that it should not transfer data across the interface on interchange Circuit BA.

The ON condition of Circuit CB is a response to the occurrence of a simultaneous ON condition on Circuits CC (DCE Ready) and Circuit CA (Request to Send), delayed as may be appropriate for the DCE to establish a data communication channel. This includes the removal of the MARK HOLD clamp from the Received Data interchange circuit of the remote DCE.

Where Circuit CA (Request to Send) is not implemented in the DCE with transmitting capability, Circuit CA shall be assumed to be in the ON condition at all times, and Circuit CB shall respond accordingly.

*Circuit 106*—Ready for Sending
Direction: From DCE

Signals on this circuit indicate whether the DCE is prepared to accept data signals for transmission on the data channel or for maintenance test purposes under control of the DTE.

The ON condition indicates that the DCE is prepared to accept data signals from the DTE.

The OFF condition indicates that the DCE is not prepared to accept data signals from the DTE.

The Clear to Send signal means slightly different things in different modems. In full-duplex modems not equipped with an error-detection system, it indicates that the carrier is being received from the distant modem and is thus a fairly good indication that a suitable communications channel exists. In full-duplex modems equipped with an error-detection system, it indicates that internal buffers within the modem are ready to accept data for transmission. In some older modems (Bell 103 series), Clear to Send and Carrier Detect are tied together or may function separately if the "CB–CF Separate" option has been installed. Further details may be found in Appendix B.

In half-duplex modems, even when used on full-duplex facilities, Clear to Send is merely a delayed version of Request to Send. The modem interface control asserts Request to Send, and a timer in the modem, upon detecting this assertion, waits for up to 200 milliseconds (depending on option arrangements) and then asserts Clear to Send back to the modem interface. In this case, Clear to Send is really "Probably Clear to Send."

|  |  |
|---|---|
| **EIA-232-D**<br>**Definitions** | **CCITT V.24**<br>**Definitions** |

*Circuit CC*—DCE Ready (CCITT 107)
Direction: From DCE

*Circuit 107*—Data Set Ready
Direction: From DCE

Signals on this circuit are used to indicate the status of the local DCE.

Signals on this circuit indicate whether the DCE is ready to operate.

The ON condition on this circuit is presented to indicate that:

a) the local DCE is connected to a communication channel ("OFF HOOK" in switched service),

AND

b) the local DCE is not in talk (alternate voice) or, in switched service, is not in dial mode,*

AND

c) in switched service, the local DCE has completed, where applicable—

The ON condition, where circuit 142 (Test Indicator) is OFF or is not implemented, indicates that the signal converter or similar equipment is connected to the line and that the DCE is ready to exchange further control signals with the DTE to initiate the exchange of data.

The ON condition, in conjunction with the ON condition of circuit 142, indicates that the DCE is prepared to exchange data signals with the DTE for maintenance test purposes.

*The DCE is considered to be in the dial mode when circuitry directly associated with the call origination function is connected to the communication channel. The call origination function includes signaling to the central office (dialing) and monitoring the communication channel for call progress or answer back signals.

| EIA-232-D | CCITT V.24 |
|---|---|
| **Definitions** | **Definitions** |

*Circuit CC (Cont.)*

*Circuit 107 (Cont.)*

1. any timing functions required by the switching system to complete call establishment, and
2. The transmission of any discrete answer tone, the duration of which is controlled solely by the local DCE.

Where the local data communication equipment does not transmit an answer tone, or where the duration of the answer tone is controlled by some action of the remote DCE, the ON condition is presented as soon as all the other above conditions (a, b, and c-1) are satisfied.

The ON condition of this circuit shall not be used to indicate the status of any but the local DCE. It shall not be interpreted as either an indication that a communication channel has been established to a remote DCE or the status of any other DCE.

The OFF condition indicates that the local DCE

1. is not ready to operate,
2. has detected a fault condition (which may be network or DCE dependent) which has lasted longer than some fixed period of time, such period being network dependent, or,
3. in switched service, has detected a disconnect indication from the remote station or from the network.

The OFF condition, in conjunction with the ON condition on circuit 106, (Ready for Sending) indicates that the DCE is ready to exchange data signals associated with the programming or control of serial automatic calling DCEs.

The OFF condition, in conjunction with the OFF condition on circuit 106, indicates:

1. that the DCE is not ready to operate in the data transfer phase,
2. that it has detected a fault condition which may be network or DCE dependent, or
3. that it has detected a disconnect indication from the remote station or from the network.

NOTE—Provision of the capability defined in 2) and 3) above is a matter for Administrations unless it is specified in a DCE Recommendation.

*Operation of Circuits 107 and 108/1\* and 108/2\**

Signals on Circuit 107 (Data Set Ready) are to be considered as responses to signals which initiate connection to line, e.g., Circuit 108/1 (Connect Data Set to Line). However, the conditioning of a data channel, such as equalization and clamp removal, cannot be expected to occur before Circuit 107 is turned ON.

When the DCE is conditioned for automatic answering of calls, connection to the line occurs only in response to a combination of the calling signal and an

---

\*Circuits 108/1 and 108/2 are discussed in Chapter 9.

## EIA-232-D
### Definitions

In switched service, when the OFF condition occurs during the progress of a call before Circuit CD is turned OFF, the DTE shall interpret this as a lost or aborted connection and take action to terminate the call. Any subsequent ON condition on Circuit CC is to be considered a new call.

In a dedicated service, when the OFF condition occurs, the DTE shall interpret this as a hard failure, shall clamp Circuit BA to MARK and shall terminate any communication sessions in progress over the affected communications channel.

In switched service, when the DCE is used in conjunction with Automatic Calling Equipment (ACE), the OFF to ON transition of Circuit CC shall not be interpreted as an indication that the ACE has relinquished control of the communication channel to the DCE. Indication of this is given on the appropriate lead in the ACE interface (see EIA Standard EIA-366).

NOTE—Attention is called to the fact that, on a dedicated service, if a data call is interrupted by alternate voice communication, Circuit CC will be in the OFF condition during the time that voice communication is in progress. The transmission or reception of the signals required to condition the communication channel or DCE in response to the ON condition of interchange Circuit CA (Request to Send) of the transmitting DTE will take place after Circuit CC comes ON, but prior to the ON condition on Circuit CB (Clear to Send) or Circuit CF (Received Line Signal Detector).

## CCITT V.24
### Definitions

ON condition on circuit 108/2 (Data Terminal Ready).

A wiring option shall be provided within the DCE to select either Circuit 108/1 or Circuit 108/2 operation. In certain leased line applications, Circuit 108 might not be implemented, in which case the condition on this circuit is assumed to be permanently ON.

Under certain test conditions, both the DTE and the DCE may exercise some of the interchange circuits. Thus, when Circuit 107 (Data Set Ready) is OFF, and circuit 108/1 or 108/2 is OFF, the DTE is to ignore the conditions on any interchange circuit from the DCE except those on Circuit 125 (Calling Indicator) and the timing circuits, and the DCE is to ignore the conditions on any interchange circuit from the DTE.

The OFF condition on Circuit 108/1 or 108/2 shall not disable the operation of Circuit 125 (Calling Indicator).

When circuit 108/2 (Data Terminal Ready) is in the ON condition and circuit 107 (Data Set Ready) is in the OFF condition, the DTE may communicate with serial automatic calling DCEs on circuits 103 (Transmitted Data) and 104 (Received Data). This state is recognized by an ON condition on circuit 106 (Ready for Sending).

Under the loop test conditions defined in Recommendation V.54, circuit 107 (Data Set Ready) shall be in the OFF condition and not respond to circuit 108/1 or 108/2 when the DTE is not involved with maintenance testing. Circuit 142 (Test Indicator) shall be in the ON condition and circuit 107 shall respond to

| **EIA-232-D**<br>**Definitions** | **CCITT V.24**<br>**Definitions** |
| --- | --- |
| | *Operations (Cont.)* |

<table>
<tr><td></td><td>

circuit 108/1 or 108/2 when the DTE is involved in maintenance testing with the local or remote DCE.

When Circuit 108/1 or 108/2 (Data Terminal Ready) is turned OFF, it shall not be turned ON again until Circuit 107 (Data Set Ready) is turned OFF by the DCE and the OFF state of circuit 107 has been recognized by the DTE.

In the case where the DCE turns circuit 107 OFF first (see Note), the DTE shall consider the call aborted and shall proceed as described below: (Note—The provision of this mode of operation is a matter for Administrations unless it is specified in a DCE Recommendation.)

In the case of circuit 108/1 (Connect Data Set to Line), the DTE shall turn this circuit OFF with a minimal delay and shall hold the circuit in the OFF condition for a minimum of 500 ms and until it is ready to initiate a new call, or to answer an incoming call.

In the case of circuit 108/2, selection of a preferred protocol is left for further study. Administrations, manufacturers, and users are cautioned that protocols developed for this case may involve "lock-up" situations or unauthorized access to data bases.

</td></tr>
</table>

| *Circuit CF*—Received Line Signal Detector (CCITT 109)<br>Direction: From DCE | *Circuit 109*—Data Channel Received Line Signal Detector<br>Direction: From DCE |
| --- | --- |
| The ON condition on this circuit is presented when the DCE is receiving a sig- | Signals on this circuit indicate whether the received data channel line signal is |

| EIA-232-D Definitions | CCITT V.24 Definitions |
|---|---|
| nal which meets its suitability criteria. These criteria are established by the DCE manufacturer. | within appropriate limits, as specified in the relevant Recommendation for DCE. |
| The OFF condition indicates that no signal is being received or that the received signal does not meet the DCE's suitable criteria. | The ON condition indicates that the received signal is within appropriate limits. |
| The OFF condition of Circuit CF (Received Line Signal Detector) shall cause Circuit BB (Received Data) to be clamped to the Binary One (Marking) condition. | The OFF condition indicates that the received signal is not within appropriate limits. |
| The indications on this circuit shall follow the actual onset or loss of signal by appropriate guard delays. | |
| On half-duplex channels, Circuit CF is held in the OFF condition whenever Circuit CA (Request to Send) is in the ON condition and for a brief interval of time following the ON to OFF transition of Circuit CA (See Circuit BB.). | |

Received Line Signal Detector, commonly called "Carrier Detect," indicates that there is an appropriate tone being received from the distant modem. In a full-duplex arrangement, it is on whenever the communications channel exists and the distant modem has its Request to Send lead asserted—i.e., is transmitting. In half-duplex applications, it is on whenever carrier (tone) is on the line and the local modem's Request to Send lead is OFF; if the local modem is not transmitting the tone must be from the other modem. One exception to this rule is the Bell System 202C modem. In the modem the Carrier Detect lead is independent of the state of the local Request to Send lead and thus is on whenever either the local or distant modem has its transmitter on.

The Carrier Detect lead usually has an immunity to very short losses of carrier. Losses of less than 20 ±10 milliseconds are, as a rule, not reflected in the Carrier Detect lead.

There are a substantial number of EIA and CCITT circuits not described in the preceding lists, which are intended to provide a basis on which other chapters will build as further applications are discussed.

In the past three chapters, various technical details of the facilities used for getting data from one place to another have been discussed. Chapter 6 returns to the simple interface discussed in Chapter 2 but adds leads associated with the transmission facilities—in particular, modem control and status leads. The more complicated case of modem control and status for switched network use is treated in Chapter 9. A completely different concept in modem control and status—serial signaling using CCITT Recommendations X.20 and X.21—is discussed in Chapter 27.

# 6

## A Single Line Asynchronous UART with Private Line Modem Control

In Chapter 2, Figure 2–1 presented a block diagram of a single line asynchronous UART. Address selection logic was provided to gate the contents of the receiver buffer and various registers onto a microprocessor bus via "bus drivers," and to record the data from the microprocessor bus receivers into designated registers during write operations directed toward those registers. The interrupt control logic permitted the program running in the microprocessor to be notified whenever a received character arrived or whenever the transmitter was capable of transmitting another character.

Figure 6–1 is a reprint of Figure 2–1, but a Request to Send control lead has been added, along with three new status leads—Clear to Send, Carrier Detect, and Data Set Ready. Underlining in Figure 6–1 emphasizes the position of these leads in the block diagram. Also shown in Figure 6–1 is a change in the leads that enter the Interrupt Control Logic. In addition to the Receiver Interrupt lead and Transmit Interrupt lead, a Modem Interrupt lead is provided.

The register bit assignments for the single line interface shown in Figure 2–1 and the single line interface with control for private line modems shown above are compared in Figure 6–2. Figure 6–2 also includes underlining to emphasize the new signal leads that have been added. Bit 15 has been assigned as "Data Set Change Interrupt" (DS INT) and is set whenever the Clear to Send lead, the Carrier Detect lead, or the Data Set Ready lead changes state. The program may examine the current state of those leads by reading bits 13 (CTS), 12 (DCD), and 09 (DSR) of this register. The

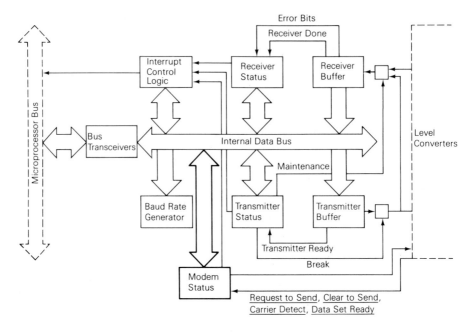

Figure 6–1   Block Diagram of a Single Line UART with Private Line Modem Control

| 15 | 14 | 13 | 12 | 11 | 10 | 09 | 08 | 07 | 06 | 05 | 04 | 03 | 02 | 01 | 00 |
|----|----|----|----|----|----|----|----|----|----|----|----|----|----|----|----|
| DS INT | | CTS | DCD | | | DSR | | RCVR DONE | RCVR IE | DS IE | | | RTS | | |

Figure 6–2   Sample Bit Assignments for a Single Line UART with Private Line Modem Control

setting of bit 15, indicating a change of state of these leads, causes an interrupt if the generation of interrupts for data set lead changes is enabled—i.e., if bit 05, Data Set Change Interrupt Enable (DS IE), is set.

The program also may control the state of the Request to Send lead by setting bit 02 (RTS) to assert the Request to Send lead to the ON state or by clearing bit 02 to put the Request to Send lead in the OFF state.

The simplified interface shown in Chapter 2 is connected to the following circuits:

• CCITT 102 (AB), Signal Ground
• CCITT 103 (BA), Transmitted Data
• CCITT 104 (BB), Received Data

The interface described in this chapter connects to these circuits and adds:

- CCITT 105 (CA), Request to Send
- CCITT 106 (CB), Ready for Sending (Clear to Send)
- CCITT 107 (CC), Data Set Ready
- CCITT 109 (CF), Data Channel Received Line Signal Detector (Carrier Detect)

This accounts for all the modem control leads defined in Chapter 5. Circuits 108/1 and 108/2 were mentioned but will not be defined until Chapter 9.

So far, all discussion of computer interfaces for data communications has dealt with interfaces for a single communications line. Multiline applications often use somewhat different arrangements, as is discussed in Chapter 7.

# 7

## Asynchronous Multiplexers

Previous chapters have described UARTs that allow asynchronous transmission and reception of characters on a communications line attached to a computer. Characters arriving in bit serial fashion are assembled into characters, an interrupt is generated to a microprocessor to indicate that a received character is ready, and a path is set up to transfer the character into the memory associated with the microprocessor. In like fashion, the UART indicates by means of an interrupt to the microprocessor that it can transmit a character, the microprocessor loads a character into the UART, and the UART serializes the character onto the line. Figure 7–1 shows a simplified view of the UART function.

There are many applications in which it is desirable to connect to a number of asynchronous lines. The connection of user terminals to a mid-size or large computer is a traditional example. Connection of terminals to a terminal concentrator or terminal server associated with a local area network (Chapter 28) is another example. The connection of a plurality of asynchronous devices to a personal computer or workstation is a third example.

Depending on the number of lines to be connected and the amount of traffic they handle, UARTs may simply be added to the microprocessor bus, and the microprocessor may still have time to perform services for the terminal users in addition to receiving and transmitting characters. At some point, however, the data communication tasks will leave no time for the processor to do anything else. At this point, a microprocessor specifically devoted to communications tasks is required. Further, that microprocessor

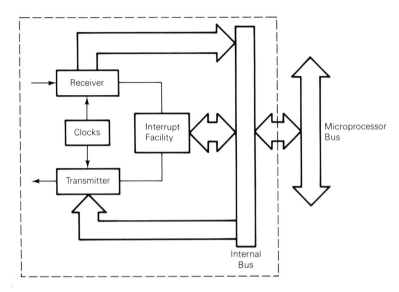

Figure 7–1   Simplified View of the UART Function

may require hardware assistance in accomplishing its task of handling messages to and from another computer or a network. A device for serving the communications needs of a multiple number of lines is called a "multiplexer." A multiplexer permits a number of UARTs to share the same intelligence (microprocessor and other logic) and interface to a larger computer or network. A simplified diagram of a typical asynchronous multiplexer is shown in Figure 7–2.

Here, each line has its own UART, but all other components are shared. Two new components are added, a scanner and a first-in first-out buffer (FIFO). The scanner (a counter in hardware or a program in the microprocessor) sequentially checks each receiver for a character available flag (or responds to a receiver interrupt generated by a UART). When it sees a flag, it automatically loads the character, along with its line number and any error flags (such as Overrun or Framing Error) into the FIFO, which is an area of memory. The scanner counter/program also checks the transmitters for flags (or responds to transmitter interrupts) indicating that a transmitter holding buffer is empty. Upon finding such a flag, the scanner loads a character from a buffer in memory (a separate buffer for each line) into the transmitter for that line. The number of UARTs served by a single multi-

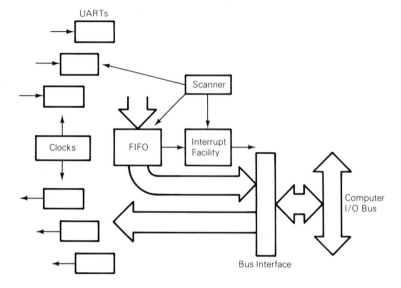

Figure 7–2   Block Diagram of a Multi-Line Asynchronous Interface (Multiplexer)

plexer is usually a power of two for convenience in presenting the line numbers in binary form. Four-line, eight-line, and sixteen-line multiplexers are common. Because the crystal for generating baud rates, the microprocessor, the memory, and the interface to the larger computer or network are not repeated for each line, cost is saved not only in components, but also in printed circuit board space. It is possible to build a four- or eight-line multiplexer on a card that previously housed just a single line interface.

The choice of multiplexer size is influenced by the packaging that the computer manufacturer uses and the number of lines his customers typically buy. While the cost benefits are greatest with larger multiplexers, users who typically install a dozen lines on their computer systems will not be enthused about a 256-line multiplexer, no matter how low the cost per line.

Because the complicated equipment can be shared in a multiplexer, it is possible to include features that would not be economical in single line interfaces. Among these are full modem control for many or all of the interface leads, character recognition, direct deposition of characters into computer memory, and the FIFO buffer.

Of the features mentioned above, one of the more common is the FIFO buffer. It resembles, in concept, a farm silo where silage is placed in the top and falls as far down the silo as possible before coming to rest on other accumulated silage. The silage is retrieved from the bottom of the silo as needed, and as some is withdrawn, the remaining silage moves down to take its place. A FIFO may be implemented as a specialized chip or as an area of memory where a microprocessor reads and writes characters at locations designated by pointers.

In the case of a FIFO chip, characters are loaded in by the scanner hardware/program, and they propagate as far toward the output as they can until they encounter another stored character. One flag indicates to the scanner that there is room in the FIFO to store a character (typical capacity is 64 characters), and another indicates that there is a character available at the output of the FIFO. This second flag can be connected to the interrupt facility and is used to indicate to the microprocessor that it can read the "bottom" of the FIFO to obtain a received character.

In the case of a FIFO implemented as an area of memory, characters are loaded in by the scanner program at a location specified by the "write pointer." When a character has been loaded, the write pointer is advanced to the next location after the program has checked to make sure that the next location is still part of the area in the memory assigned for the FIFO function. If the end of the FIFO area is reached, the write pointer is moved around to the beginning of the FIFO area, and a check is made to see whether the character previously stored there has been read. There is also a "read pointer," which indicates where the next character to be read is located. If the write and read pointers point to the same place, the program knows that there are no characters stored. As with the write pointer, the program must check for "end conditions"—i.e., the beginning and end of the FIFO area—before moving the other pointer. While the implementation of a FIFO in ordinary memory is more complex than implementation as a special chip, the cost per bit stored and the board area taken are much less.

Regardless of implementation, the FIFO permits the microprocessor to delay character processing for a substantial time without data being lost. Note, however, that the microprocessor must keep up with the arriving character rate on a long-term basis, or the FIFO will eventually fill. A less obvious feature of the FIFO is that it improves throughput in some cases.

When a computer responds to an interrupt, it must store certain information relative to the task it was performing at the time, and it must then execute various instructions associated with entering the "interrupt service routine." This process must be repeated in reverse order for exiting from the interrupt service routine. The time spent to do this is essentially useless overhead, as no computation is done. Thus, if each received character generates an interrupt, this overhead is incurred for each character received. If, however, an interrupt occurs whenever there are characters in the FIFO, and the interrupt service routine processes all the characters in the FIFO before exiting the routine, chances are good that several characters will be processed on each interrupt. The overhead is therefore spread out over more characters. Best of all, as the processing load increases, and the computer subsequently becomes more tardy in responding to the interrupt, more characters accumulate in the FIFO while waiting for the computer to respond. Since this results in more characters being serviced on each interrupt service routine, the overhead per character is even more drastically reduced. The system actually becomes more efficient as the load on the computer increases!

While a FIFO is a very helpful and simple device to have on the receiver side of a multiplexer, a FIFO common to all lines cannot be added to the transmitter side. A high-speed line would want to withdraw its characters quickly, while a low-speed line would want to withdraw its characters slowly; thus, the characters for both types of line could not be stored one behind the other in the same FIFO. A separate FIFO could be provided for each line, however. Such an arrangement would allow the overhead of transmit interrupts to be averaged over a greater number of characters. Care in design would be necessary to make sure that transmission could be suspended when necessary (for example, when XOFF was received).

The primary benefits of multiplexers are: (1) lower cost per line than single line interfaces, (2) availability of special features, especially those that improve throughput, (3) reduced space and power requirements, and (4) reduced electrical loading on the computer input/output bus due to fewer bus interfaces.

The drawbacks are: (1) if the manufacturer sells $n$-line multiplexers and you need $n + 1$ lines, you may have to buy two $n$-line multiplexers, (2) the programming of a multiplexer is generally more complicated, and (3) if the multiplexer fails, a lot of lines go down.

In Chapter 2, a very simple interface was presented. In Chapters 3, 4, and 5, some properties of data transmission facilities were discussed, which led to the more sophisticated interfaces treated in Chapters 6 and 7. It is now time to go a step further and discuss a much more complicated data transmission facility, the switched telephone network.

# 8

## Telephone Switching Systems

In the early days of telephony, people bought telephones in pairs. Doctor Smith would have one for himself and one at the other end of the line for the pharmacy. The harness maker would have one for himself and one for the livery stable. Soon all the doctors in town were on a common line with Doctor Smith and the pharmacy. Similar professional common interest groups had similar telephone hookups. After a while the various groups wanted to talk to one another and residential telephone subscribers wanted to talk to all the various professionals and businesses. Thus was born the need for the telephone switchboard.

Early telephone instruments obtained the power for their transmission from batteries located near the telephone. A bell associated with the telephone alerted subscribers that someone was trying to reach them. When more than one person had a telephone on the same line (as was the usual case), coded ringing, such as one long ring followed by two short rings, identified which of the parties on the line was being contacted. In addition, a hand-cranked magneto (or generator) was installed in the telephone, which permitted each subscriber to signal the others by applying ringing current to the line.

When switchboards were first utilized, a person wishing to make a call would first ring the operator, who would place a plug in the jack of the caller's line to talk to him or her. After learning to whom the caller wished to speak, the operator would place another plug in the jack of that person's line and ring the line with the appropriate ringing code.

When the conversation was over, the two parties would apply ringing to the line again, signaling the operator that the connection could be taken down. Because the batteries that supplied the power were local to the telephone instruments and because of the type of signaling used, such arrangements were called "magneto local battery" systems. Such systems left their mark on telephony in such terms as "drop," "ring off," and "take down the connection."

To aid operators in identifying the lines that were trying to get their attention, each line jack had a metallic flag that dropped down when the subscriber rang the line. This flag was called a "drop," and the term is still used to refer to the line to a subscriber's home, in particular the part from the pole to the house. The wire used to make that connection is even called "drop wire."

The phrase is rarely used anymore, but at one time people who were about to terminate their telephone conversations would often say, "Well, I think I'll ring off now," referring to the practice of ringing at the end of a call to signal the operator to "take down the connection." The latter term refers to switchboard construction. Subscriber lines appear as jacks on a vertical panel, in front of which is a shelf containing "cord sets." These are two plugs connected by a cord and a bit of circuitry to bring the operator's telephone in and out of the connection. Taking down a connection refers to removing the plugs from the vertical panel and restoring the operator's cord set to its rest position.

Local battery magneto systems were followed by "common battery manual" systems. In the common battery system, all telephone instruments received their power from a common battery located on the telephone company's premises near the switchboard. By placing sensitive relays in the circuit between the subscriber telephones and the battery, it became possible to determine when a telephone was "on-hook" (drawing no current) and when it was "off-hook" (drawing current). The telephone subscriber did not have to ring the operator to place a call; the caller simply lifted the receiver off the hook to start drawing current. The relay for his or her line would then signal the operator by means of a light over the appropriate line jack on the switchboard. In similar fashion, relays placed in the cord circuit between the two plugs used to connect callers could determine when the two parties hung up their telephones and alert the operator to take down the connection.

The process of determining whether a telephone is off-hook or on-hook is called "supervision" and is one of the most important concepts in telephony (especially when the subscribers pay to place calls). The principal contribution to the telephonic lexicon from common battery switchboards was the identity of the conductors used to make the connections at the switchboard. The plug used to make a connection to a subscriber's line jack had a "Tip" portion, which was of positive potential, and a "Ring" portion, for the negative side of the line. The terms Tip and Ring are still used to identify the two conductors of a telephone line.

In the late 1880s, a number of efforts were made to automate the switching of telephone calls. The first truly successful system was that devised by Almon B. Strowger, an undertaker. How an undertaker came to design the world's longest lasting, and at one time most pervasive, telephone switching system is a classic story. Almon Strowger was one of two undertakers in a small town in the midwestern United States, and the other undertaker's wife was the town telephone operator. When town residents suffered a death in the family, they would often ask the operator for "an undertaker" and would of course be connected to the operator's husband. Strowger saw that his prospects for business were few unless he could eliminate the operator, so he devised a simple rotary switch mechanism using a celluloid shirt collar and some common pins as a sample. He subsequently sold his idea to the Automatic Electric Company, which refined and developed it. The Strowger system was called "step-by-step" by the Bell System, which also manufactured and used the Strowger design.

Subsequent switching systems have gradually centralized the control logic, moving it from each switch, where it was in the Strowger system, to a progressively smaller number of more sophisticated controllers. A number of texts, several of which are listed at the end of this chapter, describe the Strowger and subsequent systems in great detail. The aspects of telephone switching systems that are of primary interest to the data communication system designer are call setup time, traffic capacity, circuit characteristics, noise, and multiline hunt groups.

As was indicated in the brief outline of common battery manual telephone systems, a telephone that is on-hook is an "open circuit" and one that is off-hook appears as a resistance (about 50 ohms) between the Tip and Ring conductors of the telephone line. In electromechanical systems, the presence of that resistance causes current flow, which is detected by a "line relay." In some electronic systems, the current flow saturates a magnetic element, which is periodically scanned by a computer. Once the off-hook condition has been detected, the switching system connects the line to apparatus suitable for recording the dialed digits. When the digit recording apparatus has been connected to the subscriber's line, a "dial tone" is returned to the subscriber to indicate that he may proceed to dial. (It is general North American telephone practice to return a dial tone within three seconds on 90 percent of all subscriber call attempts.)

The selection of the number to be called is performed either by interrupting the current through the subscriber telephone in a precisely timed way (dial pulsing) or by means of tone generators within the subscriber telephone set. The pulsing rate for telephone dials must be uniform and within the range of 8 to 11 pulses per second (10 pulses per second nominal). Each pulse consists of an interval of "break" followed by an interval of "make." The break portion must be 58 to 64 percent of the pulse interval. The pulses that represent a dialed digit are separated from the pulses that represent the next dialed digit by a period known as the "interdigital interval." The interdigital interval must be at least 600 milliseconds long for the switching equipment to determine where one digit (string of pulses) ends and the next digit (string of pulses) begins. Using the above figures, an average digit of five pulses, at a 10 pulse per second rate, will be completed in 500 milliseconds (1/2 second) plus the 600 millisecond interdigital time—roughly 1.1 seconds per digit dialed.

Tone signaling from subscriber sets, also referred to as dual tone multifrequency (DTMF) signaling, consists of two sinusoidal signals. One signal is from a high group of three frequencies and one from a low group of four frequencies; together they represent one of the 12 characters shown in Table 8–1.

The frequencies are required to be within 1.5 percent of their nominal values, but 1.2 percent accuracy is preferred. The minimum duration of a

Table 8–1   Touch Tone™ Frequency Assignment

|  |  | 1209 | 1336 | 1477 |
|---|---|---|---|---|
| Nominal | 697 | 1 | 2 | 3 |
| Low-Group | 770 | 4 | 5 | 6 |
| Frequencies | 852 | 7 | 8 | 9 |
| (Hz) | 941 | * | 0 | # |

two-frequency signal is 50 milliseconds, and the minimum interdigital time is 45 milliseconds. The mathematics does not quite work out, but the minimum cycle time is one digit per 100 milliseconds. Note that this is one-eleventh of the time necessary to dial pulse the same information if the digit 5 is dialed.

So far we have discussed the delay in receiving a dial tone and the time required to dial digits by dial pulsing or tone signaling. The remaining topic is the amount of time necessary to complete the call. In the Bell System 1969–1970 Switched Telecommunications Network Connection Survey, measurements were taken of the time that elapsed between dialing the last digit of the telephone number and receiving a test tone supplied by automatic answering equipment at that number. For connections over short distances (about 200 miles or less), call completion took about 11 seconds. For moderate distances (about 200 to 700 miles), call completion took about 15 seconds. For long distances (about 800 to 3000 miles), call completion took about 14 seconds. Since the time when this survey was done, the switched network has undergone substantial change as a result of the divestiture of the Bell System. While some of these changes have made call completion more complex, an unrelated change in switching technology has compensated for the increased complexity. That change is the introduction of common channel interoffice signaling (CCIS), which has improved call connection times by transferring signaling information directly over high-speed data channels between the processors that control electronic switching systems. This signaling system is described in detail in Volume VI of the CCITT *Red Book* and is called CCITT Signaling System #7. As a result of all these changes, the 1969–1970 survey information is largely obsolete and should be thought of as an upper bound on connection times.

The second aspect of telephone switching systems of interest to data communication system designers is traffic capacity. While the high degree of success in completing calls may lead one to believe that there is ample telephone equipment to handle all possible traffic, this is not the case. On the contrary, many telephone systems will accommodate the origination of calls by only about 10 percent of the subscribers. If that 10 percent calls another 10 percent, 20 percent of the subscribers could be on the telephone simultaneously. In business telephone systems, especially in businesses where the telephone is used a lot, capacity is usually provided for 15 to 20 percent of the subscribers to originate calls. The arrangement of telephone equipment to serve what appears to be such a small percentage is based on economics. If the present arrangements deny service on only 1 or 2 percent of the call attempts during the busiest hour of the day, will the subscribers be willing to pay twice as much to reduce that denial to 0.5 percent or some similar small figure? In general, the answer is that they will not.

These economic considerations are, to a large degree, based on mechanical switching technology, where additional capacity takes up additional equipment and floor area. In many electronic switching systems, notably time division multiplex switching systems, conversations are sampled, and these samples are placed in "time slots" on a common electrical bus. The equipment associated with the person to whom you are talking is then synchronized so as to sample the signal on the bus at the appropriate time. In such a system, the cost of additional call handling capacity is the cost of bandwidth on the common bus. This cost does not rise as steeply as the cost of equipment in mechanical "space division" switching systems where each call takes up physical space. Thus, in future communications systems, call carrying capacity will probably be less of a design problem.

A call handling capacity of 10 percent of the subscribers originating calls was mentioned above. It must be noted that in common control systems, such as the non-Strowger electromechanical systems and most electronic systems, the number of subscribers that can be simultaneously dialing is substantially less than the number that can be simultaneously carrying on conversations on calls that they placed. This latter number is the 10 percent cited above. The number of simultaneous "dialers" that can be accommodated varies from system to system, but a figure of 60 in a 10,000 subscriber system would not be uncommon. It is therefore important that computer systems employing automatic dialers not use programs that permit more than a dozen or so to be active at once, since that computer system might otherwise have a noticeable effect on local telephone service.

In similar fashion, large quantities of terminating traffic may be a problem. It is important to talk with the local telephone company people as soon as possible when planning the installation of a large computer system that will be receiving a high volume of incoming calls. The availability of suitable telephone service should be as carefully considered as are heat, light, floor space, and rental rates. Too often people assume that, because the telephone company has no trouble putting a telephone in a home, putting 32 lines in a computer center should not be substantially more difficult. This is decidedly not the case.

Noise is another characteristic of switching systems that should be considered. There are many possible sources of noise in telephone systems. Some of the noise sources, such as crosstalk between conductors in cables, will exist both in private lines and in switched network connections. Other sources of noise, usually impulse type noise, are introduced primarily by switching systems. Once a telephone call is in progress in an electromechanical switching system, a dozen or more movable electrical contacts may be involved, even on a local call. As other calls are handled by equipment adjacent to any of these contacts, vibration from that equipment may cause the contacts to move slightly. Since the contacts are not ultraclean, noise is introduced. Electronic switching systems either use contacts that are sealed in airtight glass capsules or use no contacts at all. Hence, data communication through electronic offices has noticeably less switching noise than data communication through electromechanical offices.

One other source of noise in switching systems is the battery supply used to power the telephone transmitters in typical voice conversations. Although there is no need for telephone instrument transmitters in most data communication, a battery is still needed to establish "loop current" to the calling and called parties so that off-hook and on-hook conditions can be detected. The battery in the telephone company's central office also is used to power the switching equipment, and various electrical noises from the switching equipment can be present on the battery. As with contact noise, the battery noise in electronic switching systems is less than the battery noise in electromechanical systems—yet another reason electronic switching systems are preferred for data communication.

Finally, use of the public switched telephone network for data communication presents the data communication system designer with the problem of varying circuit characteristics. The variability of circuit characteristics is related to the variability of telephone call routing. To understand call routing, a brief look at the structure of the U.S. telephone network is in order. While the paragraphs that follow are specific to the United States, the general concepts apply to other nations as well.

Effective January 1, 1984, telephone service in the United States was broken up into "Local Access and Transport Areas" (LATAs). The boundaries of these areas were generally the same as the area code boundaries.

The Bell System was broken up into seven "Regional Bell Operating Companies" (RBOCs), each of which was responsible for telephone service *within* several LATAs, but none of which was permitted to offer service *between* LATAs. Service between LATAs could be provided only by "Inter-LATA Carriers" (ICs, or "long-distance carriers"). RBOCs were required by the court to provide their subscribers with equal access to all the long-distance carriers, one of which was their former parent company, AT&T.

For telephone calls where the subscriber elected to use AT&T as their long-distance carrier, the nationwide telephone network appears as the hierarchy shown in Figure 8–1. Five classes of telephone switching office are indicated in the figure, the top three of which are owned and operated

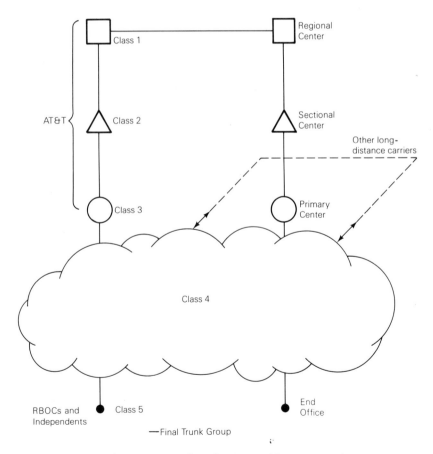

Figure 8–1  Switching System Classification and Interconnection

by the long-distance carrier, in this case AT&T. The Class 4 offices are shown as a "cloud" because it is at this point that the RBOCs provide access to and from the long-distance carriers. The complexity of this connection is beyond the scope of this text. The Class 5 offices are the offices to which the subscribers' telephones connect; they are owned and operated by the RBOCs or by independent telephone companies.

To give some idea of the number of offices involved, AT&T has 12 Class 1 or Regional Center offices in the United States and Canada. There are approximately 75 Class 2 offices, approximately 265 Class 3 offices, 1400 Class 4 offices, and 18,000 Class 5 offices, also known as "end offices."

A local call from a home to the butcher shop is typically within the same end office—i.e., 234-5678 to 234-7654. A call to a person in another town (but within the same LATA) is handled differently. If the two towns are close enough together, or if there are a lot of calls between the two towns, there might be direct circuits from one end office to the other. Such a group of circuits is called a "high-usage" group. If these circuits are busy or simply do not exist, the call is "route advanced" to a "tandem" office (essentially a Class 4 office) associated with the Class 5 office for which the call is destined.

Figure 8–2 shows a typical routing pattern within the AT&T network, with high-usage groups shown as heavy dashed lines. The importance of this figure is that calls between two end offices, especially those located in different LATAs, may travel through a half dozen or more transmission and switching systems. While the long-distance carriers attempt to achieve consistently acceptable connections, there may be differences between various calls due to different routing being used.

In addition to switching plans, the long-distance carriers also have transmission plans. The transmission plans are designed to achieve a high degree of user satisfaction by controlling loss, noise, and echo.

While noise and echo are evil, loss is not always undesirable. In fact, there is a relationship between loss and echo that is of interest to the data communication system designer. Connections between four-wire and two-wire transmission facilities (see Chapter 4) and other connections between various transmission media often produce echoes. Studies have shown that these echoes are not annoying to telephone users unless they are loud or occur after a substantial delay. To control the adverse effects of echoes, telephone companies intentionally introduce loss into telephone connec-

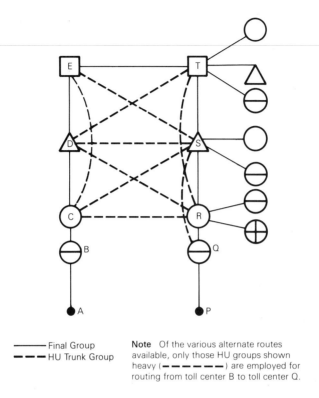

——— Final Group
— — — HU Trunk Group

**Note** Of the various alternate routes available, only those HU groups shown heavy (— — — — —) are employed for routing from toll center B to toll center Q.

Figure 8–2　Typical Routing Pattern (AT&T)

tions. Two plans are used for doing this. One is called the "Via Net Loss" (VNL) plan and is used for analog circuits. The other is called the "Switched Digital Network" (SDN) plan and is used for digital circuits. The VNL plan allocates various amounts of loss to various links of the switching hierarchy shown in Figure 8–1, while the SDN plan uses a fixed amount of loss inserted in the digital-to-analog conversion process. Because the delays and noise associated with digital switching are much less than those associated with analog systems, the use of a compromise value is acceptable. As the switched telephone network becomes more and more digital, the use of the SDN plan will predominate.

On very long connections (more than 1850 miles), echoes returning after a long delay are a problem. To solve this problem, echo suppressors are installed. Echo suppressors are devices that detect which party is talking louder and allow transmission only from the speaker to the other party; thus the echoes, which are traveling in the opposite direction, are not heard.

The effect of echo suppressors is not usually noticeable unless an earth satellite is in the connection or a volume level or echo suppressor sensitivity problem causes noise on one side of the communications channel. In the former case, the delays involved make the echo suppressor action noticeable; in the latter, the noise triggers the echo suppressor, cutting up the conversation of the distant party.

For full-duplex data transmission, the echo suppressors must be disabled. While this keeps them from functioning, filters or echo cancelers within the modems keep the echoes from interfering with transmission. To disable the echo suppressors, a single frequency tone, with a level 0 to 5 db below the maximum specified data signal level within the band 2010 to 2240 Hz, is applied for at least 400 milliseconds. No other tone or signal should be applied during this period. The echo suppressor remains disabled if the data signal (or other energy of similar magnitude) is applied within 100 milliseconds after the disabling tone is removed from the line. Any interruptions in the subsequent signal over 100 milliseconds in duration will permit the echo suppressor to become enabled again. The 2225 Hz tone applied to the line by a typical low-speed asynchronous modem answering a call meets the specifications for echo suppressor disabling.

Returning to the figures concerning the hierarchical nature of the telephone system, it should be noted that subsequent calls may take different routes, due to changing traffic conditions. Also, AT&T uses a technique called "network management" to maximize utilization of its facilities. When it is 9 A.M. in New York City and Miami, it is only 6 A.M. in San Francisco, so additional call capacity between New York and Miami at that hour of the day may be obtained by routing calls to San Francisco and back. The routes used have low transmission loss and are at the top of the hierarchy shown in Figure 8–2. Furthermore, they are available for use because no one is calling between San Francisco and any East Coast points at that time. During general periods of high traffic, this type of routing is not normally used; while a few people would be happy to get their calls through, the facilities used to get those calls through could have been used to place several shorter distance calls.

Routing is important to the data communication system designer because the circuit delay between two simultaneously placed calls, or between two calls placed at different times of day, may vary. In the first case, the variation is due to changed routing caused by momentary traffic fluctuations; in the second, it is due to network management.

Now that the data transmission facility has been discussed, it is time to deal with the modems and modem controls that work with it.

## References

1. "Notes on the BOC Intra-LATA Networks," Document Number TR-MPL-000275. Available from Bell Communications Research, 60 New England Avenue, Room 1B252, Piscataway, NJ 08854, (201)699-5800.
2. Fike, John L., and George E. Friend. *Understanding Telephone Electronics.* Dallas: Texas Instruments Learning Center, 1983. (Available at many Radio Shack stores.)
3. Hobbs, Marvin. *Modern Communications Switching Systems.* Blue Ridge Summit, PA: Tab Books, 1974.
4. Rubin, Murray, and C.E. Haller. *Communications Switching Systems.* Huntington, NY: Krieger Publishing, 1974.
5. Talley, David. *Basic Telephone Switching Systems.* Rochelle Park, NJ: Hayden Books, 1979.
6. Talley, David. *Basic Electronic Switching for Telephone Systems.* Rochelle Park, NJ: Hayden Books, 1975.

# 9

## Modem Control for Switched Network Use

The modem interface leads defined in Chapter 5 are shown again in Table 9–1. Briefly reviewed, Circuit 102 provides a ground connection for electrical reference. The data that the computer wishes the modem to transmit over the communications channel is applied to the Transmitted Data lead. The data being received over the communications channel is delivered by the modem to the computer over the Received Data lead. The Request to Send lead is provided to turn the modem transmitter on and off for half-duplex applications. The readiness of the modem to accept data for transmitting over the communications channel is reflected by the Clear to Send lead. The DCE Ready (Data Set Ready) lead indicates that the modem is connected to the communications channel and not in voice or test mode. Finally, reception of signals from the distant modem is indicated by the

Table 9–1   Interface Leads for Low-Speed Asynchronous Full-Duplex Private Line Modem

| Designation | | Name |
| EIA | CCITT | |
| --- | --- | --- |
| AB | 102 | Signal Ground |
| BA | 103 | Transmitted Data |
| BB | 104 | Received Data |
| CA | 105 | Request to Send |
| CB | 106 | Clear to Send |
| CC | 107 | Data Set Ready |
| CF | 109 | Data Channel Received Line Signal Detector |

Data Channel Received Line Signal Detector (Carrier Detect). With the exception of this last signal, each of the signal names is quite simple and very descriptive of the lead's function. Even the phrase "Received Line Signal Detector" is self-explanatory; it basically means "I hear something that sounds like a modem talking to me."

While the above signals are sufficient to permit the control of asynchronous modems on private lines, the use of modems on the switched telephone network requires some additional leads, notably DTE Ready (Data Terminal Ready) and Ring Indicator. The definitions for these leads are given below. These definitions are taken from EIA Specification EIA-232-D and are reproduced here by permission of EIA. The CCITT definitions are taken from Recommendation V.24 and are reproduced here by permission of the CCITT. In some instances, notes have been added in brackets [ ].

| **EIA-232-D**<br>**Definitions** | **CCITT V.24**<br>**Definitions** |
|---|---|
| *Circuit CD*—DTE Ready (CCITT 108/2) [Formerly called Data Terminal Ready]* Direction: To DCE | *Circuit 108/2*—Data Terminal Ready Direction: To DCE |
| Signals on this circuit are used to control switching of the DCE to the communication channel. The ON condition prepares the DCE to be connected to the communication channel and maintains the connection established by external means (e.g., manual call origination, manual answering, or automatic call origination). | Signals on this circuit control switching of the signal-conversion or similar equipment to or from the line.<br><br>The ON condition, indicating that the DTE is ready to operate, prepares the DCE to connect the signal-conversion or similar equipment to the line and maintains this connection after it has been established by supplementary means. |
| When the station is equipped for automatic answering of received calls and is in the automatic answering mode, con- | The DTE is permitted to present the ON condition on Circuit 108/2 whenever it is ready to transmit or receive data. |

*An important note to this definition is that the relationship of the OFF condition of Data Terminal Ready to the completion of transmitted data transfer is not an automatic function of the modem. The modem is merely a level conversion device and does not interpret the meaning of the bit stream passing through. Thus, the modem does not know when transmission is over. The program that has control of the DTE Ready lead must decide when to bring it to the OFF state. The use of double-buffered transmitters such as those found in the UART requires that two character times elapse between the time the UART transmitter is loaded with the final character and the time the final character has been shifted out onto the line. Some modems require even more additional time before the modem control program brings DTE Ready to the OFF state.

**EIA-232-D**
**Definitions**

*Circuit CD (Cont.)*

nection to the line occurs only in response to a combination of a ringing signal and the ON condition of Circuit CD (DTE Ready): however, the DTE is normally permitted to present the ON condition on Circuit CD whenever it is ready to transmit or receive data, except as indicated below.

The OFF condition causes the DCE to be removed from the communication channel following the completion of any "in process" transmission. See Circuit BA (Transmitted Data). The OFF condition shall not disable the operation of Circuit CE (Ring Indicator).

In switched network applications, when circuit CD is turned OFF, it shall not be turned ON again until Circuit CC (DCE Ready) is turned OFF by the DCE.

*Circuit CE*—Ring Indicator (CCITT 125—Calling Indicator)
Direction: From DCE

The ON condition of this circuit indicates that a ringing signal is being received on the communication channel.

The ON condition shall appear approximately coincident with the ON segment of the ringing cycle (during rings) on the communication channel.

The OFF condition shall be maintained during the OFF segment of the ringing cycle (between "rings") and at all other times when ringing is not being received. The operation of this circuit shall not be disabled by the OFF condition on Circuit CD (DTE Ready).

**CCITT V.24**
**Definitions**

*Circuit 108/2 (Cont.)*

The OFF condition causes the DCE to remove the signal-conversion or similar equipment from the line, when the transmission to line of all data previously transferred on Circuit 103 [Transmitted Data] and/or Circuit 118 [Transmitted Backward Channel Data] has been completed.

*Circuit 125*—Calling Indicator
Direction: From DCE

Signals on this circuit indicate whether a calling signal is being received by the DCE.

The ON condition indicates that a calling signal is being received.

The OFF condition indicates that no calling signal is being received, and this condition may also appear during interruptions of a pulse-modulated calling signal.

The interaction of all these leads can best be appreciated by comparing the receipt of a typical telephone call at home. When the telephone rings (Circuit CE [125]—Ring Indicator), you hear the ring. If you wish to answer, you pick up the handset and into the off-hook state, a step similar to asserting Circuit CD (108/2)—DTE Ready. You say "hello" and await a response, a process similar to monitoring Circuit CF (109)—Data Channel Received Line Signal Detector (Carrier Detect). If you hear nothing, hang up (negate DTE Ready). If you hear someone, converse and hang up later when you are done. An automatically answered call from one low-speed full-duplex asynchronous modem to another functions this way.

These three leads, Ring Indicator, DTE Ready, and Data Channel Received Line Signal Detector, are the minimum required for switched network operation of modems. Circuit CC (107), DCE Ready, also should be provided to meet the requirement of EIA-232-D and CCITT V.24 that "when DTE Ready is turned OFF, it shall not be turned ON again until DCE Ready is turned OFF by the DCE." Most European PTTs forbid connection of modem interfaces that do not do this.

As indicated above, DTE Ready may be left on, allowing incoming calls to be answered. This suggests the possibility of leaving DTE Ready on at all times. While this would work for answering the call, a problem arises when the call is to be terminated. Some types of switching equipment provide a line polarity reversal to the called party when the calling party hangs up at the end of a call. This causes the called modem to disconnect from the line. This cannot be relied on, however, so conservative design procedure and European PTT regulations call for program control of the DTE Ready lead so that it may be negated at the end of the call and may remain negated until DCE Ready is negated (as mentioned above). Furthermore, some modems use a circuit that works differently from DTE Ready. This circuit is CCITT Circuit 108/1, Connect Data Set to Line.

| EIA-232-D<br>Definitions | CCITT V.24<br>Definitions |
|---|---|
| No EIA equivalent to this circuit. | *Circuit 108/1*—Connect Data Set to Line<br>Direction: To DCE<br><br>Signals on this circuit control switching of the signal-conversion equipment to and from the line. |

| EIA-232-D | CCITT V.24 |
|---|---|
| **Definitions** | **Definitions** |

*Circuit 108/1 (Cont.)*

The ON condition on this circuit may also be used to initiate a direct call facility for automatic calling DCEs [i.e., assertion of this signal could be used to cause an automatic dialer to dial a stored number and connect this modem to the line after doing so].

The OFF condition causes the data communication equipment to remove the signal-conversion or similar equipment from the line, when the transmission to the line of all data previously transferred on Circuit 103 [Transmitted Data] and/or Circuit 118 [Transmitted Backward Channel Data] has been completed.

This lead is essentially the same as the DTE Ready/Data Terminal Ready (Circuit 108/2) previously described, except that no interlocking with the Ring/Calling Indicator circuit is involved. Thus, when this type of circuit is used, assertion of the lead in advance of call reception is not permitted. This would be equivalent to a person taking his or her phone off the hook and leaving it that way. Instead, the program that controls the computer/modem interface must wait to receive a Calling Indicator signal and then may assert Connect Data Set to Line. North American practice is to use the DTE Ready/Data Terminal Ready (Circuit 108/2) lead, while European practice varies.

In summary, computer interface hardware for modem control for switched network use must allow the program to control the state of the DTE Ready lead. Computer software may choose to assert DTE Ready and wait for Ring Indicator, or it may wait for Ring Indicator and then assert DTE Ready. The latter approach is more universal, as it also works in those cases where Connect Data Set to Line is used instead of DTE Ready. Also, the latter approach solves one problem that the first approach sometimes has: the modem control misses the assertion of a very short ring signal that is sufficient to be recognized by the modem, thus allowing an unannounced call answer.

The Ring/Calling Indicator lead is important for three reasons. First, it is necessary in the case where Circuit 108/1 (Connect Data Set to Line) is used, in order that the program know when to assert 108/1. Second, if either DTE Ready or Connect Data Set to Line is used, Ring/Calling Indicator is needed to define when to start looking for Data Channel Received Line Signal Detector to differentiate between a voice call and a data call. Third, Ring/Calling Indicator is needed to safeguard user files in time-sharing systems by enabling the computer system software to determine the difference between a temporary interruption in transmission and a new call.

The first of the above reasons for Ring/Calling Indicator has already been explored in detail. The second requires some elaboration, which will explain one of the uses for Data Channel Received Line Signal Detector in switched network modems. One of the problems of a data communication system attached to the switched network is that of misdirected voice telephone calls. Assume that a person making an ordinary voice telephone call accidentally reaches a modem. Ring/Calling Indicator is asserted to the modem interface, and the computer program directs the assertion of DTE Ready from the interface to the modem. The modem answers the call. At this time, appropriately written computer software starts a software timer (typically about 15 seconds) to check for the assertion of carrier from the calling modem. Since in this case the caller is a person, not a modem, there will be no carrier forthcoming. No Data Channel Received Line Signal Detector assertion will occur, and the software timer will expire. Another method is for the program to send a "Who are you?" message and await a reply. In either case, the important feature of the Ring/Calling Indicator lead is to alert the computer program that it should enter this routine.

The third reason for the use of the Ring/Calling Indicator is related to the possibility of momentary losses of carrier during data transmission. When the carrier returns after such a loss, a question could arise as to whether the caller is the same one that was there before the carrier outage. If it is, the system program may allow the caller to resume work on the files that he or she was manipulating. If the identity of the caller has changed, this is not permissible. The Ring/Calling Indicator solves this dilemma by announcing new calls.

This description of the function of the Ring/Calling Indicator may seem at odds with previous statements that manipulation of the DTE Ready lead is required to terminate an existing call. Strictly speaking it is, but the objective here is to mention what could happen; with some types of switching systems it is possible for a call to disappear momentarily. The most conservative programming practice would be to close out a user's job automatically and drop DTE Ready on any line suffering a carrier loss (negation of Data Channel Received Line Signal Detector) for more than 500 milliseconds. Certainly the arrival of a new call (assertion of the Ring/ Calling Indicator) on a line that the software believes already has a job in progress is a sure sign that that job should be terminated.

The preceding discussions have already mentioned one use of DCE Ready (EIA CC, CCITT 107): to confirm that the negation of DTE Ready has been successful in disconnecting the modem from the line. Since this lead indicates that the modem is connected to the line and is in operational mode (rather than voice, dialing, or test mode), it also can be used to announce incoming calls. It could thus be used in place of Ring/Calling Indicator by adopting the convention that a positive transition of this signal indicates an incoming call. There is one exception: when a serial autodialer is being used to make an outgoing call. In that case, the placement of the call will assert DCE Ready. A program utilizing this signal to announce an incoming call should ignore this signal when a call is being placed. The question then arises, "What if a call arrives just as call placement is beginning?" The answer is that either the calling device should send a "Call Arriving" status indication to the modem per CCITT Recommendation V.25 *bis*, or the Ring/Calling Indicator should be used for this purpose. In many ways, provision of both DCE Ready and the Ring/Calling Indicator is the ideal solution.

The interface leads required for switched network operation of a low-speed (300 bps) modem on the switched network are summarized in Table 9–2. Such modems typically divide the available bandwidth into two channels, a high-frequency channel for transmission in one direction and a low-frequency channel for transmission in the other direction. Frequency shift keying (see Chapters 5 and 10) is then used to transfer the data.

When it becomes desirable to transmit and receive data at higher speeds on the switched network, the task of the data communication system designer becomes more complex. Some higher speed full-duplex switched network modems continue to utilize a high-frequency channel and a low-frequency channel but substitute complex modulation schemes for the

Table 9–2   Interface Leads for Low-Speed Asynchronous Full-Duplex Switched Network Modem

| Designation | | |
|---|---|---|
| *EIA* | *CCITT* | *Name* |
| AB | 102 | Signal Ground |
| BA | 103 | Transmitted Data |
| BB | 104 | Received Data |
| [CA] | [105] | (see Note 1) |
| CB | 106 | Clear to Send (see Note 2) |
| CC | 107 | Data Set Ready (see Note 3) |
| CD | 108/1 | Connect Data Set to Line, or |
| | 108/2 | Data Terminal Ready |
| CF | 109 | Data Channel Received Line Signal Detector (Note 2) |
| CE | 125 | Ring/Calling Indicator (Note 3) |

Notes

1. Request to Send is not required in low-speed asynchronous full-duplex switched network modems.

2. In low-speed asynchronous modem interfaces, provision of either Clear to Send or Data Channel Received Line Signal Detector is sufficient. However, if the modem has serial automatic calling or error-correction features, or if PTT regulations dictate use of Clear to Send, that signal will be required.

3. For a minimum-feature modem interface, Data Set Ready is not necessary unless PTT regulations indicate otherwise. Alternatively, Data Set Ready can be retained and Ring/Calling Indicator not used.

simple frequency shift keying system used in the low-speed modems. These modems have the benefit of using the same interface just described for low-speed modems, minimizing or eliminating the need for interface or programming changes. The "Bell 212A" and its equivalents are examples of this type of modem and operate at 1200 bps full duplex.

More sophisticated modems provide a simple asynchronous interface but use synchronous transmission methods on the telephone line. These are discussed in Chapter 22.

For those who do not wish to use the new higher speed full-duplex modems or who cannot because of availability or PTT regulations, speeds above 300 baud will require the use of half-duplex operation. Modems that operate at 600 and/or 1200 baud half duplex use simple frequency shift keying transmission schemes similar to those previously described. They use the full bandwidth available in the switched telephone connection, however, rather than separating it into two chunks by means of filters. Filters are still used on the transmitters, but these are to eliminate the unwanted by-products of the modulation process.

Speeds of 600 and 1200 baud were used relatively early in data communication with the advent of the high-speed paper tape sender. Companies would batch together data or other messages and transmit to other plants, saving money on the telephone call cost by means of the increased line transmission speed. One of the features of high-speed paper tape transmission systems was error correction. The characters transmitted were grouped in blocks of 128 characters, and each block was followed by a block check character computed from the ones and zeros of the preceding characters. This was called a Longitudinal Redundancy Check (LRC) block check character; the LRC method of block checking is described in greater detail in Chapter 13. The receiving station would read the data received over the communications line and perform the same calculation on the characters as was being done simultaneously at the transmitting station. When the transmitting station sent the block check, the receiving station would check that against the result it had calculated. If the block check did not agree, it would ask for retransmission. All the calculating and checking was done in the DTE, not in the DCE (modem).

The modem became involved with the request for retransmission. One way to request retransmission is to have the transmitting station relinquish control over the communications channel at the end of each message, then have the receiving station seize the channel and send back a retransmission request. This is rather elaborate and time-consuming.

A better method is to use a low-speed channel from the receiving station to the transmitting station to indicate that data blocks are being received satisfactorily. The speed requirements of this channel can be determined as follows. At a 1200 bps rate, assuming 10 bits per character, 120 characters per second are being sent. Hence a block of 128 characters is completed only once every second, and the OK/not OK signal needs to be sent only once every second.

Some modems perform this function by providing a single frequency tone (387 Hz), which can be keyed on and off by the receiving station to indicate whether the block check is acceptable. Other modems provide a higher speed capability by frequency shift keying between two very low frequencies. Since the information is being supplied in a direction that is opposite that of the main data channel, this signaling facility is called the "reverse channel," "backward channel," or "supervisory channel."

EIA specification EIA-232-D describes the associated leads as follows (reproduced with permission of the EIA):

*Circuit SBA*—Secondary Transmitted Data (CCITT 118) [pin 14]
Direction: To DCE

This circuit is equivalent to Circuit BA (Transmitted Data) except that it is used to transmit data via the secondary channel.

Signals on this circuit are generated by the DTE and are connected to the local secondary channel transmitting signal converter for transmission of data to remote DTE.

The DTE shall hold Circuit SBA (Secondary Transmitted Data) in marking condition during intervals between characters or words and at all times when no data are being transmitted.

*Circuit SBB*—Secondary Received Data (CCITT 119) [pin 16]
Direction: From DCE

This circuit is equivalent to Circuit BB (Received Data) except that it is used to receive data on the secondary channel.

*Circuit SCA*—Secondary Request to Send (CCITT 120) [pin 19]
Direction: To DCE

This circuit is equivalent to Circuit CA (Request to Send) except that it requests the establishment of the secondary channel instead of requesting the establishment of the primary data channel.

*Circuit SCB*—Secondary Clear to Send (CCITT 121) [pin 13]
Direction: From DCE

This circuit is equivalent to Circuit CB (Clear to Send) except that it indicates the availability of the secondary channel instead of indicating the availability of the primary channel.

*Circuit SCF*—Secondary Received Line Signal Detector (CCITT 122) [pin 12]
Direction: From DCE

This circuit is equivalent to Circuit CF (Received Line Signal Detector) except that it indicates the proper reception of the secondary channel line signal instead of indicating the proper reception of a primary channel received line signal.

CCITT Recommendation V.24 defines these circuits as follows (reproduced with permission of the CCITT):

*Circuit 118*—Transmitted Backward Channel Data [see ISO 2110 for pinning]
Direction: To DCE

This circuit is equivalent to Circuit 103 [Transmitted Data] except that it is used to transmit data via the backward channel.

*Circuit 119*—Received Backward Channel Data [see ISO 2110 for pinning]
Direction: From DCE

This circuit is equivalent to Circuit 104 [Received Data] except that it is used for data received on the backward channel.

*Circuit 120*—Transmit Backward Channel Line Signal [see ISO 2110 for pinning]
Direction: To DCE

This circuit is equivalent to circuit 105 [Request to Send], except that it is used to control the backward channel transmit function of the DCE.

The ON condition causes the DCE to assume the backward channel transmit mode.

The OFF condition causes the DCE to assume the backward channel non-transmit mode, when all data transferred on circuit 118 have been transmitted to line.

*Circuit 121*—Backward Channel Ready [see ISO 2110 for pinning]
Direction: From DCE

This circuit is equivalent to circuit 106 [Ready For Sending], except that it is used to indicate whether the DCE is conditioned to transmit data on the backward channel.

The ON condition indicates that the DCE is conditioned to transmit data on the backward channel.

The OFF condition indicates that the DCE is not conditioned to transmit data on the backward channel.

*Circuit 122*—Backward Channel Received Line Signal Detector [see ISO 2110 for pinning]
Direction: From DCE

This circuit is equivalent to Circuit 109 [Data Channel Received Line Signal Detector], except that it is used to indicate whether the received backward channel line signal is within appropriate limits, as specified in the relevant Recommendation for DCE.

An early Bell System 202-series modem, the 202C, controlled the supervisory channel via Circuit SA, Supervisory Transmitted Data, on pin 11 and reported the status of the received supervisory channel via Circuit SB, Supervisory Received Data, on pin 12. This utilization of signal names and pins conflicted with the EIA and CCITT definitions. Newer 202-series modems, such as the 202S and 202T, control the supervisory channel via Secondary Request to Send (SCA) on pins 11 and 19, while reporting the status of the received supervisory channel via Secondary Received Line Signal Detector (SCF) on pin 12. Thus, it should be noted that secondary channel pinning may not follow the standards in all modems.

The important concepts of the reverse/secondary channel are summarized in Figure 9–1. Note that a computer interface must have four leads for data transfer to handle such a modem: Transmitted Data, Received Data, Secondary Transmitted Data, and Secondary Received Data. In the case of the 202-series modems utilizing a reverse/backward channel of only five baud capability, the reverse channel data may be transmitted and received by

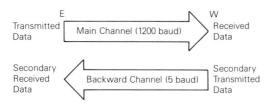

Figure 9–1a   East-to-West Transmission

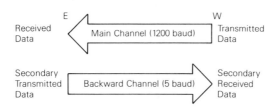

Figure 9–1b   West-to-East Transmission

simple program toggling of a bit for transmission and program sampling of a bit for reception. The UART type of receiver/transmitter, such as that described in Chapter 2, is not required. However, the backward channel is not always only five baud.

CCITT Recommendation V.23 describes a 600/1200 baud modem for switched network use that utilizes a 75 baud backward channel. A backward channel of that capability permits use of the backward channel not only for circuit assurance (i.e., indication that the receiving station is still there) and requests for retransmission such as previously described, but also for actual keyboard input. This is especially so if some buffering is provided to smooth out the rapidity with which a typist can type certain trigrams, such as t-h-e. There are two disadvantages to such a use. First, a full 75 baud signaling rate requires using a UART on the Backward Channel Transmit and Backward Channel Received leads rather than depending on program bit sampling. (This problem may be avoided if the one modem always transmits at the high speed and the other always transmits at the low speed. Such an arrangement may be thought of as "asymmetrical full duplex" and only a single UART, capable of "split baud rate operation" is required at each end.) Second, a problem with all half-duplex systems is that the data cannot be looped around from the transmitter to the receiver of the same modem to check the circuitry—i.e., one cannot create the configuration shown in Figure 9–2.

Loopback 1 permits one to ascertain that the data is leaving the DTE correctly. Loopback 1A checks that the data is arriving at the near end modem correctly. Loopback 2 permits one to ascertain that the data is being received and demodulated correctly by the distant modem. These tests and various intermediate loopbacks, which may be possible depending on the specific hardware used, permit the easy location of faults. This type of loopback is not possible (except at a 75 baud speed) in the type of modem just described, since the main channel will accommodate 1200 baud in only one direction at a time.

Before the advent of 1200 baud full-duplex modems for switched telephone network use, efforts were made to build modems with a 1200 baud main data channel and a 150 baud backward channel. While these worked quite well technically, the problems of loop-around testing and the lack of an industry standard inhibited widespread adoption of those modems. The

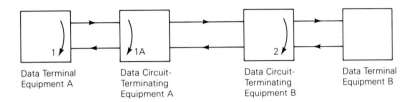

Figure 9–2  Maintenance Loopbacks

idea of split-speed modems has enjoyed a rebirth with the proposed Recommendation V.33 9600/300 baud modem.

So far, only the control leads for switched network modems have been discussed. To appreciate the function of the control leads fully, it might be useful to explore the internal operation of simple switched network modems; that is the subject of the next chapter.

# 10

## Asynchronous Modems for Switched Network Use

An idealized presentation of the typical frequency response of a switched network telephone connection is shown in Figure 10–1. The presence of a signaling tone at 2600 Hz makes use of this frequency undesirable, as a single tone of this frequency will cause the telephone call to be disconnected. This and the relative unpredictability of the frequency response characteristics in the 2600 to 3000 Hz area have caused modem designers to use tones between 300 and 2400 Hz.

As shown in Figure 10–2, 300 baud asynchronous modems (often referred to as "103-type") provide full-duplex operation over two-wire telephone circuits by use of frequency division multiplexing (FDM). With FDM, two data channels are obtained by operating in separate frequency bands, one for each direction of transmission. In the case of 103-type modems, these frequency bands are centered at 1170 Hz and 2125 Hz. The close proximity

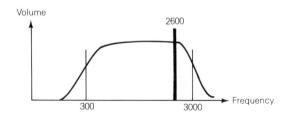

Figure 10–1   Location of Signaling Tone in
Switched Network Frequency Response

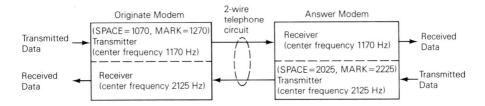

Figure 10–2   U.S. Low-Speed Asynchronous Full-Duplex Modem Frequency Assignments

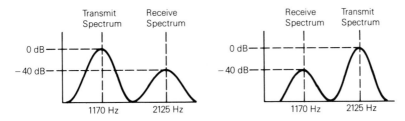

Figure 10–3   U.S. Low-Speed Asynchronous Full-Duplex Modem Frequency Spectra

of the transmit and receive spectra of both modems is illustrated in Figure 10–3 to emphasize the importance of channel separation filter quality.

Two types of modems are required for operation on separate frequency bands: originate mode modems (transmit on 1070/1270) and answer mode modems (transmit on 2025/2225). This nomenclature has come into use because the Bell 103A modem and its successors are automatically switched into the originate mode when a call is originated and into answer mode when a call is answered. For private line applications, as discussed in Chapter 5, the network configuration is known, and the operating mode of each modem must be specified in advance.

For applications where terminals always call the computer, savings can be obtained by having the modem at the terminal be an originate-only variety and the modem at the computer be an answer-only variety. Originate-only and answer-only modems are simpler because they do not have to be able to change their transmitters, receivers, and filter arrangements from transmit 1070/1270 and receive 2025/2225 to transmit 2025/2225 and receive 1070/1270. Low-speed asynchronous modems are so inexpensive, however, that many users prefer the flexibility of originate/answer capability and are willing to pay the very modest increase in price.

An interesting problem arises in the case of a "booked call" in which a telephone operator is asked to establish a call and then to call the originating party when she has the called party available. If this is done with modems, the operator is calling both modems, and they both go into the answer mode. In countries where this is a problem, a "booked call" button ensures that the originating modem stays in originate mode despite the fact that it receives a call from the operator.

Figures 10–4 and 10–5 are repeats of Figures 10–2 and 10–3, but with the frequency assignments of CCITT Recommendation V.21: "300 Bits Per Second Modem Standardized for Use in the General Switched Telephone Network." Note that not only are the frequency assignments different, but also the higher frequencies of each pair represent the SPACE state rather than the MARK.

There are a variety of implementations for a low-speed asynchronous modem of the "103-type," many of which use digital techniques. An analog design is shown in block diagram form in Figure 10–6.

Transmit Data (EIA BA/CCITT 103) is applied to the Frequency Shift Keying (FSK) oscillator, which responds by shifting its frequency in accordance with the MARK/SPACE data. The output of the oscillator is applied

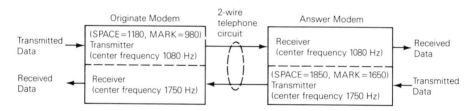

Figure 10–4   CCITT Low-Speed Asynchronous Full-Duplex Modem Frequency Assignments

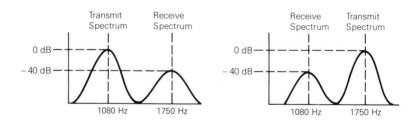

Figure 10–5   CCITT Low-Speed Asynchronous Full-Duplex Modem Frequency Spectra

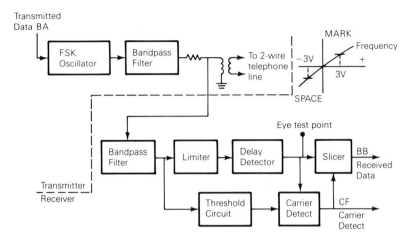

Figure 10–6   Block Diagram of Low-Speed Asynchronous Modem

to a bandpass filter, which restricts the sidebands of the oscillator output. (The process of shifting back and forth between 1070 and 1270 [or 2025 and 2225] produces additional frequencies that should not be applied to the telephone line.) The bandpass filter output is coupled to the telephone line by a line matching transformer.

At the receiver, the signal from the telephone line comes in through the line matching transformer and is applied to a bandpass filter. This filter attenuates out-of-band noise and the adjacent transmit signal by passing only frequencies of approximately 1800 to 2400 Hz (originate modem) or 900 to 1500 Hz (answer modem). The filter output is applied to a limiter, which eliminates amplitude variations of the signal. The limiter functions over a large enough volume range for its output to vary only in frequency, not in volume. The output of the limiter is connected to the delay detector, which compares the signal to a delayed version and produces an output voltage proportional to frequency.

As shown in Figure 10–6, the output of the delay detector is referred to as the eye test point. If random data is sent, an eye pattern can be observed at this point. Figure 10–7a shows an eye pattern for a line receiving error-free data, while Figure 10–7b shows an eye pattern for a line upon which data errors are occurring. (The pattern is called an eye pattern because of its resemblance to a human eye.) Note that in the good eye pattern (Figure 10–7a), transitions from the top of the eye to the bottom are smooth and cross a center line drawn from left to right cleanly and without wavering.

Figure 10–7a   Good Eye Pattern          Figure 10–7b   Bad Eye Pattern

This center line is implemented by a circuit called a "slicer," into which the eye pattern is fed. The slicer converts the analog signal that comes out of the delay detector back to MARK/SPACE digital data for the Receive Data lead (BB/104). Note that the slicer output (BB/104) is under the control of the Carrier Detect (CF/109) signal. For the slicer to operate normally, Carrier Detect must be on. Whenever CF/109 goes off, the slicer output is forced to a MARK, preventing erroneous data from appearing on the Receive Data lead. This operation will now be explained in somewhat more detail.

As shown in Figure 10–6, signals for Carrier Detect operation are picked off two separate points in the Receive Data channel. The first point feeds a threshold circuit that turns off CF whenever the receive signal drops below a certain threshold, such as −45 dbm. The second point monitors the delay detector output to determine whether the incoming signal is valid data or noise. Since the frequency spectra of valid, randomly keyed data and noise are quite similar, the Carrier Detect circuit must average for a relatively long time to distinguish between the two signals. Waveforms that illustrate the operation of the Carrier Detect circuit are shown in Figure 10–8. Note that CF/109 stays on for a signal loss of less than 30 milliseconds (ms).* When a signal loss of greater than 30 ms occurs, CF/109 goes off after 30 ms and BB/104 is forced to a MARK condition; 150 ms* after the signal reappears, CF turns back on, and valid data is again present at BB/104. Note that BB/104 is invalid whenever the line signal is lost, but CF/109 is still on for a short period.

Figure 10–9 shows how 103-type modems use up the frequency response available in a typical switched network call. Figure 10–10 shows how a 1200 baud modem, such as the Bell System 202, uses that same frequency response.

Like the 103-type modem, the 202-type modem transmits data by means of frequency shift keying, using a tone of 2200 Hz to represent a SPACE and a tone of 1200 Hz to represent a MARK. As indicated in Figure 10–10,

*These numbers are from a particular company's version of 300 baud asynchronous modem.

the frequency spectrum produced by such keying uses most of the available frequency response of the telephone connection, and transmission is therefore possible only in one direction at a time. Some information transmission is possible in the reverse direction by means of the receiving modems transmitting a 387 Hz tone back to the transmitting modem. This tone, when present, indicates that the circuit between the two modems is still there. It also can be used for the receiving station to inform the transmitting

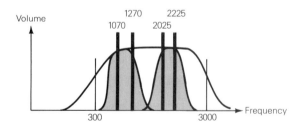

Figure 10–8  Carrier Detect Operation During Dropouts

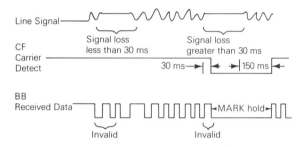

Figure 10–9  Frequency Utilization for 300 Baud Full-Duplex Modem

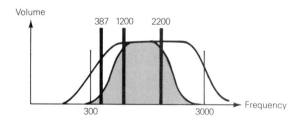

Figure 10–10  Frequency Utilization for 1200 Baud Half-Duplex Modem with Reverse Channel

station that the previous message contained errors and to request retransmission of that message.

The international version of the 202-type modem is the "600/1200 Baud Modem Standardized for Use in the General Switched Telephone Network," as described in CCITT Recommendation V.23. The modulation rates and frequencies for the main data transmission channels are:

|  | *MARK* | *SPACE* |
|---|---|---|
| Mode 1 (up to 600 baud) | 1300 Hz | 1700 Hz |
| Mode 2 (up to 1200 baud) | 1300 Hz | 2100 Hz |

Note that, as with the 103-type modem, the international version uses closer frequency spacing than its North American counterpart.

The CCITT V.23 modem also differs from its North American counterpart in that the reverse channel has a 75 baud capability and uses real FSK rather than ON/OFF keying. On the reverse channel, 390 Hz represents a MARK, and 450 Hz represents a SPACE. The interface is arranged so that if no interface lead is provided, the reverse channel sends a MARK.

The 202-type modem has some characteristics that may be of interest to programmers. Some versions of the 202-type modem leave the receiver circuitry on while transmission is taking place. Since the frequencies used by the transmitter are identical to those used by the receiver, the receiver sees the line signal being produced by the transmitter, demodulates it, and produces a copy of the Transmitted Data for delivery to the Received Data lead. This feature is called "local copy." In addition, the Carrier Detect lead is asserted whenever either the local or distant modem is transmitting.

Recently, the cost of electronics has become low enough for it to be economically feasible to use advanced modulation techniques to create more sophisticated modems for both asynchronous and synchronous use. These modems are discussed in Chapter 22.

# 11

## Automatic Calling Units

Previous chapters have dealt with data communication between two computers connected by private lines and have discussed data communication over the switched telephone network with the calls being answered automatically by the computer. In addition to these arrangements, it is also possible to have systems where the computer automatically originates the calls. One of the applications is inventory control systems where the computer calls various warehouses or retail stores, usually after business hours, and reaches a computer that has inventory or sales information stored in it. If the computer is ready to transmit the data, it automatically answers the call and allows the central computer to read the data. Thus, the computer must be designed so that not just any person calling the number will elicit transmission of the data.

A second application is the automatic establishment of a "dial back-up" circuit when a private line fails. In this application, the software in a computer system detects that a private line between it and another computer or terminal has failed. Automatic calling is used to dial up a port on the other computer and reestablish communications, although often at a reduced signaling rate.

For many years, the most common automatic dialing units were the Bell System (Western Electric) 801A Automatic Calling Unit (dial pulse) and 801C Automatic Calling Unit (Touch Tone™). Independent equipment manufacturers and various PTT authorities throughout the world offered similar units. Calling units of this type utilized a parallel interface, over which dialing commands were passed from the computer to the calling unit and call status information was passed from the calling unit to the computer. Modern automatic calling units use a serial interface to perform these tasks.

Parallel interface calling units generally conform to CCITT Recommendation V.25 and EIA Specification EIA-366. Serial interface calling units follow several differing standards, with CCITT Recommendation V.25 *bis* and the Hayes Protocol being the most common.

For both parallel and serial interface calling units, the computer and its associated interface to the automatic calling unit are responsible for:

1. Ensuring that the data communication equipment (i.e., the calling unit and the line) is available for operation.
2. Providing the telephone number to be dialed.
3. Deciding to abandon the call if it is not successfully completed.
4. Supervising the call to determine when to take down the connection. (In general, the supervision task is handed over to the modem when the call has been established.)

Before discussing serial interface calling units, let's review parallel units, with an emphasis on how they accomplish the four tasks outlined above.

Two leads are provided to perform the first task. One of these indicates that the calling unit has its power on and is called "PoWer Indicator" (PWI, CCITT Circuit 213). The second circuit indicates whether the communications line is currently in use, either by a person using the associated telephone set (if there is one) or by a previously established data call. This lead is called "Data Line Occupied" (DLO, Circuit 203). To seize the communications line to place a call, the "Call Request" lead is provided (CRQ, Circuit 202).

Thus, to obtain a dial tone, the computer/interface checks to see that PWI/213 is ON and that DLO/203 is OFF, then asserts CRQ/202. Data Terminal Ready (Circuit 108/2) also may be asserted by the interface to the modem at this time.

The communications line is now placed in the off-hook condition by the calling unit, and the telephone switching equipment returns a dial tone to the calling unit. In the Bell System 801A and some similar units, the detection of a dial tone requires a special alteration to the telephone line called "Ground Start." The 801C uses a tone detection circuit that responds to the 350/440 Hz precise tones that represent dial tone in Bell System switching offices where Touch Tone service is provided.

All calling units requiring Ground Start lines, and some with tone detectors, have problems in applications where detection of a second dial tone is required. For example, in systems where "9" is dialed for an outside (city) trunk, and a wait for a city trunk dial tone is involved, the second wait may have to be timed by system software, and after a reasonable interval the receipt of a dial tone must be assumed. In some calling units, unused codes on the dialed digit leads are assigned to indicate that the calling unit should wait for a dial tone, thus obviating the need for software timing. Automatic dialers built to CCITT Recommendation V.25 provide a delay when the Separation (SEP) code (1101) is applied to the digit leads.

Once the automatic calling unit has seized the line and recognized a dial tone, it is time for the interface to undertake the second task: providing the telephone number to be dialed. A lead called "Present Next Digit" (PND, Circuit 210) is provided from the calling unit to the computer/ interface, which, when asserted, indicates that the calling unit is ready to be told a digit to dial. This information is presented from the interface to the calling unit over four digit leads referred to as NB1, NB2, NB4, and NB8 (Circuits 206, 207, 208, and 209, respectively). See Table 11–1.

The transfer of information on the digit leads is done in parallel, just as described in Chapter 1. The "clock" or "strobe" signal is provided by an additional lead from the interface to the calling unit, called "Digit Present"

Table 11–1   Automatic Calling Unit Digit Leads

| Digit | 209 NB8 | 208 NB4 | 207 NB2 | 206 NB1 | *CCITT Designations* 801 Designations |
|-------|-----|-----|-----|-----|-------------------|
| 1 | Off | Off | Off | On | |
| 2 | Off | Off | On | Off | |
| 3 | Off | Off | On | On | |
| 4 | Off | On | Off | Off | |
| 5 | Off | On | Off | On | |
| 6 | Off | On | On | Off | |
| 7 | Off | On | On | On | |
| 8 | On | Off | Off | Off | |
| 9 | On | Off | Off | On | |
| 0 | On | Off | On | Off | |
| EON | On | On | Off | Off | End of Number |
| SEP | On | On | Off | On | SEParation |

(DPR, Circuit 211). The calling unit indicates that it has accepted the digit for dialing by negating the PND/210 lead. The digit lead information and the DPR/211 signal must not be changed until this negation occurs.

The automatic calling unit reasserts PND/210 when it has completed dialing that digit. The interface may then present new information on the digit leads (which may be changed as soon as PND negates) and may assert DPR/211 to indicate that the new digit should be dialed.

The process of presenting digit information proceeds until the last digit has been dialed. The interface then places the End of Number (EON) code on the digit leads and asserts DPR/211. This step is unnecessary if modems with recognizable answer tones are used and the calling unit is equipped with the "Detect Answer" option.

Having dialed the number, the automatic calling unit and its associated interface are now ready for the third task: abandoning the call if it is not successfully completed. There are three possible ways this can be done. The CCITT Recommendation V.25 method is for the "abandon call timer" to begin operating when the calling unit has negated PND/210 in response to receiving the EON code on the digit leads. If the call is answered by a data terminal, a tone is received by the calling unit, and the abandon call timer is turned off. If the call is not answered or is answered by something or someone other than a data terminal, the timer continues running. After 10 to 40 seconds (selectable), the calling unit asserts "Abandon Call" (ACR, Circuit 205), which directs the interface to disconnect the call; it does so by dropping Call Request (CRQ/202). If the call is successfully answered by a data terminal, the calling unit asserts the signal "Distant Station Connected" (Circuit 204), and the control of the telephone line is passed to the modem. The modem continues to hold the connection intact under the control of the Data Terminal Ready lead (Circuit 108/2), which must be asserted by the interface by this time. The Call Request lead may then be dropped without disconnecting the call. The modem interface, in conjunction with the computer software, then controls the assertion of Data Terminal Ready and disconnects the call when appropriate.

The second method of checking for call completion is used by 801-type calling units. As with the CCITT Recommendation V.25 method, the EON operating mode is used, but an option called "Do Not Stop ACR When DSS Goes On" is used instead of "Stop ACR." This option is necessary because the 801-type calling units differ from V.25 units by having a signal called

Data Set Status instead of Distant Station Connected. The Data Set Status signal in the 801 indicates that the modem has control of the telephone line, rather than indicating anything about the status of distant stations. A further difference between the 801 and a V.25 calling unit is that when the 801 is used in EON operation, the modem is connected to the line immediately when the EON code is presented. Data Set Status, meaning the modem has control of the line, is immediately asserted. The abandon call and retry timer is allowed to expire, and the assertion of the ACR/205 lead is used to notify the computer program that it should send a "Who are you?" or some other kind of inquiry on the communications line to see whether a call has been successfully established.

The third method of call control is used when 801-type calling units are placing calls to modems that answer with a tone in the 2000 to 2400 Hz range. The sequence of events is again similar to that described for Recommendation V.25, except that "Detect Answer" operation is used rather than EON codes. The 801 looks for an answer tone (2000 to 2400) after completion of each dialed digit, and upon detecting one, it transfers control of the call to the modem (the "Terminate Call After DSS Goes On, Via Data Set" option is required). If no answer tone is detected within the ACR interval after dialing the last digit, the ACR/205 lead is asserted, indicating failure to complete the call.

The final task of an automatic calling unit, supervising the call, is performed by the associated modems.

Now that a thorough background in parallel interface automatic calling units has been established, serial interface calling units can be easily understood. Serial interface calling units use special character sequences on the Transmit Data and Receive Data interface leads to control the dialing function and to report on call status. Serial interface calling units are usually housed within the associated modem as an additional circuit board, as an additional chip, or within the modem chip itself. The international standard for these units is CCITT Recommendation V.25 *bis*, which allows two modes of operation:

1. The "addressed call and/or answer authorized by DTE (circuit 108/2) mode."
2. The "direct call and/or answer controlled by the DTE (circuit 108/1) mode."

The discussion that follows will deal only with the "addressed call" mode, as that is both the most interesting and the most common mode. The interface leads required to implement the addressed call mode of V.25 *bis* are listed below, and their functions are outlined briefly:

*Circuit 103*—Transmitted Data
The commands issued during the automatic dialing procedure are transmitted from the interface to the modem over this lead.

*Circuit 104*—Received Data
The modem's responses to commands are received over this lead.

*Circuit 106*—Ready for Sending
The modem will turn this circuit ON in response to the interface having turned ON Data Terminal Ready (Circuit 108/2). During call establishment, the modem will turn this signal OFF when a call has been established and an answer tone has been detected. During the ensuing call, this signal will operate in response to Request to Send (Circuit 105). At the conclusion or aborting of a call, the modem will turn this circuit OFF if the interface turns Data Terminal Ready OFF.

*Circuit 107*—Data Set Ready
During call establishment, the modem will turn this signal ON when a call has been established and an answer tone has been detected. At the conclusion or aborting of a call, the modem will turn this circuit OFF if the interface turns Data Terminal Ready OFF.

*Circuit 108/2*—Data Terminal Ready
The interface controls this circuit and turns it ON to allow the modem to dial or answer a call automatically. If the interface does not wish to do either of these things or wishes to abort a call in progress, it will turn this signal OFF.

*Circuit 125*—Calling Indicator
The modem uses this signal to indicate an incoming call. If the calling unit detects assertion of this signal, it will not attempt to place an outgoing call but rather will answer the incoming call. Use of this signal by the interface is optional because V.25 *bis* modems also provide an indication message on the Received Data lead (Circuit 104).

While the state of other interface signals is not prescribed by Recommendation V.25 *bis*, two other signals are of possible interest:

*Circuit 109*—Data Channel Received Line Signal Detector
(Commonly called "Carrier Detect")
Signals on this circuit usually indicate that the received line signal is within appropriate limits for the modem to be able to decode the data being received. However, to facilitate using common software routines for handling both "real" data and the data used to control a serial automatic calling unit, it is also desirable to have this signal asserted during the exchange of data signals between a computer and a calling unit.

*Circuit 105*—Request to Send

Signals on this circuit control the transmit function of the modem. The hardware or software in the computer may wish to assert this signal during the programming or control of a serial automatic calling unit, but the calling unit is not required to recognize this signal.

Recommendation V.25 *bis* provides a powerful vocabulary of commands that can be used by a computer to control a dialer. One set of commands, called "program commands," allows the computer to preprogram various memory locations within the dialer with numbers to be dialed (and the calling number, if required). Another set of commands, called "call request commands," requests that the dialer retrieve a designated number from memory and dial it or that the dialer accept a number provided by the computer. Additional commands direct the dialer to list the contents of its memory locations, disregard incoming calls, or answer calls. The dialer responds to these commands with "valid" or "invalid" indications to indicate that the command was (or was not) properly formatted. In addition, the caller may respond with call status indications, such as "busy," "ring tone time out" (i.e., no answer), "abort time out" (i.e., no ring or busy signal received), or "answer tone not detected" (i.e., a person answered). If an incoming call was received before the line was seized to make the outgoing call, an "incoming call" indication will be given.

A list of commands and indications for Recommendation V.25 *bis* dialers is given in Table 11–2. The characters listed in the table are from International Alphabet Number 5 (CCITT Recommendation T.50), sometimes abbreviated IA5. When asynchronous transmission is used, the character format is one START element, a seven-bit IA5 character, an even parity bit, and one STOP bit. The command or indication and its associated parameters are followed by a carriage return and a line feed. Synchronous operation can be used, but format information will not be given here, as synchronous protocols have not yet been discussed.

One of the indications listed in the table, "delayed call," is worthy of special note. In many countries, it is illegal for an automatic calling unit to make repeated unsuccessful (i.e., no data transferred) call attempts to the same number more frequently than every $x$ minutes (where $x$ varies from country to country). Some automatic calling units provide an automatic enforcement of this by declining to accept call attempts to the same number more frequently than every $x$ minutes. The V.25 *bis* "delayed call" indication essentially says, "It is illegal to call now, please wait." It is

Table 11–2   Commands and Indications for Recommendation V.25 *bis* Dialers

| Command/Indication | Characters | Parameters |
|---|---|---|
| Call Request with: | | |
|   Number provided | CRN | Number to be dialed |
|   Number provided with identification number | CRI | Number to be dialed, identification number |
|   Memory Address | CRS | Memory address where number to be dialed is stored |
| Program: | | |
|   Normal | PRN | Memory address and number to be dialed when a CRS command is given for this address |
|   Identification | PRI | Identification number |
| List Request of: | | |
|   Stored Numbers | RLN | |
|   Forbidden Numbers | RLF | |
|   Delayed Call Numbers | RLD | |
|   Identification Number | RLI | |
| Disregard Incoming Call | DIC | |
| Connect Incoming Call | CIC | |
| Call Failure Indication | CFI | Call Failure Parameters |
| Delayed Call | DLC | Time Duration in minutes |
| Incoming Call | INC | |
| Valid | VAL | |
| Invalid | INV | |
| List of: | | |
|   Stored Numbers | LSN | Memory address and number to be dialed |
|   Forbidden Numbers | LSF | Memory address and number to be dialed |
|   Delayed Call Numbers | LSD | Memory address and number to be dialed |
|   Identification Number | LSI | Identification number |

important to note, however, that not all calling units have this feature, yet many countries require it. Therefore, it is highly recommended that this feature be provided in the computer software that is used for controlling the calling unit.

While V.25 *bis* is the international standard for serial interface calling units, another widely used standard is the Hayes AT Command Set. This command set is summarized in Table 11–3, reproduced by permission of Hayes Microcomputer Products, Inc.

When using the AT Command Set to set up a connection, commands are given as a "command line" preceded by an AT and concluding with a carriage return. For example, to dial 1-617-555-1212, the sequence would be ATD16175551212, followed by a carriage return. If the number were being dialed from a PBX line where dialing "9" and awaiting a dial tone was necessary, the sequence would be ATD9,16175551212. In these examples, the AT is the attention prefix, the D is the dial command, and the dialed digits follow (with a comma inserted if a pause to wait for a second dial tone is required). The carriage return indicates the end of the command line. If one wishes to use the Hayes AT Command Set during an established call (to change modem parameters, for example), an "escape sequence" is necessary to reconnect the calling unit logic to the Transmit Data and Received Data leads. As indicated in Table 11–3, this sequence is +++.

When a command line is executed, a "Result Code" is returned on the Received Data lead. These codes are summarized in Table 11–4, also reproduced by permission of Hayes Microcomputer Products, Inc. For example, a typical call would receive an OK response, indicating that the command had been executed, followed by a CONNECT response if the call were successful, a BUSY response if the called line was busy, or a NO CARRIER response if the call was answered by something or someone other than a modem.

The commands available in the Hayes AT Command Set also allow a computer to alter the option settings of the associated modem. Among the options that can be controlled are the following:

1. A choice of whether the modem is Bell 212A compatible or CCITT compatible when operated at 1200 bps.

2. Delay between Request to Send and Clear to Send.

3. Pulse dialing or tone dialing and the timing characteristics of the alternative chosen.

Table 11–3   Command Summary

---

| | |
|---|---|
| AT | Attention prefix; precedes all commands except + + + (escape) and A/ (repeat) |
| A/ | Repeat last command |
| + + + | Go to command state (Escape Code) |
| ATO | Go to on-line state |

*Dialing and Answering Commands*

| | |
|---|---|
| D | Dial |
| P | Pulse-dial subsequent calls |
| T | Touch-tone dial subsequent calls |
| , | Pause |
| ; | Return to command state after dialing |
| R | Reverse mode (dial, then go into answer mode) |
| A | Answer |
| H0 | Hangup |
| H1 | Line and auxiliary relays off hook |
| H2 | Line relay only off hook |

*Configuration Commands*

| | |
|---|---|
| C0 | Transmit carrier off |
| **C1** | **Transmit carrier on** |
| E0 | Command state echo disabled |
| **E1** | **Command state echo enabled** |
| F0 | On-line echo enabled |
| **F1** | **On-line echo disabled** |
| M0 | Speaker always off |
| **M1** | **Speaker on until carrier detected** |
| M2 | Speaker always on |
| **Q0** | **Result codes displayed** |
| Q1 | Result codes not displayed |
| Sr? | Requests current value of register r |
| Sr=n | Sets value of register r equal to n |
| V0 | Numerical result codes |
| **V1** | **Verbose result codes** |
| Z | Software reset; restores default configuration |

---

**Bold** indicates default setting.

Commands entered with null parameters assume the parameter 0. For example, M is the same as M0.

Source: Hayes Microcomputer Products, Inc., Norcross, Georgia. Reprinted with permission.

Table 11–4   Result Codes

| | | |
|---|---|---|
| 0 | OK | Command executed |
| 1 | CONNECT | Carrier detected |
| 2 | RING | Ringing signal detected |
| 3 | NO CARRIER | Carrier signal not detected or lost |
| 4 | ERROR | Illegal command |
| | | Error in command line |
| | | Command line exceeds buffer (40 characters, including punctuation) |

Source: Hayes Microcomputer Products, Inc., Norcross, Georgia. Reprinted with permission.

4. Modem response during modem test situations.

5. Carrier Detect response time and amount of time to wait before hanging up when a carrier loss occurs.

6. Whether or not to answer incoming calls automatically.

In contrast, Recommendation V.25 *bis* leaves the details of modem options to the recommendation associated with the particular modem being used. There are probably three reasons for this. First, modem options have traditionally been accomplished by means of metal jumper straps in the modem, and program selectable options are a new concept. Second, in many countries modem options are set at installation by government post and telegraph personnel and are not intended to be user changeable. Third, detailed modem option selection can quickly become product specific, as can be appreciated by reviewing Appendix H.

In addition to a differing treatment of modem options, Recommendation V.25 *bis* and the Hayes Protocol also differ in the following ways:

1. V.25 *bis* enters the "dialer active" state by means of a unique set of modem control lead states, whereas the Hayes Protocol uses an escape sequence.

2. V.25 *bis* enters the "call connected" state by means of modem control lead states, whereas Hayes uses an indication message.

Finally, on a historical note, earlier dialers, such as the Vadic VA831 and the Digital Equipment DF03-AC, used a simpler protocol than either Recommendation V.25 *bis* or the Hayes AT Command Set. This simpler protocol is shown in Table 11–5.

Table 11–5   Special Character Sequences Used on Interface Circuits of a Non-Bell Automatic Calling Unit

| Character | ASCII Code | Function |
| --- | --- | --- |
| STX (Control B) | 002 | Condition the automatic calling unit for reception of numeric input. |
| Digits | 060–071 | String of numbers representing the telephone number to be dialed. If the initial digit is used within a PBX to access an "outside line," use of a "pause" character (see below) is necessary. |
| = | 075 | Pause—this character is equivalent to the SEParation code defined in V.25. It allows time to obtain a second dial tone. |
| SI (Control O) | 017 | Buffer Limit (Vadic VA831) |
| ETX (Control C) | 003 | End of numeric input. Dialing can begin in Vadic VA831 (dialing occurs simultaneously with input in the Digital DF03-AC). |
| SOH (Control A) | 001 | Abort the call attempt (for use before the automatic calling unit returns Response A—Data Set Status). |
| < | 074 | Transfer telephone line to modem after the telephone number has been dialed without waiting for an answer tone. This is equivalent to the use, in an 801, of the "End of Number" option rather than the "Detect Answer" option. |

The automatic calling unit responds with the following possible responses:

| Character | ASCII Code | Function |
| --- | --- | --- |
| A | 101 | Data Set Status—the telephone line has been transferred to the modem. |
| B | 102 | Abandon Call and Retry—the call attempt did not succeed. |
| D | 104 | Framing Error (VA831 only) |
| E | 105 | Parity Error (VA831 only) |
|   |   | The above two errors indicate that the serial data transferred to the VA831 had the types of errors indicated. |
| F | 106 | Overrun (VA831 only) |
|   |   | A number consisting of too many digits was loaded between the STX and SI characters. |
| G | 107 | Data Line Occupied—a fault condition. |

Note: Signals are appropriate to a Vadic VA831 RS232/801 adapter and Digital Equipment Corporation DF03-AC dialer.

# 12

# Asynchronous Multiplexers with Modem Control

It was noted in Chapter 7 that computer systems with a number of asynchronous communications lines connected to them can generally profit from the introduction of multiplexers. This is so both because a large number of communications lines can share a single bus interface and because other features that all of the lines could use can be added economically. The features most commonly added are direct memory transfers and modem control. Some of these features, notably modem control, are also found in single line interfaces, but they are more commonly found in multiplexers.

Both single line interfaces and multiplexers provide programmable formats and speeds, but this feature is more important in multiplexers. Programmable formats and speeds enable a multiplexer to answer a switched network telephone call, then adjust itself, perhaps with program assistance, to the operating characteristics of the terminal on the other end of the telephone call. Appendix E lists some of the possible formats for asynchronous data transmission.

To provide a wide variety of features for multiple lines, a multiplexer uses a more complex register arrangement than the single line interfaces discussed in Chapters 2 and 6. The starting point is the base control and status register shown in Figure 12–1. Like the single line counterpart, there is a "transmitter ready" bit (XMIT ACTION, Bit 15) and a "receiver done" bit (RCVR DONE, Bit 07). Each of these bits may generate an interrupt request if its associated interrupt enable bit (bits 14 and 6, respectively) is

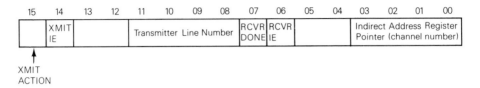

Figure 12–1   Base Control and Status Register

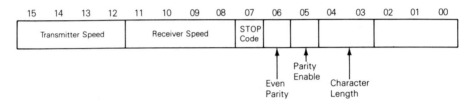

Figure 12–2   Line Parameter Register

set. Since there are multiple sources for the transmit interrupt, bits 11–08 are used to identify the line generating the transmitter interrupt. The line number for the receiver interrupt is given in a different fashion, which will be discussed later. Finally, bits 03–00 are used as line number selection bits that must be conditioned to select a particular line before addressing some of the registers described below.

Returning to the subject of multiplexer features, registers associated with each line implement the programmable formats and speeds function. The register is called the line parameter register and is arranged as shown in Figure 12–2. This register is loaded after the program has loaded a line selection register to indicate the line number to which this information applies.

The transmitter speed is controlled by bits 15–12 and the receiver speed may be independently set in bits 11–08. Both of the four-bit speed selection groups use speeds from Table 12–1.

The speeds shown in Table 12–1 have the following significance:

50, 75   Used in some low-speed applications, especially with Baudot (five-bit) code. Generally obsolete.

110   Used in Teletype Corporation's Model 33 and Model 35 teleprinters. Generally obsolete.

134.5   Used for IBM Model 2741 and Model 1050 terminals. Generally obsolete.

| 150 | Used for printing terminals using electronic rather than mechanical transmitter/receiver units. Generally obsolete. |
| --- | --- |
| 300 | Top speed of V.21, 103-series, and similar full-duplex switched telephone network modems. |
| 600 | Slower speed used in 600/1200 bps asynchronous modems built according to CCITT Recommendation V.23. |
| 1200 | Top speed of V.23, 202-series, and similar half-duplex modems on switched network service. Top speed of V.22, 212-series, and similar full-duplex modems for switched network service. |
| 1800 | Top speed of 202-series and similar half- and full-duplex asynchronous modems for private line service. Not a common speed. |
| 2000 | A speed used by a long-obsolete Bell synchronous modem that used internal clocks and thus never required this speed. This speed is a mistake propagated by baud rate generator chip manufacturers. |

Table 12–1   Speed Selection Table

|  |  | Bit |  |  |  |
| --- | --- | --- | --- | --- | --- |
| *Transmitter* | *15* | *14* | *13* | *12* |  |
| *Receiver* | *11* | *10* | *09* | *08* |  |
|  | 0 | 0 | 0 | 0 | 50* |
|  | 0 | 0 | 0 | 1 | 75 |
|  | 0 | 0 | 1 | 0 | 110 |
|  | 0 | 0 | 1 | 1 | 134.5 |
|  | 0 | 1 | 0 | 0 | 150 |
|  | 0 | 1 | 0 | 1 | 300 |
|  | 0 | 1 | 1 | 0 | 600 |
|  | 0 | 1 | 1 | 1 | 1200 |
|  | 1 | 0 | 0 | 0 | 1800 |
|  | 1 | 0 | 0 | 1 | 2000 |
|  | 1 | 0 | 1 | 0 | 2400 |
|  | 1 | 0 | 1 | 1 | 4800 |
|  | 1 | 1 | 0 | 0 | 7200 |
|  | 1 | 1 | 0 | 1 | 9600 |
|  | 1 | 1 | 1 | 0 | 19,200 |
|  | 1 | 1 | 1 | 1 | 38,400 |

*Speed in bits per second (bps)

| 2400 | Top speed of V.22 *bis*, V.26 *bis*, and V.26 *ter* full-duplex modems for switched network service. |
| 4800 | Top speed of V.27 *ter* full-duplex modems for switched network service. |
| 9600 | Top speed of V.32 and V.33 full-duplex modems for switched network service. |
| 19,200<br>38,400 | Terminal speeds sometimes used when close enough to the computer for line drivers rather than modems to suffice. |

Since baud rate generator chips are very cheap and since baud rate generation is often built into UARTs, most terminals have all the speeds mentioned in the above chart. Some multiplexers provide unused speed codes, which can be used for special clocks if desired.

Returning to the explanation of Figure 12–2, bit 07 determines whether a single STOP unit follows the data bits (bit 07 clear) or whether two STOP units are used (1.5 STOP units in the case of five-bit codes). If parity operation is selected (see bit 05), the type of parity used is determined by the state of bit 06, Even Parity. When set, bit 05 indicates that the line will be operated with the transmitter affixing a parity bit to each character transmitted and the receiver checking each received character for proper parity. Bits 04 and 03 determine the length of the characters transmitted and received, according to Table 12–2. The character lengths in Table 12–2 do not include the parity bit.

A second feature made possible by the common equipment sharing permitted by multiplexer design is direct memory transfers. This feature permits a program to specify to the multiplexer that a message, beginning at a particular address in memory and of a specified length, is to be sent on a selected line. The multiplexer, upon receiving these details, directly transfers the characters from the memory location to the communications line,

Table 12–2   Character Lengths

| Bit | | |
|---|---|---|
| *04* | *03* | *Character Length* |
| 0 | 0 | 5 bits |
| 0 | 1 | 6 bits |
| 1 | 0 | 7 bits |
| 1 | 1 | 8 bits |

as the transmitter for that line becomes available. It will not take any of the program's time until the job is completed; the multiplexer then notifies the program, by means of an interrupt, that the task has been completed.

The hardware required is a scratchpad memory that will hold the "transmit buffer address" for each line and the "transmit direct memory access (DMA) buffer count" for each line. The transmit buffer address is the memory address at which the next character to be sent is located. The transmit buffer address is initially loaded by the computer program to specify the location of the first character of the message. Once the multiplexer begins the transmission, it obtains the character stored at that location, loads it into the transmitter unit of the appropriate line, and increments the buffer address value so that it will obtain the next character from the next location. The transmit DMA buffer count is a count of the number of characters to be transmitted (assuming that characters have been stored one character per eight-bit byte). Like the buffer address, the buffer count register contains a value initially loaded by the program. Unlike the buffer address, however, the value in the byte count register is decremented each time a character is sent, with an interrupt being given when the buffer count reaches zero, indicating that all the characters have been sent. Alternatively, if an error condition occurs during transmission (such as an attempt to load a character from a location beyond the memory address limits) or a suspension of transmission is requested by the program, an interrupt is generated, and the buffer count register indicates the number of characters remaining to be sent.

To provide DMA transmission, three additional registers would be required, in addition to the line parameter register previously discussed. These are shown in Figures 12–3, 12–4, and 12–5.

These three registers must be replicated for each line. Thus, before loading them, a program must first select the line number whose current address and byte count registers it wishes to access. This permits the hardware to store the information in random access memory and to use the line numbers as addresses to select the desired information.

While the transmit DMA buffer counter register and the transmit buffer address register number 1 have been discussed, the transmit buffer address register number 2 in Figure 12–5 merits further mention. Bits 1 and 0 are used to provide additional addressing bits. Bit 7 is used as a "go" bit; when set, it enables the start of DMA transfers. Thus, of the three registers

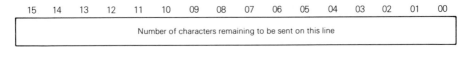

Figure 12–3   Transmit DMA Buffer Counter Register

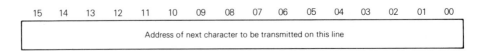

Figure 12–4   Transmit Buffer Address Register Number 1

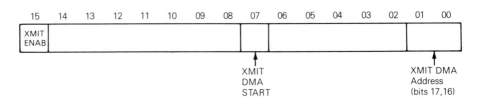

Figure 12–5   Transmit Buffer Address Register Number 2

discussed, this register should be loaded last. When the multiplexer has completed (or aborted) a DMA transfer, it will clear this bit, in addition to giving status indications via registers not yet described. To complete the DMA logic, the appropriate circuitry to control the computer bus during the data transfers from memory is required.

Obviously, a similar set of registers can be provided to accommodate a similar process on the receiver side. Many computer operating systems use special characters, however, which immediately connect the terminal operator to a higher level program and cease the execution of the current program, or which stop the output of characters to their terminal. These special characters must be recognized immediately when they are typed. In addition, some operating systems echo back each character to the terminal as it is typed to confirm to the terminal operator that the computer received the information he or she thinks it did. When these types of operating systems are used, it is often of little advantage to use DMA transfers in the receiver section of a multiplexer. Rather, it is preferable to either have a multiplexer smart enough to do character recognition or to have the receiver section of the multiplexer be a simple interrupt operated silo (FIFO) system, such as that described in Chapter 7. Chapter 21 explores character recognition and other multiplexer enhancements in some detail.

The third feature most commonly added to multiplexers is modem control. While single line interfaces are also built with modem control, the equipment sharing allowed with multiplexers permits the construction of some rather interesting implementations of modem control.

As indicated in Chapter 9, any modem control must include control of DTE Ready (CCITT 108/2) or Connect Data Set to Line (CCITT 108/1). This lead must be asserted to maintain a call connection in switched network service, but it must be negated to drop that connection at the conclusion of data transmission. Either the DCE Ready lead (CCITT 107) or the Ring Indicator lead (CCITT 125) also must be monitored so that a computer program will know when a new call has been established and will treat the new caller accordingly. A Clear to Send lead (CCITT 106) must be provided so that the transmitter will know when it is safe to begin transmission, and a Carrier Detect lead (Data Channel Received Line Signal Detector, CCITT 109) must be provided to advise the receiver logic of the likely validity of the data on the Received Data lead (CCITT 103). If half-duplex modems or multipoint line operation are envisioned, a Request to Send lead (CCITT 105) will be needed to turn the transmitter section of the modem off and on. Further, since the program may wish to ignore modem leads for lines subject to extreme noise conditions or connected to faulty modems, an enable bit to permit the program to ignore modem lead transitions is a useful feature.

The control leads mentioned above can all be arranged in a line control register, one of which would be provided for each line in the multiplexer. In a similar fashion, the status leads mentioned above can all be arranged in a line status register, one of which would be provided for each line in the multiplexer. The program can condition some line selection bits (not shown) to determine which line it wishes to change (or monitor) before addressing the line control register (or line status register).

A possible bit arrangement for a line control register is shown in Figure 12–6. The abbreviations used are RTS for Request to Send and DTR for Data Terminal Ready. A possible bit arrangement for a line status register is shown in Figure 12–7. The abbreviations used are DSR for Data Set Ready, RI for Ring Indicator, DCD for Carrier Detect, and CTS for Clear to Send.

| 15 | 14 | 13 | 12 | 11 | 10 | 09 | 08 | 07 | 06 | 05 | 04 | 03 | 02 | 01 | 00 |
|----|----|----|----|----|----|----|----|----|----|----|----|----|----|----|----|
|    |    |    | RTS |    |    | DTR | Link Type |    |    |    |    |    |    |    |    |

Figure 12–6   Line Control Register

| 15 | 14 | 13 | 12 | 11 | 10 | 09 | 08 | 07 | 06 | 05 | 04 | 03 | 02 | 01 | 00 |
|----|----|----|----|----|----|----|----|----|----|----|----|----|----|----|----|
| DSR |    | RI | DCD | CTS |    |    |    |    |    |    |    |    |    |    |    |

Figure 12–7   Line Status Register

Returning to Figure 12–6, there is an additional bit that performs the enable/disable feature for modem lead transition reporting mentioned a few moments ago. Bit 08, Link Type, controls the presentation of the line status information (Figure 12–7) to the transition detection system. If this bit is clear, the state of the modem status leads is reflected in the line status register only. If this bit is set, the state of the modem status leads is reflected in the line status register and monitored by the modem change detection logic described below.

One of the simplest ways to detect transitions on any signal lead is to build the circuit shown in Figure 12–8. The symbol shown is for an exclusive-OR (XOR) gate, whose output Y is related to the inputs A and B, as shown in the table accompanying Figure 12–8.

In this circuit, the present state of the lead is compared by the XOR gate with the state of the lead some time ago. "Some time" is determined by the value of the delay line—50 nanoseconds is a common value. When the present and the past are different (i.e., there has been a transition), the output of the XOR gate is asserted. After the delay time has expired, lead

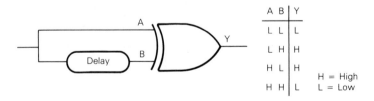

| A | B | Y |
|---|---|---|
| L | L | L |
| L | H | H |
| H | L | H |
| H | H | L |

H = High
L = Low

Figure 12–8   Transition Detector

B changes to the new value; since the signals at points A and B are then identical, the output of the XOR gate is no longer asserted. The output of the XOR gate is thus asserted for a length of time equal to the length of the delay line associated with point B. This output is typically used to set a bit in a register to indicate that a transition has occurred. Lead A is usually wired to another register to give the program information about the present status of the lead. The line status register shown in Figure 12–7 is an example of such a register.

A transition detector such as that shown in Figure 12–8 works well, but monitoring Data Set Ready, Ring, Carrier Detect, and Clear to Send in a 16-line multiplexer requires 64 copies of the Figure 12–8 circuit, an arrangement that consumes both space and money.

Because the frequency of the transitions of modem control leads is very slow relative to computer processing speeds, the circuit shown in Figure 12–9 can be used to detect transitions of the Clear to Send lead (for example) on 16 lines. The circuitry in Figure 12–9 works as follows: At Clock 1 time, the Line Counter is incremented, causing the scanner to sample the state of the Clear to Send lead for a new line. At the same time, the previous state of the Clear to Send lead for that line is read out from a memory containing 16 addressable entries, each one bit wide—i.e., storage of the previous Clear to Send lead state for each of the 16 lines. At Clock 2 time,

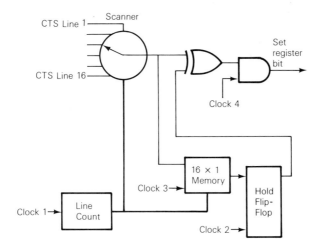

Figure 12–9   Multiple Line Transition Detector

the previous state of Clear to Send as read from the memory is recorded in the Hold flip-flop and the XOR gate compares that previous state with the present state obtained from the scanner. The truth table for the XOR gate is the same as that shown in Figure 12–8, and if the present state differs from the past state, the output of the XOR gate is asserted. This assertion is sampled at Clock 4 time and used to set a bit in a register as well as to stop the clocking system so that a computer program can read the setting of the line counter to determine which line has a transition of its Clear to Send lead. At Clock 3 time (which would occur between Clock 2 time and Clock 4 time), the new state of Clear to Send is recorded in the appropriate memory location.

This circuit may appear to have a great many more elements than the Figure 12–8 circuit, and indeed it does—but not 16 times as many. Further, the same line counter can be used to run additional scanners that look at Data Set Ready, Ring, and Carrier Detect. Since the Hold flip-flop, 16 × 1 Memory, and XOR gate are normally packages with four such units in one integrated circuit, the amount of logic needed to implement four versions of Figure 12–9 is far less than the amount needed to implement sixty-four versions of Figure 12–8. As with all apparent panaceas, there are some drawbacks. In particular, the computer must restart the scanner after processing in information concerning the transition of a lead, and a hardware system must be devised that will, on power-up, clear the 16 × 1 memories. A modem control using the transition detection system shown in Figure 12–9 could present the transition information in a "modem change register."

When a multiplexer contains one or more microprocessors, a further optimization of the modem control is possible. Specifically, the microprogram can perform the function described in Figure 12–9. At intervals of every ten milliseconds,* the microprogram examines the current state of Data Set Ready, Ring Indicator, Carrier Detect, and Clear to Send for each line. These states are then compared to the previously stored state for each line via an XOR instruction, rather than via an XOR gate. Changes are

---

*A question may arise as to why Figure 12–8 uses a 50 nanosecond delay and the paragraph discussing microprogram implemented modem scanning uses a 10 millisecond delay. The reason is that it is desirable to keep the delay line in Figure 12–8 physically small for economy and space reasons. With a microprogram, however, it is desirable to sample infrequently so that the microprogram can accomplish other tasks in addition to modem control. Since modem control leads change infrequently, a sampling rate of once every 10 milliseconds is permissible.

noted, and the current state for each line is stored in place of the previously stored state for each line. The appropriate line status register is updated with the current state, and if the Link Type bit in the line control register so directs, the changes are reported. This method of reporting modem status changes can require very little hardware if the changes are reported to the program in the same FIFO that is being used to report received characters. Like the received characters, a line number must accompany the modem status change information, and a code indicating that this is a modem status change rather than a received data character also must be supplied.

Figure 12–10 gives bit assignments for a receiver buffer register that reports both received characters and modem status changes. In this register, bits 07–00 are used for either received characters or for modem lead transition reporting. Bits 11–08 are used to report the line number on which the character was received or upon which the modem lead transitions occurred. Bits 14–12 indicate Overrun Errors, Framing Errors, or Parity Errors, as were discussed in Chapter 1. A code of 111 in these bits is reserved to indicate that the bits shown in 07–00 represent modem lead change information. Finally, since this register is serving 16 lines, upon which several characters can be received and several modem leads can change in a short period of time, it is best implemented as a FIFO buffer of many entries (for example, 256). Bit 15 is used as a "Data Valid" bit so that a program responding to an interrupt indicating that there are FIFO entries can read this register, obtaining characters and modem change information on successive reads until the clear state of the Data Valid bit indicates that there are no more FIFO entries to be read. In this way, the interrupt service routine entry and exit time can be averaged over several received characters and modem transitions. Further, the program can determine which characters were received during which states of the modem leads, and hence which may be of suspect validity.

A final note on multiplexers concerns the use of per-line registers that are selected by first loading a "line select" register and then reading a single

| 15 | 14 | 13 | 12 | 11 | 10 | 09 | 08 | 07 | 06 | 05 | 04 | 03 | 02 | 01 | 00 |
|----|----|----|----|----|----|----|----|----|----|----|----|----|----|----|----|
| Data Valid | OE | FE | PE | ← Receiver Line Number → | | | | ← Received Character or Modem Lead Transitions → | | | | | | | |

Figure 12–10   Receiver Buffer Register

address that is a common "window" for all lines. The line control registers and line status registers discussed above were of this type. These registers are sometimes referred to as "secondary registers."

Why are these used rather than having all registers made directly accessible to the program? The principal reason is the widespread use of semiconductor memories in which a large number of bits are stored in an ordered array in a small number of integrated circuits. The ordered array is addressed by address selection leads that are decoded inside the integrated circuit. The most convenient and economical way to use such a memory is to tie the address selection leads to a register that the program loads with the address in the ordered array to or from which it wishes to transfer data. The addressed location is then a secondary register.

Not only are secondary registers a packaging convenience, but they also reduce the computer address space required for various peripherals. It may be desirable in some systems to use as much addressing capability as possible for addressing memory and as little as possible for addressing peripheral devices such as asynchronous multiplexers. A scheme that employs secondary registers requires only two addresses in the computer's peripheral address space (plus a line selection section of another register) for all 16 line control registers and all 16 line status registers.

The drawback to the use of secondary registers is that the programming becomes more complicated. Interrupt service routines must in general save the contents of the register that is being used to select among the secondary registers. This is because the service routine is apt to change the register in the process of servicing interrupts; the routine will have to restore the register before going back to the main program, so the main program will be "pointing" to the same register(s) to which it was pointing before it was interrupted.

# 13

# Error Detection

In all electrical information transmission systems, due consideration must be given to the effects of noise. Noise is any unwanted signal and may originate from sources as spectacular as lightning strikes or as mundane as dirty contacts on telephone switching equipment.

The most important characteristic of noise in telecommunications systems is the relatively long duration of the disturbances. A noise burst of .01 second duration is not uncommon and sounds like a simple click during a voice conversation. If the .01 second noise burst occurs during a 9600 bps data transmission, the "simple click" is the death knell for 96 data bits. Thus, when noise causes bits to be received in error, it generally causes a great number of bits to be affected. The periods of high error rate are generally separated by relatively long intervals of low-noise, low-error rate data reception. Thus, the error rate averaged over an hour is typically 1 error bit in 100,000 bits received. The "bursty" nature of errors in telecommunications systems is very important in considering error detection.

To determine whether the bits in a character have been properly received, it would be quite simple to append an additional bit to each character and to have that bit be a one or a zero according to the rule that "all transmitted characters shall have an odd number of ones." Thus, for example, the character 01001100 would be expanded to 001001100 and the character 01101100 would be expanded to 101101100. The added, underlined bit is called the "parity," bit and using it to make the number of ones odd is called "odd parity." (Plainly, one could make the number of ones even and call it "even parity.") In a parity system, the transmitter unit calculates the state of the parity bit and appends it to the character during transmission.

The receiving unit calculates the state of the parity bit and compares the calculated value to the value actually received. If they disagree, the receiver knows that a bit has been received in error.

Let's assume that the transmitter sends 101101100. Parity is odd; everything is OK. Let's assume that the second and third bits (counting from the right) are received erroneously. The received character is then 101101010. The parity is still odd, and things appear OK despite the double error. The lesson to be learned is that parity on each character can detect only errors that affect a single bit (or three, or five, etc.). Errors that affect two (or four, or six, etc.) bits will not be detected. This problem exists regardless of whether "odd parity" or "even parity" is used.

Consider transmission of the six characters in Figure 13–1. Each bit (except the left-most) in the check character has been computed such that it and the bits immediately above it in characters 1 through 5 total an odd number of ones. For example, the right-most bit in the check character is a zero because three of the right-most bits in the characters above it are ones; hence there is an odd number of ones. In all characters, including the check character, the left-most bit is a parity bit, as described above.

Let's assume that the transmitter sends 101101100 (character 1). Parity is odd; everything is OK. Let's assume that the second and third bits (counting from the right) are received erroneously. The received character is then 101101010. The parity is still odd, and things appear OK despite the double error. This time, however, there is a check character being sent. The error just described increases the number of ones in the second column from three to four (an even number) and decreases the number of ones in the third column (counting from the right) from four to three (excluding the check character).

When the check character sent by the transmitter is compared in the

| | |
|---|---|
| 101101100 | Character 1 |
| 110101111 | Character 2 |
| 001110101 | Character 3 |
| 111100010 | Character 4 |
| 100010111 | Character 5 |
| 010111100 | Check Character |

Figure 13–1   Sample Transmission

receiver to what the receiver has calculated from summing the ones in the various "columns" of the received characters, the second and third bit positions will be incorrect. The computed check character will require the second bit from the right to be a one to increase the number of ones in that column from four to five and will require the third bit to be a zero, as the receiver has received only three "1" bits in that column. Thus, the calculated check character and the transmitted check character will disagree in the second and third bit positions, which are indeed where the errors occurred.

Lest one embrace this scheme as foolproof, consider the case where characters 1 and 3 are received with errors in the second and third bit positions. Now there will be two more ones in the second column and two fewer ones in the third column. The number of ones in each column is now such that the receiver's calculated block check character and that sent by the transmitter will be the same.

Thus, in the same way that a parity check within the character was defeated by a double error in the character, parity on the columns (referred to as a Longitudinal Redundancy Check, or LRC) is defeated if a double error occurs in a column. There are numerous possibilities for double bit errors in characters to occur simultaneously with double bit errors in columns in such a fashion that neither the character parity (referred to as Vertical Redundancy Check, or VRC) nor the column parity (LRC) will indicate that the errors have occurred. This is an especially important problem since errors in communications transmission systems tend to occur in bursts, as noted above.

The detection systems most effective at detecting errors in communications systems with a minimal amount of hardware (but more than VRC/LRC systems) are the Cyclic Redundancy Checks (CRCs). CRC calculations are customarily done in a multisection shift register, which feeds into an exclusive-OR (XOR) gate whose output feeds back to other XOR gates located between the sections of the shift register. An XOR gate is one where the output is zero if the inputs are both zero or are both one. If the inputs differ, the output of the XOR gate is a one. Figure 13–2 shows a typical arrangement.

The placement and quantity of the XOR gates vary for CRC-12, CRC-16, and CRC-CCITT, which are the most common CRCs. The block check

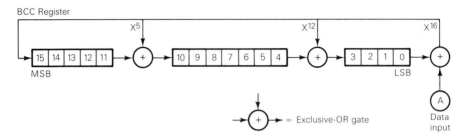

Figure 13–2   Block Check Register Implemented with Shift Registers and Exclusive-OR Gates

register example shown in Figure 13–2 is the implementation of CRC-CCITT. Note that the terms MSB and LSB used in the figure refer to the most significant and least significant bits of the *register*; the LSB end of the register is sent first but corresponds to the $X^{15}$ term of the CRC.

When the logic shown in Figure 13–2 is used in a transmitter circuit, it is initialized to all zeros. As each bit is presented to the communications line, it is also applied to the point marked "A" in Figure 13–2, and a shifting pulse is applied to the shift register. Figure 13–3 shows the contents of the shift register, assuming that the first bit transmitted was a one. Note what a dramatic effect this single bit has and how that effect is spread throughout the register.

As the "1" bits shown in Figure 13–3 get shifted on through the segments of the shift register during the transmission of subsequent bits, they will eventually reach some of the XOR gates between the segments of the shift register. Here they will affect the state of the "feedback bits" coming from the XOR gate on the far right-hand side of the diagram. The general effect to be recognized is that the effect of any bit is reflected in the various bits of the shift register for a considerable time after that bit is transmitted.

In a CRC-equipped system, a logical arrangement identical to that used in the transmitter (Figure 13–3) is used in the receiver. Again the register is initialized to zero, and data *from* the communications line is applied to point A, while the shift register contents are shifted once for each bit received. At the conclusion of the message, the transmitting station sends the contents of the transmitter CRC shift register to the receiving station. The receiving station applies the incoming bit stream to point A of the CRC logic, just as it did with the preceding data bits. The properties of XOR gates shown in Figure 13–4 are reviewed below.

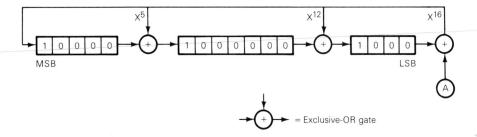

Figure 13–3   Propagation of a "1" Bit into Block Check Register

As the first bit of the received CRC character is applied to point A of the receiver CRC logic, the XOR gate obeys Rule 1 in Figure 13–4 and produces a zero if the first bit of the calculated CRC matches the first bit of the CRC being received. All the other XOR gates in the Figure 13–3 style of CRC logic will obey Rule 2 in Figure 13–4 and will become essentially "transparent"; a zero will be shifted into the left end of the shift register. As long as the calculated CRC contained in the receiver CRC shift register continues to match the CRC being received from the transmitting station, the output of the right-most XOR gate will continue to be zero and the other XOR gates will continue to be "transparent." When all the CRC bits have been shifted, the CRC shift register bits will all be zeros. This will be true regardless of the placement of the XOR gates and hence true for all types of CRC. An exception is that Synchronous Data Link Control (SDLC) and High (level) Data Link Control (HDLC) start with a preset value in the shift register and end with a special nonzero result.

The most important property of CRCs is that, due to the feedback arrangements, the exact state of the shift register is dependent on a great deal of past history. Thus, it is highly unlikely that a burst of errors could

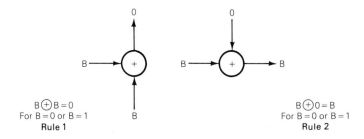

Figure 13–4   Logical Rules for Exclusive-OR Gates

produce a CRC calculation that was the same as that for the data as originally transmitted before the errors occurred.

CRC requires no bit per character as parity does, but there are two check characters at the end of each block of characters, since the CRC shift register is two character lengths long. So that the reader may correlate this simplified presentation with various trade journal articles that discuss CRC polynomials in mathematical terms, a mathematical presentation follows.

A cyclic code message consists of a specific number of data bits and a Block Check Calculation (BCC). Let $n$ equal the total number of bits in the message and $k$ equal the number of data bits; then $n - k$ equals the number of bits in the BCC.

The code message is derived from two polynomials that are algebraic representations of two binary words, the generator polynomial P($X$) and the message polynomial G($X$). The generator polynomial is the type of code used (CRC-12, CRC-16, and CRC-CCITT); the message polynomial is the string of serial data bits. The polynomials are usually represented algebraically by a string of terms in powers of $X$ such as $X^n \ldots + X^3 + X^2 + X + X^0$ (or 1). In binary form, a one is placed in each position that contains a term; absence of a term is indicated by a zero. The convention followed in the following presentation is to place the $X^0$ bit at the right. For example, if a polynomial is given as $X^4 + X + 1$, its binary representation is 10011 (third and second degree terms are not present).

Given a message polynomial G($X$) and a generator polynomial P($X$), the objective is to construct a code message polynomial F($X$) that is evenly divisible by P($X$). It is accomplished as follows:

1. Multiply the message G($X$) by $X^{n-k}$ where $n - k$ is the number of bits in the BCC.
2. Divide the resulting product $X^{n-k} [G(X)]$ by the generator polynomial P($X$).
3. Disregard the quotient and add the remainder C($X$) to the product to yield the code message polynomial F($X$), which is represented as $X^{n-k} [G(X)] + C(X)$.

The division is performed in binary without carries or borrows. In this case, the remainder C($X$) is always one bit less than the divisor. The remainder C($X$) is the BCC, and the divisor is generator polynomial P($X$); therefore, the bit length of the BCC is always one less than the number of bits in the generator polynomial P($X$).

A simple example is explained below.

1. Given:
   Message polynomial $G(X) = 110011$ $(X^5 + X^4 + X + X^0)$.
   Generator polynomial $P(X) = 11001$ $(X^4 + X^3 + 1)$.
   $G(X)$ contains 6 data bits.
   $P(X)$ contains 5 bits and will yield a BCC with 4 bits; therefore, $n - k = 4$.

2. Multiplying the message $G(X)$ by $X^{n-k}$ gives:
   $X^{n-k}[G(X)] = X^4 (X^5 + X^4 + X + X^0) = X^9 + X^8 + X^5 + X^4$
   The binary equivalent of this product contains 10 bits and is 1100110000.

3. This product is divided by $P(X)$.

$$
\begin{array}{r}
100001 \leftarrow \text{quotient} \\
P(X) \rightarrow \quad 1001 \overline{\smash{\big)}\ 1100110000} \leftarrow X^{n-k}[G(X)] \\
\underline{11001} \\
10000 \\
\underline{11001} \\
1001 \leftarrow \text{remainder} = C(X) = \text{BCC}
\end{array}
$$

4. The remainder $C(X)$ is added to $X^{n-k}[G(X)]$ to give $F(X) = 1100111001$.

The code message polynomial $F(X)$ is transmitted. The receiving station divides it by the same generator polynomial, $G(X)$. If there is no error, the division will produce no remainder, and it is assumed that the message is correct. A remainder indicates an error. The division is shown below.

$$
\begin{array}{r}
100001 \\
P(X) \rightarrow \quad 11001 \overline{\smash{\big)}\ 1100111001} \leftarrow F(X) \\
\underline{11001} \\
11001 \\
\underline{11001} \\
00000 \leftarrow \text{no remainder}
\end{array}
$$

A more practical example of generating a BCC by long division is shown in Figure 13–5. Generation of a BCC for the same message by use of a shift register is shown in Figure 13–8, page 135.

In typical data communication hardware, the BCC is computed and accumulated in a shift register. The configuration of the register is based on the CRC code to be implemented. The number of stages in the register is equal to the degree of the generating polynomial; the number of XOR elements is also a function of the polynomial. In the subsequent examples,

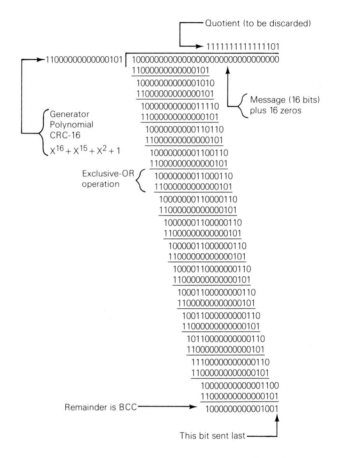

Figure 13–5   BCC Computation Using Long Division
Method with CRC-16 as Generator

a unique register configuration is shown for each CRC code (CRC-12, CRC-16, and CRC-CCITT).

1. *CRC-12*

CRC-12 is applied to synchronous systems that use 6-bit characters. The BCC accumulation is 12 bits. The generator polynomial is $X^{12} + X^{11} + X^3 + X^2 + X + 1$ with prime factors of $(X + 1)$ and $(X^{11} + X^2 + 1)$. It provides error detection of bursts up to 12 bits in length.

Figure 13–6 shows a block diagram configuration of a BCC register for use with CRC-12. A step-by-step shift pattern is shown as the data is serially applied to the register. Initially, the register contains all zeros. A 12-bit data word (a one followed by eleven zeros) is the input to the register. Prior to the first shift, the first data bit or least significant bit (LSB), which is a one, is XORed with the zero from the LSB of the register. The result on the serial quotient line is a one, which is sent via the feedback paths to the following places: bit 11 and the XORs between bits 11 and 10, bits 10 and 9, bits 9 and 8, and bits 1 and 0. When the feedback settles down, the first shift takes place and produces the register states in the line labeled 1 under the Shift Number column. The shift also presents the next data bit to the input. The process repeats until all 12 data bits are encoded. The BCC is the contents of the register after shift number 12. The most important fact to remember is that the XOR of the LSB of the BCC register and the input data bit set up the feedback path prior to the shifting operation. The result of this operation is shown in the area labeled "Feedback before shift." When the shift takes place, the results of the XOR operations are shifted into the register.

The subsequent examples, which show the BCC accumulation for CRC-CCITT and CRC-16, can be analyzed the same way; register length, data word length, and feedback paths are different, but the process is the same.

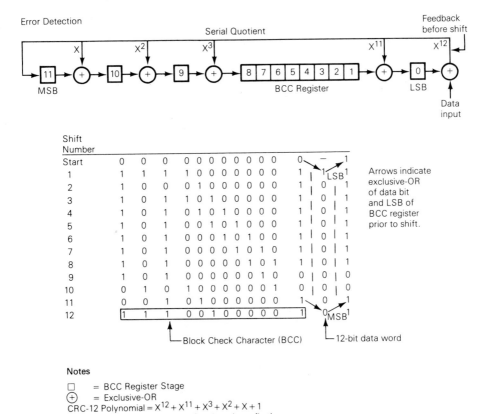

Figure 13–6  BCC Accumulation Using CRC-12, Transmit Sequence

2. *CRC-CCITT*

CRC-CCITT is the standard method used to compute a BCC for European systems. When operating with eight-bit characters, the BCC accumulation is 16 bits. The generator polynomial is $X^{16} + X^{12} + X^5 + 1$. It provides error detection of bursts up to 16 bits long. In addition, more than 99 percent of error bursts greater than 12 bits can be detected.

Figure 13–7 shows a BCC accumulation using a 16-bit data word (a one followed by fifteen zeros).

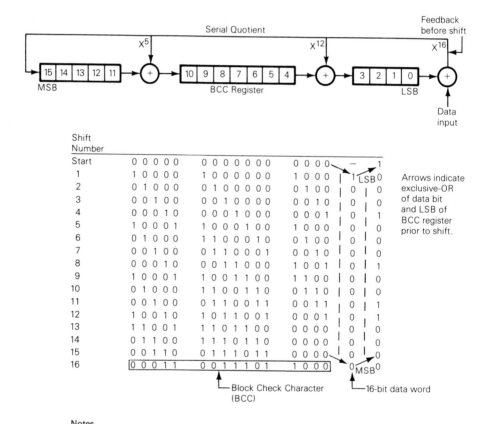

Figure 13–7   BCC Accumulation Using CRC-CCITT, Transmit Sequence

3. *CRC-16*

CRC-16 is applied to synchronous systems that use eight-bit characters. The BCC accumulation is 16 bits. The generator polynomial is $X^{16} + X^{15} + X^2 + 1$. It provides error detection of bursts up to 16 bits in length. In addition, more than 99 percent of error bursts greater than 16 bits can be detected.

Figure 13–8 shows a BCC accumulation using a 16-bit data word (a one followed by fifteen zeros).

The three CRC examples (Figures 13–6, 13–7, and 13–8) show BCC accumulations that are to be used in a transmission sequence. Figure 13–9 shows the

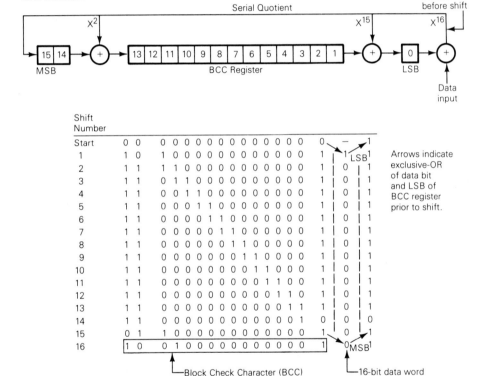

Figure 13–8   BCC Accumulation Using CRC-16, Transmit Sequence

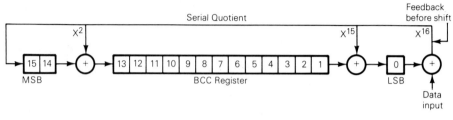

| Shift Number | 15 14 | 13 12 11 10 9 8 7 6 5 4 3 2 1 | 0 | |
|---|---|---|---|---|
| Start | 0 0 | 0 0 0 0 0 0 0 0 0 0 0 0 0 | 0 | — 1 |
| 1 | 1 0 | 1 0 0 0 0 0 0 0 0 0 0 0 0 | 1 | 1 LSB 1 |
| 2 | 1 1 | 1 1 0 0 0 0 0 0 0 0 0 0 0 | 1 | 0 \| 1 |
| 3 | 1 1 | 0 1 1 0 0 0 0 0 0 0 0 0 0 | 1 | 0 \| 1 |
| 4 | 1 1 | 0 0 1 1 0 0 0 0 0 0 0 0 0 | 1 | 0 \| 1 |
| • | • • | • | • | • \| • |
| • | • • | • Same as CRC-16 transmit | • | • \| • |
| • | • • | • sequence | • | • Data • |
| • | • • | • | • | • \| • |
| 13 | 1 1 | 0 0 0 0 0 0 0 0 0 0 0 1 1 | 1 | 0 \| 1 |
| 14 | 1 1 | 0 0 0 0 0 0 0 0 0 0 0 0 1 | 0 | 0 \| 0 |
| 15 | 0 1 | 1 0 0 0 0 0 0 0 0 0 0 0 0 | 1 | 0 \| 1 |
| 16 | 1 0 | 0 1 0 0 0 0 0 0 0 0 0 0 0 | 1 | 0 MSB 1 |
| 17 | 0 1 | 0 0 1 0 0 0 0 0 0 0 0 0 0 | 0 | 1 LSB 0 |
| 18 | 0 0 | 1 0 0 1 0 0 0 0 0 0 0 0 0 | 0 | 0 \| 0 |
| 19 | 0 0 | 0 1 0 0 1 0 0 0 0 0 0 0 0 | 0 | 0 \| 0 |
| 20 | 0 0 | 0 0 1 0 0 1 0 0 0 0 0 0 0 | 0 | 0 \| 0 |
| 21 | 0 0 | 0 0 0 1 0 0 1 0 0 0 0 0 0 | 0 | 0 \| 0 |
| 22 | 0 0 | 0 0 0 0 1 0 0 1 0 0 0 0 0 | 0 | 0 \| 0 |
| 23 | 0 0 | 0 0 0 0 0 1 0 0 1 0 0 0 0 | 0 | 0 \| 0 |
| 24 | 0 0 | 0 0 0 0 0 0 1 0 0 1 0 0 0 | 0 | 0 BCC 0 |
| 25 | 0 0 | 0 0 0 0 0 0 0 1 0 0 1 0 0 | 0 | 0 \| 0 |
| 26 | 0 0 | 0 0 0 0 0 0 0 0 1 0 0 1 0 | 0 | 0 \| 0 |
| 27 | 0 0 | 0 0 0 0 0 0 0 0 0 1 0 0 1 | 0 | 0 \| 0 |
| 28 | 0 0 | 0 0 0 0 0 0 0 0 0 0 1 0 0 | 1 | 0 \| 0 |
| 29 | 0 0 | 0 0 0 0 0 0 0 0 0 0 0 1 0 | 0 | 1 \| 0 |
| 30 | 0 0 | 0 0 0 0 0 0 0 0 0 0 0 0 1 | 0 | 0 \| 0 |
| 31 | 0 0 | 0 0 0 0 0 0 0 0 0 0 0 0 0 | 1 | 0 0 |
| 32 | 0 0 | 0 0 0 0 0 0 0 0 0 0 0 0 0 | 0 | 1 MSB 0 |

Arrows indicate exclusive-OR of data bit and LSB of BCC register prior to shift.

If the BCC register is all 0s the received message is assumed to be correct.

16-bit data word and BCC register

**Notes**

☐  = BCC Register Stage
⊕  = Exclusive-OR
CRC-16 Polynomial $= X^{16} + X^{15} + X^2 + 1$
LSB  = Least Significant Bit of register (sent first)
MSB  = Most Significant Bit of register (sent last)

Figure 13–9   BCC Accumulation Using CRC-16, Receive Sequence

BCC accumulation performed on a message that has been received along with a BCC. The message and the computed BCC have been taken from Figure 13–8— i.e., a BCC accumulation using CRC-16. In Figure 13–9, the accumulation process is the same as that shown in Figure 13–8 through shift number 16. Starting with shift number 17, the BCC is sent to the data input, LSB first. A correct transmitted BCC results in all zeros in the BCC register at the end of the computation. In effect, this is a comparison of the transmitted BCC with the one computed at the receiving station. A correct comparison yields a zero remainder, or all zeros in the BCC register.

In addition to the shift register implementations of the CRCs that are shown in the preceding discussion, it is relatively simple to implement CRC calculation on a byte-wise basis. The first step in understanding this approach is to consider, for example, the BCC accumulation using CRC-16 shown in Figure 13–9. Rather than assigning specific binary values to the initial state of the BCC register and to the arriving byte as was done in the figure, let's assign variables. Let the bit positions of the BCC register be labeled $R_{15}$ (most significant bit, MSB) through $R_0$ (least significant bit, LSB), and let $C_{15}$ through $C_0$ be the initial values of the bits in those positions before any shifts due to the input byte. Let $M_0$ through $M_7$ be the bits of the arriving input byte, with $M_0$ being the first bit received.

Before the first shift, the contents of the BCC register will be as shown in Figure 13–10. After the first shift, the contents of the BCC register will be as shown in Figure 13–11. After some amount of tedious computation, the contents of the BCC register after eight shifts will be as shown in Figure 13–12.

| $R_{15}$ | $R_{14}$ | $R_{13}$ | $R_{12}$ | $R_{11}$ | $R_{10}$ | $R_9$ | $R_8$ | $R_7$ | $R_6$ | $R_5$ | $R_4$ | $R_3$ | $R_2$ | $R_1$ | $R_0$ |
|---|---|---|---|---|---|---|---|---|---|---|---|---|---|---|---|
| $C_{15}$ | $C_{14}$ | $C_{13}$ | $C_{12}$ | $C_{11}$ | $C_{10}$ | $C_9$ | $C_8$ | $C_7$ | $C_6$ | $C_5$ | $C_4$ | $C_3$ | $C_2$ | $C_1$ | $C_0$ |

Figure 13–10   Initial Contents of BCC Register

| $R_{15}$ | $R_{14}$ | $R_{13}$ | $R_{12}$ | $R_{11}$ | $R_{10}$ | $R_9$ | $R_8$ | $R_7$ | $R_6$ | $R_5$ | $R_4$ | $R_3$ | $R_2$ | $R_1$ | $R_0$ |
|---|---|---|---|---|---|---|---|---|---|---|---|---|---|---|---|
| $C_0$ $\oplus$ $M_0$ | $C_{15}$ | $C_{14}$ $\oplus$ $C_0$ $\oplus$ $M_0$ | $C_{13}$ | $C_{12}$ | $C_{11}$ | $C_{10}$ | $C_9$ | $C_8$ | $C_7$ | $C_6$ | $C_5$ | $C_4$ | $C_3$ | $C_2$ | $C_1$ $\oplus$ $C_0$ $\oplus$ $M_0$ |

($\oplus$ = Exclusive-OR)

Figure 13–11   Contents of BCC Register after First Shift

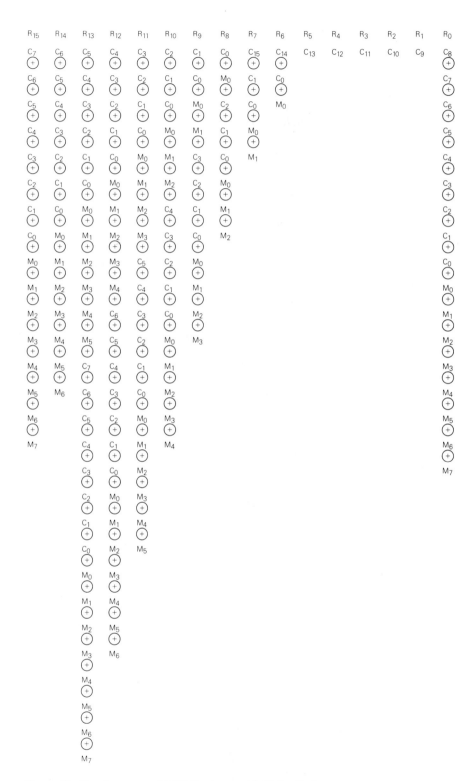

Figure 13–12   Contents of BCC Register with Eight Shifts

To simplify Figure 13–12, the following four properties of the XOR function can be employed:

$$A \oplus A = 0$$
$$A \oplus 0 = A$$
$$A \oplus B = B \oplus A$$
$$A \oplus B \oplus C = A \oplus C \oplus B$$

Further, since the combination $C_0 \oplus M_0$ appears so often, let us replace $C_0 \oplus M_0$ with $X_0$. In similar fashion, we will replace $C_1 \oplus M_1$, with $X_1$, and so on, up through $C_7 \oplus M_7$, which is replaced with $X_7$. The $Xi$ terms merely represent the XOR of the $i$th term of the arriving character with what was in the $i$th position of the BCC register before the character arrived. The result of these simplifications is shown in Figure 13–13.

A very fast method of computing CRC would be to construct a special piece of hardware using a parallel arrangement of XOR gates and two registers. The CRC accumulated to date is stored in Register 1. The character just received is stored in Register 2. A network of XOR gates arranged according to Figure 13–13 combines the contents of Registers 1 and 2, and the result is recorded back into Register 1. Other BCC calculations, includ-

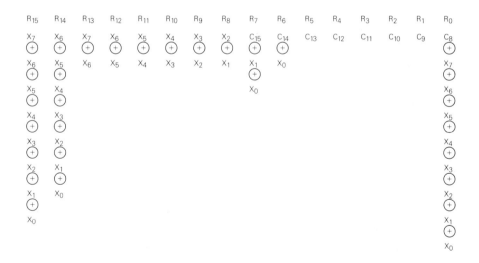

Figure 13–13   Contents of BCC Register after Eight Shifts (Simplified)

ing CRC-CCITT and LRC, could be performed with modest additions to the same hardware (the $X_7 \ldots X_0$ terms are LRC, for example).

Perez [1983] contains a more complete explanation of how to get to Figure 13–13 and describes how to use software algorithms to achieve the results of Figure 13–13. Perez first redraws the figure, as shown in Figure 13–14. He goes on to note that the top line of the figure consists solely of the high byte of the accumulated CRC, shifted eight bits to the right. The low byte of the accumulated CRC does not appear directly in the figure but rather is XORed with the input byte to create the $X_7 \ldots X_0$ terms from which the remainder of Figure 13–14 can be calculated. Since there are only eight bits $X_7 \ldots X_0$, there are only 256 possible values for the bottom portion of Figure 13–4. As examples, if the $X$ terms are all zeros, Figure 13–14 reduces to:

| $R_{15}$ | $R_{14}$ | $R_{13}$ | $R_{12}$ | $R_{11}$ | $R_{10}$ | $R_9$ | $R_8$ | $R_7$ | $R_6$ | $R_5$ | $R_4$ | $R_3$ | $R_2$ | $R_1$ | $R_0$ |
|---|---|---|---|---|---|---|---|---|---|---|---|---|---|---|---|
| 0 | 0 | 0 | 0 | 0 | 0 | 0 | 0 | $C_{15}$ | $C_{14}$ | $C_{13}$ | $C_{12}$ | $C_{11}$ | $C_{10}$ | $C_9$ | $C_0$ |
| $\oplus$ | $\oplus$ | $\oplus$ | $\oplus$ | $\oplus$ | $\oplus$ | $\oplus$ | $\oplus$ | $\oplus$ | $\oplus$ | $\oplus$ | $\oplus$ | $\oplus$ | $\oplus$ | $\oplus$ | $\oplus$ |
| 0 | 0 | 0 | 0 | 0 | 0 | 0 | 0 | 0 | 0 | 0 | 0 | 0 | 0 | 0 | 0 |

If the $X$ terms are all ones, Figure 13–14 reduces to:

| $R_{15}$ | $R_{14}$ | $R_{13}$ | $R_{12}$ | $R_{11}$ | $R_{10}$ | $R_9$ | $R_8$ | $R_7$ | $R_6$ | $R_5$ | $R_4$ | $R_3$ | $R_2$ | $R_1$ | $R_0$ |
|---|---|---|---|---|---|---|---|---|---|---|---|---|---|---|---|
| 0 | 0 | 0 | 0 | 0 | 0 | 0 | 0 | $C_{15}$ | $C_{14}$ | $C_{13}$ | $C_{12}$ | $C_{11}$ | $C_{10}$ | $C_9$ | $C_0$ |
| $\oplus$ | $\oplus$ | $\oplus$ | $\oplus$ | $\oplus$ | $\oplus$ | $\oplus$ | $\oplus$ | $\oplus$ | $\oplus$ | $\oplus$ | $\oplus$ | $\oplus$ | $\oplus$ | $\oplus$ | $\oplus$ |
| 0 | 1 | 0 | 0 | 0 | 0 | 0 | 0 | 0 | 1 | 0 | 0 | 0 | 0 | 0 | 0 |

Thus, the algorithm becomes:

1. Exclusive-OR the input byte with the low byte of the accumulated CRC to get the $X$ terms.

2. Shift the accumulated CRC eight bits right.

3. Exclusive-OR the (shifted) accumulated CRC with the contents of a 256-entry, 16-bit-wide table, using the value of $X_7 \ldots X_0$ as an index.

4. Repeat the above steps for each input byte.

The performance of this table-driven algorithm operating on bytes is roughly five times that of bit-wise calculation, although it takes substantially more memory. In Perez, a compromise algorithm that calculates the values of Figure 13–4 without resorting to tables is outlined. That algorithm offers more than three times the performance with the same memory requirements as the bit-wise approach.

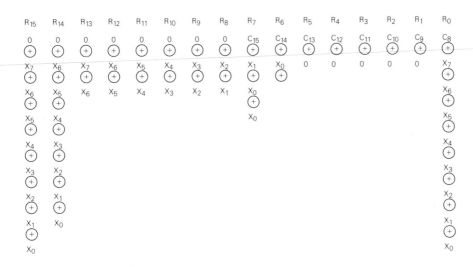

Figure 13–14   Contents of BCC Register after Eight Shifts (Redrawn)

## References

1. Boudreau, P., and R. Steen. "Cyclic Redundancy Checking by Program." *AFIPS Proceedings*, vol. 39 (1971).
2. Digital Equipment Corporation. *KG11 Manual*.
3. Higginson, P., and P. Kirstein. "On the Computation of Cyclic Redundancy Checks by Program." *The Computer Journal* (British), vol. 16, no. 1 (February 1973).
4. Lee, R. "Cyclic Code Redundancy." *Digital Design*, July 1981, pp. 77–85.
5. Martin, J. *Teleprocessing Network Organization*. Englewood Cliffs, NJ: Prentice-Hall, 1970.
6. Marton, A., and T. Frambs. "A Cyclic Redundancy Checking (CRC) Algorithm." *Honeywell Computer Journal*, vol. 5, no. 3 (1971).
7. Pandeya, A.K., and T.J. Cass. "Parallel CRC Lets Many Lines Use One Circuit." *Computer Design*, September 1975.
8. Perez, A. "Byte-wise CRC Calculations." *IEEE MICRO*, June 1983.
9. Peterson, W., and D. Brown. "Cyclic Codes for Error Detection." *Proceedings of the IRE*, January 1961.
10. Peterson, W. *Error Correcting Codes*. Cambridge, MA: MIT Press, 1961.
11. Wecker, S. "A Table-Lookup Algorithm for Software Computation of Cyclic Redundancy Check (CRC)." Digital Equipment Corporation memorandum (130-959-002-00), January 1974.

# 14

## Synchronous Communications

In Chapter 1, the format for a typical character being transmitted in an asynchronous transmission system was discussed. This format is repeated in Figure 14–1. Although modern asynchronous receivers do not require a STOP interval for mechanism coasting purposes, they do require a STOP interval to guarantee that each character will begin with a 1-to-0 transition, even if the preceding character was entirely zeros. The requirement for a 1-to-0 transition to indicate the beginning of each character causes an eight-bit data character to require ten bit times to transmit. Twenty percent of the line time is being used strictly for timing purposes.

Synchronous communications require either a separate clock lead from the transmission point to the reception point, in addition to the data lead, or a modem that includes the clock information in the modulation process that encodes the data. In typical synchronous modems, phase shift keying is used. The clock is recovered from the sidebands of the received signal and is brought out of the modem on a separate lead that indicates to the data communication hardware (typically a computer interface) the appropriate instant to sample the data on the "Received Data" lead. The inclusion of the clock with or "beside" the data stream keeps the transmitter and receiver in synchronism—hence the term "synchronous communications."

Since START and STOP bits are not required in synchronous communications, all bits are used to transmit data; this eliminates the 20 percent waste characteristic of asynchronous communications. The character "framing" information provided by the START and STOP bits is absent, however, so another method of determining which groups of bits constitute a character must be provided.

142

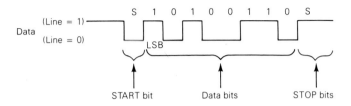

Figure 14–1   Asynchronous Data Character Format

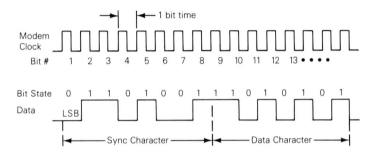

Figure 14–2   Synchronous Data Character Format

Figure 14–2 shows the character format for synchronous transmission. Bits 1–8 might be one character and bits 9–13 part of another character, or bit 1 may be part of one character, bits 2–9 part of a second character, and bits 10–13 part of a third character, etc. The delimiting or framing of each actual character is accomplished by defining a synchronization character, commonly called "sync." The sync character is usually chosen so that its bit arrangement is significantly different from that of any of the regular characters being transmitted and it has an irregular pattern (i.e., not 01010101). Thus, when a sync character is preceded and followed by regular characters, there is no likely successive pattern of bits that equals the bit pattern of the sync character except those eight bits that are actually the sync character. The sync character used in ASCII is 10010110 (226 octal).

Typical synchronous receiver units are placed in a "sync search" mode by either hardware or software whenever a transmission begins or whenever a data dropout has occurred and the hardware or software determines that resynchronization is necessary. In the sync search procedure, the hardware shifts a bit into the receiver shift register, compares the contents of the receiver shift register with the sync character (stored in another register), and, if no match occurs, repeats the process. If a match occurs, the receiver begins shifting in bits and raising a "character available" flag every eight bits. For even greater certainty that synchronization is occurring properly, most communications systems require that the receiver identify two successive sync characters before raising "character available" flags every eight bits.

It is fairly likely that the first sync character transmitted will be mangled in some fashion by the time it arrives on the Received Data lead of the receiving modem. Transients on the telephone line, start-up problems in the receiving modem, and a variety of other effects will contribute to the likelihood of damage to the first sync character. Therefore, it is absolutely necessary in systems where the receiver reaches synchronization on receipt of one sync that at least two be sent, and in systems where the receiver "syncs up" on two syncs that at least three be sent.

Systems that require the receiver to recognize two successive sync characters to achieve synchronization are less prone to go into synchronization prematurely (i.e., less likely to be fooled by a bit pattern that looks like sync but is a combination of other characters). The requirement that two sync characters be recognized poses some interesting problems.

Assume that the string of three sync characters shown in Figure 14–3 is received. Slashes (/) have been inserted for the reader's convenience, and the first two bits received have been replaced with Xs to indicate that they were received in error. This example is exactly the case described above: The first character has been damaged, but the transmitter has sent three syncs, and thus there are still two left for the receiver to recognize.

Now assume reception of the characters in Figure 14–4. In this example, the second character contains an erroneous bit. There are no two syncs in a row, thus the receiver cannot synchronize. This particular problem could be solved by sending four syncs, as illustrated in Figure 14–5.

Now, despite the erroneous bit in the second character, there are two good sync characters following, and the receiver can achieve synchronization. In this case, the receiver's ability to synchronize on the remaining

X X 1 0 1 0 0 0/0 1 1 0 1 0 0 0/0 1 1 0 1 0 0 0          0 1 1 0 1 0 0 0/0 1 X 0 1 0 0 0/0 1 1 0 1 0 0 0

Figure 14–3   Receipt of Three Sync
Characters with Error in First Character

Figure 14–4   Receipt of Three Sync
Characters with Error in Second
Character

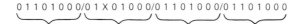

Figure 14–5   Receipt of Four Sync Characters with
Error in Second Character

two syncs will depend on how the receiver logic recovers from the erroneous
second character. If the receiver, upon receiving each bit, does a comparison
against a 16-bit register that contains two sync characters, the receiver will
be able to resynchronize using the final two sync characters in this example.
If the receiver, upon receiving each bit, does a comparison against an eight-
bit register that contains a sync character, then sets a flag that it has "seen
a sync," the receiver must shift in eight more bits and choose between the
following alternatives:

• If this set of eight bits is also a sync, set the "synchronization achieved" flag.

• If this set of eight bits is not a sync, clear the "seen a sync" flag and start over
  again looking at one bit at a time.

• If this decision process takes too long, the third sync character will be on its way
  into the receiver, and a decision to resume bit-at-a-time sampling will occur too
  late for the first bit of the third sync character to be included in this sampling
  process.

Thus, the receiver will not see two more complete sync characters and will
not resynchronize. To cover this situation and to cover the possibility of
two bits (last bit of second sync and first bit of third sync) being erroneous,
conservative programming practice calls for the transmission of five sync
characters. Of course, there is no rule that says one cannot transmit 20
sync characters at the beginning of each message, but to do so for a 100-
character message would result in a 20 percent waste of line time, which
would be just as inefficient as asynchronous transmission.

In addition to its different method for delineating characters, synchronous
transmission also differs from asynchronous transmission in the type of
error correction, line speeds, and modems commonly used.

Because bits arrive at a steady, predictable rate in synchronous systems,
modems that use phase modulation and other techniques dependent on
constant data flow can be utilized. These modems are substantially more
expensive than the simple frequency shift keying modems discussed previously, but the line speeds achieved are also substantially higher. Whereas
1200 or 1800 bps is the top operating speed for frequency shift keyed
asynchronous modems operating on voice grade telephone lines, bps rates

of 4800, 9600, or more are achieved with phase modulated and phase/amplitude modulated synchronous modems. A classical synchronous modem, the Bell System 201B, will be treated in block diagram form below.

First, however, a brief review of modulation processes is in order. Most people are familiar with the two types of modulation used for commercial radio broadcasts: amplitude modulation (AM) and frequency modulation (FM). In both these modulation processes, a signal of characteristics appropriate for propagation over long distances is used, and that signal is altered at the transmitting station to convey information to someone receiving the signal. The signal used is called the "carrier," and the process of altering it is called "modulation." Getting the information back at the receiving station involves a process called "demodulation." By way of review, it is a combination of the words *mod*ulation and *dem*odulation that gives us the word "modem."

If one were to measure the output of a radio station during a moment when the announcer was not saying anything and observe that output with a device that could plot voltage as a function of time (an oscilloscope), one would see only the carrier, as shown in Figure 14–6. If the announcer then began to speak, the appearance of the signal would depend on whether the radio station was an AM station or an FM station. If it were an AM station, the oscilloscope would show a signal similar to that in Figure 14–7. If it were an FM station, Figure 14–8 would apply.

In the case of the AM station, the information has been applied to the carrier by altering its amplitude. In the FM case, the information has been applied to the carrier by altering its frequency. The asynchronous modems discussed in Chapter 4 performed frequency shift keying to apply infor-

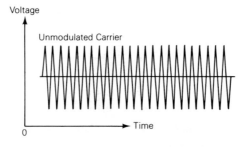

Figure 14–6   Unmodulated Carrier

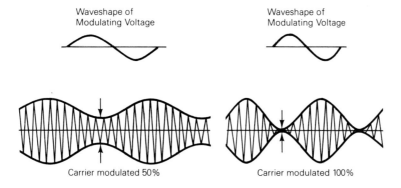

Figure 14–7   Amplitude Modulation

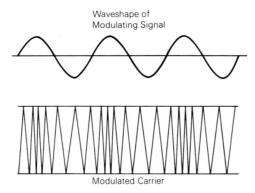

Figure 14–8   Frequency Modulation

mation to the carrier and were thus a simplified case of FM. There are, however, methods other than AM and FM that can be used to alter the carrier to convey information. Phase modulation is the most widely used of these methods.

The concept of "phase" may best be understood by comparison to the moon, an object widely known to have phases. Figure 14–9 shows one and a quarter cycles of the moon. The waveform shown under the faces of the moon could just as well represent the carrier signal discussed in previous paragraphs. Figure 14–10 illustrates the concept of phase modulation.

The waveform shown in Figures 14–9 and 14–10 is one that is commonly generated by electronic equipment. It is called a sine wave because its magnitude varies in exactly the same fashion as the geometric function sine. Thus, it is possible to label the horizontal axis of Figure 14–9 with

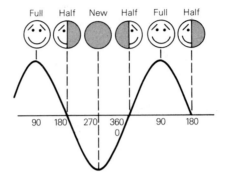

Figure 14–9   Phases of Moon

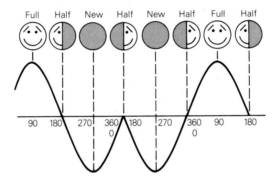

Figure 14–10   Phase Modulation Example

the 90-, 180-, 270-, 360/0-, 90-, and 180-degree markings to indicate that a sine waveform is being used. Furthermore, it is possible to represent the same information shown in Figure 14–9 in a phase diagram, such as that shown in Figure 14–11. In addition to the moon phases (or signal phases) shown, any intermediate phase can be represented by a pointer, such as the one drawn for a 45-degree phase angle. Using the phase angle representation system, it is possible to represent the phase change shown in Figure 14–10 as a phase angle change of 180 degrees (see Figure 14–12).

Phase angle changes are what convey information in phase modulation. Assume a signaling arrangement where phase angle changes of 45°, 135°, 225°, and 315° are used to represent the data being transmitted. Since four different phase angle changes are possible, bit combinations of 11, 10, 00, and 01 can be transmitted. In the 201B modem, these two-bit combinations are referred to as "dibits" and are transmitted at a rate of 1200 dibits per second, or 2400 bps. Thus, every 1/1200 of a second, the carrier being produced by a 201B is changed in phase 45°, 135°, 225°, or 315°, depending on whether a 11, 10, 00, or 01 dibit is to be transmitted. The phase changes listed are measured relative to the phase at the beginning of the previous dibit, rather than from the end of one dibit to the beginning of the next. This distinction becomes important in those cases where there is not an integral number of carrier cycles per dibit. Note that the "baud rate" is 1200 baud, despite the 2400 bps data transmission rate.

Data is recovered in the 201B by using "product modulators," despite their being used in the demodulator. A product modulator multiplies two input signals. The mathematics is as follows, assuming an input signal of Cos $\omega t$ and another signal of Cos($\omega t + \Theta$). (Cosines are used in this example, but a similar presentation can be done with sines.)

$$\text{Cos } x \text{ Cos } y = 1/2 \ [\text{Cos}(x+y) + \text{Cos } (x-y)]$$

$$\text{Cos } (\omega t + \Theta) \text{ Cos } \omega t = 1/2 \text{ Cos } (2\omega t + \Theta) + 1/2 \text{ Cos } \Theta$$

This result is expressed schematically in Figure 14–13. The signal shown as Cos $\omega t$ is the carrier at the end of the previous dibit and the signal shown as Cos($\omega t + \Theta$) is the carrier at the end of the present dibit.

Thus, phase angle $\Theta$ is the 45°, 135°, 225°, or 315° change of phase that represents receipt of dibit 11, 10, 00, or 01. The first term in the output of the product modulator is proportional to $2\omega t$ and is called a "double frequency term." It is not useful in this application and may be removed by

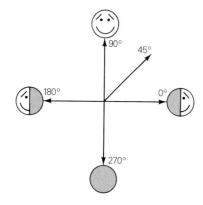

Figure 14–11   Phase Angle Representation of Phase of Moon

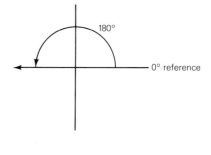

Figure 14–12   Phase Angle Representation of the Phase Change Shown in Figure 14–10

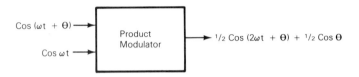

Figure 14–13   Product Modulator

passing the signal through a filter that allows only low frequencies to get through. This type of filter is called a low-pass filter and is abbreviated LPF in subsequent diagrams. The second term does not contain a time ($t$) term at all and is called the "d.c. term." This term produces a positive output voltage when $\Theta$ is either 45 or 315 degrees. To determine which of the two is the value of $\Theta$, a second product modulator is used whose inputs are Cos $\omega t$ and Cos($\omega t + \Theta - 90$ degrees). If the output of this second product modulator is also positive, the angle $\Theta$ must have been 45 degrees, as 45 degrees minus 90 degrees is 315 degrees, which is also positive. If the output of the second modulator is negative, $\Theta$ must have been 315 degrees. The same circuitry also can detect whether $\Theta$ has a value of 135 or 225 degrees, since both those values will produce a negative d.c. term, while only the 225 degree value for $\Theta$ will remain negative despite a −90-degree shift.

Modern modems make extensive use of digital signal processors to perform many of the functions described above. Another difference between modern modems and the (now obsolete) Bell 201B is that modern modems scramble the data before transmission (and descramble it at the receiving modem) so that repeated bit patterns such as 010101 are far less likely to occur than in normal data. This is done because some repeated bit patterns produce signal spectra on the line that make clock recovery very difficult.

By extension of the general principles described above, it is possible to transmit bits three at a time (tribits), using eight different phase angles. Together with an increase in the line signaling rate from 1200 baud to 1600 baud, this results in a bit rate of 4800 bps. As was the case with frequency shift keying, the modulation procedure has limits. First, the receiver cannot discern the difference between different signaling indications if they occur too rapidly or are too similar. In addition, phase shift keying eventually is limited by the performance of carrier transmission systems. These systems do not transmit the actual carrier used to perform the modulation; they just transmit the results of the modulation process. For example, a telephone conversation of 300 to 3000 Hz would be transmitted as 200,300 Hz to 203,000 Hz, but the 200,000 Hz signal itself would not be transmitted.

To perform demodulation at the receiving station, the carrier must be reinserted. The reinserted carrier may vary slightly relative to the carrier used in the modulation process at the transmitting station. The difference between the carrier used for modulation and the carrier used for demodulation shows up as a phase change in the signal being transmitted through the carrier system. In voice communications a change of phase is not noticeable. With phase shift keyed modems, however, the phase change introduced by the carrier system may affect the ability of the receiving modem to perceive the phase changes from the transmitting modem that contain the data transmission information.

Predivestiture Bell System surveys indicated that the magnitude of the phase shifts introduced by carrier systems was rather small. This effect, however, is one of the reasons that modems designed to achieve 9600 bps transmission speeds use amplitude modulation in addition to phase modulation, rather than simply doubling the number of phase angles used in 4800 bps transmission. Some 9600 bps modems use twelve phase angles, four of which have two amplitude values. The line signaling speed is 2400 baud. Figure 14–14 shows the phase angles used.

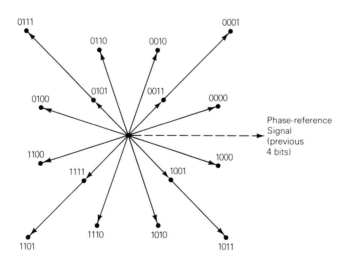

Figure 14–14   Phase Angles for 9600 Bit-per-Second Transmission

The modems discussed in this chapter are sensitive not only to phase changes but also to noise. They are not necessarily more sensitive to noise than slower modems, but the operating speeds in synchronous communications are high enough that line disturbances lasting only a few milliseconds are sufficient to invalidate substantial quantities of data. Hence, simple character parity error detection systems are insufficient, and either a combination of Longitudinal and Vertical Redundancy Checks (LRC/VRC) or a Cyclic Redundancy Check (CRC) must be used.

One more point about synchronous versus asynchronous transmission should be noted. It is not always true that asynchronous is slow and synchronous is fast. Some terminals operate over short distances at an asynchronous rate of 38,400 bps, while others operate at 1200 bps synchronous.

Synchronous modems typically have the following interface leads, the functions of which are described in Chapters 5 and 9:

|  | *Reference*<br>*Designation* |  |
|---|---|---|
| *EIA* | *CCITT* | *Function* |
| AB | 102 | Signal Ground or Common Return |
| BA | 103 | Transmitted Data |
| BB | 104 | Received Data |
| CA | 105 | Request to Send |
| CB | 106 | Clear to Send |
| CC | 107 | Data Set Ready |
| CD | 108/2 | Data Terminal Ready |
| CE | 125 | Ring Indicator |
| CF | 109 | Received Line Signal Detector |

In addition, interface leads unique to synchronous modems are provided (except as noted).

|  | *Reference*<br>*Designation* |  |
|---|---|---|
| *EIA* | *CCITT* | *Function* |
| CG | 110 | Signal Quality Detector |
| CH | 111 | Data Signal Rate Selector (DTE Source)* |
| CI | 112 | Data Signal Rate Selector (DCE Source)* |
| DA | 113 | Transmitter Signal Element Timing (DTE Source) |
| DB | 114 | Transmitter Signal Element Timing (DCE Source) |
| DD | 115 | Receiver Signal Element Timing (DCE Source) |

The definitions of the additional modem leads are reprinted below (with permission of the EIA and the CCITT):

| EIA-232-D Definitions | CCITT V.24 Definitions |
|---|---|

*Circuit CG*—Signal Quality Detector (CCITT 110)
Direction: From DCE

*Circuit 110*—Data Signal Quality Detector
Direction: From DCE

Note: Use of circuit CG—Signal Quality Detector is not recommended for new designs.

Signals on this circuit are used to indicate whether or not there is a high probability of an error in the received data.
An ON condition is maintained whenever there is no reason to believe that an error has occurred.

An OFF condition indicates that there is a high probability of an error. It may, in some instances, be used to call automatically for the retransmission of the previously transmitted data signal. Preferably the response of this circuit shall be such as to permit identification of individual questionable signal elements on Circuit BB (Received Data).

Signals on this circuit indicate whether there is a reasonable probability of an error in the data received on the data channel. The signal quality indicated conforms to the relevant DCE Recommendation.

The ON condition indicates that there is no reason to believe that an error has occurred.

The OFF condition indicates that there is a reasonable probability of an error.

*Circuit CH*—Data Signal Rate Selector (DTE Source) (CCITT 111)
Direction: To DCE

*Circuit 111*—Data Signaling Rate Selector (DTE Source)
Direction: To DCE

Signals on this circuit are used to select between the two data signaling rates in the case of multirate synchronous DCEs or the two ranges of data signaling rates in the case of dual range nonsynchronous DCEs.

An ON condition shall select the higher data signaling rate or range of rates.

Signals on this circuit are used to select one of the two data signaling rates of a dual rate synchronous DCE, or to select one of the two ranges of data signaling rates of a dual range asynchronous DCE.

The ON condition selects the higher rate or range of rates.

*The signal rate selection circuits are also used in some asynchronous modems, particularly in Europe.

| EIA-232-D Definitions | CCITT V.24 Definitions |
|---|---|

*Circuit CH (Cont.)*

The rate of timing signals, if included in the interface, shall be controlled by this circuit as may be appropriate.

*Circuit CI—Data Signal Rate Selector (DCE Source) (CCITT 112)*
Direction: From DCE

Signals on this circuit are used to select one of two data signaling rates or ranges of rates in the DTE to coincide with the data signaling rate or range of rates in use in multirate synchronous or dual range nonsynchronous DCEs.

An ON condition shall select the higher data signaling rate or range of rates.

The rate of timing signals, if included in the interface, shall be controlled by this circuit as may be appropriate.

*Circuit DA—Transmitter Signal Element Timing (DTE Source) (CCITT 113)*
Direction: To DCE

Signals on this circuit are used to provide the transmitting signal converter with signal element timing information.

The ON to OFF transition shall nominally indicate the center of each signal element on Circuit BA (Transmitted Data). When Circuit DA is implemented in the DTE, the DTE shall normally provide timing information on this circuit whenever the DTE is in a POWER ON condition. It is permissible for the DTE to withhold timing information on this circuit for short periods provided Circuit CA (Request to Send) is in the OFF condition. (For example, the temporary withholding of timing information may

*Circuit 111 (Cont.)*

The OFF condition selects the lower rate or range of rates.

*Circuit 112—Data Signaling Rate Selector (DCE Source)*
Direction: From DCE

Signals on this circuit are used to select one of the two data signaling rates or ranges of rates in the DTE to coincide with the data signaling rate or range of rates in use in a dual rate synchronous or dual range asynchronous DCE.

The ON condition selects the higher rate or range of rates.

The OFF condition selects the lower rate or range of rates.

*Circuit 113—Transmitter Signal Element Timing (DTE Source)*
Direction: To DCE

Signals on this circuit provide the DCE with signal element timing information.

The condition on this circuit shall be ON and OFF for nominally equal periods of time, and the transition from ON to OFF condition shall nominally indicate the center of each signal element on Circuit 103 (Transmitted Data).

| EIA-232-D | CCITT V.24 |
|---|---|
| **Definitions** | **Definitions** |

*Circuit DA (Cont.)*

be necessary in performing maintenance tests within the DTE.)

*Circuit DB*—Transmitter Signal Element Timing (DCE Source) (CCITT 114)
Direction: From DCE

*Circuit 114*—Transmitter Signal Element Timing (DCE Source)
Direction: From DCE

Signals on this circuit are used to provide the DTE with signal element timing information. The DTE shall provide a data signal on Circuit BA (Transmitted Data) in which the transitions between signal elements nominally occur at the time of the transitions from OFF to ON condition of the signal on Circuit DB. When Circuit DB is implemented in the DCE, the DCE shall normally provide timing information on this circuit at all times that the DCE is capable of generating it. However, the withholding of timing information may be necessary under some conditions, e.g. the performance of maintenance routines in the DCE [See Section 4.3.2 of EIA-232-D.]

Signals on this circuit provide the DTE with signal element timing information.

The condition on this circuit shall be ON and OFF for nominally equal periods of time. The DTE shall present a data signal on Circuit 103 (Transmitted Data) in which the transitions between signal elements nominally occur at the time of the transitions from OFF to ON condition of Circuit 114.

*Circuit DD*—Receiver Signal Element Timing (DCE Source) (CCITT 115)
Direction: From DCE

*Circuit 115*—Receiver Signal Element Timing (DCE Source)
Direction: From DCE

Signals on this circuit are used to provide the DTE with received signal element timing information. The transition from ON to OFF condition shall nominally indicate the center of each signal element on Circuit BB (Received Data). Timing information on Circuit DD shall normally be provided by the DCE at all times that the DCE is capable of generating it. However, the withholding of timing information may be necessary under some conditions, e.g. the performance of maintenance routines in the DCE [See Section 4.3.2 of EIA-232-D.]

Signals on this circuit provide the DTE with signal element timing information.

The condition of this circuit shall be ON and OFF for nominally equal periods of time, and a transition from ON to OFF condition shall nominally indicate the centre of each signal element on Circuit 104 (Received Data).

# 15

# A Single Line Synchronous USRT

As with asynchronous communications, the required functions for synchronous communications are performed by a single integrated circuit. Unlike the asynchronous case, however, no single computer manufacturer led the way, nor did the migration of personnel from a single integrated circuit company spread a standard component pinning across the industry. Instead, some early manufacturers produced one chip that was a synchronous/ asynchronous transmitter and a second that was a synchronous/ asynchronous receiver. Other early designs combined a transmitter and a receiver in a single chip but offered only synchronous capability. Present designs offer both synchronous and asynchronous capabilities with built-in baud rate generators, extensive modem control, and support of numerous communications protocols. (Protocols are discussed in the next four chapters.)

Despite the availability of chips that provide both synchronous and asynchronous capabilities (Universal Synchronous Asynchronous Receiver Transmitters, or USARTs), this chapter will discuss a hypothetical chip that provides only synchronous capabilities (USRT). The provision of asynchronous capabilities in a chip is discussed in Chapter 2, and discussion of a chip with combined functionality becomes very confusing. Further, the discussion will be limited to USRTs that support character-oriented protocols; expansion to support bit-oriented protocols will be shown in Chapter 20.

Like a UART, the USRT converts a serial stream of bits arriving over a single wire into a character that can be read in parallel form by a microprocessor connected to the USRT by a parallel bus. In a symmetrical fashion, the microprocessor can load characters in parallel form into the USRT and have those characters converted into a serial bit stream.

The parallel bus connections also allow the microprocessor to access additional registers within the USRT besides those containing characters involved in the reception/transmission process. The additional registers contain bits that provide status information and bits that control various operating characteristics of the USRT. For example, some status bits indicate that a received character is available for reading, while others indicate that the transmitter is available for the microprocessor to load a character for transmission. Additional status bits provide Overrun and Underrun Error indications.

As in the asynchronous case, an Overrun Error occurs when the characters are not read out of the receiver register as fast as they are received. This results in a character arriving and the receiver having no place to store it. Underrun occurs when a transmitter can transmit characters faster than they are being loaded into the transmitter. This results in the transmitter having nothing to send. This latter condition is not fatal in asynchronous communications, as the stop interval is merely made longer. Hence, asynchronous receivers do not report an error under these circumstances. Underrun can be fatal in synchronous communications, however, and the conditions under which this is true are explained in the chapters describing the various protocols. Since Underrun conditions at a transmitting station can cause messages to be negatively acknowledged by the receiving station, it is important that an Underrun Error indication be provided.

Like the UART, USRT registers include bits that determine the number of bits per character and whether or not parity operation is enabled. If parity is used, the registers include bits that determine whether that parity is odd or even.

Figure 15–1 shows a block diagram of a single line synchronous interface implemented with a USRT. At the left of the drawing is a microprocessor input/output bus, typically a structure of several dozen conductors. Some of the conductors in that bus are "address leads." Circuitry connected to the USRT, but not shown in the drawing, monitors those leads and enables the "bus transceivers" whenever the address assigned to the USRT chip appears. In a typical installation, a few address leads are also brought into the USRT chip to allow the microprocessor to select which register will be read or written. When a register is to be read, the address leads within the

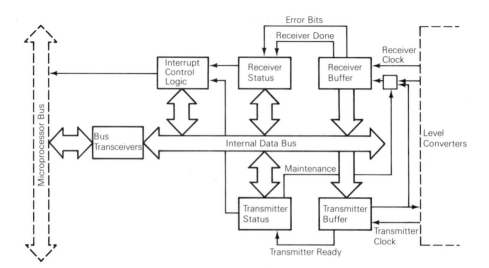

Figure 15–1   Block Diagram of a Single Line USRT

USRT gate the contents of the receiver buffer, the receiver status register, or the transmitter status register onto the leads labeled "Internal Data Bus." This permits the bus transceivers to place the data that has been read onto the microprocessor bus. When a register is to be written, data on the microprocessor bus is received by the bus transceivers and is presented to the receiver status register, the transmitter status register, or the transmitter buffer register via the internal data bus. One of the leads in the microprocessor bus is typically a strobe signal, which is passed through the bus transceivers and used to record the data into the register selected by the address leads. The bit assignments for these registers are shown in Figure 15–2.

Two blocks in the diagram remain to be explained: interrupt control logic and level conversion. The interrupt control logic is provided to eliminate the need for the microprocessor to examine the receiver and transmitter status registers continually to see whether there are characters to be handled. Instead, the interrupt logic (if enabled) will alert the microprocessor whenever the receiver has assembled a character or the transmitter is ready to accept a character for transmission.

Some USRTs (and especially USARTs) provide interrupt logic that will recognize an "interrupt acknowledge" signal from the microprocessor and place an "interrupt vector" on the data leads. The interrupt vector provides an address at which a pointer, which will direct the microprogram to an "interrupt service routine" appropriate to the USRT, can be found.

The one remaining block to be explained is labeled "Level Converters." As was mentioned in conjunction with a similar figure in Chapter 2, data communication are seldom done at transistor–transistor logic levels (TTL) once a signal lead is outside the box containing the computer and/or computer communications interface. Thus, USRTs connect to level converter circuits, which convert the TTL logic levels to EIA-232-D voltage levels. Since the EIA-232-D specification is applicable only up to 20,000 bps, data rates above this must use some other type of interface. High-speed interfaces commonly used include the combined voltage level/differential interface specified in CCITT Recommendation V.35 and the differential interface described in the EIA-422-A specification.

In Chapter 2, the UART presented in Figure 2–1 has the bit assignments shown in Figure 15–2. With the exception of the bit designated in parentheses, which will be commented on below, a USRT can use, as a starting

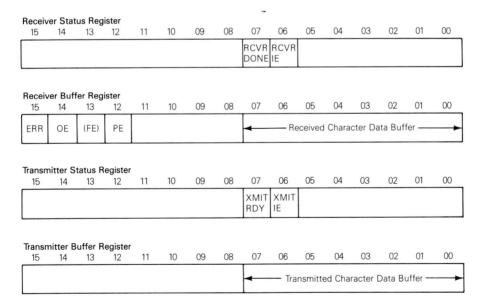

Figure 15–2   Sample Bit Assignments for Single Line Synchronous Interface

point, the exact same bits as the asynchronous interface (which is why combined UART/USRT, or USART, chips are so popular). The meaning of each bit assignment is the same as those explained in Chapter 2. Receiver Done (RCVR DONE) indicates that a character has been received. If Receiver Interrupt Enable (RCVR IE) is also a one at the time this occurs, the setting of RCVR DONE will cause an interrupt in the microprocessor. The character that has been received is presented in the receiver buffer register, along with any error flags that may have accompanied it. Transmitter Ready (XMIT RDY) indicates that the transmitter is ready to be loaded with a character for transmission, and the microprocessor may load such a character by writing it into the transmitter buffer register. Like the Receiver Done flag, the Transmitter Ready flag will generate an interrupt if the program has previously indicated the desirability of this by setting the interrupt enable bit (XMIT IE).

One of the bits shown in Figure 15–2 has its designation enclosed in parentheses. This bit, Framing Error (FE), is associated only with asynchronous communications and will be dropped from further discussions and figures. It should be noted, however, that Framing Error is used when asynchronous format characters (i.e., those delineated with START and STOP bits) are sent with a clocking connection between the transmitter and receiver. This method of sending asynchronous format data by synchronous means is called "isochronous" transmission.

Some manufacturers offer simple UART-based interfaces, without modem control, similar to the interface described in Chapter 2. Some of these are an integral part of a microprocessor. The market for synchronous communications equipment, however, includes a much higher percentage of applications where modems are required. Thus, most USRTs include some type of modem control facility. This requires that the bit assignments of Figure 15–2 be expanded to those shown in Figure 15–3. Note that only the receiver status register and the transmitter status register have had bits added. The receiver buffer register and transmitter buffer register have not been changed.

In the same way that bit 15 of the receiver buffer register is set whenever any receiver error condition is reported (OE or PE), bit 15 of the receiver status register sets whenever there is a change in modem (data set) status. This bit is called the Data Set Change Interrupt (DS INT) bit and, if set, will generate an interrupt—provided that bit 05, the Data Set Change In-

**Receiver Status Register**

| 15 | 14 | 13 | 12 | 11 | 10 | 09 | 08 | 07 | 06 | 05 | 04 | 03 | 02 | 01 | 00 |
|----|----|----|----|----|----|----|----|----|----|----|----|----|----|----|----|
| DS INT | RING | CTS | DCD | RCVR ACT |  | DSR | ST SY | RCVR DONE | RCVR IE | DS IE | SCH SYN |  | RTS | DTR |  |

**Receiver Buffer Register**

| 15 | 14 | 13 | 12 | 11 | 10 | 09 | 08 | 07 | 06 | 05 | 04 | 03 | 02 | 01 | 00 |
|----|----|----|----|----|----|----|----|----|----|----|----|----|----|----|----|
| ERR | OE |  | PE |  |  |  |  | ◄——— Received Character Data Buffer ———► | | | | | | | |

**Transmitter Status Register**

| 15 | 14 | 13 | 12 | 11 | 10 | 09 | 08 | 07 | 06 | 05 | 04 | 03 | 02 | 01 | 00 |
|----|----|----|----|----|----|----|----|----|----|----|----|----|----|----|----|
| DNA | Maintenance System | | | | | XMIT ACT |  | XMIT RDY | XMIT IE | DNA IE | SEND | HALF DPLX |  |  |  |

**Transmitter Buffer Register**

| 15 | 14 | 13 | 12 | 11 | 10 | 09 | 08 | 07 | 06 | 05 | 04 | 03 | 02 | 01 | 00 |
|----|----|----|----|----|----|----|----|----|----|----|----|----|----|----|----|
|  |  |  |  |  |  |  |  | ◄——— Transmitted Character Data Buffer ———► | | | | | | | |

Figure 15–3  Expanded Bit Assignments for a Synchronous Interface

terrupt Enable (DS IE), also is set. The modem leads that are monitored for changes are Ring, Clear to Send, Carrier Detect, and Data Set Ready. The status of these leads is reflected at any given moment by the status of bits 14, 13, 12, and 09, respectively. The functions of these leads are described in detail in Chapter 9 but are reviewed briefly here. Ring indicates that the modem is being signaled by the telephone switching equipment that a call is being made to the line. Clear to Send is an indication to the computer interface that data applied to the Transmitted Data lead of the modem by the transmitter section of the interface will probably succeed in reaching the receiving station. Carrier Detect, also called Data Channel Received Line Signal Detector, is an indication that carrier is being received from the distant modem. Data Set Ready indicates that the modem is connected to the line and is ready to transfer data.

The Receiver Status word also provides the capability for the computer program to control two of the leads that go to the modem: Request to Send and Data Terminal Ready. This is accomplished by bits 02 and 01, respectively. Request to Send is used to turn on the modem's transmitter section to initiate the transmission of data from this modem to the distant modem.

In addition to turning on its transmitter, the modem responds by asserting Clear to Send (bit 13) in response to the assertion of Request to Send. The delay between Request to Send and Clear to Send can be selected (in the modem) to be 0 to 250 milliseconds. By this time, the modem should have propagated its signal (carrier) to the distant modem. The Data Terminal Ready lead is used to answer calls to this modem and to maintain calls that have been originated or answered by this modem. When the computer program negates Data Terminal Ready by clearing this bit, the interface drops the assertion of Data Terminal Ready toward the modem, and the modem drops the telephone line connection. (This applies to switched telephone service only; it is not used in private line applications.)

There are two remaining bits in the receiver status register whose function has not been explained. These bits are not associated with modem operation but have to do with the peculiarities of synchronous transmission. Bit 08 is Strip Sync (ST SY). Since the receiver has the ability to recognize which received characters are sync characters (this is necessary to achieve synchronization), and since sync characters received in addition to those used to synchronize are of little use, it would be convenient to be able to ignore the unnecessary sync characters. Consider a case where five sync characters are transmitted and the reception of two syncs places the receiver in synchronization. If the line has relatively little noise, the first two syncs received will place the receiver in synchronization. What happens to the next three sync characters? Barring any special features, these three characters arrive, generate interrupts, and are serviced by the interrupt service routine portion of the computer program. Chances are that the program is arranged to throw those characters away once they are recognized as syncs, as they are unnecessary for any purpose but synchronization. The computer program could be saved from wasting its time with these extra sync characters if the USRT were to throw away any sync characters received between synchronization and receipt of the first nonsync character. This is the purpose of the Strip Sync bit and its associated logic. It is not a good idea to throw away sync characters that appear in the midst of messages, as they might be part of a "transparent text stream." This will be explained more fully in Chapters 16 and 17.

The other unexplained bit is 04, Search Sync (SCH SYN). When set, this bit forces the receiver logic to go out of synchronization and to resume the search for sync characters. It does this by shifting in a bit at a time and comparing the most recently received eight bits against the sync character stored within the receiver. The Search Sync bit is set by the computer program whenever it believes, based on high error rates or lack of messages, that the receiver is out of synchronization. When the receiver again recognizes the appropriate number of sync characters, the receiver logic clears Search Sync.

As mentioned in conjunction with the Underrun bit in the USRT, the inability of a computer program to feed characters to a transmitter at a sufficient rate will cause the transmitter to send an idling character, such as sync. This extra character can cause the receiving station to acknowledge the message negatively, depending on the protocol being used and the circumstances at the time the extra character is sent. While it might be stated that it does not matter whether a few extra errors are thus introduced since the telephone line will be causing a fair number of errors anyway, it is often necessary to determine exactly what is causing the negative acknowledgments in a malfunctioning communications system. For this reason, the existence of an underrun bit is important. This is bit 15 of the transmitter status register, where it is called Data Not Available (DNA). The setting of this bit generates an interrupt if the program indicates that this is desirable, which it can do by leaving Data Not Available Interrupt Enable (DNA IE, bit 05) set.

One of the bits in the transmitter status register is devoted to maintenance and loops the transmitted data and clocks to the received data and clocks. During loopback, no characters are transmitted to, or received from, points outside the USRT.

In addition to a loopback test within the USRT, many modems include loop-around features, which permit the transmitted data to pass into the modem, be converted to the voltage levels used within the modem (but not be converted to tones), and be converted back to interface voltages and sent back to the Received Data lead of the USRT. Use of such a loop-around and remote loop-around provisions at a distant modem are extremely useful in pointing out exactly where the trouble lies. When communications interfaces, modems, and transmission facilities are all provided by different vendors, such loop-around capability reduces finger pointing.

An additional bit, indirectly associated with modem control, appears in the transmitter status register. This bit is called Transmitter Active. The Transmitter Active bit is provided to indicate to the program when it is safe to drop the Request to Send lead in the modem control. Transmitter Active is set whenever the transmitter unit is serializing data onto the communications line and for one-half bit time thereafter. When the bit clears, the transmitter is idling MARK onto the line, and Request to Send for most modems can be dropped.

Some USRTs provide a bit for operation with half-duplex modems, shown here as bit 03 of the transmitter status register. When set, this bit blinds the receiver logic whenever the transmitter is in use. In this way, if the modem produces a copy of the transmitted data on the Received Data lead, that data will not disturb the receiver logic. Figure 15–4 illustrates the function of this lead.

The modulator and demodulator sections of the modem are both connected to the telephone line, and since the frequencies and modulation methods used by the modulator are exactly the same as those used by the demodulator, the demodulator sees everything the modulator transmits and delivers it to the receiver logic. The Half-Duplex Control lead solves this problem of extraneous data entering the receiver logic by blinding the receiver logic while the transmitter is operating.

Many modems solve this problem by interlocking the demodulator with the Request to Send lead and thus not running the demodulator while the modulator is on. When a synchronous interface is being used with this type of modem, there is no need for the half-duplex bit, although its use would not do any harm.

So far, all discussion of a USRT has emphasized its similarity to the UARTs described in Chapters 2 and 6. This analogy can only be carried so far, and it is now time to discuss features specific to synchronous com-

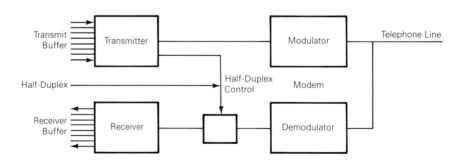

Figure 15–4   Half-Duplex Lead Logic

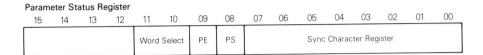

Figure 15–5    Parameter Status Register

munications. One of these features is the ability to select the character that will be used for achieving synchronization, the sync character.

To select the sync character, it is necessary to add a register to those listed in Figure 15–3. Such a register would provide not only programmable sync characters, but also programmable character length and programmable parity features. Figure 15–5 is a possible format for a parameter status register containing this information.

Bits 10 and 11 are used to select whether character length is five, six, seven, or eight bits per character. When bit 09 is set, parity operation is enabled. All characters sent have a parity bit added, and all characters received are expected to have a parity bit. The parity bit makes each character one bit longer than the length specified in bits 10 and 11.

When the Parity Enable bit is set, the sense of the parity (odd or even) is controlled by bit 08. When bit 08 is set, even parity is generated by the transmitter and checked for by the receiver. The program does not have to supply a parity bit to the transmitter; this is performed by the transmitter logic. When bit 08 is cleared, odd parity is generated and checked.

Bits 00–07 of the parameter status register may be loaded by the program to specify the sync character. The sync character is used by the receiver logic to detect received sync characters and thereby to achieve synchronization. The sync character is also used by the transmitter as an idling character when it has not been provided with anything else to send.

While on the subject of idling characters, it should be noted that a moderate amount of care is required when shutting down a transmission on a synchronous line. If the transmission facility is full duplex, the transmitter can be allowed to idle sync characters between messages. This has the benefit of keeping the receiving station in synchronization between messages. The program at the receiving station has to have some expedient means of disposing of the syncs received, however. Idling sync characters can create a problem, in rare cases, that line noise can cause the receiver to think a new message has started. For half-duplex lines, the transmission must be shut down and the line "turned around." Shutdown is normally accomplished by the transmission of End of Transmission (EOT), followed by two PAD characters (all ones). The PAD characters ensure that, when the Request to Send lead is negated and the modem turns off its transmitter, the transmitter in its last gasps will not be sending data that could be mistakenly interpreted at the receiving station.

When the receiving station recognizes the End of Transmission, it checks to see whether it has information to send; if so, it asserts its Request to Send lead, which starts a timer in the modem. After the timer has expired (up to one-quarter second later), the modem returns a Clear to Send signal, and the transmitter begins transmission of sync characters. What has previously been called the receiving station is now the transmitting station. The major time delay in this line turnaround process is caused by the echo suppressors (see Chapter 8). When it is known that no echo suppressors exist in the communications facility, the Request to Send/Clear to Send delay in the modem can be selected to be a much smaller value, increasing the line utilization by allowing faster turnaround.

As indicated earlier in this chapter, the USRT discussed above handles only character-oriented protocols. Before discussing the capabilities of more complex chips, it is necessary to discuss the protocols with which such chips must deal. The next four chapters do this. A more complex USRT is discussed in Chapter 20.

# 16

## Protocols

The tasks of a data communication system include delivery of information that is correct, in proper sequential order, and understandable to the recipient. To accomplish these functions, electrical circuits (Chapters 1–4), modems and their interfaces (Chapters 5–12), error detection systems (Chapter 13), and other hardware/software subsystems (not yet discussed) must all perform in a cooperative fashion following a set of rules or protocols.

Dictionaries define "protocol" as being a set of rules and ceremonies by which diplomats and heads of state communicate. The rules of diplomatic protocol ensure that communications are completely and correctly understood by both parties. In data communication, protocols perform a similar function, and their use is almost as complex as the use of diplomatic protocols.

As indicated above, many functions must be performed to accomplish the tasks of data communication, and there is generally a protocol for each of these functions. For example, the protocols for EIA-232-D interface operation are discussed at some length in Chapter 5 and include rules concerning electrical signal levels and those concerning what the assertion of various signals means and under what conditions those signals are to be asserted. In Chapter 13, some protocols for error correction are discussed. A family of protocols covering all aspects of data communication is necessary to do the complete job of transferring correct, time sequential, understandable data.

To assist people in designing protocol families, the International Organization for Standardization (ISO) has developed a model in which each protocol that makes up the family is a "layer" that performs certain functions for the protocol (layer) above it. The ISO model does not specify the exact details of each protocol,* but it does specify a way of designing protocol families—that is, which layers should be present and what functions each layer should perform. Two protocol families that are "ISO compatible" may not necessarily communicate with each other. Furthermore, many protocol families only loosely follow the ISO model.

The idea that protocols are arranged as layers is a bit difficult to grasp, but anyone who has ever sent a letter has used layered protocols without realizing it. In writing a letter, it is customary (i.e., according to protocol) to acknowledge receipt of previous correspondence and then to discuss whatever topics one chooses. The text of the letter is preceded by a greeting ("Dear John") and concluded with a closing ("Sincerely"). The completed letter is then packaged according to postal regulations (another protocol) and sent to the post office. Note that there is a protocol for what is in the text, a protocol for framing the text between a greeting and a closing, and a protocol for physically transporting it. Figure 16–1 shows these three protocols in a block diagram.

An important part of the concept of layered protocols is the idea that each layer provides a service for the layers above it. In the letter-writing example, the post office provides the letter-delivery service and the postal protocol ensures the rapid and economical delivery of the correct letter to the correct party by specifying envelope sizes that fit the sorting machines and by specifying address formats that can be conveniently read by humans or machines.

The formatting protocol specifying a greeting and a closing ensures that the message is for the intended party and verifies the identity of the sender. If you receive a letter that begins "Dear John" and your name is Larry, you know that the sender placed the wrong letter in the envelope. Similarly, receiving a letter with a stranger's signature may indicate that something has gone wrong.

The "protocol for what is said and in what order" guides both the message sender and the message recipient. For example, specifying that previous correspondence be acknowledged ensures that the two correspondents realize when a message is lost. If the letter begins "Received yours of May

---

*Although the ISO model does not specify individual protocols, the ISO organization does specify and approve protocols.

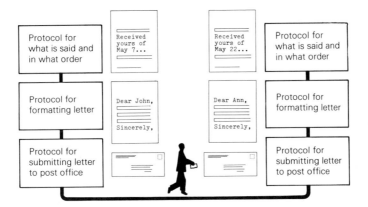

Figure 16–1   Postal Service Protocols

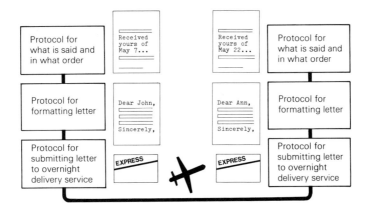

Figure 16–2   Overnight Delivery Service Protocols

7" and the recipient knows he or she sent another letter on May 20, there is reason to suspect that a letter is missing.

The layering of protocols permits services to be substituted with minimal impact. For example, the correspondents might prefer to have their letters delivered by an overnight package delivery service rather than by the post office. In that case, Figure 16–2 would then apply. Figure 16–2 differs from Figure 16–1 only at the lowest level. The typical differences are the type of envelope used, the pickup and delivery points, and the rate paid. The higher level protocols remain unchanged. One might presume that any overnight service that required its customers to change some higher level protocol, such as the message format or content, would not have very many customers.

Several protocol layers might be altered, however, if the substitution of services occurred at a higher level. Consider the case of a telephone call. Like the postal protocol, the "telephone protocol" includes an addressing function (dialing), and a service charge is collected. Like the format of a written message, the format for a telephone call includes a greeting ("hello") and a closing ("good-bye"). The top level of communications, the "protocol for what is said in what order," is often unchanged between a letter and a telephone call, at least in terms of the broad outline of acknowledging previous correspondence and announcing the reason for or subject of this correspondence.

In summary, even such ordinary everyday correspondence as letters and telephone calls follows a layered protocol. The layers provide an ordering of services that makes the correspondence more accurate and easier to understand. Furthermore, the layering allows for the substitution of services if special circumstances demand it. ("This has to be there overnight" or "I must communicate right now.")

Data communication protocols also are layered. The ISO model specifies the following layers, as diagrammed in Figure 16–3.

### Physical Layer

As with the "postal protocols" discussed above, the lowest layer of the ISO model concerns the physical process of getting the data from one point to another. As with the postal case, there can be several choices for the transmission method, such as direct connections using the EIA interfaces discussed in Chapters 3 and 4 or modem-equipped connections using EIA-232-D and the modems discussed in Chapters 5, 10, and 14.

### Data Link Layer

During the process of getting from one point to another, data bits may be subject to errors. Also, it may be desirable to send bits for a variety of purposes; for example, some bits may be user data and others may be for control purposes. To ensure that transmission errors can be detected, and to permit user data bits and control bits to be sent over the same physical layer, data communication systems send bits in groups called "frames" or

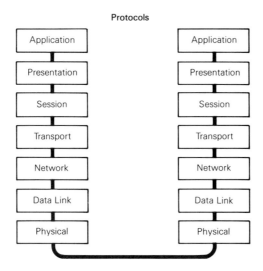

Figure 16–3   ISO Layered Model for
Protocols

"packets." The assembly and transmission of frames is accomplished by the data link layer and are together referred to as the "framing process." However, discussion of various data link protocols refers to these entities as "packets," so that term will be used from here on.

Error control is usually included in the data link layer, although there may be additional forms of error control in the upper layers. The error control in the data link layer is implemented as part of the process of dividing the data into frames. The frames are analogous to the letters delivered by the post office, in the sense that they have a "greeting" (called a "header") and a "closing" (called a "frame check sequence"). The headers contain packet numbering that indicates the number of the packet being transmitted and the number of the last good packet received (or in some cases the number of the next packet expected). The frame check sequences are (usually) 16- or 32-bit quantities that are the result of specific mathematical operations performed on the bits that constitute the packet (see Chapter 13 for details). If the frame check sequence contained in the packet agrees with the frame check sequence generated by the receiving station on the basis of the received data, the receiving station sends a positive acknowledgment to the transmitting station, either immediately or as part of a subsequent transmitted packet header. If the frame check sequence does not agree, a negative acknowledgment (or in some cases no acknowledgment) is sent. The transmitting station responds to this situation, possibly after a time-out period, by retransmitting the packet.

An additional task that could be performed in the data link layer is flow control for the transmission system, which could be useful in networks with transmission links of varying speeds. (Transmission flow control also can be accomplished by higher level software.) In networks where the host computers are of varying speed, there must be flow control between the hosts, but that is provided in a higher layer rather than in the data link layer.

Choices for implementing the physical layer and the data link layer are often influenced by the hardware being used, but the functions of the layers above these are usually hardware independent, as they are implemented in firmware or software.

## Network, Transport, Session, and Presentation Layers

The network, transport, session, and presentation layers each provide a service for the layers above them, and the functions delegated to each layer vary somewhat in different protocols. Among the services provided are the following:

1. *Route Selection.* A "global" address for the destination may be added—i.e., an address that will specify the destination no matter which combination of transmission links is used.

2. *Congestion control for the links.* The number of packets queued up for transmission over various links may be limited.

3. *Creation of an error-free sequenced stream.* Many networks require a reliable, sequenced, error-free stream of data between the two ends of the connection (a "virtual circuit"). Other services can use more primitive facilities. For example, in some cases ("datagrams"), it may be acceptable to have data delivered with only a certain probability of success, and applications may use data that is delivered out of order. If a reliable, sequenced, error-free stream is needed, it is provided by the middle layer protocols, usually those in the transport layer.

4. *Multiplexing.* It is possible to utilize multiple network connections for high throughput or to multiplex several transport connections onto the same network connection for economy. Either case must be transparent to the next higher layer.

5. *Congestion control for the hosts.* As indicated in conjunction with the data link discussion, additional flow control functionality, primarily associated with keeping fast hosts from overrunning slow hosts, can exist at a higher level of the protocol.

6. *User interface.* One of the higher levels of the protocol, usually the session layer, is the user's interface to the network and contains the software necessary for a user to establish a connection with another host. The user can then log on and become an interactive user on that machine, or the user can access that machine simply to transfer a file.

7. *Packet format interpretation.* One of the higher layers may define the meaning of bytes in the packets delivered by the lower layers. For example, the presentation layer might contain a program for interpreting the packets destined for a file handling program operating in the application layer. The interpretation program would tell the file handling program, "The first bytes of the packet contain a file name, followed by a carriage return and line feed. The next bytes contain the user name of the file owner, followed by a carriage return and line feed. After that comes the file itself, followed by an end of file delimiter."

## Application Layer

The application layer contains the programs that perform the tasks desired by the users. Examples include programs for providing file, printer, and mail services.

## Protocol Alternatives for the Data Link Layer

As indicated above, choices for implementing the physical layer and the data link layer are often influenced by the hardware being used. Some of the physical layer alternatives are discussed in preceding chapters. In the three chapters that follow, alternatives for the data link layer are discussed, and chapters beyond those discuss hardware appropriate to those alternatives.

While looking at the various protocol alternatives for the data link layer, the following operating problems should be considered:

1. *Framing.* The determination of which eight-bit groups constitute characters and, most important, which groups of characters constitute packets.

2. *Error control.* The detection of errors by means of the Longitudinal, Vertical, or Cyclic Redundancy Checks described in Chapter 13; the acceptance of correct packets; and the request for retransmission of faulty packets.

3. *Sequence control.* The numbering of packets to eliminate duplicate packets, avoid losing packets, and identify packets that are retransmitted by the error control system.

4. *Transparency.* The transmittal of information (such as instrumentation data) that contains bit patterns resembling the control characters used to solve problems 1, 2, and 3 above, without the receiving station identifying those bit patterns as control characters.

5. *Line control.* The determination, in the case of a half-duplex or multipoint line, of which station will transmit and which will receive.

6. *Special cases.* Solving the problem of what a transmitter sends when it has no data to send.

7. *Time-out control.* Solving the problem of what to do if packet flow suddenly ceases entirely.

8. *Start-up control.* The process of getting transmission started in a communications system that has been idle.

It is beyond the scope of this book to describe how each of the data link layer protocols commonly in use solves the problems in each of the above areas, but the following chapters highlight some of the methods used.

Data link layer protocols may be divided into three categories according to the packet framing techniques used. These are character-oriented, byte count-oriented, and bit-oriented. A character-oriented protocol uses special characters, such as STX to indicate the beginning of a packet and ETB to indicate the end of a block of text (i.e., the imminent arrival of the block check characters). The classic character-oriented protocol is IBM's Binary Synchronous Communications Protocol, known as BISYNC.

Byte count–oriented protocols use a header that includes a beginning special character followed by a count that indicates how many characters follow in the data portion of the packet and some control information, such as which packets have been received correctly to date. The data portion, which comes next, is the specified length and is followed by block check characters. Digital Equipment Corporation's Digital Data Communication Message Protocol (DDCMP) is an example of this type of protocol, as is Kermit, a widely used file transfer protocol for personal computers.

Finally, it is possible to create a protocol that delineates which bits constitute packets by separating those packets with a special flag character, such as 01111110. This type of protocol specifies that there shall never be six "1" bits in a row except for the transmission of a flag. Thus, when the receiving station receives a flag character, it knows that the previous 16 bits were the block check character and that the bits between those 16 and the previous flag constitute the packet. This type of protocol is a "bit-stuffing" or bit-oriented protocol. IBM's Synchronous Data Link Control (SDLC) and ISO's High (level) Data Link Control (HDLC) are examples.

Protocols of each of the three major types are discussed in greater detail in the following chapters.

# References

1. Davies, D.W., et al. *Computer Networks and Their Protocols*. New York: John Wiley & Sons, 1979.
2. International Organization for Standardization (ISO). *Information Processing Systems—Open Systems Interconnection—Basic Reference Model*. Draft International Standard ISO/DIS 7498, 1982.
3. McNamara, John E. *Local Area Networks—An Introduction to the Technology*. Bedford, MA: Digital Press, 1985.
4. Tanenbaum, Andrew S. *Computer Networks*. Englewood Cliffs, NJ: Prentice-Hall, 1981.

# 17

# BISYNC and Character-Oriented Protocols

One of the most widely used protocols in the industry is IBM's Binary Synchronous Communications Protocol, known as BISYNC. It has been in use since 1968 for transmission between IBM computers and batch and video display terminals. BISYNC is a character-oriented protocol; it uses special characters to delineate the various fields of a packet and to control the necessary protocol functions.

The overall format of a BISYNC packet is shown in Figure 17–1. The header is optional, but if a header is used, it begins with SOH (Start of Header) and ends with STX (Start of Text). SOH and STX are special characters, and the bit combinations to form these characters may be found in character sets for ASCII, EBCDIC, and Six Bit Transcode, the three codes most commonly used with BISYNC. The contents of the header are defined by the user, except that polling and addressing for multipoint lines are not done by the header but rather by a separate control packet. The text portion of the packet is variable in length and may contain transparent data—i.e., bits that are to be treated as data (e.g., data from a measuring instrument) and not as characters. This feature requires that the character recognition logic of the receiver be turned off so that a data pattern resembling either ETX (End of Text) or one of the other special characters will not confuse the receiver logic. To turn off the character recognition at the receiver, the transparent data is delimited by DLE (Data Link Escape) STX and DLE ETX (or DLE ETB). Regardless of whether the text field ends with ETX, ETB, DLE ETX, or DLE ETB, these special characters indicate the end of the text field and the beginning of the trailer section, which contains only the block check character(s).

176

BISYNC employs a rigorous set of rules for establishing, maintaining, and terminating a communications sequence. A typical exchange between a terminal station and a computer on a point-to-point private line is illustrated in Figure 17–2.

As mentioned above, BISYNC supports ASCII, EBCDIC, or Six Bit Transcode for coding the information. Certain bit patterns in each set have been set aside for the required control characters: SOH, STX, ETB, ITB, ETX, EOT, NAK, DLE, and ENQ. Some controls are two-character sequences— ACK0, ACK1, WACK, RVI, and TTD. All these control character abbreviations are defined below.

*SOH—Start of Heading*

*STX—Start of Text*

*ETB—End of Transmission Block.* ETB indicates the end of a block of characters that starts with SOH or STX and indicates that the block check is coming next. ETB requires a response from the receiving station indicating its status: ACK0, ACK1, NAK, WACK, or RVI.

*ITB—End of Intermediate Transmission Block* (called IUS in EBCDIC and US in ASCII). ITB is used to separate the packet into sections for error detection purposes without causing a reversal of transmission direction. The transmission of ITB indicates that the block check is coming next. While the block check is checked at this point and reset to zero, the receiving station does not reply to the transmitting station until a final block, ending in ETB or ETX, is received. Except for the first intermediate block, or a boundary between a heading block and a text block, the intermediate blocks need not begin with STX. One further exception is the use of intermediate blocks in transparent data transfer; these must all start with DLE STX.

*ETX—End of Text.* Terminates a block of characters that was transmitted as an entity and started with SOH or STX. Its function is the same as ETB, except it also means there are no more data blocks to be sent.

*EOT—End of Transmission.* EOT indicates the end of a packet transmission that may contain a number of blocks, including text and headings. EOT is also used

Direction of serial data flow

Figure 17–1  BISYNC Message Format

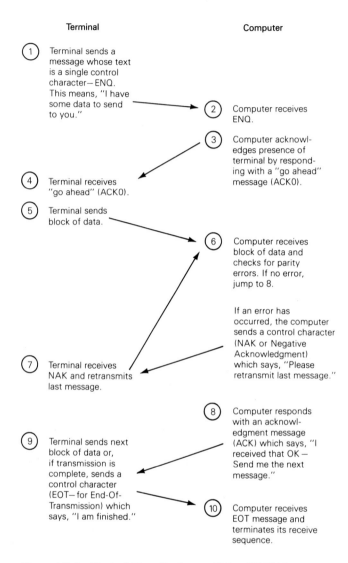

Figure 17–2  Typical Data Exchange Using BISYNC

to respond "nothing to transmit" to a polling request and can be used as an abort signal.

*NAK—Negative Acknowledgment.* NAK indicates that the previous block was received in error.

*DLE—Data Link Escape.* One of the uses of DLE is in the creation of WACK, ACK0, ACK1, and RVI, which are two-character sequences. For example, in EBCDIC,

RVI is sent as DLE. DLE is primarily used for control character sequences in transparent data transfer. The sequence DLE STX is used to initiate transparent text, and DLE ETX, DLE ITB, and DLE ETB are used to terminate transparent text. In addition, DLE ENQ, DLE DLE, and DLE EOT are used for control purposes during transparent text transmissions.

*ENQ—Enquiry.* ENQ is used to bid for the line when using point-to-point connections; it indicates the end of a poll or selection sequence. It also is used to request retransmission of the ACK/NAK response if the original response was garbled or not received when expected.

*ACK0, ACK1—Affirmative Acknowledgment.* These replies indicate that the previous block was accepted without error and that the receiver is ready to receive the next block. ACK0 is used to acknowledge multipoint selection, point-to-point line bid, and even numbered blocks. ACK1 is used to acknowledge odd numbered blocks.

*WACK—Wait Before Transmit Positive Acknowledgment.* A WACK reply indicates that the previous block was accepted without error but that the receiver is not ready to receive the next block. The usual response from the transmitting station is ENQ, and the receiving station continues to respond with WACK until it is ready to receive.

*RVI—Reverse Interrupt.* Like ACK0, ACK1, and WACK, RVI is a positive acknowledgment. It is also a request that the transmitting station terminate the current transmission because the receiving station has a high-priority packet that it wishes to send to the transmitting station and thus needs to turn the line around.

*TTD—Temporary Text Delay (STX ENQ).* TTD is used by a transmitting station that is not quite ready to transmit but wishes to retain the line. The receiving station responds with NAK, and the transmitting station may again send TTD if it is still not ready.

To detect and correct transmission errors, BISYNC uses either Vertical or Longitudinal Redundancy Checks (VRC/LRC) or a Cyclic Redundancy Check (CRC), depending on the information code being used. For ASCII, a VRC check is performed on each character (i.e., parity) and an LRC on the whole packet. In this case, the block check in the trailer field of the packet is a single eight-bit character. If the code is EBCDIC or Six Bit Transcode, no VRC (parity) check is made; rather, a CRC is calculated for the entire packet. CRC-16 is used with EBCDIC. This results in a block check that is 16 bits long and is transmitted as two eight-bit characters; the lowest order eight bits are transmitted first. With Six Bit Transcode, CRC-12 ($X^{12} + X^{11} + X^3 + X + 1$) is used, resulting in a block check character that is 12 bits long. This is transmitted as two six-bit characters, lowest order bits first. If the block check character transmitted does not agree with the block check calculated by the receiver, or if there is a VRC error, then a negative acknowledge (NAK) sequence, such as that shown in Figure 17–2, is sent back to the data source. To correct errors, BISYNC requires the retransmission of a block when an error occurs. Retransmission will typically be attempted several times before it is assumed that the line is in an unrecoverable state.

When a transmitted block check does match the receiver's calculated block check, the receiver sends a positive acknowledgment: ACK0 for an even numbered block or ACK1 for an odd numbered block. This alternating between ACK0 and ACK1 checks for sequence errors to detect duplicated or missing blocks. The acknowledgment packets are sent as separate control packets rather than being incorporated in a data packet.

The operation of the BISYNC protocol can best be appreciated from a state flow diagram, such as that shown in Figure 17–3. There are five states for transmission, two of which apply to transmission of ordinary data and three of which apply to transmission of transparent data.

For ordinary nontransparent data, transmission begins in State 3 for the transmission of any header date or the ENQ control character. A header begins with SOH, which has some special rules associated with it. The first SOH or STX to follow a line turnaround causes the BCC to reset. All succeeding STX or SOH characters (until a line turnaround) are included in the BCC. ITB, ETB, and ETX characters are always included in the BCC and are followed by the BCC. When an STX or ITB delimiter occurs in State 3, transmission progresses to State 4, the text transmission mode. When the transmitter has sent the entire data block, the character count (byte count) reaches zero, and transmission returns to State 3 for transmission of the next data block.

For transparent data, transmission begins in State 0, where any ACK, RVI, or WACK control characters sent are prefixed with a DLE. The transmission of an STX is also prefixed with a DLE and shifts the transmission into State 1, the transparent data transmission state. The transmission stays in State 1 until all characters have been sent (character count/byte count reaches zero), then switches to State 2, the end of transparent block state. In State 2, the transmission of an ITB DLE STX sequence causes a return to State 1 for transmission of the remainder of the data block. Using ETB

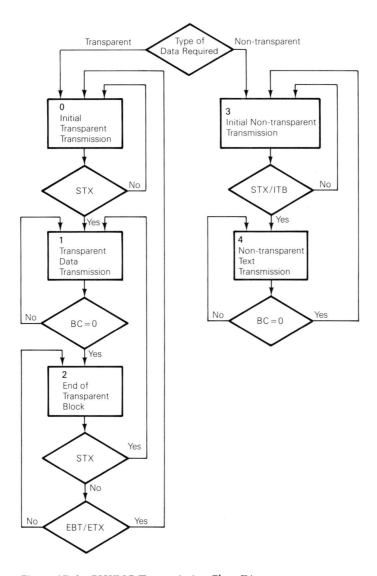

Figure 17–3   BISYNC Transmission Flow Diagram

or ETX in the above sequence causes a return to State 0 to enable trans-mission of the next data block.

Figure 17–4 is a state flow diagram for the BISYNC reception control process. States 0 and 2 are used to handle ordinary data reception, while States 3, 4, and 5 are used to handle transparent data reception. State 1 is

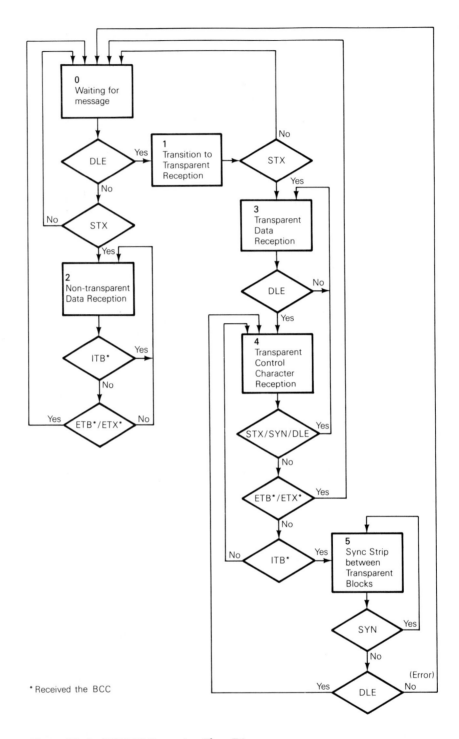

* Received the BCC

Figure 17–4   BISYNC Reception Flow Diagram

a transition state between ordinary data reception and transparent data reception.

While waiting for a packet, the receiver is in State 0. When the first control character arrives, the response of the receiver depends on which control character is received:

*ENQ.* Generate an interrupt to the computer to record the ENQ and to set up a buffer to store the expected data. Remain in State 0.

*DLE.* Go to State 1 (transition to transparent reception).

*STX or SOH.* Go to State 2 (ordinary data reception).

*EOT.* Generate an interrupt to the computer to announce the end of packet. Remain in State 0.

*NAK.* Generate an interrupt to the computer to inform the program that it will have to retransmit. Remain in State 0.

The most interesting reception case is transparent data reception. As indicated in the above list, the first step toward transparent data reception is the receipt of DLE, placing the receiver into State 1. When a receiver is in State 1, the next character, in other than error situations, is STX. The receipt of STX after DLE completes the entry into State 3, the transparent data reception state.

At this point it would be useful to compare State 2, ordinary data reception, with State 3, transparent data reception. In State 2, the following characters are significant: ITB, ETB, ETX, ENQ, and SYN. Reception of any of the first three is an indication to the receiver that it should notify the computer program by means of an interrupt and that it should expect the block check next. Reception of ENQ is an error condition, and reception of SYN is ignored. In State 3, however, all characters except DLE are received, stored, and included in the block check, as State 3 is transparent data reception. If a DLE is received, it is discarded, but it accomplishes its purpose: changing the receiver to State 4.

Control characters received in the transparent data stream are processed in State 4. The usual control characters are the block delimiters: ITB, ETB, or ETX. These are included in the block check, which is received immediately after them. The reception of ITB causes a transition to State 5, whereas ETB or ETX indicates the end of the transparent text block and sends the receiver back to the initial state, State 0. The other interesting characters to be received while in this state are DLE and SYN. A received

DLE is stored and included in the block check and returns the reception to State 3. This is how BISYNC solves the problem of sending a data pattern equivalent to DLE while in transparent mode. A DLE is "stuffed" in front of the data pattern to alert the receiver that a special character is coming, then the special character is checked. Upon finding it to be a bit pattern equivalent to DLE, the receiver treats it as a transparent data entry and returns to transparent data reception. Note that the "stuffed" DLE is not included in the block check, but the DLE-like data pattern is.

A SYN message received while the receiver is in State 4 is completely disregarded, except that the receiver is returned to State 3. Like the DLE–DLE combination, the use of DLE SYN is a BISYNC special case. Earlier, in the discussion of synchronous communications (Chapter 14), it was mentioned that a transmitter that has no data to send must send something. The usual "something" is SYN, as that keeps the line in synchronization and is customarily discarded by the receiver. The problem arises when a transmitter is in the midst of sending transparent data and temporarily runs out of things to send. If the transmitter sends SYN, the receiver has every reason to believe that the bits representing SYN are data. It will, therefore, include them in the stored buffer and in the block check, causing a block check error. The solution to this problem is for the transmitter to send DLE SYN, thus alerting the receiver via DLE that something special is coming. The receiver can then recognize the SYN as SYN, discarding both the DLE and SYN and including neither of them in the block check.

This problem and its solutions are important for two reasons. First, some of the integrated circuits used to implement synchronous communications have a mechanism for automatically idling SYN when the transmitter is not supplied with data at a sufficient rate; they do not provide, in all cases, a mechanism for idling DLE SYN. Second, the idling of SYN, DLE SYN, or anything else is fatal in byte count–oriented protocols (DDCMP) or bit-oriented protocols (SDLC). In short, allowing a transmitter to idle is possible only in a character-oriented protocol such as BISYNC and even then only if one is very careful.

The final reception state to be considered is State 5, which is used after the receipt of DLE ITB during transparent reception. This state is used to permit the syncs received between intermediate text blocks to be discarded without inclusion in the block check. SYN is ignored, and DLE moves the reception back into State 4.

Computer users have developed other character-oriented protocols, but they use different control characters or a subset of the BISYNC rules. The most commonly used subsets are those that leave out the transparent data transmission and reception features.

Readers interested in a more authoritative and complete explanation of BISYNC are referred to the reference listed below.

## Reference

IBM Corporation. "Binary Synchronous Communications—General Information" (GA27-3004 File TP-09).

# 18

## DDCMP and Byte Count-Oriented Protocols

An examination of the Binary Synchronous Communications Protocol (BISYNC) transmission and reception state flow diagrams in Chapter 17 reveals that much of the complication associated with that protocol is a result of the special procedures used to achieve transparent transmission and reception. Even with those procedures, some difficult situations arise. An example is the termination of transparent text containing bit combinations equivalent to DLE and ETX (see Chapter 17 for definitions) and being sent in the following order:

$$\text{DLE ETX DLE ETX DLE ETX} \tag{1}$$

If the receiver is to interpret this data stream correctly, the transmitting unit must send:

$$\text{DLE DLE ETX DLE DLE ETX DLE DLE ETX} \tag{2}$$

Since this is the end of the block, the transmitter also wishes to affix a "real" DLE ETX to indicate the end of the text. Thus, the final data stream, as it appears on the communications facility, will be:

$$\text{DLE DLE ETX DLE DLE ETX DLE DLE ETX DLE ETX} \tag{3}$$

A hardware or software system sending this message must be quite careful, since the rules for sending the final DLE ETX are different from sending the others. No DLE is prefixed to DLE ETX the last time because that DLE ETX is supposed to be interpreted by the receiver as DLE ETX; only the first three are to have DLE stuffed in front of them. The only solution is to treat the last DLE ETX separately. It could be placed in a different packet buffer or sent after an interrupt indicating that the previous transparent text containing the three DLE ETXs had been sent. If the "actual" DLE ETX is going to be kept in a separate buffer and sent only when the block of transparent text has all been sent, how does the transmission software or hardware know when that is? The answer is by keeping track of the character count, referred to frequently as the "byte count" (because many computers store one character per eight-bit "byte").

It is possible to devise a protocol that, by keeping track of byte count, solves the transparency problems without the use of DLE or other control characters. One of the widely used protocols that does this is Digital Equipment Corporation's Digital Data Communication Message Protocol (DDCMP) protocol (see Figure 18–1).

DDCMP is a very general protocol; it can be used on synchronous or asynchronous, half- or full-duplex, serial or parallel, and point-to-point or multipoint systems. Most applications involving protocols are half- or full-duplex transmissions in a serial synchronous mode; that operating environment is emphasized in this description.

As indicated in Figure 18–1, the format is somewhat similar to BISYNC in that the packet is broken into two parts: a header containing control information and a text body. Unlike BISYNC, however, the header is not optional. It is the most important part of the packet, as it contains the packet sequence numbering information and the character count, the two most important features of DDCMP. Because of the importance of the header information, it merits its own Cyclic Redundancy Check (CRC), indicated in the figure as CRC 1. Packets that contain data rather than just control information have a second section that contains any number of eight-bit characters (up to a maximum of 16,363) and a second CRC indicated in the figure as CRC 2.

| SYN | SYN | Class | Count (14 bits) | Flag (2 bits) | Response (8 bits) | Sequence (8 bits) | Address (8 bits) | CRC 1 (16 bits) | Information (up to 16,363 8-bit characters) | CRC 2 (16 bits) |
|-----|-----|-------|-----------------|---------------|-------------------|-------------------|------------------|-----------------|---------------------------------------------|-----------------|

Figure 18–1   DDCMP Message Format

Before the packet format is discussed in greater detail, the packet message sequencing system should be explained, as most of the header information is directly or indirectly related to the sequencing operation. In the DDCMP protocol, any pair of stations that exchange packets with each other number those packets sequentially starting with packet number 1. Each successive data packet is numbered, using the next number in sequence, modulo 256. Thus, a long sequence of packets would be numbered 1,2,3, . . . 254,255,0,1, . . . . The numbering applies to each direction separately. For example, Station A might be sending its packets 6, 7, and 8 to Station B while Station B is sending its packets 5, 6, and 7 to Station A. Thus, in a multipoint configuration where a control station is engaged in two-way communication with ten tributary stations, there are twenty different packet number sequences involved—one for packets from each of the ten tributaries to the control station and one for packets from the control station to each of the ten tributaries.

Whenever a station transmits a packet to another station, it assigns its next sequential packet number to that packet and places that number in the "Sequence" field of the packet header. In addition to maintaining a counter for sequentially numbering the packets it sends, the station also maintains a counter of the packet numbers received from the other station. It updates that counter whenever a packet is received with a packet number exactly one higher than the previously received packet number. The contents of the received packet counter are included in the "Response" field of the packet being sent, to indicate to the other station the highest sequenced packet that has been received.

When a station receives a packet containing an error, that station sends a negative acknowledge (NAK) packet back to the transmitting station. DDCMP does not require an acknowledgment for each packet, as the number in the response field of a normal header or the number in either the special NAK or positive acknowledgment (ACK) packet specifies the sequence number of the last good packet received. For example, if packets 4, 5, and 6 have been received since the last time an acknowledgment was sent and packet 6 is bad, the NAK packet specifies number 5, which says, "Packets 4 and 5 are good and 6 is bad." When DDCMP operates in the full-duplex mode, the line does not have to be turned around; the NAK is simply added to the packets for the transmitter.

When a station receives a packet that is out of sequence, it does not respond to that packet. The transmitting station will detect this from the response field of the packets it receives, and if the "reply wait" timer expires before the transmitting station receives an acknowledgment, the transmitting station will send a "REP" packet. The REP packet contains the sequence number of the most recent unacknowledged packet sent to the distant station. If the receiving station has correctly received the packet referred to in the REP packet (as well as the packets preceding it), it replies to the REP by sending an ACK. If it has not received the packet referred to in sequence, it sends a NAK containing the number of the last packet it received correctly. The transmitting station will then retransmit all data packets after the packet specified in the NAK. The numbering system for DDCMP packets allows up to 255 unacknowledged packets outstanding, a useful feature when working on high-delay circuits such as those using satellites.

With this background, it is now time to explore the various DDCMP packet formats in full detail, as shown in Figure 18–2. The first character of the packet is the class of packet indicator, represented in ASCII with even parity. There are three classes of packets: Data, Control, and Maintenance. These are indicated by class of packet indicators SOH, ENQ, and DLE, respectively. The next two characters of the packet are broken into a 14-bit field and a 2-bit field. The 14-bit field is used in Data and Maintenance packets to indicate the number of characters that will follow the header and form the information part of the packet. In Control packets, the first 8 bits of the 14-bit field are used to designate what type of control packet it is, and the last 6 bits are generally all zeros. The exception is in NAK packets, where these 6 bits are used to specify the reason for the NAK. The 2-bit field contains the quick sync and select flags.

The quick sync flag is used to inform the receiving station that the packet will be followed by sync characters. The receiver may wish to set its associated synchronous receiver hardware into "sync search" mode and "strip sync" mode. This will reestablish synchronization, and syncs will be discarded until the first character of the next packet arrives. The purpose of this is to permit the receiving station to engage any hardware sync-stripping logic it might have and prevent it from filling its buffers with sync characters. The select flag is used to indicate that this is the last

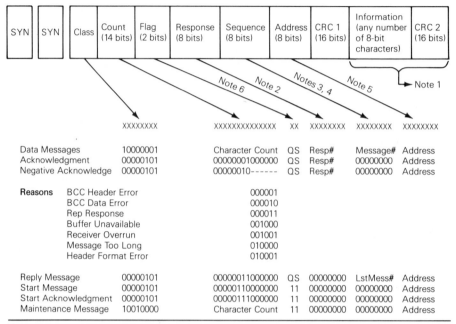

| Data Messages | 10000001 | | Character Count | QS | Resp# | Message# | Address |
| Acknowledgment | 00000101 | | 00000001000000 | QS | Resp# | 00000000 | Address |
| Negative Acknowledge | 00000101 | | 00000010------ | QS | Resp# | 00000000 | Address |

| **Reasons** | BCC Header Error | | 000001 |
| | BCC Data Error | | 000010 |
| | Rep Response | | 000011 |
| | Buffer Unavailable | | 001000 |
| | Receiver Overrun | | 001001 |
| | Message Too Long | | 010000 |
| | Header Format Error | | 010001 |

| Reply Message | 00000101 | | 00000011000000 | QS | 00000000 | LstMess# | Address |
| Start Message | 00000101 | | 00000110000000 | 11 | 00000000 | 00000000 | Address |
| Start Acknowledgment | 00000101 | | 00000111000000 | 11 | 00000000 | 00000000 | Address |
| Maintenance Message | 10010000 | | Character Count | 11 | 00000000 | 00000000 | Address |

**Notes**

1. Only the Data Message and the Maintenance Message have character counts, so only these messages have the information and CRC 2 fields shown in the message format diagram above.

2. "Resp#" refers to Response Number. This is the number of the last message received correctly. When used in a negative acknowledge message, it is assumed that the next higher numbered message was not received, was received with errors, or was unaccepted for some other reason. See "Reasons."

3. "Message #" is the sequentially assigned number of this message. Numbers are assigned by the transmitting station modulo 256; i.e., message 000 follows 255.

4. "LstMess#" is the number of the last message transmitted by the station. See the text discussion of REP messages.

5. "Address" is the address of the tributary station in multipoint systems and is used in messages both to and from the tributary. In point to point operation, a station sends the address "1" but ignores the address field on reception.

6. "Q" and "S" refer to the quick sync flag bit and the select bit. See text.

Figure 18–2   DDCMP Message Format in Detail

packet the transmitting station is going to transmit and that the addressed station is now permitted to begin transmitting. This flag is useful in half-duplex or multipoint configurations, where transmitters need to get turned on and off.

The response field contains the number of the last packet correctly received. This field is used in Data packets and in the positive and negative acknowledge types of Control packet. Its function should be evident from the preceding discussion of sequence control.

The sequence field is used in Data packets and in the REP type of Control packet. In a Data packet, it contains the sequence number of the packet as assigned by the transmitting station. In a REP packet, it is used as part of the question: "Have you received all packets up through packet number (specify) correctly?"

The address field is used to identify the tributary station in multipoint systems and is used in packets both to and from the tributary. In point-to-point operation, a station sends address "1" but ignores the address field on reception.

In addition to the positive and negative acknowledgment and REP types of Control packet, there are also start and start acknowledge Control packets. These are used to place the station that receives them in a known state. In particular, they initialize the packet counters, timers, and other counters. The start acknowledge packet indicates that this has been accomplished.

Figure 18–2 also shows the Maintenance packet. This is typically a bootstrap packet containing load programs in the information field. A complete treatment of bootstrap packets and start-up procedures is beyond the scope of this book.

DDCMP is able to do the following: run on full- or half-duplex transmission facilities; run on many existing hardware interfaces; support point-to-point and multipoint lines; run on synchronous, asynchronous, or parallel systems; and provide multiple acknowledgments per ACK packet (up to 255 packets are acknowledged by one ACK packet).

DDCMP has two drawbacks. First, the header is relatively short, and the higher level operating system must therefore have a buffer of the appropriate size ready on relatively short notice. Second, the transmitting station must not idle a sync in the middle of a packet, as that will cause the character count to come out wrong and produce a bad CRC check. The first problem is inherent in every protocol. Most get around it by agreeing that packets will not be more than *n* characters long; this can also be done in a DDCMP system. The second problem is shared by DDCMP, Transparent Mode BI-SYNC, and Synchronous Data Link Control (SDLC). In each case, the error detection and recovery systems permit recovery, and the only consequence is an apparently higher line error rate than really exists. An error logging system that checks the Data Not Available flags in the synchronous transmitter units is able to detect the difference between this type of failure and a line error.

The principal advantages of DDCMP include simplicity (especially for transmissions requiring data transparency) and generality (usable on synchronous or asynchronous, half- or full-duplex, serial or parallel, and point-to-point or multipoint systems). The attributes of simplicity and generality are especially important in personal computers, where a simpler protocol has been developed for file transfers between diverse brands of computer. This protocol, developed at Columbia University, is called "Kermit," and is shown in Figure 18–3.

The Kermit format is similar to DDCMP in that the packet is broken into two parts: a header containing control information and a text body. Like DDCMP, the header contains the packet sequence numbering information and the character count. Unlike DDCMP, however, the header does not have its own block check but is protected by the block check that covers the entire packet (exclusive of the MARK and the block check itself).

Before the packet format is discussed in greater detail, the packet sequencing system should be explained, as it differs somewhat from that of DDCMP. In the Kermit protocol, any pair of stations that exchange packets with each other number those packets sequentially starting with packet number 1. Each successive data packet is numbered using the next number in sequence, modulo 64. Thus, a long sequence of packets would be numbered 1,2,3, . . . 62,63,0,1, . . . . The numbering applies to each direction separately. For example, Station A might be sending its packets 6, 7, and 8 to Station B while Station B is sending its packets 5, 6, and 7 to Station A.

Whenever a station transmits a packet to another station, it assigns its next sequential packet number to that packet and places that number in the "Sequence" field of the packet header. If it receives an ACK, it sends a new packet with a sequence number one higher than the last packet. If it receives a NAK, or no response (as determined by a time-out), it retransmits the previous packet. When a station receives a correct packet, it responds by transmitting an ACK. When a station receives a packet containing an error, that station sends a NAK packet back to the transmitting station. As with any data link level protocol, there is some danger that the ACK may get lost on its way back to the transmitting station. When this happens in Kermit, the transmitting station "times-out" awaiting the ACK, then re-

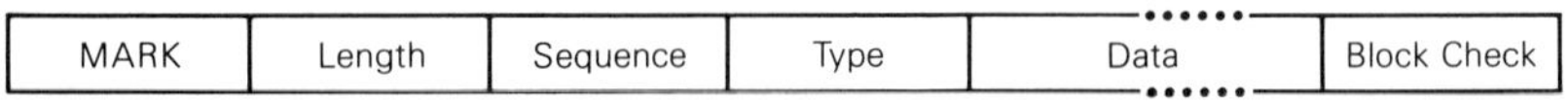

| MARK | Length | Sequence | Type | Data | Block Check |
|------|--------|----------|------|------|-------------|

**Note**  The packet shown is typically followed by an end of line delimiter, such as carriage return. This is not a protocol requirement, but is frequently an implementation requirement.

Figure 18–3   Kermit Packet Format

transmits the packet. The receiving station recognizes that the sequence number is the same, sends back an ACK (if the block check is correct), and discards the packet, since it has a previously received good copy already stored. Transmission and reception then resume normally. Thus, unlike DDCMP, Kermit requires an acknowledgment for each packet, as there is no equivalent to the DDCMP "response" field in a Kermit packet.

With this background, let's explore the Kermit packet format in greater detail. As shown in Figure 18–3, the first character of the packet is the "MARK," by convention a Control A (SOH, ASCII 001), although it may be redefined. The second character is the length field. The length field contains a count of the number of characters that follow this field, up to and including the block check. Since the Kermit protocol requires that all header characters be printing characters, the length is expressed in "excess-32" notation (excess-40 if you prefer octal). Therefore, the shortest possible packet, which is three characters (Sequence, Type, and Block Check), has a length field entry of # (ASCII 43). The longest possible packet, which is 94 (136 octal) characters (Sequence, Type, 91 data characters, and Block Check), has a length indicator of _ (ASCII 176). The third character is the sequence field, discussed in the previous paragraph. As with the length field, the sequence field is modified to be in the range of printable characters. The 0 value is translated to SPACE (ASCII 40) and the 63 value (77 octal) is translated to (ASCII 137). The fourth character is the type field and is encoded as shown in Table 18–1.

The data field comes next and contains the text of the packet, if the packet is of a type that carries text. The block check character follows the data field and is an arithmetic sum of all the characters between, but not including, the MARK and the block check itself. Bit 7 of the control and data characters is not included in the calculations if it is being used for parity, but it is included if it is being used for data. As with the other control fields, some manipulation is necessary to make the result a printing

Table 18–1   Basic Kermit Packet Types

| | |
|---|---|
| S | Send Initiation |
| F | File Header |
| D | File Data |
| Z | End of File |
| B | Break Transmission |
| Y | Positive Acknowledgment (ACK) |
| N | Negative Acknowledgment (NAK) |
| E | Fatal Error |

character. The manipulation takes the following form: Bits 6 and 7 of the final value are added to the quantity formed by bits 0–5, and the result is expressed in "excess-32."

Additional information about Kermit, including packet types beyond those listed in Table 18–1 and various protocol options may be found in da Cruz (1987).

## References

1. Digital Equipment Corporation. "Digital Data Communication Message Protocol."
2. da Cruz, Frank. *Kermit, A File Transfer Protocol.* Bedford, MA: Digital Press, 1987.

# *19*

## SDLC and Bit-Oriented Protocols

It is not the intent of this chapter to be a definite source on Synchronous Data Link Control (SDLC), but rather to describe enough of its operation for the reader to get the general idea and to be able to more readily understand more detailed references on the subject.

First, a few definitions are needed. Any data communication link involves at least two participating stations. The station that is responsible for the data link and issues the commands to control that link is called the "primary station." The other station is a "secondary station." It is not necessary that all information transfers be initiated by a primary station. Using SDLC procedures, a secondary station may be the initiator.

The basic format for SDLC is a "frame," shown in Figure 19-1. The information field is not restricted in format or content and can be of any reasonable length (including zero). The maximum length is that which can be expected to arrive at the receiver error-free most of the time and is hence a function of communications channel error rate.

The two flags that delineate the SDLC frame serve as reference points for the position of the address and control fields and initiate the transmission error checking. The ending flag indicates to the receiving station that the 16 bits just received constitute the Frame Check. The ending frame could be followed by another frame, another flag, or an idle. Note that this means that when two frames follow each other, the intervening flag is simultaneously the ending flag of the first frame and the beginning flag of the next frame. Since the SDLC protocol does not use characters of defined length but instead works on a bit-by-bit basis, the 01111110 flag may be recognized at any time.

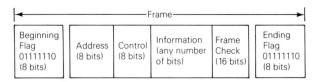

Figure 19–1   Basic SDLC Frame

So that the flag might not be sent accidentally, SDLC procedures require that a binary 0 be inserted by the transmitter after any succession of five continuous ones. The receiver then removes a zero that follows a received succession of five ones. Inserted and removed zeros are not included in the transmission error check.

The address field is eight bits long and designates the number of the secondary station to which the command from the primary station is being sent. The control field is an additional eight bits and can have three formats: "information transfer format," "supervisory format," and "nonsequenced format." The only thing the three formats have in common is the Poll/ Final (P/F) bit. A frame with the P bit set is sent from a primary station to a secondary station to authorize transmission, and a frame with the F bit set is sent by the secondary station in response to the poll. Typically, the primary station will send a number of frames to a particular secondary station, each frame having the P/F bit set at 0, until the primary station is finished and ready for the secondary station to respond. At this time, the primary station will send a frame having the P/F bit set at 1. The secondary station will recognize that the primary station desires a response and will reply, perhaps with a number of frames, each having the P/F bit at 0. When the secondary station is completing its response to the "poll," it will send a "final" frame, which has the P/F bit set at 1.

The three control formats are summarized in Table 19–1. The information format is used for ordinary data transmission and is the only one of the three formats that uses frame sequence numbering. Each frame transmitted in this format is numbered so that the receiving station can tell whether any are missing; when retransmission is required, the receiving station can tell the transmitting station which frame to start with in the retransmission. A station that transmits sequenced frames counts and numbers each frame. This count is known as "Ns." A station receiving sequenced frames counts each error-free sequenced frame it receives; the receiver count is called "Nr." The Nr count advances when a frame is checked and found to be error-free; Nr thus becomes the count of the "next expected" frame and should agree with the next incoming Ns count. Returning to the format shown in Table 19–1, the initial "0" bit indicates that this control field is in information format, the three Ns bits say "This is the message number I am sending," the P/F bit is set if the station is concluding its poll or its response to a poll, and the three Nr bits say "This is the message number I am expecting next."

The supervisory format is used in conjunction with the information format to initiate and control information transfer in the information format. The first two bits sent, 1 and 0, designate that this control field is in supervisory format. The next two bits indicate which command this is: Receive Ready (RR), Receive Not Ready (RNR), or Reject (REJ). An RR can be sent by either a primary or a secondary station and indicates that all sequenced frames up through Nr − 1 have been received correctly, and that the originating station is ready to receive more. RNR also can be sent by

Table 19–1   SDLC Control Field Formats

| Format | | Bits | | | Acronym |
|--------|-----|-----|-----|-----|---------|
| Information | Nr | P/F | Ns | 0 | I |
| Supervisory | Nr | P/F | 00 | 01 | RR |
| | Nr | P/F | 01 | 01 | RNR |
| | Nr | P/F | 10 | 01 | REJ |
| Nonsequenced | 000 | P/F | 00 | 11 | NSI |
| | 000 | F | 01 | 11 | RQI |
| | 000 | P | 01 | 11 | SIM |
| | 100 | P | 00 | 11 | SNRM |
| | 000 | F | 11 | 11 | ROL |
| | 010 | P | 00 | 11 | DISC |
| | 011 | F | 00 | 11 | NSA |
| | 100 | F | 01 | 11 | CMDR |
| | 001 | 1 | 00 | 11 | ORP |

Sent Last ———

Sent First ———

either a primary or a secondary station and acknowledges messages up through Nr − 1. Unlike RR, however, RNR indicates a temporary busy condition in which no additional frames that require buffer space can be accepted. REJ is a command/response that may be transmitted to request transmission or retransmission. It acknowledges successful receipt of frames up through Nr − 1 and requests Nr and following frames.

The nonsequenced format is used for setting operating modes, initializing stations, and so on. As the name implies, nonsequenced communications are not sequence checked and do not use the Nr and Ns system. The first two bits sent, 11, indicate a nonsequenced format, the P/F bit has its usual meaning, and the remaining five bits in the control field are used for encoding the various commands and responses.

The commands and responses encoded in the nonsequenced format control field are listed below.

*NSI (Nonsequenced Information).* This indicates that the information that follows in the variable length information field is being sent separately from any sequenced message currently in progress.

*RQI (Request for Initialization).* This is transmitted by a secondary station when it wants the primary station to send a SIM command. If the primary station sends something other than SIM, the secondary station sends another RQI.

*SIM (Set Initialization Mode).* This command initiates system-specified procedures at the receiving secondary station for the purposes of initializing. Nr and Ns counts are set to zero at both the primary and secondary stations. The expected response to SIM is NSA.

*SNRM (Set Normal Response Mode).* This command subordinates the receiving secondary station to the transmitting primary station, and the secondary station is not expected to initiate any transmissions unless requested to do so by the primary station. The Nr and Ns counts at both the primary and the secondary stations are reset to zero. The secondary station remains in this mode until it receives a DISC or SIM command. The expected response to SNRM is NSA.

*ROL (Request On-Line).* This is transmitted by a secondary station to indicate that it is disconnected.

*DISC (Disconnect).* This command places the secondary station effectively off-line. That station cannot receive or transmit information frames and remains disconnected until it receives a SNRM or SIM command. The expected response to DISC is NSA.

*NSA (Nonsequenced Acknowledgment).* This is the affirmative response to SNRM, DISC, or SIM.

*CMDR (Command Reject).* This is the response transmitted by a secondary station in normal response mode when it receives an invalid command. A frame with

CMDR in the control field is followed by an information field arranged in a fixed format that reports the station's present Ns, the station's present Nr, and four bits that indicate 1) an invalid or nonimplemented command, 2) an information field associated with a command that is not supposed to have one, 3) an information field that was so long it caused buffer overrun, or 4) the Nr received from the primary station does not make sense, given the Ns that was sent to it.

*OPR (Optional Response Poll)*. This command invites transmission from the addressed secondary stations.

While SDLC is simpler in most aspects than previously discussed protocols, the block check calculations are a good deal more complex. The first difference is that the transmitting station begins with a "remainder value" of all ones rather than the customary all zeros. The binary value of the transmission is premultiplied by $X^{16}$ and divided by the generating polynomial $X^{16} + X^{12} + X^5 + 1$. The quotient digits are ignored, and the transmitter sends the complement of the resulting remainder value, with the high-order bit first.

One other feature that should be discussed is the procedure for prematurely terminating a data link. This is called "abort" and is accomplished by the transmitting station's sending eight consecutive "1" bits. The abort pattern may be followed by a minimum of seven additional ones to idle the data link, or it may be followed by a flag. The purpose of a flag following an abort is to clear the Cyclic Redundancy Check (CRC) function at the receiver.

The preceding has been a rather condensed description of SDLC, and the reader is advised to read the references listed below for further information about SDLC and High (level) Data Link Control (HDLC), a similar protocol.

## References

1. IBM Corporation. "Synchronous Data Link Control—General Information" (GA27-3093 File GENL-09).
2. International Organization for Standardization (ISO). "High Level Data Link Control (HDLC)" (DIS 3309.2 and DIS 4335).

# 20

# A Single Line USRT
# for Bit-Oriented Protocols

The single line Universal Synchronous Receiver Transmitter (USRT) discussed in Chapter 15 has all the receiver flag, receiver buffer, transmitter
flag, and transmitter buffer features of a typical data communication interface. Added to those features were modem control and status signals that
allowed the USRT to play the role of "Data Terminal Equipment" (DTE)
in data transmission involving both private line and switched network
modems. A block diagram of a single line USRT is shown in Figure 20–1.

The simplest possible USRT has program addressable registers, such as
those shown in Figure 20–2. Addition of the modem control and status
features would expand the bit assignments to those illustrated in Figure
20–3. In addition to the modem control bits located in the receiver status
register, a parameter status register has been added to permit the program
to load a sync character into the USRT. This sync character is used by the
receiver logic to determine which eight-bit groups constitute characters and
is used by the transmitter as an idling character. The parameter status
register also provides bits that permit the USRT to operate in other than
eight bit per character mode by selecting various settings for the Word
Select (bits 10 and 11). Parity operation and parity sense are selected by
various settings of bits 08 and 09. Finally, a maintenance loopback has been
added, and a Data Not Available flag indicates that the transmitter idled a
character. A Transmitter Active bit (XMIT ACT) also has been added. A
more complete review of the bit assignments for the USRT shown in Figure
20–3 may be obtained by reading Chapter 15.

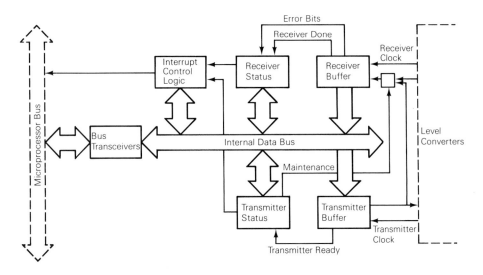

Figure 20–1　Block Diagram of a Single Line USRT

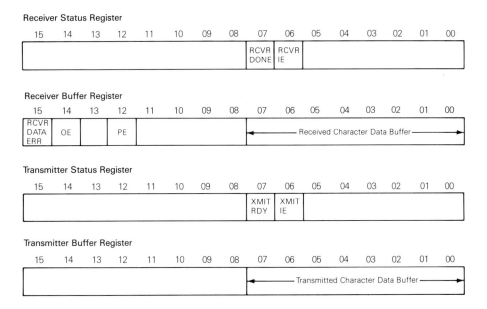

Figure 20–2　Program Addressable Registers—Simple USRT

A USRT designed to handle bit-oriented protocols such as Synchronous Data Link Control (SDLC) and High (level) Data Link Control (HDLC) must have at least the bit assignments shown in Figure 20–3, except that Strip Sync, Search Sync, and, to some degree, the entire parameter status register are unnecessary. In the USRT to be discussed, Strip Sync and Search Sync will be retained, however, so that the chip may handle character-oriented and byte count-oriented protocols. The parameter status register will have a bit added (bit 15) that will determine whether the bits function as shown in Figure 20–3 or whether some of them are redefined for bit-oriented protocol use. With these changes, the resultant USRT will be able to handle all three types of protocol discussed in the past three chapters. The new bit assignments and those old bit assignments that undergo a change of function are shown underlined in Figure 20–4.

The first bit to be considered is the Cyclic Redundancy Check (CRC) Error bit, which is bit 12 in the receiver buffer register. This is the bit

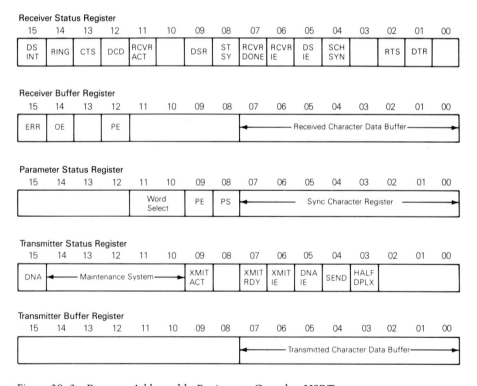

Figure 20–3   Program Addressable Registers—Complex USRT

position occupied in Figure 20–3 by the Parity Error bit. When a flag character arrives in SDLC, the receiver is supposed to check the accumulated CRC to see whether it is 0001110100001111 ($X^{15}$ through $X^0$, respectively), indicating an error-free message. This requires that the receiver hardware accumulate a CRC calculation on the incoming data and be prepared to present it to a number comparison circuit when the message is complete. If the CRC does not equal 0001110100001111 at that time, the CRC Error bit in the receiver buffer register is set, along with an End of Message (EOM) indication in bit 09 when the last data character of the message is presented. When the USRT is being operated in this fashion, the setting of CRC Error also causes Receiver Data Error, bit 15, to be set The EOM, CRC Error, and Receiver Error flags remain set until the program reads the receiver buffer register to obtain the final data character.

Since CRC calculation logic has been installed in the USRT for the benefit of the SDLC protocol, a slight modification in bit definition can be

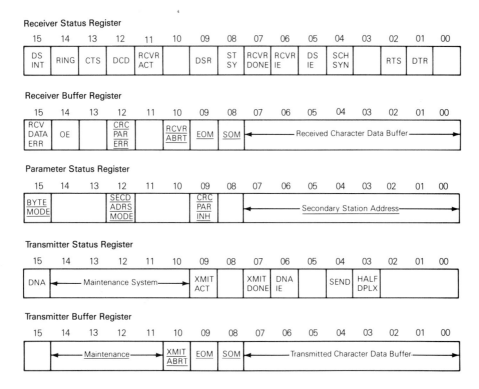

Figure 20–4   Program Addressable Registers—Bit Oriented Protocol USRT

made to permit use of the CRC logic with simplified versions of Binary Synchronous Communications Protocol (BISYNC) and with byte count protocols such as Digital Data Communication Message Protocol (DDCMP). This is done by redefining the function of the CRC Error bit when using protocols other than SDLC or HDLC. Under the new definition, when the Byte Mode bit is set, the CRC Error bit is set whenever the accumulated CRC is equal to zero and the state of the CRC Error bit no longer affects the Receiver Data Error bit. When the receiver handling program wishes to check the received CRC, on the basis that either a special character has been received or the byte count has reached zero, it checks the CRC Error bit when the last character of the message (which has been stored in the USRT while the CRC check takes place) is presented in the receiver buffer register. If the arrival of CRC has caused the accumulated CRC to reach zero, the preceding message was error-free. The sense of this bit may seem confusing in the "new definition," as the SET state is the "everything is OK" state. This sense was chosen so that in SDLC and other protocols characters received at times other than at the end of the message would have this bit and all other error bits clear. Only when the last portion of the message is being processed does this bit assume the "1" state. (There is some chance that the accumulated CRC will reach zero during a message, but this is very unlikely.)

It should be noted that, even with the definition flexibility of the CRC Error bit, this USRT cannot perform CRC checking of messages in BISYNC. The rules regulating which characters are included in the CRC and which are not are so complicated that a more sophisticated USRT is required.

Bits 08, 09, and 10 of the receiver buffer register are strictly associated with SDLC/HDLC protocols. The setting of the Received Abort (RCV ABRT) bit indicates that an abort sequence (eight or more consecutive ones) has been received. Receiver Data Error also will set. The EOM bit indicates that a flag character has arrived, terminating the present message. It is then time for the program to look at the CRC Error bit. The Start of Message (SOM) bit indicates that the character presented in bits 00–07 is the first character of an SDLC/HDLC message. Of the three bits just described, SOM and EOM are the only ones accompanied by valid data in bits 00–07.

Note that bits 08, 09, and 10 of the transmitter buffer register in Figure 20–4 are also labeled Start of Message, End of Message, and Abort. When the program sets the Abort bit (as well as the Send bit described below) the transmitter section of the USRT sends an abort character (eight ones) as soon as it has finished transmitting any character being serialized. When the program sets EOM (and Send), the transmitter completes transmission of any characters it has, sends the accumulated CRC, and sends flag characters until the next message is initiated. If the transmitter is not active, the program initiates messages by setting SOM and clearing EOM. If the transmitter is active (this includes sending flags), the next message is initiated by clearing EOM and loading data into the transmitter buffer register. The transmitter buffer register, as illustrated in Figure 20–4, also contains a loopback maintenance bit.

The parameter status register is next in line when discussion of the registers in top to bottom order is resumed. Bit 15 of this register is called "Byte Mode," and when set it conditions the USRT logic to operate with character-oriented and byte count-oriented protocols. When this bit is clear, the USRT is arranged to operate with bit-oriented protocols. This bit affects the definition of the CRC Error bit, as previously discussed, and also influences the operation of the SOM bit in the transmitter buffer register. When the Byte Mode bit is clear, the SOM bit operates as indicated above. When the Byte Mode bit is set, the SOM bit is used to facilitate the transmission of sync characters at the beginning of the message without including them in the transmitter CRC. This is done because the receiving station misses some syncs, uses some to synchronize, and "receives" some number less than was transmitted. Thus, the syncs at the beginning of a message are never included in CRC calculations at either the transmitting station or the receiving station. It is relatively easy for the receiving station logic to recognize the initial sequence of syncs at the beginning of a message and keep them out of the CRC calculation. Some method must be found, however, to ensure that the transmitting apparatus also keeps the syncs out of its CRC calculation. This can be accomplished by using the Byte Mode bit, along with the rule that a sync loaded into the transmitter buffer at the same time SOM is loaded is not included in the CRC. Further, as long as SOM remains set and a sync remains in the transmit buffer, syncs will continue to be transmitted. As soon as the program wishes to send data, it loads the transmit buffer with that data and simultaneously loads a zero into the SOM bit.

The Secondary Address Mode Selection bit (parameter status register bit 12) allows the USRT to function as a secondary station in multipoint systems. When this bit is cleared, the USRT operates as a primary station. All data subsequent to the last received flag character is presented to the program until the termination flag is received. Secondary station operation is in effect when this bit is set. In this mode, only messages that are prefixed with the correct secondary station address are presented to the program. The Secondary Station Address must have been loaded into the 00–07 bits of this register before the Receiver Enable bit was set by the program. The actual address character is not presented to the program in the secondary mode. If extended secondary addresses are used (i.e., 16 bit), the first eight bits of the address can be detected by the hardware. The software would have to confirm the second eight bits of the address.

The ninth bit of the parameter status register is the CRC Inhibit bit. When that bit is set, transmission of the CRC is inhibited, and the CRC error-detection logic is not operated during reception.

The function of bits 00–07 has already been discussed in conjunction with Secondary Mode operation. When these bits are not used for that purpose and the Byte Mode bit is set, these bits are used to store the sync character that will be used to achieve line synchronization.

# *21*

## Multiplexer Enhancements

An asynchronous multiplexer with Direct Memory Access (DMA) and modem control is discussed in Chapter 12. The registers and bit arrangements therein are reviewed in Figure 21–1.

Since modern multiplexers have one or more microprocessors located within them, some interesting enhancements are possible. One of these enhancements is a self-test diagnostic that checks the operational capabilities of the multiplexer. The self-test is invoked when power is applied to the multiplexer or when the Reset bit is set by the program. Bit 05 of the control and status register is the Reset bit, which remains set during the self-test to indicate that the self-test is in progress. At the conclusion of the self-test, bit 13 (Diagnostic Fail) will indicate whether an error occurred during the test. Results of the diagnostic can be reported via the received character First In/First Out (FIFO) buffer. If desired, the self-test can be skipped; this is accomplished by setting bit 04 (Skip) at the same time as setting bit 05. Figure 21–2 shows a control and status register with these new bits added.

Another enhancement would be a FIFO timer. As indicated in Chapter 12, FIFOs have the desirable property that during periods of high activity, when the processor is delayed in responding to an interrupt from the FIFO, there are more characters to be processed when the interrupt service routine finally gets around to emptying the FIFO. Thus, more characters are handled on a single interrupt handling transaction, and system efficiency improves. It is also possible to capitalize on this effect by deliberately delaying the presentation of the interrupt via a FIFO timer ("Receiver Timer"). A possible bit arrangement for a receiver timer register is shown in Figure 21–3.

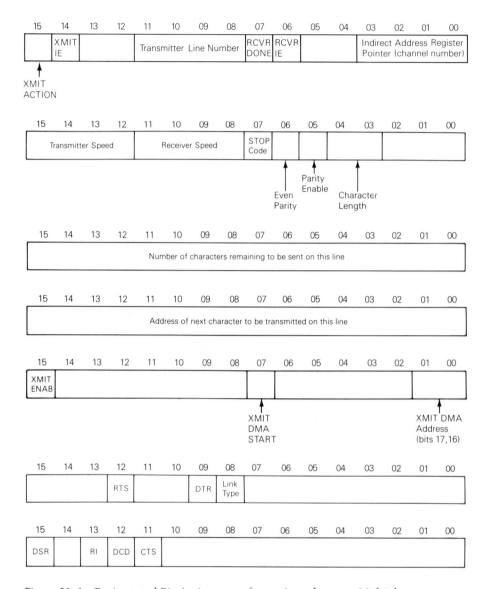

Figure 21–1   Register and Bit Assignments for an Asynchronous Multiplexer

In this register, a setting of 0 causes the interrupt to be generated only when the FIFO is three-quarters full or a modem status change entry is made—i.e., the time-out (for reception of a few characters) is theoretically infinite. A setting of 1 causes an immediate interrupt whenever anything is entered into the FIFO. Settings of 2 through 255 delay interrupts for 2 through 255 milliseconds, respectively.

A more complex enhancement is the automatic generation of, and automatic response to, flow control characters (XON and XOFF). Figure 21–4 shows a line control register with bit 01 assigned as "I Auto." When I Auto is set, the multiplexer automatically sends an XOFF character when a character arrives that will cause the FIFO to be more than three-quarters full. If characters continue to arrive after that, an XOFF will be sent in response to every other arriving character. When the FIFO has been drained to the one-half full mark, an XON will be sent (if an XOFF was previously sent on this line). The program may also send an XOFF by setting bit 05 (Force XOFF); if this bit is set, the FIFO reaching a state of half full or less will not cause an XON to be sent. The program also may send XOFFs and XONs in the data stream, but doing so with I Auto and/or Force XOFF set produces unpredictable results.

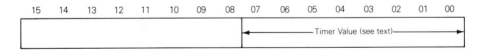

Figure 21–2   BASE Control and Status Register with Diagnostic Bits Added

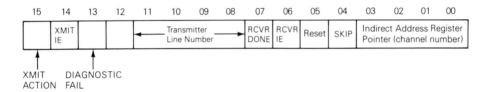

Figure 21–3   Receiver Timer Register

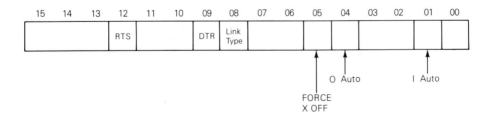

Figure 21–4   Line Control Register with XON/XOFF Control Bits Added

Figure 21–4 also shows a bit called O Auto (bit 04). When this bit is set, the multiplexer will check the incoming data stream for XON and XOFF characters and will control its transmitted character stream appropriately.

A final enhancement is the addition of FIFO-buffered transmission. Despite its performance benefits, DMA transmission does have some drawbacks. If the average transmission length is small and the program complexity of setting up DMA transmissions is large, or if the computer system contains bus hardware that poses difficulties to DMA transmission, transmission using interrupts may be preferable. The same virtues of a receiver FIFO appear in a transmitter FIFO: ability to delay in responding to an interrupt and less interrupt overhead per character handled. Unlike a receiver FIFO, however, which can be shared by many lines (as long as each entry includes a line number), transmitter FIFOs must be supplied on a per-line basis. The reason for this is that each line may operate at a different speed, and a fast line would have to wait for slower lines to withdraw their characters if the FIFO were shared. Fortunately, microprocessors are excellent at keeping track of multiple read and write pointers in a Random Access Memory (RAM), and various sections of RAM can be used as FIFOs for various lines.

As with most nifty features, there are some problems. First, if the program wishes to send an XOFF, there may be considerable delay, as there could be several dozen characters in the transmit FIFO. For this reason, a multiplexer that offers FIFO-buffered transmitters should offer automatic XOFF transmission and the Force XOFF bit (discussed above), as these permit the microprocessor within the multiplexer to insert an XOFF at the output of the FIFO. A second problem concerns suspension or aborting of transmission. With a DMA transfer, the process can be stopped and the program can decide whether to resume from the same spot or switch to another buffer. For a FIFO-buffered transmission, it is much more difficult to determine which characters have been sent and which have not. Some multiplexers clear the transmit FIFO if transmission on a line is aborted.

The previous discussion has mentioned FIFO-buffered reception, FIFO-buffered transmission, and DMA transmission. No mention has been made of DMA reception. For the reception of asynchronous characters (for example, from a terminal keyboard), a multiplexer is generally required to recognize some special characters, especially when an editor is being used. This could be handled by a microprocessor-based character detection system that looks for special characters before depositing the typed characters into memory on a DMA basis. In synchronous communications, use of DMA reception is a bit more complicated, but the rewards are very attractive.

Most synchronous communications use some type of error detection. As described in Chapter 13, error detection typically involves the calculation of a Cyclic Redundancy Check (CRC) by the transmitting station while it is transmitting the characters and the sending of that check as a two-character group following the last character of the message. The receiving station performs a similar calculation, and the reception of the check character(s) should yield a specific result in the receiver calculation circuitry. This all seems simple enough, but the various protocols in use have special rules about which characters in a message are to be included in the block check calculation and which are not. Further, it is necessary for both the receiver and the transmitter to know where the messages start and end so that they can perform the check character calculations correctly. In addition to these problems with the block check calculations, special characters or sequences of characters often are required to generate interrupts.

While it is rarely done, one method of accomplishing "intelligent" DMA for asynchronous or synchronous reception is to use an associative memory in which are stored various special characters or two-character sequences. The incoming data stream is then compared with the contents of the associative memory; when a match is found, block check character calculation begins, ends, or skips these characters, as appropriate. Alternatively, the finding of a match might generate an interrupt. A similar system could be used for transmission.

A related method of accomplishing intelligent DMA is to use the received characters as numerical offsets in a memory table. Such a table contains entries that indicate what to do when that character is received, such as whether to include it in the block check or whether to generate an interrupt. This method is especially suited to detecting sequences of special characters. The received eight-bit characters can have "mode bits" appended to stretch them into nine-, ten-, or eleven-bit characters, thus permitting indexing into memory tables with different entries for the same character; the different entries are used depending on what sequence of characters preceded the character in question. The basic operation of this kind of multiplexer is shown in Figure 21–5.

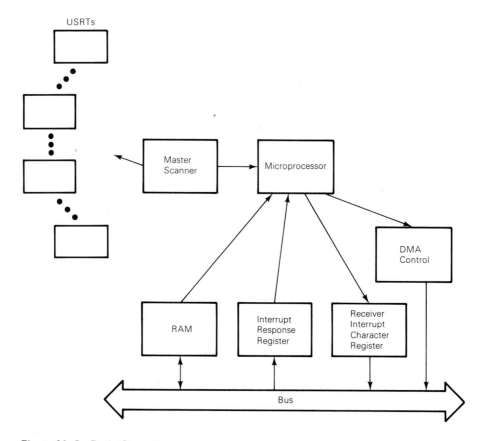

Figure 21–5  Basic Operation

In sixteen USRTs, receivers assemble characters received from serial communications lines and assert a flag as each character is received. The USRT transmitters disassemble characters and transmit them on serial communications lines and assert a flag whenever they can accept another character for transmission. A hardware scanner, separate from the microprocessor, sequentially checks the USRTs for each line to see whether a flag exists.

The microprocessor handles all characters received or transmitted. The microprocessor system includes a 128-character FIFO buffer. While most characters received will propagate through this buffer and be directly transferred to memory by means of a DMA transfer, the occasion may arise when the attention of the computer program is required before this is done.

To prevent the receivers from experiencing data overruns during the interval that the multiplexer is awaiting program attention, the microprocessor will continue to load the received characters into the FIFO buffer. The action of the microprocessor in withdrawing characters from the buffer will cease, however, until the computer program responds to the interrupt caused by the special character at the bottom of the FIFO buffer. The character that requires program attention is copied into the receiver interrupt character register at the time the interrupt is generated.

The receiver interrupt character register is used by the microprocessor to show the computer program any received character, along with line number and error flags, for which the control logic requires assistance in processing. The interrupt response register is used to instruct the microprocessor how to process the character in the receiver interrupt character register. The DMA control is the hardware that is used to store received characters, obtain characters for transmission, and obtain control bytes that direct the character processing.

The microprocessor RAM contains current addresses and character counts used in the DMA transfers. The initial values are loaded by the computer program, and these values are subsequently updated by the microprocessor. The RAM also contains a line protocol word for each line, which the program uses to specify what action is to be taken when the byte count reaches zero and what type of block check polynomial should be used.

Reception is shown in greater detail in Figure 21–6. Line synchronization and character assembly are accomplished in the USRTs by comparing groups of eight bits received on each line with the preselected sync character. When line synchronization has been achieved, subsequently received characters are placed into a 128-character FIFO buffer. Each line receiver appends the line number (four bits) and any error flags (two bits—Parity Error and Overrun Error) to the character prior to placing it in the receiver storage buffer.

The microprocessor removes characters from the FIFO, along with their line number and error flags. If there is an error flag (as a result of the Parity Error or Overrun Error detected by the receiver), the character is placed in the receiver interrupt character register, and an interrupt request is generated. If there is no error flag, the processing depends on whether a character-oriented protocol (for example, Binary Synchronous Communications Protocol, or BISYNC) or a byte count-oriented protocol (for example, Digital Data Communication Message Protocol, or DDCMP) is being used.

## Character-Oriented Protocol Reception

If there is no error flag, the microprocessor affixes three mode bits at the high-order end of the received eight-bit character. This eleven-bit character is then used as an offset in the control table in memory (either main computer memory or an on-board RAM, depending on multiplexer design) to obtain a control byte that will indicate to the microprocessor what mode is to be used for subsequent reception on this line and any special handling information appropriate to this character (such as whether to generate an interrupt, whether to include the character in a block check computation, or whether to store the character in a message buffer).

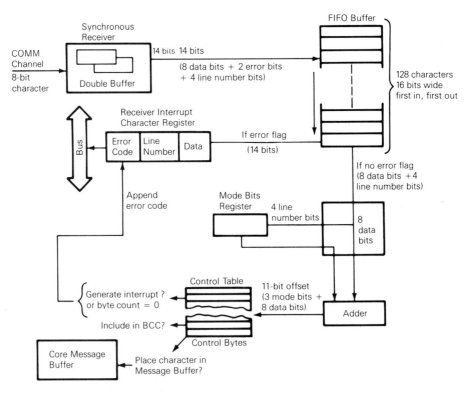

Figure 21–6   Reception

If the generation of an interrupt is indicated, the character and the line number are moved to the receiver interrupt character register, along with an error bit code. The error bit code indicates that this interrupt is being generated because a control table control byte has indicated that this is a special character.

If the control byte indicates that this character should be included in a block check, the microprocessor performs the appropriate calculation (LRC, CRC-16, or CRC-CCITT—see Chapter 13). If the control byte directs that a received character be discarded, the character is discarded. If it indicates that the character be stored, the microprocessor obtains the current address from the RAM and uses that address to store the received character in a message buffer. The microprocessor then increments the current address for that line. In addition, the microprocessor adjusts the byte count for that line. If the storage of the character caused the byte count to reach its final value, the microprocessor checks to see whether special actions associated with byte count run-out have been requested. Having accomplished any actions requested, a copy of the character is moved to the receiver interrupt character register, along with the error bits that indicate that a new receive message buffer must be established for this line. In all cases where a character is moved to the receiver interrupt character register, an interrupt is generated, and the microprocessor ceases to withdraw characters from the receiver FIFO buffer until the program indicates that such withdrawal can proceed.

## Byte Count-Oriented Protocol Reception

If a byte count-oriented protocol is used, the microprocessor skips the control byte process described above, includes all characters in the block check calculation, and stores all characters (except BCC1 and BCC2). Details of character storage are the same as indicated above.

The receiver throughput in the multiplexer is dependent on the number of characters identified in the control bytes as being special (interrupt generating) and the size of the message buffers for received characters. It is intended that the ability of control bytes to accomplish reception mode changes relieves the necessity for received special characters generating an interrupt. When a receiver interrupt is generated, received characters are accumulated in a 128-character FIFO buffer until the interrupt is handled. Assuming arrival of characters at a 19,200 character per second rate, it would take approximately 6.6 milliseconds for a FIFO overflow to occur. Thus, substantial worst-case interrupt latency can be accommodated.

## Character-Oriented Protocol Transmission

Transmission is shown in Figure 21–7. For each line there is a double-buffered serial transmitter. Whenever the transmitter buffer is empty, a flag is raised. The microprocessor scans for transmitter flags, and when it finds one, it checks a "worksheet" to determine whether any special action must be taken (e.g., "send a block check character"). If no special action is required, the microprocessor checks to see whether the transmitter "GO" bit for the line is set. If it is set, the microprocessor uses the transmitter current address register to perform a DMA transfer and obtain—from a message buffer—a character to be transmitted. The processing of this character depends on whether a character-oriented protocol such as BISYNC or a byte count-oriented protocol such as DDCMP is being used.

Before transmitting the character, the microprocessor copies it, adds mode bits to the high-order end, and obtains a transmit control byte from a control table. This byte contains information indicating what new modes are to be used, whether to include the character in the block check, and whether to prefix the transmission of the character with a Data Link Escape (DLE) (performed by the microprocessor).

## Byte Count-Oriented Protocol Transmission

If a byte count-oriented protocol is used, the microprocessor skips the control byte process described above and includes all characters in the block check calculation. The characters are transmitted as described below.

The microprocessor loads the character to be transmitted into the appropriate line transmitter and adjusts the byte count. It then checks the byte count to determine whether it has reached its final value. If it has, a check is made to determine whether any special action has been requested. Having accomplished any actions requested, the microprocessor switches to the other set of tables (i.e., from principal to alternate, or vice versa). If, after the switch in registers, the microprocessor finds the new byte count is zero, it will clear "Transmit Go" in the line state register and idle sync (or MARK).

There are several ways of arranging transmit buffers so that a program can manage them conveniently and a microprocessor in a high-performance

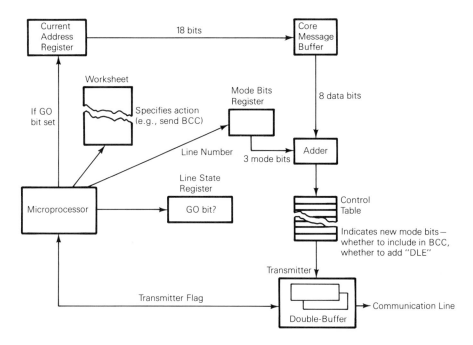

Figure 21–7   Transmission

interface can progress from buffer to buffer without pause. One method is to alternate between two buffers—a "primary buffer" and an "alternate buffer." The program loads message text into each buffer and tells the microprocessor which one to start with. The microprocessor completes transmission from one buffer and proceeds to the other, generating an interrupt. The program now knows that it is safe to replace the text in the first buffer and establish a new byte count for that buffer. When the microprocessor finishes sending from the second buffer, it returns to the first, generating an interrupt. The process continues until there is no more text to send.

Another method of sending successive buffers involves the use of linked lists. In a linked list, blocks of memory are set aside for "linked list headers." A linked list header contains four pieces of information:

1. The address of the next header.

2. The address of the message text buffer.

3. The size of the message text buffer.

4. Control bits indicating special actions to be taken before or during the transmission of the text.

When the microprocessor begins transmission of a text buffer, it picks up these four pieces of information and stores them in its memory. When the first text buffer has been completed, it uses the "address of next header" information to find the next header and repeat the process. If the "address of next header" is zero, the end of the list of buffers has been reached, and there is no more text to send.

Yet another method is the use of ring buffers. In the ring buffer system, a block of memory is set aside containing, for example, eight of the headers listed above. The "address of next header," however, is replaced with a status bit that is one if the microprocessor has not picked up the buffer information and zero if it has. Thus, the microprocessor rotates through the header blocks, taking the information and acknowledging receipt of that information by changing status bits from one to zero. The computer program managing the buffers checks the status bits for changes from one to zero and installs new headers upon discovering zeros.

# 22

# Sophisticated Modems

The two tables in this chapter summarize the CCITT V-Series Recommendations for modems (excluding acoustic couplers, parallel interface modems, medical analog modems, and wideband modems).

Table 22–1 is a list of those modem recommendations that have been widely accepted and implemented. Most modem manufacturers offer modems that will operate in several of the following modes: Bell 103, Bell 212, V.21, V.22, and V.22 *bis*.

Table 22–2 lists the CCITT recommendations about which there is considerably more controversy. A number of companies use different forms of these modems. Further, the 9600 bps modems have fallback rates of 7200 and 4800 bps, and some modems that interoperate at the 9600 bps rate do not interoperate at the fallback rates. Persons leasing or purchasing these modems should attempt to obtain all of them from one vendor. If multiple vendors are required, tests should be conducted, including operation at fallback rates. Do not assume that because both are "compatible" with the same CCITT recommendation that they will interoperate.

Despite this somewhat cloudy picture, user enthusiasm for 9600 baud operation is high, and modem manufacturers are working on 14,400 bps full-duplex modems for switched network operation and 38,400 bps half-duplex modems for switched network operation. The principal motivation for so much research in the switched network area is that leased lines are becoming more expensive and more difficult to obtain.

Several sophisticated transmission methods are used, either alone or in combination. One of these is echo canceling. Echo canceling is best understood by considering a conversation between two people in a room that has

Table 22–1   Widely Accepted and Implemented Modem Recommendations

| | |
|---|---|
| V.21 | 300 bps duplex modem standardized for use in the general switched telephone network<br>[This is the European version of the Bell 103-series modems. It is similar in capabilities to the 103 but uses different frequencies.] |
| V.22 | 1200 bps duplex modem standardized for use in the general switched telephone network and on point-to-point two-wire leased telephone-type circuits<br>[This is the European version of the Bell 212 modem. It is similar in capabilities to the 212 but uses different frequencies.] |
| V.22 *bis* | 2400 bps duplex modem using the frequency division technique standardized for use in the general switched telephone network and on point-to-point two-wire leased telephone-type circuits |
| V.23 | 600/1200 baud modem standardized for use in the general switched telephone network<br>[This modem was once very popular in Europe, as it offered 1200 baud half-duplex operation at a very low cost.] |

a lot of echo. Each person's hearing system rejects echoes of that person's own voice and listens for sounds that do not match the frequency, intonation, and information content of what they are saying. The other sounds must be the other person's speech. Typically, it takes a few moments for the mind to adjust to the echo conditions. An exactly parallel situation occurs with echo canceling modems, where digital signal processors perform the "brain" function of subtracting delayed and distorted versions of the transmitted signal from the received signal. As with humans, a training interval (in addition to the line equalization training interval) is required before the signal processor can function correctly.

An additional sophisticated transmission method is trellis coding. In a trellis-coded modem, the data stream to be transmitted is broken into four-bit groups (quadbits), which we will designate as Q1, Q2, Q3, and Q4. Since these groups arrive one after another, let's designate successive groups of arriving bits as Q1a, Q2a, Q3a, Q4a, Q1b, Q2b, Q3b, Q4b, Q1c, etc. The first two bits in time (Q1, Q2) of each group are differentially encoded by the modem to produce two new bits Y1, Y2. The differential encoding is

Table 22–2   Other Modem Recommendations

| | |
|---|---|
| V.26 | 2400 bps modem standardized for use on four-wire leased telephone-type circuits<br>[Not common] |
| V.26 *bis* | 2400/1200 bps modem standardized for use in the general switched telephone network |
| V.26 *ter* | 2400 bps duplex modem using the echo cancellation technique standardized for use in the general switched telephone network and on point-to-point two-wire leased telephone-type circuits |
| V.27 | 4800 bps modem with manual equalizer standardized for use on leased telephone-type circuits<br>[This is the European version of the Bell 208 but is not compatible.] |
| V.27 *bis* | 4800/2400 bps modem with automatic equalizer standardized for use on leased telephone-type circuits |
| V.27 *ter* | 4800/2400 bps modem standardized for use in the general switched telephone network |
| V.29 | 9600 bps modem standardized for use on point-to-point four-wire leased telephone-type circuits<br>[This is the European version of the Bell 209 but is not compatible.] |
| V.32 | A family of two-wire duplex modems operating at data signaling rates of up to 9600 bps for use on the general switched telephone network and on leased telephone-type circuits |

done according to a table that produces Y1c, Y2c (for example) by comparing bits Q1c, Q2c with previously encoded bits Y1b, Y2b. Bits Y1b, Y2b were, in turn, produced by comparing bits Q1b, Q2b with Y1a, Y2a. In other words, the encoding process continually produces new Y bits by comparing the newly arrived Q1, Q2 bits with the old Y1, Y2 bits. The Y bits produced by this process are used as input to a systematic convolutional encoder, which generates a redundant bit Y0. This redundant bit and the four information bits Y1c, Y2c, Q3c, and Q4c (for example) are then mapped into the coordinates of the signal element to be transmitted according to a "signal space diagram," as shown in Figure 22–1. The binary numbers in the figure

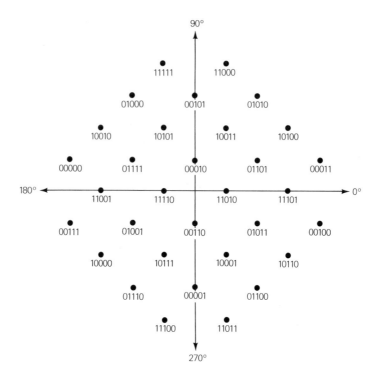

Figure 22–1   Signal Space Diagram for Trellis-Coded Modem

denote Y0, Y1, Y2, Q3, Q4. The signal space diagram resembles a trellis, hence the name trellis coding.

The important feature of trellis coding is not the unusual signal space diagram, but rather the robustness produced by encoding a redundant bit into the transmitted signal. Trellis-coded modems are able to tolerate a 4 db poorer signal-to-noise ratio than conventional modems.

An interesting modem that differs from all those listed above is the Telebit Trailblazer. Rather than using one or two carrier frequencies, up to 512 carriers spaced 7.8 Hz apart are used. Each carrier conveys two, four, or six signaling elements at a 7.5 baud rate. The modem measures the signal-to-noise ratio of each carrier to determine how many signaling elements to send. With an average of 400 usable carriers and 6 bits per carrier, the modem will transmit a packet of 2400 bits every 1/7.5 second for an 18,000 bps data rate (half duplex).

Also of interest are modems that operate in asymmetrical full duplex— 9600 bps in one direction and 300 bps in the other. For many applications these modems provide satisfactory throughput at a cost substantially below that of true full-duplex 9600 bps modems.

Modems are not only becoming faster, they are becoming "smarter." Error-correcting modems are examples of smart modems. In Chapter 14, it was noted that the two principal advantages of synchronous over asynchronous operation were improved efficiency due to the elimination of START and STOP bits and improved error performance due to the use of protocols that included error detection. In addition, synchronous modems were noted as being able to operate at higher bit rates due to the use of line signaling methods that depend on the continual bit flow characteristic of synchronous operation. Error-correcting modems take advantage of all three of these advantages of synchronous operation to provide an apparently asynchronous pair of modems between which few if any errors occur. (They can provide a synchronous interface, but the advantages of their operation are more apparent when they provide an asynchronous interface.)

Figure 22–2 is a block diagram of a pair of error-correcting modems. The UARTs in the diagram provide interfaces that look to the user like asynchronous modems despite the fact that the signal on the communications line is actually synchronous. Characters received from the user of Station 1 are converted to parallel form and deposited in FIFO 1T. The USRT (synchronous UART) at the bottom of FIFO 1T withdraws the characters and forms them into a message in a synchronous protocol (for example, Synchronous Data Link Control, or SDLC) for delivery to the modem sec-

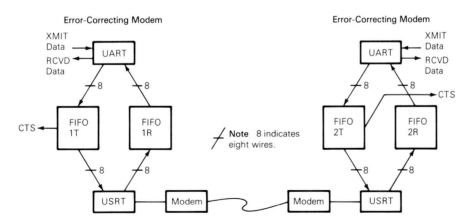

Figure 22–2   Block Diagram of Two Error-Correcting Modems Communicating

tion (typically a V.22 *bis* modem). The message is transmitted to Station 2, where another V.22 *bis* modem section delivers the serial stream to a USRT, which converts the data into parallel form and deposits it into FIFO 2R. The characters are withdrawn from FIFO 2R and placed in a UART, from which they are serialized for reception by Station 2. Characters from Station 2 to Station 1 follow a similar path involving FIFO 2T and FIFO 1R.

Readers familiar with SDLC (Chapter 19) will realize that there is protocol overhead consisting of header information and a Cyclic Redundancy Check (CRC). There is even more overhead if the CRC is found to be incorrect and a request for retransmission is required. The line efficiency has been increased 20 percent, however, by eliminating the START and STOP bits that surround a typical eight-bit data character in asynchronous transmission. Further, the input process is through a FIFO buffer. If things become too bad, the FIFO will fill and the Clear to Send lead (EIA: CB, CCITT: 106) will be negated or an XOFF will be sent. Note that Clear to Send has usually been associated with half-duplex modems or synchronous modems utilizing a training sequence. The use of error-correcting modems is a case where a "simple" full-duplex interface (not usually requiring Clear to Send) now requires it (unless XON/XOFF is used). If characters are arriving over the communications channel too quickly, a Receive Not Ready or similar indication is sent to the transmitting USRT, and a negation of Clear to Send or an XOFF is used to suspend transmission at the distant station.

Once one has Clear to Send (or XOFF) for indicating whether the FIFO can accept characters, it is a short step to the idea of using Clear to Send or XOFF to permit the operating speed of the UART and the operating speed of the line to differ. The Data Terminal Equipment (DTE) speed must, however, match the UART speed. Further, in some error-correcting modems, the modem (when receiving a call) will adjust the UART to match the UART at the distant station. Therefore, the DTE should have the capability to "autobaud" and detect the operating speed of the UART in the modem (in the same way the operating speed of the distant UART must be determined when ordinary modems are used).

Since error correcting involves protocols, and since protocols can have many levels (Chapter 16), error correcting is available as a protocol family of many levels. The following chart indicates the available levels of the Microcom Networking Protocol (MNP):

| MNP Class | Transmission Type | Duplex | Effective Line Speed |
|-----------|-------------------|--------|----------------------|
| 1 | Async, byte-oriented | half | 70% of 2400 bps |
| 2 | Async, byte-oriented | full | 84% of 2400 bps |
| 3 | Sync, bit-oriented | full | 110% of 2400 bps |
| 4 | Class 3 plus adaptive packet assembly and data phase optimization | | 122% of 2400 bps |
| 5 | Class 4 plus two types of data compression | | 200% of 2400 bps |
| 6 | Class 5 plus universal link negotiation and statistical duplexing | | ≥ 200% of 2400 bps |

The first four classes are in the public domain, and the last two are proprietary. Adaptive packet assembly refers to the use of shorter packets on noisy lines. Data phase optimization refers to reducing the number of header bits. The data compression techniques used in Class 4 are run-length encoding and Huffman encoding. Universal link negotiation and statistical duplexing involve alterations to the modulation methods used and allocating bandwidth according to traffic density.

Many of the operating modes for a typical error-correcting modem can be changed via serial autodialing commands (see Chapter 11). An explanation of the operating modes is beyond the scope of this book.

# *23*

---

# Digital Transmission

In previous chapters, the electrical properties of telephone switching networks and transmission systems have been discussed. As is evident from these discussions, the electrical properties of existing telephone systems have been optimized for the transmission of voice signals. While modems have made data transmission over the telephone system very workable, there are nonetheless certain properties of the telephone network that will always work against its total usefulness for data transmission. Chief among these are limited speed and high error rates.

Interestingly enough, while more and more modems are being used to carry digital data over the analog telephone network, the analog telephone network has been turning increasingly to the use of digital techniques to transfer analog signals (voice). It is very common for digital data from a computer to be converted into analog signals by a modem, only to be converted back to digital within the telephone transmission system. The data is then converted back to analog at the end of the transmission system, converted to digital by another modem, and used by a second computer.

As with many other aspects of data communication, this unusual situation has its roots in history and tradition. Specifically, digital transmission systems in the United States are based on technology developed by the Bell System to provide more economical telephone service by conveying multiple telephone conversations on a single pair of wires, a process referred to as "multiplexing." A brief historical review of this process follows.

By the end of the nineteenth century, telephone companies had established a modest network of central offices within large cities and had established some "long-distance" connections. Unfortunately, each conversation taking place between these offices required its own pair of wires. Not only was such an arrangement unsightly, it also was very expensive. The use of telephone cables solved much of the appearance problem, but cost was still a factor.

The telegraph industry had faced the problem of wire cost several decades earlier and had solved it by multiplexing several signals over the same wire. In fact, research into telegraph multiplexing led to the invention of the telephone.

In 1914, the Bell System extended the concept of multiplexing to include telephone transmission and installed an experimental system that used voice signals to alter (modulate) a high-frequency signal called a "carrier." This process was similar to the one used by radio stations. In the same way that many radio stations could occupy the frequency spectrum between 550 kHz and 1600 kHz, multiple telephone conversations could be transmitted on the same wire. Because this system conveyed the conversations on carrier frequencies, it and subsequent systems have been referred to as "carrier systems."

Four years later, the first commercial carrier system was placed in service between Pittsburgh and Baltimore. This design was designated as "Type A Carrier," beginning a Bell tradition of alphabetic designations. During the next 50 years, a series of improved systems was developed, including types C, D, G, H, J, K, L, M, N, O, and ON, although not in that order.

In 1962, the Bell System began installation of a completely new type of carrier system, designated as "T1 carrier." This system did not divide the bandwidth of the transmission facility into various frequencies, but instead divided the time available into time slots.

The theoretical foundation for the T1 system was laid almost 30 years earlier by Harry Nyquist, who determined that an electrical signal could be faithfully reconstructed by sampling it at twice the maximum frequency contained therein, transmitting the samples, and reconstructing the original signal from the samples. The sampling process is shown in Figure 23–1a. Applied to telephone work, this theory meant that a telephone conversation utilizing frequencies between 0 and 4000 Hz could be faithfully reproduced by samples taken at an 8000 Hz rate. These samples were analog samples, however, and could have an indeterminate number of amplitude values. Transmitting such samples would be no easier than transmitting the original conversation. To facilitate transmission of the samples, Bell engineers

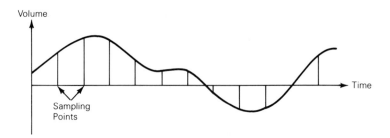

Figure 23–1a   Sample of a Voice Signal

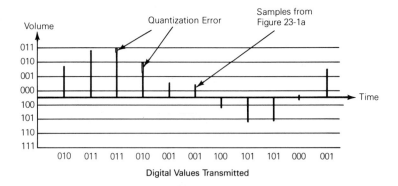

Figure 23–1b   Digital Coding of Analog Samples

chose 255 amplitude values and assigned each an eight-bit binary number. When a voice sample was to be transmitted, it would be assigned the amplitude value nearest its actual amplitude, and the corresponding eight-bit number would be transmitted. This concept is shown in simplified form, using only eight amplitude values and three bit numbers, in Figure 23–1b.

In a T1 system built to the original design, 24 voice channels are carried simultaneously. Since each of the 24 voice samples has to be encoded into 8 bits, 192 (24 x 8) bits are sent. The 8 bits for the first channel are sent, then the 8 bits for the second channel, and so on. This poses a problem for the receiving equipment, which has to deliver the proper bits to the proper channel despite noise and other interruptions in the incoming bit stream. To assist the receiving equipment, an extra bit is added. This bit is called the "framing bit" because it allows the receiver to divide the incoming bits into 193-bit "frames" representing 8-bit samples from each of the channels in proper order. The bit arrangement of a typical 193-bit T1 frame is shown in Figure 23–2.

The framing bit is transmitted in a special pattern: 001110110001. The receiver can then follow an algorithm similar to this:

1. Record a bit.
2. Count to 193.
3. Record that bit.
4. Have the bits recorded thus far matched a portion of the framing pattern?
    If yes, go to 5.
    If no, discard accumulated bits, count to 194, and go to 3.
5. Have 12 bits matching the framing pattern been received?
    If yes, we are in synchronization.
    If no, go to 1.

Once synchronization is achieved, the receiving station will know which bits are to be delivered to which channel. The per-channel equipment in the receiver then converts the digital signals back to analog samples and then to a voice signal. (Note: The framing pattern described here is being replaced by an "Extended SuperFrame Format," described in AT&T Technical Reference PUB 54016.)

Regardless of whether the original framing format or the Extended SuperFrame Format is used, each frame in a T1 system contains 192 sample bits (8 for each of 24 channels) plus a framing bit. Since the samples are being generated at an 8000 Hz rate, a 193-bit frame has to be sent 8000 times per second. This requires a transmission rate of 1.544 megabits per second (Mbps) (8000 × 193).

Each of the 24 channels carries an 8-bit sample 8000 times per second, for a bit rate of 64,000 bps. The bit rate that can be conveyed over a channel, however, is sometimes quoted as 56,000 bps rather than 64,000. The reason

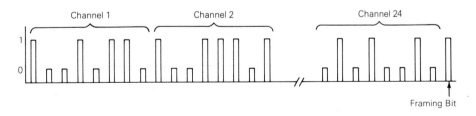

Figure 23–2   Bit Arrangement of Typical T1 Frame

for this is that the original T1 systems used some of the bits in the voice channels for signaling.

Signaling is very important in telephone systems. For example, when a call originates, a signal must be sent so that equipment for recording the number of the called party can be connected. If dial pulses are being used to convey the number of the called party, the dial pulses must be conveyed by some signaling method. When the called party answers, that information must be signaled to the originating end so that billing may commence. Likewise, when either party hangs up, that information must be exchanged via signaling.

In the original T1 system, signaling functions were accomplished by conveying the "on-hook/off-hook" status of the calling and called telephones within the voice channels. This was done by periodically robbing one of the bits normally used for encoding the voice samples. Specifically, every six frames, each voice sample would be seven bits rather than eight bits, producing an unnoticeable degradation in voice quality for that sample. The eighth bit would convey signaling information, including the status of the calling telephone (on-hook or off-hook). Since those utilizing a T1 channel for data transmission had no way of knowing when the eighth bit would be stolen for signaling, only seven bits could be relied on for data transmission. The "reliable" seven bits were transmitted 8000 times per second, therefore the bit rate available for data transmission was 56,000 bps.

In modern T1 systems, an entire channel is devoted to signaling, and the remaining channels have all 64,000 bps available for data transmission. T1 systems with this capability are referred to as having "clear channel capability." Further, it is not necessary that the channel containing the signaling information be routed through the same T1 transmission facility as the voice channels being controlled by that signaling information. The separation of the signaling function from the voice or data transmission function is referred to as Common Channel Interoffice Signaling (CCIS) and is beyond the scope of this chapter.

There is one other aspect of T1 systems that should be discussed: the recovery of clocking information from the transmitted signal. In T1 a "1" bit is represented by a pulse on the line, and a "0" bit is represented by the absence of a pulse. The receiving apparatus uses the incoming pulses to recover the clocking information necessary to determine the appropriate times to sample the state of the received signal, an important task when "0" bits are being received, as there are no pulses to indicate their presence. A bit stream with several ones makes this an easy task, as there are many pulses, but a bit stream with large groups of "0" bits may cause the clocking to be lost, as there are insufficient pulses to keep the clock recovery circuit running properly. Because this poses a problem in the T1 system, steps must be taken to ensure that large groups of "0" bits do not occur. Encoded voice samples are inverted so that low signal levels are represented by codes rich in ones. Data transmission from customers may be passed through "Channel Service Units," which ensure an adequate density of ones but reduce the channel capacity available to the customer. When direct connections are permitted, customers are advised that certain densities of ones are required.

This problem is now being solved by altering the existing T1 systems. Normally, the pulses representing the "1" bits are transmitted in alternating polarity—that is, if the last pulse transmitted was positive, the next pulse will be negative. This is done to prevent the line from slowly charging itself up to a positive voltage and is referred to as Alternate Mark Inversion (AMI). The AT&T version of the modified T1 system detects when eight successive "0" bits are about to be transmitted and substitutes an 8-bit block in which there are two 1-bit pulses (in specific bit positions) that violate the AMI rule. The receiving station notices the violations, but further notices that they occur in the "magic" bit positions. Recognizing this as a special signal, the receiving apparatus substitutes a block of eight "0" bits for the 8-bit block containing the bipolar violations. This modification to the T1 system is referred to as Block 8 Zero Suppression (B8ZS). Other manufacturers and carriers have proposed an alternative called Zero Byte Time Slot Interchange (ZBTSI).

The problems of 56,000 versus 64,000 bps, and customer ones density requirements versus B8ZS may or may not be a problem, depending on the rapidity of conversion of T1 systems from the original design to the newer designs. In addition to the 1.544 Mbps T1 transmission systems, a hierarchy of T carrier systems is available, including T2, which operates at 6.312 Mbps.

Time division multiplex (TDM) systems are also used in Europe, where 32 channels at 64,000 bps are operated over a line running at 2.048 Mbps. Only thirty of the channels are used for voice and data; the remaining two channels contain signaling and framing information. This is sometimes referred to as the CEPT system.

Digital multiplex systems provide other benefits in addition to the ability to carry a large number of conversations on a single pair of wires. One of the principal benefits is better transmission quality. In an analog telephone transmission system, the received signal differs from the transmitted signal because of crosstalk, noise, intermodulation, and other distortion. Once the disturbance has been introduced, it cannot be eliminated, and the information content of the signal is thus degraded. Ultimately, the system performance is limited by these degradations. In a digital transmission system, however, a receiver needs only to decide whether the signal present on the line at a given moment is a one or a zero. This task is very easy unless there is a great deal of noise. Most important, however, is the fact that a digital signal can be regenerated before signal degradation becomes so severe that the receiver will be unable to discern the ones and zeros. Thus, while an analog amplifier cannot improve the quality of a signal passing through it, a digital amplifier can restore the signal to an exact replica of the transmitted signal. With digital regenerative repeaters there is theoretically no limit to the transmission distance, and the signal-to-noise ratio of the facility over which the system is operating may be as poor as 12 db. (An analog system would require 60 db.)

The high capacity and reasonable error rate of digital carrier systems has enabled telecommunications common carriers all over the world to offer a variety of digital transmission services, both on a switched and a private line basis. Synchronous data rates of 2400, 4800, 9600, 56,000, and 64,000 bps are typical. For some service offerings, a Data Service Unit provides the customer interface and is designed to provide plug-for-plug interchangeability with existing modems using the EIA-232-D or V.35 interface, depending on the speeds used. Interface specifications for some of the AT&T digital service offerings are contained in the following AT&T Technical References:

PUB 41450    Digital Data System—Data Service Unit Interface Specification

PUB 41451    High Capacity Terrestrial Digital Service

PUB 41451A   High Capacity Satellite Digital Service

PUB 41458    Special Access Connections to the AT&T Communications Public Switched Network or New Service Applications

These publications are available from AT&T Customer Information Center, Commercial Sales Representative, P.O. Box 19901, Indianapolis, IN 46219. A good starting point is to order the Catalog of Communications Technical Publications (PUB 10000), available free of charge. It contains a list of all AT&T Communications technical publications, their prices, and an order form.

Digital transmission has led to many interesting service offerings, including packet switching networks and the Integrated Services Digital Network (ISDN), discussed in the next two chapters.

# 24

## Packet Switching

The best way to explain packet switching and its pros and cons is to contrast it with other methods. Telephone systems and telex (switched teleprinter) systems use circuit switching. In circuit switching a person or terminal places a call by entering the directory listed number of the person or terminal to be called into the switching system; the switching system then sets up a connection. Every piece of information entered at the calling point is immediately conveyed to the called point with a delay equal only to the speed of light in the transmission medium used. The connection between the two points is used solely by the two communicating parties. Although some multiplexing may take place in portions of the transmission system, the parties will not notice this. The connection will exist until the two parties decide to hang up.

Message telegram systems use message switching, in which a message is sent to a switching center, where it is stored. When facilities become available to send it on to another switching center closer to the destination, the message is forwarded over those facilities to be stored at the next point. The storing and forwarding process continues until the message reaches its destination. Message switching is also called "store and forward" switching.

Circuit switching has several advantages over message switching. First of all, it is interactive. If a person asks a question, the other person answers right away. In addition, each person can tell immediately whether the other person is happy, sad, or angry. Second, it is full duplex for low-speed data transmission. Finally, the speed of service is nearly immediate, except for occasional blocking in the switching systems involved, and connection to the distant party is confirmed when that party answers.

Message switching is more efficient than circuit switching, however. Because a switched circuit is in place between the two conversing parties or terminals throughout the conversation, there are frequent intervals in which little is said or little data is transferred. Thus, the channel is not very efficient. A message could have been sent over that channel, occupying the channel at full capacity just long enough to send the message; the channel could then have been made available for some other use. The ability of a message switching system to store messages during traffic peaks and send them on their way later also makes a message switching system much more efficient. Unlike circuit switching, no traffic peaks must be taken care of immediately. Since all service requests are handled on a "blocked calls delayed" basis rather than a "blocked calls lost" basis, the service can be offered at far less cost than a system designed for busy hour loads. Since a higher percentage of attempted calls is completed, more revenue is collected for a given capital investment.

Other factors involved in contrasting telephone systems with telegram systems include the greater ease of using the telephone terminal apparatus and the emotional appeal of a loved one's voice compared with his or her typed words. While these two factors make a case for the telephone, the value of a written record and the ease of operating written message systems across half a world of time zones make a strong case for the telegram in many applications. None of these factors is important in data switching, however, as both circuit and message switching involve the same apparatus and written communications.

The critical points of comparison for data transmission systems are speed of operation and cost. The efficiencies of line time utilization and the traffic peak smoothing effects inherent in message switching make message switching very attractive from a cost standpoint. Speed of operation is a drawback, however.

A message switching system operating at 100 percent capacity will have substantial delays, regardless of message length. A message switching system operating at 80 percent capacity will have short delays, providing there are no long messages in the system that might block certain routing paths and delay other messages. If all messages are limited to 1000 information bits and 9600 bps transmission facilities are used, no message occupies the line for more than about 100 milliseconds. Application of this rule requires that messages longer than 1000 bits be broken up into separate messages or "packets," hence the term "packet switching." Each packet must have some additional bits added for address and administrative purposes.

By designing the message switching system so that it never has to operate at or near design capacity, and by limiting the length of the messages, packet switching systems provide speed close to that of circuit switching, and do so at an attractive cost. There are some problems, however. The principal one is that long messages must be broken up into a great many packets, each of which has its own address/administrative header. Had that long message been sent through a circuit switching system, the addressing information would have been presented only once and the "overhead" would have been much less. Thus, packet switching is most effective when most of the messages handled fit in a small number of packets, preferably one.

Because very short messages have a high overhead in both packet and circuit switching systems, this is not an item of comparison between the two systems. It is worthwhile to note that 1000-bit or similar size packets are too short to be circuit switched effectively because of the time taken within circuit switching systems and between circuit switches (signaling) to set up a call. The call setup period involves the greatest utilization of elaborate and expensive equipment, particularly in common control switching systems. The call setup period also makes the most demands on the signaling equipment. Because of the high cost of setting up a call and the lack of revenue accrual during this period, most common carriers and telecommunications authorities charge more for the initial connection period than for subsequent equal intervals of time. For this reason, transmission of data as separate short calls is not economical, and the packet concept is applied only to networks of message switching processors connected by private lines. Some packet switching systems have access ports that are reached by dialing numbers in the circuit switched telephone network, but these are provided principally as a convenience for low-use terminal users.

While the most commonly cited packet switching network is ARPANET, the first packet switching network offered as a service to the general public was Telecom Canada's Datapac™. The Datapac network uses a selected set of option and feature capabilities from the 1980 version of CCITT Recommendation X.25. Conversion to the 1984 version will take place in late 1988. More details concerning the Datapac network offerings may be obtained by writing to: Datapac Resource Centre, Room 1890, 160 Elgin

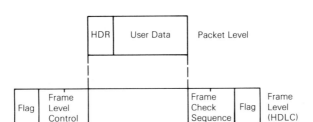

Figure 24–1    Framing Formats in X.25

Street, Ottawa, Ontario, Canada K1G 3J4. A brief review of Datapac and its use of CCITT Recommendation X.25 is included here, but this is not a complete presentation.

Recommendation X.25 transfers packets in frames in the High (level) Data Link Control (HDLC) format (see Figure 24–1). The packets are sent from the customer's Data Terminal Equipment (DTE), typically a computer, programmable terminal controller, or intelligent terminal, to the Datapac network over a point-to-point private line operating in synchronous mode at 1200, 2400, 4800, 9600, or 19,200 bps. While asynchronous operation and dial-in facilities are available via Packet Assembly-Disassembly (PAD) devices, only the X.25 service (Datapac 3000™) is discussed here.

The line from the X.25 DTE to the Datapac network is time division multiplexed to provide the capability of handling traffic on a number of virtual circuits. A "virtual circuit" is a bidirectional association between a pair of DTEs over which all data transfers take the form of packets. Transmission facilities are assigned only when data packets are actually being transferred. The association between two DTEs may be permanent (a "permanent virtual circuit") or temporary (a "switched virtual circuit"). The only important difference between these two types of circuit is that the switched virtual circuit requires that the DTEs and the Datapac network exchange call setup packets to establish the call, and call clearing packets to take down the connection when the call is complete. This process is explained in greater detail below, but first let's look at the transmission facility between a typical DTE installation and the Datapac network.

In most time division multiplex systems, the transmission facility transmits a sample of one channel for a moment, then the next channel, then the next, and so on until all channels have been sampled. At that time it starts over with the first channel. Each channel is sampled, and the result of that sample is placed on the line, whether the channel is handling traffic or not. The Datapac network does not do this. Instead, Asynchronous Time Division Multiplexing is used. In this system, the fact that a typical virtual circuit to a remote DTE may actually be carrying data only a small percentage of the time is exploited by dynamically allocating the transmission facility to an active virtual circuit. The bit rate of the physical circuit must be chosen based on queuing delay considerations to handle the average busy period loads for the virtual circuits being multiplexed. In Datapac 3000, 255 virtual circuits can be handled over one physical circuit (access line). The Asynchronous Time Division Multiplexing of virtual channels is shown in Figure 24–2.

The logical channel identifiers shown in Figure 24–2 are used only between the DTE and the Network Node to which it is connected. In the example shown, logical channel identifiers 1 and 2 are in permanent use for permanent virtual circuits to DTEs B and C, respectively. Identifiers 3 and 4 are in use only as long as the switched virtual circuits to DTEs D and E are in use. When either of those connections is released, the associated virtual circuit number will be available for other outgoing or incoming calls.

Establishing a connection between two DTEs over switched virtual circuits in the Datapac network is accomplished by the calling station sending a Call Request packet, which the network sends on to the called station. If the called station accepts the call, it sends a Call Accepted packet back to the network. This is forwarded to the calling station as a Call Connected

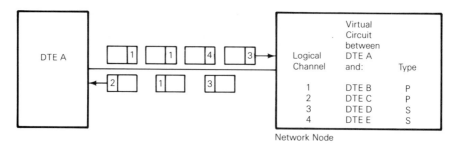

Figure 24–2   Packet Flow

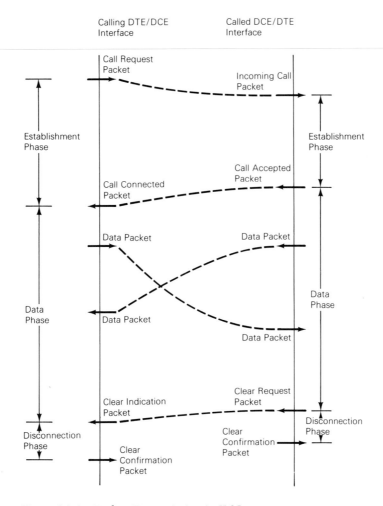

Figure 24–3   Packet Transmission in X.25

packet (assuming there is no network congestion). Data transfer can then take place. At the conclusion of data transfer, either station can cause the connection to be taken down by sending a Clear Request packet into the network. The network responds by giving a Clear Confirmation packet back. The network also sends a Clear Indication packet to the other station, and that station responds with a Clear Confirmation packet. This is summarized in Figure 24–3.

The packets used in Figure 24–3 to establish and clear calls over switched virtual circuits have prescribed formats consisting of three or more eight-

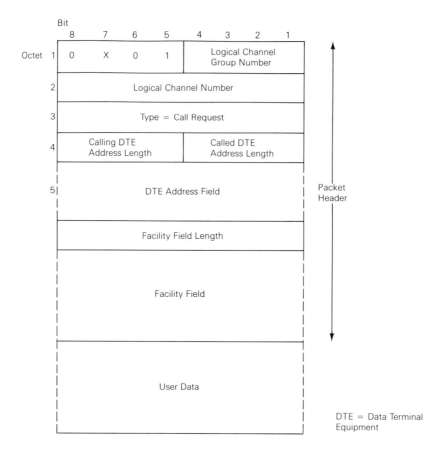

Figure 24–4   Call Request Packet Format

bit groupings called "octets" rather than characters. Bits of an octet are numbered 8 to 1, where bit 1 is the low-order bit and is transmitted first. Octets are numbered consecutively starting with 1 and are transmitted in that order. The X.25 (1984) Call Request packet format is shown in Figure 24–4.* Note that this format contains some of the features of the Digital Data Communication Message Protocol (DDCMP) discussed in Chapter 18, in that Octet 4 contains the length of the address field. This is followed by the address field. The same procedure is used with the facility field. This is somewhat similar to the character count in DDCMP, which is followed by an information field of the length specified by the count.

*The Datapac 3000 packet formats differ very slightly from the X.25 (1984) packet formats. The packet formats shown here are for X.25 (1984).

The facility field provides for some interesting features. Codes indicating that the call is "collect"—i.e., that the recipient pays the telecommunications costs—may be placed in this field. Codes that identify the calling DTE as part of a closed user group, may also be placed there, as the called terminal might accept calls only from members of that group.

While the size of the packet header in Figure 24–4 may seem large, the packet headers for the other types of signaling packets used, such as Clear Request, are typically much smaller (see Figure 24–5). The packet header for data packets, shown in Figure 24–6, is the shortest of all, as might be

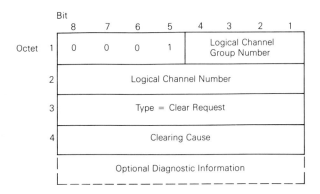

Figure 24–5   Clear Request Packet Format

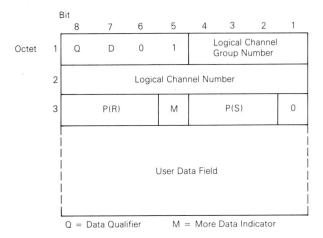

Figure 24–6   DTE Data Packet Format

expected. This permits minimum overhead. The Data Qualifier bit is used to distinguish between data and control information headed for a terminal controller. The More Data bit indicates that an additional packet that contains more of the same message follows. P(R) and P(S) are the Packet Receive Sequence number and Packet Send Sequence number, respectively. Their function is similar to the Response and Sequence fields in DDCMP and identical to the Nr and Ns sequence numbers in Synchronous Data Link Control (SDLC).

In addition to the packets shown here, a number of flow control, restart, and reset packets are designed for use in special circumstances. These are beyond the scope of this text but are described completely in CCITT Recommendation X.25 and in the Datapac 3000 (X.25[80]) Specification.

# 25

## Integrated Services Digital Network

Chapter 23 mentions that data transmission over the public switched telephone network frequently goes from digital at the user's location through a modem to become analog and then becomes digital again inside the telephone system. This wasteful situation could be eliminated if the telephone system could provide digital transmission capability at the user's location. Further, in some countries there are separate switching networks for teleprinters, special arrangements for Videotext services, and special networks for data transmission. If all of these services could be performed by a single network, substantial savings in costs would result. Thus, it would benefit both the telecommunications service user and provider if network services could be provided by an Integrated Services Digital Network (ISDN).

The CCITT defines an ISDN as follows: "An ISDN is a network, in general evolving from a telephone IDN, that provides end-to-end digital connectivity to support a wide range of services, including voice and non-voice services, to which users have access by a limited set of standard interfaces."

The two most important standard interfaces are the Basic Rate Interface and the Primary Rate Interface. The Basic Rate Interface is the one that would be provided to every home and to every desk. The preferred implementation thereof provides two "bearer" channels (B channels), each capable of 64 kilobits per second (kbps), and one "data" channel (D channel) capable of 16 kbps. This arrangement is sometimes referred to as "2B + D." The 64 kbps B channels would each be capable of handling voice or data (analog-to-digital conversion for voice would be done in the telephone set). The D channel would use packets to convey signaling and/or operational, administrative, and maintenance (OAM) messages. Since typical installations would use one B channel for voice and one for data, some refer to ISDN as "64 kbps to your desk." The Basic Rate Interface would connect to either an ISDN central office or to an ISDN Private Branch Exchange (PBX).

The other important interface is the Primary Rate Interface, which is based on the T1 carrier in the United States and Japan and the 32-channel carrier elsewhere. The T1 carrier version consists of 23 B channels and one 64 kbps D channel. This arrangement is referred to as "23B + D." As with the Basic Rate Interface, the B channels may be used for either voice or data. In addition, six B channels may be grouped together to form a 384 kbps H0 channel. Further, if more than one T1 system is in use between the same two points, the D channel of one T1 system can serve several other T1 systems, allowing them to contain 24 B channels. This latter arrangement permits formation of a 1.536 megabits per second (Mbps) H11 channel. The Primary Rate Interface can link host processors and ISDN PBXs to each other and to ISDN central offices.

The European version of the Primary Rate Interface must reserve one channel for framing, leaving 31 channels available. A 30B + D arrangement will be the most common allocation of channels, but other combinations will be possible, including not only the H0 and H11 discussed above, but also a 1.920 Mbps H12 channel.

The D channel in both interfaces will conform to the ISO model discussed in Chapter 16. In general, ISDN signaling will provide the services of the first three layers of the seven-layer ISO Reference Model. In particular, the signaling messages in the third layer are very powerful and flexible and are the key to many of the new services ISDNs will offer. Among these services are advanced versions of the "800" service, identification of the calling party, and automatic callback of the last person who called you.

Since existing telephones and terminals are not designed for direct connection to the Basic Rate Interface, a number of interfaces have been standardized. Figure 25–1 shows some of these. Several of the abbreviations in this figure require explanation. "NT1" stands for "Network Termination 1," which includes functions broadly equivalent to layer 1 of the ISO Reference Model. These functions involve the proper electromagnetic and physical termination of the network. Line transmission termination, layer

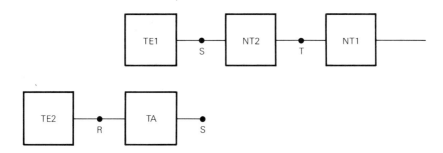

Figure 25–1   ISDN Interfaces

1 maintenance and performance monitoring functions, timing, power transfer, and layer 1 multiplexing are among the functions performed.

"NT2" stands for "Network Termination 2," which includes functions broadly equivalent to layer 1 (and higher layers) of the OSI Reference Model (see CCITT Recommendation X.200). Examples of equipment that provide NT2 functions include PBXs, local area networks, and terminal controllers. NT2 functions include interface termination and other layer 1 functions, protocol handling and multiplexing for layers 2 and 3, switching, concentration, and maintenance functions. However, all NT2s are not created equal. A simple PBX can provide NT2 functions for the first three layers; a simple terminal concentrator can service only the first two layers, and a simple time division multiplexer can service only level 1.

"TE" stands for "Terminal Equipment," which (like NT2) includes functions broadly equivalent to layer 1 (and higher layers) of the Recommendation X.200 Reference Model. Digital telephones, Data Terminal Equipment (DTE), and integrated workstations are examples of equipment that performs the TE functions, which include protocol handling, maintenance functions, interface functions, and connections to other equipment. If the terminal equipment performs DTE functions and has an interface that complies with ISDN user–network interface Recommendations, it is considered TE1 (Terminal Equipment type 1). If the terminal equipment performs DTE functions but does not have an interface compliant with ISDN user–network interface Recommendations, it is considered TE2 (Terminal Equipment type 2) and must have a TA (Terminal Adapter) interposed between it and the NT equipment. For example, terminal equipment having an X-series interface (such as X.21) or a V-series interface (such as V.24) would require a TA.

For a comprehensive treatment of ISDN interfaces, refer to Fascicle III.5 of Volume III of the CCITT *Red Book*, which contains the I-Series Recommendations. The next CCITT book will be available in early 1989, at which time the fascicles may be renumbered. It is, therefore, advisable to contact the United Nations Bookstore if ordering after that time. (See page 337 for address.)

# 26

# Special Problems

There is a children's story that tells how the lack of a nail in a horseshoe caused the horseshoe to be lost and how the loss of the horseshoe caused the horse to be lost. This in turn led to the loss of the knight on the horse, which led to the loss of a critical battle and the loss of a kingdom.

It is possible to call a nail a form of connector, since it connects the horseshoe to the horse. Thus, the king who lost his kingdom did so because of a connector problem. Men no longer ride to battle on horses, but connector problems are still with us, especially when setting up data communication systems.

Data communication interfaces, especially multiplexers, are generally designed to connect to modems. The connectors used are 25-pin male connectors that present data to be transmitted on pin 2 and expect to receive data on pin 3. This type of connector (in the United States, a DB25-P) is shown in abbreviated form in Figure 26–1. A full list of DB25-P pins is given in Appendix G.

Terminals also are generally designed to plug into modems and use a connector as shown in Figure 26–1. In most computer installations, however, terminals located close to the computer must be connected to the same multiplexer that is connected to the modem-equipped lines. This problem is shown schematically in Figure 26–2. Not only is there a problem with the sex of the connectors (both male), but there is also a problem with the pinning, as both connectors deliver data to be transmitted on pin 2.

Figure 26–3a shows one solution to this problem, the "null modem," and indicates how its use is similar to that of actual modems (Figure 26–3b). In both figures the "modem facility" provides a female connector

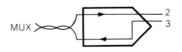

Figure 26–1   Pin Utilization
of DB25-P Connector

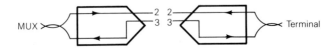

Figure 26–2   Attempted Connection of Multiplexer and
Terminal Using DB25-P Connectors

for the computer interface to plug into and another female connector for the terminal to plug into. Data applied to pin 2 of one of those connectors comes out pin 3 of the other.

The null modem may be implemented either as a length of cable with leads 2 and 3 (and some others) transposed or as a cigarette box–size container with a terminal board inside and female connectors at the ends. The cable implementation is much neater and provides some additional cable length. Many computer companies sell cables that accomplish this function but call them "cables for connection terminal to computer interface." As can be deduced from Figure 26–2, either the cable from the computer interface or the cable from the terminal can be altered to solve the connector problem.

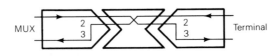

Figure 26–3a   Connection with Null Modem

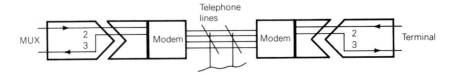

Figure 26–3b   Connection with Actual Modem

The cigarette box–type of null modem offers some advantages over the cable type, however. With a terminal strip inside the box, a number of different wiring arrangements are possible. Figure 26–4 shows a typical wiring diagram for a terminal strip.

The dashed lines indicate the connections usually provided. The two Signal Ground leads (pin 7) are connected together, and the Transmitted Data lead (pin 2) on each side is connected to the Received Data lead (pin 3) on the other side to accomplish the transposition described in conjunc-

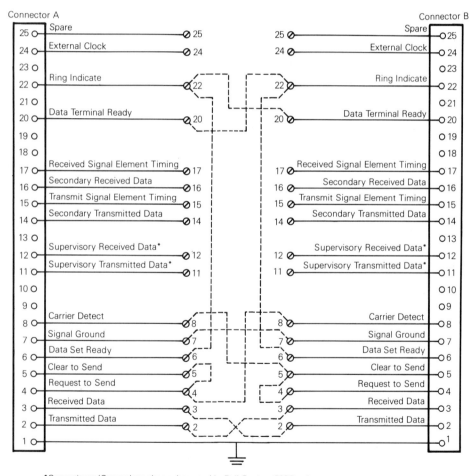

*Supervisory/Secondary channel as used in Bell System 202C only.

Figure 26–4   Null Modem Wiring Diagram

tion with Figure 26–3b. The remaining cross-connections involve control leads. To convince the devices connected to the null modem that they are dealing with a real modem, another lead causes the assertion of Request to Send by the device to be returned as an assertion of Clear to Send by the null modem. Since, under these circumstances, a real modem would send a carrier to the distant device (i.e., the other device attached to the null modem), a lead that causes the Request to Send from one device to assert Carrier Detect at the other device also is provided. Finally, a cross-connection between Data Terminal Ready of one device and both Ring Indicate and Data Set Ready of the other device permits the assertion of Data Terminal Ready (indicating a willingness to transfer data) to show as a call arrival (assertion of Ring and Data Set Ready) at the other device. The cross-connections of the control leads make the turning on of the terminal look like a call arrival to the multiplexer, and hence elicit the appropriate software response.

Due to the presence of clock leads, the interconnection of synchronous hardware by means of null modems is slightly more complicated than the case just described. Many synchronous modems provide both a transmitter clock, which tells the synchronous transmitter unit when to apply data to the Transmitted Data lead, and a receiver clock, which tells the receiver unit when to sample the data on the Received Data lead. Other modems provide only the receiver clock and require the synchronous transmitter unit to supply its own timing information along with the data.

The clock leads must obey the following definitions, reprinted here by permission of the EIA and the CCITT.

| EIA-232-D<br>Definitions | CCITT V.24<br>Definitions |
|---|---|
| *Circuit DB*—Transmitter Signal Element Timing (DCE Source) (CCITT 114) Direction: From DCE | *Circuit 114*—Transmitter Signal Element Timing (DCE Source) Direction: From DCE |
| Signals on this circuit are used to provide the DTE with signal element timing information. The DTE shall provide a data signal on Circuit BA (Transmitted Data) in which the transitions between signal elements nominally occur at the | Signals on this circuit provide the DTE with signal element timing information. The condition on this circuit shall be ON and OFF for nominally equal periods of time. The DTE shall present a data signal on Circuit 103 (Transmitted Data) in which the transitions between signal |

| EIA-232-D<br>Definitions | CCITT V.24<br>Definitions |
|---|---|

*Circuit DB (Cont.)*

time of the transitions from OFF to ON condition of the signal on Circuit DB. When Circuit DB is implemented in the DCE, the DCE shall normally provide timing information on this circuit at all times that the DCE is capable of generating it. However, the withholding of timing information may be necessary under some conditions, e.g., the maintenance routines in the DCE. [See Section 4.3.2 of EIA-232-D.]

*Circuit DD*—Receiver Signal Element Timing (DCE Source)
(CCITT 115)
Direction: From DCE

Signals on this circuit are used to provide the DTE with received signal element timing information. The transition from ON to OFF condition shall nominally indicate the center of each signal element on Circuit BB (Received Data). Timing information on Circuit DD shall be provided by the DCE at all times that the DCE is capable of generating it. However, the withholding of timing information may be necessary under some conditions, e.g., the performance of maintenance routines in the DCE. [See Section 4.3.2 of EIA-232-D.]

*Circuit DA*—Transmitter Signal Element Timing (DTE Source)
(CCITT 113)
Direction: To DCE

Signals on this circuit are used to provide the transmitting signal converter with signal element timing information. The ON to OFF transition shall nominally indicate the center of each signal element on Circuit BA (Transmitted Data). When Circuit DA is implemented

*Circuit 114 (Cont.)*

elements nominally occur at the time of the transitions from OFF to ON condition of Circuit 114.

*Circuit 115*—Receiver Element Timing (DCE Source)
Direction: From DCE

Signals on this circuit provide the DTE with signal element timing information. The condition of this circuit shall be ON and OFF for nominally equal periods of time, and a transition from ON to OFF condition shall nominally indicate the center of each signal element on Circuit 104 (Received Data).

*Circuit 113*—Transmitter Signal Element Timing (DTE Source)
Direction: To DCE

Signals on this circuit provide the DCE with signal element timing information. The condition on this circuit shall be ON and OFF for nominally equal periods of time, and the transition from ON to OFF condition shall nominally indicate the centre of each signal element on Circuit 103 (Transmitted Data).

|  | |
|---|---|
| **EIA-232-D**<br>**Definitions** | **CCITT V.24**<br>**Definitions** |

*Circuit DA (Cont.)*

in the DTE, the DTE shall normally provide timing information on this circuit whenever the DTE is in a POWER ON condition. It is permissible for the DTE to withhold timing information on this circuit for short periods provided Circuit CA (Request to Send) is in the OFF condition. (For example, the temporary withholding of timing information may be necessary in performing maintenance tests within the DTE.)

There is no EIA-232-D equivalent to Circuit 128.

*Circuit 128*—Receiver Signal Element Timing (DTE Source)
Direction: To DCE

Signals on this circuit provide the DCE with signal element timing information. The condition on this circuit shall be ON and OFF for nominally equal periods of time. The DCE shall present a data signal on Circuit 104 (Received Data) in which the transitions between signal elements nominally occur at the time of the transitions from OFF to ON condition of the signal on Circuit 128.

Frequency accuracy of clocking provided by the data communication equipment is generally required to be .005 percent or .01 percent, depending on the modem. The modem then uses phase lock loop techniques to keep in step with the clock being provided.

Pin 15 of the interface connector is used for the Transmitter Signal Element Timing when it is being provided by the modem (CCITT 114). Pin 17 is used for the Receiver Signal Element Timing when it is being provided by the modem (CCITT 115). When the Data Terminal Equipment (DTE) provides the Transmitter Signal Element Timing (CCITT 113), pin 24 is used. Receiver Signal Element Timing using the DTE as a source (CCITT 128) is done so infrequently that there is no "commonly used" pinning convention.

The problem when connecting two synchronous terminals (or a terminal with one or two multiplexers) without modems is that with no modems there is no source of clock. It is therefore important when contemplating such a configuration to ensure that there is at least one, and preferably two, devices that contain a clock source involved. Manuals describing modems refer to clocks located outside the modems as "external clocks," despite the fact that these clocks may be internal to the DTE; therefore the term "external" may often be confusing. It may be best to substitute mentally the phrase "nonmodem clock" whenever one sees the phrase "external clock."

Returning to Figure 26–4, the device that contains the nonmodem clock delivers that clock signal on lead 24. By wiring lead 24 to leads 15 and 17 of both devices connected to the null modem, operation of two synchronous devices without a modem is possible. This arrangement is rather risky, however, since one EIA/CCITT driver, the one associated with lead 24, is driving four EIA/CCITT receivers. A better arrangement is where both devices have clocks in them producing signals on lead 24 of each device. For this configuration, a wire is run from lead 24 of one device to lead 15 of the same device and lead 17 of the other device. In this way, the external clock of a given device drives that device's transmitter and the other device's receiver. The major benefit of this scheme is that each EIA/CCITT driver involved drives only two EIA/CCITT receivers. Even with this arrangement, cable lengths add up quickly; the capacitance of the leads from the driver to the null modem and from the null modem to each of the two clock receivers may become excessive.

While on the subject of clocking, it is important to note that connection of asynchronous devices can involve clocking problems, despite the fact that no clock leads are involved. Consider the case of two computers connected by an asynchronous line. Figure 26–5 shows an eight-bit character as transmitted by a computer that will be referred to as "Station A."

Figure 26–5   Sampling a Received Character by Means of a Clock Slower than That Used to Transmit the Character

If this character is received by a second computer ("Station B"), whose clock is running somewhat slower than that of Station A, the points at which Station B samples the received character will be those indicated by the arrows in Figure 26–5. Note that the sampling points move gradually from the center of the bit (bit 1) to much later in the bit (bit 8). Since the sampling points are reestablished with the 1-to-0 transition at the beginning of the next START bit, no errors will occur (assuming no other distortion exists).

In Figure 26–6, Station A is assumed to be transmitting at a rate of 1201 bps (.083 percent fast). Characters arriving at Station B are sampled as shown in Figure 26–5, and the sampling of the last data bit is substantially beyond the center. As noted in conjunction with Figure 26–5, however, no data errors will occur, assuming that no other distortion is present. The important part of the transmission from Station A to Station B is that, at a 1201 bps rate with 10 bits per character, characters are being delivered at a rate of 120.1 per second.

Now assume that the data is being transferred from Station A to Station B and thence to Station C. If the transmitter in Station B has a clock rate of 1199 bps (.083 percent slow), it will deliver characters to Station C at a rate of 119.9 characters per second (cps). Because of the speed difference between the Station A clock and the Station B clock, the Station B receiver will believe that the Station A transmitter is cheating slightly on the STOP bit lengths. This is because the 1-to-0 transition marking the beginning of the next character will come slightly early due to the higher character rate. Most asynchronous receivers are willing to accept this, and no data will be lost as a result of the apparent shortness of the STOP elements.

Instead, the sampling clock of Station B's receiver will be reestablished, permitting it to sample the next character in accordance with Figure 26–5. Station B's transmitter is bound to send the correct number of bits as STOP elements, however, as any asynchronous transmitter must send proper

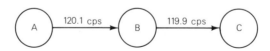

Figure 26–6   Relaying of Transmitted Characters by Stations Having Slightly Differing Clock Rates

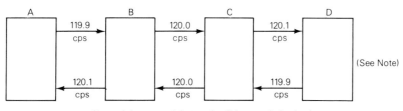

Figure 26–7   Relaying of Transmitted Characters by Stations Having Progressively Faster Clock Rates

STOP elements. Since Station B's clock is slightly slow, the bits are longer, and it will be sending longer STOP elements than it receives from Station A. In fact, it will be sending longer characters, as its character transmission rate is lower than that of Station A.

By this time the problem should be evident. Station B is accumulating characters at a rate of .2 cps. After 10 seconds, two extra characters will have accumulated at Station B, and this may be enough to cause an Overrun condition. Regardless of the storage capacity of Station B, there will be an Overrun Error condition eventually. The use of more accurate clocks helps only slightly. If the clocks used have an accuracy of .008 percent instead of .08 percent, the Overrun Error will occur in 100 seconds rather than in 10 seconds. There is only one sure hardware solution, and that is to provide progressively faster transmitter clocks, with B faster than A, C faster than B, and so on. If full-duplex transmission is envisioned, the receiver rates also must be adjusted. This is shown in Figure 26–7. To implement such an arrangement, it is necessary to have control (in a management sense) of all the hardware involved, to stock spare crystals for the various transmitters and receivers, and to be careful to put the right crystals in the right units.

A simpler scheme is to calculate a worst-case Overrun Error frequency from the clock specifications of the hardware involved and to arrange the software to provide an occasional idle interval that allows the intermediate stations to catch up. Keyboard input automatically does this because humans type so slowly, but asynchronous interprocessor communications can easily run into the clock skew problem because of the processor's ability to send long messages at full speed. The simplest solution is to simulate the keyboard by putting in an occasional idle period.

The problems of interconnection are not limited to devices with EIA/ CCITT voltage level interfaces. The same types of problems exist when dealing with current loop devices, such as teleprinters. Figure 26–8 indicates schematically the problems of trying to connect two teleprinters to each other. Figure 26–9 indicates similar problems when trying to connect two single line interfaces (the Chapter 2 interface with current loop level conversion rather than EIA-232-D) or multiplexers together.

Not only do the two teleprinters in Figure 26–8 both have male connectors, but neither has the current sources necessary to make a current loop interface work. The multiplexers in Figure 26–9 (each of which shows only one line) have a similar problem since both have female connectors. In the latter case, however, there is a surplus of current sources rather than a lack. In both the Figure 26–8 and the Figure 26–9 configurations, a transposition of the receiver leads and the transmitter leads is required to connect the keyboard of one teleprinter to the printer of the other and to connect the transmitter section of one multiplexer to the receiver section of the other. This is analogous to the transposition of the Transmitted Data lead and Received Data lead in the null modem, but in this case, two *pairs* of wires are involved rather than two wires. The device shown in Figure 26–10 will solve the problem with Figure 26–8, and the device shown in Figure 26–11 will solve the problem with Figure 26–9.

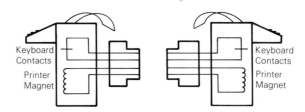

Figure 26–8   Connection Problem: Two Teleprinters

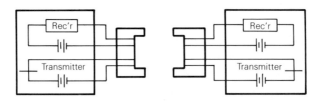

Figure 26–9   Connection Problem: Two Interfaces

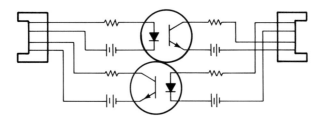

Figure 26–10   Use of Optical Coupler to Solve Connection Problem of Two Terminals

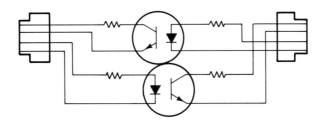

Figure 26–11   Use of Optical Coupler to Solve Connection Problem of Two Interfaces

The devices shown in circles are optical couplers, which contain a light emitting diode (LED) that will respond to current changes in one current loop, shining on a phototransistor that will alter the current flow in the second loop in response to the changes of light from the LED. The connectors shown in Figures 26–10 and 26–11 were chosen to mate with the connectors shown in Figures 26–8 and 26–9, and a transposition of the leads is provided on the right side of Figures 26–10 and 26–11 to connect the transmitters of one unit to the receivers of the other. Figure 26–10 includes current sources to supply the 20 milliampere signaling current, while Figure 26–11 provides isolation between the current loops powered by the existing Figure 26–9 current sources. These figures are for illustration purposes only, as the use of batteries is not customary in data communication and additional components may be required. The important point is that each 20 milliampere current loop circuit now contains a current source, a switching element, and a current flow sensor, the three essential elements of a current loop system.

# 27

# CCITT Recommendations X.20 and X.21

The introduction of the EIA-422-A and EIA-423-A standards discussed in Chapter 3 brought an increase in the number of interface leads used. The additional leads provided a capability for putting local and remote modems into various test modes and improved the electrical characteristics of the interface. While this capability reduced the cost of troubleshooting, it increased the number of level converters and connector pins required.

An increased number of level converters is a much more serious problem than an increased number of logic gates, flip-flops, or memory bits. Level converters have substantial power dissipation and sink a great deal of current into their ground leads; thus, they are not suitable for most large scale integration (LSI) density improvement techniques. The number of level converters per integrated circuit package has remained constant, while the numbers of gates, flip-flops, and memory bits housed in a single integrated circuit package have risen by orders of magnitude.

An increase in the number of connector pins affects price in four ways. First, more level converters are required, as mentioned above. Second, use of a larger connector means that fewer connectors can be mounted in a given space. Where a large number of communications lines is brought together, more sheet metal and more rack space are required to mount the connectors. Third, more connector pins means more wires in the cables. Fourth, more connector pins means more gold plating.

All four of these costs have remained constant or risen during the same period that logic costs have steadily declined. This suggests that an interface that uses fewer connector pins and more logic would be attractive. CCITT

Recommendation X.20 and X.21 interfaces are steps in that direction because they use only one 15-pin connector.

The X.21 interface has additional features beyond economy, however. While it does not use the large connectors associated with EIA-422-A, it does use the superior electrical characteristics of that interface. Furthermore, X.21 provides automatic calling in the same interface as the data transfer, with automatic calling features far more sophisticated than those outlined in Chapter 11. Call progress signals, calling and called line identification information, and call failure cause codes are included.

For data communication over conventional telephone networks and for point-to-point privately owned circuits, the advanced call control features of the X.20 and X.21 interfaces cannot be implemented or are unnecessary. Thus, the large number of modems that have already been installed using the EIA-232-D/V.24 interface will remain. The X.21 automatic calling and call progress features are, however, especially attractive to telecommunications authorities operating or planning to operate public data networks or Integrated Services Digital Networks, and a familiarity with these interfaces will be helpful to data communication hardware and software designers. They are summarized below:

**X.20** **Interface Between Data Terminal Equipment (DTE) and Data Circuit-Terminating Equipment (DCE) for Start-Stop Transmission Services on Public Data Networks.**

The interface consists of the following:

| | | |
|---|---|---|
| G | Signal Ground | |
| Ga | DTE Common Return | (from DTE to DCE) |
| Gb | DCE Common Return | (from DCE to DTE) |
| T | Transmit | (from DTE to DCE) |
| R | Receive | (from DCE to DTE) |

The electrical characteristics may be according to Recommendations X.26 (similar to EIA-423-A), X.27 (similar to EIA-422-A) without cable termination in the load, or V.28. A 15-pin connector is used.

When a call is being established, the sequence of operations starts with the Ready state, wherein both the T and R circuits are binary 0. To enter the Call Request state, the T circuit is changed to 1 (similar to going off-hook with a telephone). The call enters the Proceed to Select state when the R circuit changes to 1 (similar to getting a dial tone). The DTE then sends a specially formatted string of "selection characters" over the T circuit; this is the Selection Signals state (similar to dialing a telephone). In some implementations, the DCE now sends "Called Line Identification" information to the DTE by signaling on the R circuit. If the call is successful, the DCE then sends an ACK character on circuit R. Twenty milliseconds later, data transfer can begin.

For the station receiving the call, call arrival is announced by circuit R changing to 1. The station can accept the call by changing the T circuit to 1, then sending an ACK character 10 to 100 milliseconds later. As was the case with call origination, data transfer can begin 20 milliseconds after the receipt of the ACK. The DTE can request that a connection be cleared by holding the T circuit in the binary 0 condition for more than 210 milliseconds.

Recommendation X.20 contains additional information about call clearing, the sequence of events of unsuccessful calls, and formats for the call selection signals.

### X.21    General Purpose Interface Between Data Terminal Equipment (DTE) and Data Circuit-Terminating Equipment (DCE) for Synchronous Operation on Public Data Networks

The interface consists of the following:

| G | Signal Ground | |
|---|---|---|
| Ga | DTE Common Return | (from DTE to DCE) |
| T | Transmit | (from DTE to DCE) |
| R | Receive | (from DCE to DTE) |
| C | Control | (from DTE to DCE) |
| I | Indication | (from DCE to DTE) |
| S | Signal Element Timing | (from DCE to DTE) |
| B | Byte Timing (optional) | (from DCE to DTE) |

The electrical characteristics depend on the operating speed. Below 9600 bps, the circuits at the DCE are according to Recommendation X.27 (similar to EIA-422-A) without cable termination in the load. The circuits at the DTE can be the same, or they can be according to X.26 (similar to EIA-423-A), subject to some restrictions. Above 9600 bps, both the DCE and DTE must use Recommendation X.27 with cable termination in the load. In both cases, a 15-pin connector is used.

The X.21 interface is similar to the X.20 interface in that call control information is passed serially over the T and R circuits. Unlike X.20, the X.21 interface is synchronous (see Chapters 14 and 15) and thus utilizes a clock lead, referred to in the above list as circuit S, Signal Element Timing. Like other synchronous interfaces, X.21 requires that the call control information bits be aligned into characters. This is done via the transmission of "sync" characters or by manipulation of circuit B, Byte Timing, depending on the wishes of the organization providing the data transmission service.

Operation of an X.21 interface involves more states than operation of an X.20 interface, but the following paragraphs will deal only with those states that have parallels in X.20 so the two interfaces can be compared.

When a call is being established, the sequence of operations starts with the Ready state, wherein both the T and R circuits are binary 1 and both the C and I circuits are OFF. To enter the Call Request state, the T circuit is changed to 0 and the C circuit is changed to ON. The call enters the Proceed to Select state when the DCE sends two or more sync characters followed by continuous "+" characters on the R circuit. The DTE then causes entry into the Selection Signals state by sending a specially formatted string of "selection characters" over the T circuit. In some implementations, the DCE now sends "Called Line Identification" information to the DTE by signaling on the R circuit. If the call is successful, the DCE then asserts the R circuit to a binary 1 while simultaneously turning the I circuit ON. Data transfer can now begin.

For the station receiving the call, call arrival is announced by the DCE's sending two or more sync characters followed by continuous "BEL" characters on the R circuit, with the I circuit OFF. The station can accept the call by changing the T circuit to 1 and the C circuit to ON within 500 milliseconds. As was the case with call origination, data transfer can begin after the DCE asserts the R circuit to a binary 1 while simultaneously turning the I circuit ON. The DTE can request that a connection be cleared by holding the T circuit in the binary 0 condition with the C circuit OFF.

Recommendation X.21 contains additional information about call clearing, the sequence of events of unsuccessful calls, and formats for the call progress and selection signals.

For the sake of completeness, two other X-series interfaces—X.20 *bis* and X.21 *bis*—should be mentioned. These are interim interfaces that allow connection of conventional modem interfaces to public data networks. They are not serial control interfaces.

**X.20 *bis***   **V.21 Compatible Interface Between Data Terminal Equipment (DTE) and Data Circuit-Terminating Equipment (DCE) for Start-Stop Transmission Services on Public Data Networks**

(Recommendation V.21 is "300 Bits Per Second Modem Standardized for Use in the General Switched Telephone Network")

The interface consists of the following:

| | |
|---|---|
| 102 | Signal Ground or Common Return |
| 103 | Transmitted Data |
| 104 | Received Data |
| 106 | Ready for Sending |
| 107 | Data Set Ready |
| 108/x | |
| | 108/1 Connect Data Set to Line |
| | 108/2 Data Terminal Ready |
| 109 | Data Channel Received Line Signal Detector |
| 125 | Calling Indicator |

The electrical characteristics are according to Recommendation V.28, and a 25-pin connector is used.

These are the familiar EIA-232-D/V.24 signals, and they are used in the same way described in Chapters 5, 9, and 14, with minor definition and timing changes appropriate to electronic data network operation rather than switched telephone network operation. Note that X.20 *bis*, unlike X.20, does not include call selection, calling line identification, or called line identification.

**X.21 *bis***   **Use on Public Data Networks of Data Terminal Equipment (DTE) Which Is Designed for Interfacing to Synchronous V-Series Modems**

The interface consists of the following:

| | |
|---|---|
| 102 | Signal Ground or Common Return |
| 103 | Transmitted Data |
| 104 | Received Data |
| 105 | Request to Send |
| 106 | Ready for Sending |
| 107 | Data Set Ready |

108/x
      108/1 Connect Data Set to Line
      108/2 Data Terminal Ready
109   Data Channel Received Line Signal Detector
114   Transmitter Signal Element Timing (DCE)
115   Receiver Signal Element Timing (DCE)
125   Calling Indicator
142   Test Indicator (DCE)

The electrical characteristics of the DCE are according to Recommendation V.28, and a 25-pin connector is used. The electrical characteristics of the DTE may be according to Recommendation V.28 or Recommendation X.26.

When X.21 *bis* is used at a rate of 48,000 bps, the DCE will use a 34-pin connector, and the DTE interface will follow Recommendation V.35.

The call establishment and disconnection phases are controlled by Circuit 107 (Data Set Ready) and either Circuit 108/1 (Connect Data Set to Line) or Circuit 108/2 (Data Terminal Ready), according to the following tables:

*Circuit 107*—Data Set Ready
   ON Ready for Data
   OFF DCE Clear indication
   OFF DCE Clear confirmation

*Circuit 108/1*—Connect Data Set to Line (an alternative to 108/2)
   ON Call Request
   ON Call Accepted
   OFF DTE Clear indication
   OFF DTE Clear confirmation

*Circuit 108/2*—Data Terminal Ready (an alternative to 108/1)
   ON Call Accepted
   OFF DTE Clear indication
   OFF DTE Clear confirmation

Recommendation X.21 *bis* specifies that the automatic placement of calls over a switched network using addressed calling (i.e., dialing) should use the 200-series interface circuits described in Recommendation V.25 (see Chapter 11). If an automatic "direct call" (no dialing required) facility is provided, the assertion of Circuit 108/1 can be used to originate a call automatically, as is indicated in the table above, where an ON condition of Circuit 108/1 is labeled "Call Request." If the 200-series circuits are not used, or if a direct call facility is not provided, call origination must be done manually. Successful call completion is indicated when the DCE asserts Circuit 107, Data Set Ready, to the ON condition.

For the station receiving the call, call arrival is announced by the DCE's asserting Circuit 125, Calling Indicator. The station can accept the call by asserting Circuit 108/1 or Circuit 108/2, as indicated by the "Call Accepted" entries in the above tables. This must be done within 500 milliseconds after the assertion of Calling Indicator. As was the case with call origination, data transfer can begin after the DCE asserts Circuit 107, Data Set Ready, to the ON condition.

Data transmission can now begin, using Circuits 102, 103, 104, 105, 106, 109, 114, and 115. These are the familiar Recommendation V.24 signals, and they are used in the same way as described in Chapters 3, 9, and 14, with minor definition and timing changes appropriate to electronic data network operation instead of switched telephone network operation.

The DTE can request that a connection be cleared by dropping Circuit 108/1 or 108/2 to the OFF condition. The DCE will respond by dropping Circuit 107, Data Set Ready. The DCE can request that a connection be cleared by dropping Circuit 107, Data Set Ready. The DCE will respond by dropping Circuit 108/1 or 108/2 to the OFF condition.

Note that X.21 *bis*, unlike X.21, does not include call selection, calling line identification, or called line identification. Recommendation X.21 *bis* does contain a number of notes, not provided here, about alternative arrangements of interchange circuits. Readers wishing to implement any of the Recommendations discussed in this chapter should purchase the appropriate Recommendation from the United Nations Bookstore or International Telecommunications Union at the addresses given on page 00.

# *28*

## Local Area Networks

In early computer systems, users brought their problems to a computer by carrying punched cards or paper tape to the computer room and submitting the cards or tape to computer operators. It was considered a great advance when time-sharing systems and data communication made it possible for computer users to sit in a "terminal room" or in their offices and deal with the computer on an interactive basis.

Time-sharing systems have been so successful that the number of users on typical systems often grows to the point where a system's response time during periods of peak load becomes annoyingly slow. Although some users can respond to this problem by changing their work hours to avoid the busiest periods, the only viable long-term solution is to purchase more computing power.

Additional computing power can be obtained either by increasing the capacity of the central computing facility or by placing more computing capability in the hands of the user through the use of personal computers. While the power of central computing facilities is increasing, the most substantial increase in power is occurring in the personal computer area.

A look at the technologies involved suggests what is happening. Large computers are an exercise in nested packaging. Integrated circuits are mounted on printed circuit boards; printed circuit boards are mounted in card cages; card cages are bolted into cabinets; cabinets are bolted together and/or connected by cables. In contrast, personal computers are a few integrated circuits mounted on a circuit board in a box. Most important, the computational capability of the integrated circuits within the personal computer is equal to that of the large computer of less than ten years ago, due to the great progress that has been made in the design and fabrication of integrated circuits.

The progress in integrated circuits has been greater than that in computer peripherals, however. Printers, tape drives, and high-capacity removable disks have not become small enough and cheap enough to move into the office. Further, users would like to retain some "computer center" services associated with these devices, even if small, economical peripherals of all types become available. Examples of services that should be shared include file, printer, and communications services.

The need for shared file and printer services comes from the problems associated with disks and printers. Disks may crash, so they should be copied periodically ("backed up"). As users of personal computers and word processors know, one eventually gains enough confidence in the disks that making frequent back-up copies becomes too burdensome—until the day the disk is irrecoverably damaged (or physically lost) and weeks of work are lost. Using a centrally administered disk service facility solves most of this problem. There, it is someone's assigned task to do back-ups, and the disks are sealed and well cared for, rather than resting in a desk drawer or knapsack.

A central file facility also is convenient for users, as they can access desired data from any of the computers on the network. The user does not have to find a particular floppy in a particular desk drawer. A central disk service facility also reduces problems with updating data stored in duplicate on several computer systems ("distributed data bases"). It is much more likely that everyone will be working from and updating the same data base.

Using a central file facility does not mean that the personal computers have no disks. A disk is usually provided so that files may be transferred from the central file to the disk on the personal computer and subsequently referenced from the local disk to reduce delays. Further, personal computer users often like to keep sensitive data, such as salary reviews, on a disk they can physically secure at the end of the day.

Returning to the list of peripherals that should be shared, a printer on a personal computer is often an unnecessary expense. Moreover, the quality of printers cheap enough to be provided with personal computers is often disappointingly low—and the desk space consumed unexpectedly high. Personal computer users would be better off with medium-quality printers distributed throughout a building and a few centrally located high-performance printers.

Finally, a communications service should be shared by several users when the service is particularly expensive, such as a company-owned satellite link. Sharing computer services implies substantial data communication, as files are transferred rather than just keystrokes from terminals. Thus, the data rates required are far beyond the capabilities of the 9600 bps links that most of this book has discussed. Further, sharing implies a network of connections that will permit anyone to reach the file service, printer service, or shared satellite link. Fortunately, most applications requiring such connections are within the building complex of a corporation or the campus of a university—i.e., within an area that can be served by a "local area network."

A local area network is a data communication network that spans a physically limited area (generally less than a mile or two), provides high-bandwidth communications over inexpensive media (generally coaxial cable or twisted pair), provides a switching capability, and is usually owned by the user (i.e., not provided by a common carrier). Table 28–1 compares the distance, bandwidth, and cost characteristics of local area networks with those of other communications techniques.

In a local area network, the relatively short distance spanned, the high bandwidth provided, and the low-cost media used create an operating environment in which bandwidth is cheap, a substantial contrast to the tra-

Table 28–1   Comparison of Local Area Networks with
Other Communications Systems

| Distance | Bandwidth | Cost | Example |
|----------|-----------|------|---------|
| Short | Low | Low | Ordinary Wire |
| Short | Low | High | — |
| Short | High | Low | Local Area Networks |
| Short | High | High | — |
| Long | Low | Low | Public Telephone Network |
| Long | Low | High | — |
| Long | High | Low | — |
| Long | High | High | Satellite, Microwave |

ditional common carrier environment described in the rest of this book. An important consequence of these differing environments is that there are radical differences between the network topology (and the routing of traffic within that topology) for a telephone network and that for a local area network. While a telephone network generally has a hierarchical form with links placed between nodes according to traffic and cost, a local area network usually has a very regular form that is either a star (Figure 28–1a), a ring (Figure 28–1b), or a bus (Figure 28–1c). Further, the nodes of a telephone network route traffic according to complex rules (see Figure 8–2), but the nodes of a local area network do very little (if any) routing.

Each topology shown in Figure 28–1 is best suited to particular media types, has an optimum routing strategy, and has identifiable reliability characteristics. The star is a convenient topology for transmission media that are inherently simplex or cannot easily be tapped. The star permits exceptionally easy routing, as the central node knows the path to the other nodes. Since there is a central control point, access to the network can be easily controlled and priority status can be given to selected nodes. With the centralization of control come the requirements that the central node be exceptionally reliable and have the computational capacity to route all the network traffic.

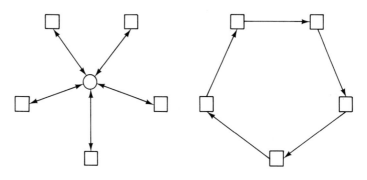

Figure 28–1a   Local Area
Network with Star Topology

Figure 28–1b   Local Area
Network with Ring Topology

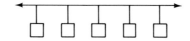

Figure 28–1c   Local Area Network with Bus Topology

A ring is another attractive topology for transmission media that are simplex or difficult to tap. The ring also permits easy routing, as each node decides whether to pass on a message or accept it, although that is a slight oversimplification. A ring may at first seem less robust than a star, as every node of a ring must work for the network to function correctly. In practice it is possible to design rings that allow a failed node to be bypassed via relays. This concept is shown in Figure 28–2a. It is also possible to extend the bypass concept one step further and utilize bypass relays and duplex connections between the nodes. Such an arrangement allows a failed node or failed ring segment to be bypassed and is shown in Figure 28–2b. The

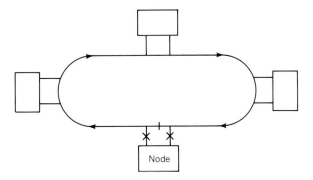

**Note**  In the figure, the connections for one node have been enlarged to show the bypass relay wiring. All nodes are similarly wired. Connections shown " × " are closed in normal operation.

Figure 28–2a   Ring Network with Bypass Relays

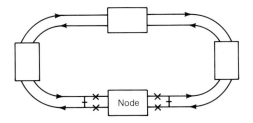

**Note**  In the figure, the connections for one node have been enlarged to show the bypass relay wiring. All nodes are similarly wired. Connections shown " × " are closed in normal operation. Connections shown " + " are closed in bypass operation.

Figure 28–2b   Ring Network with Bypass Relays between Nodes addition of a node to a ring network does pose a problem, however, because the ring must be broken for the node to be inserted, causing the network to be out of service while such changes are made. Use of relay-equipped "wire centers" reduces this time to a fraction of a second.

A bus requires a medium in which signals can flow in either direction—i.e., a full-duplex medium. Unlike the star or ring topologies, nodes associated with a bus do no routing at all. That is because the bus is a broadcast medium in which all nodes receive all transmissions. In addition, in many bus systems the nodes contend with each other for use of the medium, a scheme that distributes the control of the medium to the nodes. The lack of routing and the lack of centralized control provide substantial reliability. A major attraction of a bus is that if nodes fail, traffic can still be passed over the network, providing the node failure is not of the "babbling tributary" type (in which random signals are applied to the line).

Buses do have one drawback. The impedance irregularities caused by the installation of taps will cause signal reflections that can interfere with data transmission if the taps are placed too close to each other. Thus, bus systems often have a minimum distance between taps specified in the installation manual.

While the above paragraphs have hinted at methods of controlling access to the media for various topologies, no control systems have been discussed in detail because there is not a one-to-one relation between control schemes and local area network topology. Some schemes are more widely used with certain topologies than others, so the following discussion emphasizes the most popular control/topology combinations.

All three topologies described above were used in teleprinter networks for military, weather, and airline reservation systems long before their appearance in local area networks. A widely used control scheme for such networks is "polling," in which a master station queries each slave about whether it has traffic to send. A polling system has the advantage that all stations can receive equal access, or priority stations can be given preference by having them polled more often. Further, a polling system can be arranged to function well over extremely long distances, as it can be adjusted to compensate for long propagation delays. Polling is extremely time-consuming, however, as a substantial number of the messages on the medium are polling messages from the master station. The success of a polling system is also highly dependent on the reliability of the master station.

An efficient variation of polling, especially suitable for the ring topology, is the use of tokens. In a token system, a special bit pattern referred to as the "token" circulates around the ring. If a node has no traffic, it allows the token to pass. If the node does have traffic, it takes the token, inserts a message in front of the token, then reinserts the token. The token system provides the fairness and distance insensitivity of the polling system, while also providing far more efficient utilization of the medium. It relies on the correct performance of the nodes, however, and provision must be made to recover gracefully from failures that have caused the token to disappear. There are a number of variations of the token scheme, many of them described in the references.

Another control technique is the use of contention. While this technique is most suitable for a bus topology, the classic use of contention was the ALOHA network in Hawaii, a star topology. The ALOHA network used radio communications from the nodes around the base of a mountain to a central node atop the mountain. While the central node could communicate with the nodes at the base of the mountain, those nodes could not communicate with each other. In the control system chosen, the nodes at the base would transmit whenever they wished. If no one else was transmitting during that time, the central node would receive the message correctly; otherwise, the reception would be garbled by a transmission from some other node, an occurrence referred to as a "collision." A possible analog of this is a meeting in which all the participants talk to the chairman whenever they want. As might be imagined, the throughput of such a scheme is quite low because the medium is used for successful transmissions less than 20 percent of the time.

In the "talk whenever you want to" contention scheme, often referred to as "pure ALOHA," it is possible that a collision will occur at any time during a transmission. A collision can even occur at the end of an otherwise good message, wasting the channel time it took to send that message. A substantial improvement in channel time utilization was accomplished by creating the "slotted ALOHA" contention scheme. In slotted ALOHA, the nodes are synchronized and begin transmissions only at the beginning of a time slot, and they can transmit only for the length of the slot. As a result, some time slots contain a jumble of simultaneous transmissions, some contain no transmissions, and some contain the transmission from just one node—the successful transmission. Returning to the meeting analogy, it is as if the chairman allowed people to talk for less than a minute, starting exactly on a minute boundary. Slotted ALOHA provides roughly twice the capacity of pure ALOHA.

The contention systems described for the ALOHA network may seem strange, but the limitation that the nodes cannot hear each other is a severe constraint. If that constraint is removed, a number of more attractive techniques can be used, the simplest of which is "Carrier Sense Multiple Access," abbreviated CSMA. In CSMA, a node listens to the medium before transmitting, and if nothing is heard, it begins transmitting. There is, however, a finite probability that some other node will come to the same decision at the same time and two (or more) transmissions will commence simultaneously. The likelihood of such an event increases on long buses because a transmission can commence at one end of the bus and not propagate to the distant end before a node at that end decides to transmit. Thus, an additional feature, collision detection, is usually added to CSMA systems to create "Carrier Sense Multiple Access with Collision Detection," or CSMA/CD.

The collision detection may be accomplished by comparing transmitted data with received data to see whether the message on the medium matches the one being transmitted or by techniques that detect the presence of other transmissions by direct electrical means. Returning to the analog of a meeting, the comparison of transmitted and received data is the method actually used by meeting participants. A person listens to see whether anyone else is talking. If not, the person begins to talk while listening to see whether the sounds in the room contain voices other than his or hers. If another voice is heard, each speaker will usually back off by being silent for a few seconds, then will try talking again. In a CSMA/CD system, backing off when a collision is detected also is used. The amount of time before a retry can be random or can follow the "exponential back-off" rule. In random retry, a transmitting node that has encountered a collision will wait a random amount of time and then retry. If the retry encounters a collision, the process will be repeated, using another random time interval. In exponential back-off, the first retry occurs after a random time interval, but if collision occurs again, the node will wait twice as long before retrying. This procedure is continued until either a collision-free transmission is accomplished or a maximum retry limit is exceeded. The optimum strategy for backing off has been the subject of a number of papers.

The most famous implementation of CSMA/CD contention is the Ethernet system, and its advantages and disadvantages have become widely known. In addition to its simplicity, CSMA/CD has the advantage that control is distributed to the nodes, and in the bus topology, where the nodes are not part of the medium, a high degree of reliability is possible. CSMA/CD is more efficient than polling and does not require the "lost token recovery" features of a token system. But use of CSMA/CD on its best-suited topology, a bus, is not without drawbacks. As mentioned above, two nodes that are beginning to transmit may not recognize each other's presence (i.e., detect collision) for some time because of the amount of time (about 5 nanoseconds per meter) it takes signals from each to reach the other. If the messages are short enough, a collision may occur without either node knowing about it. Thus, there is a requirement in CSMA/CD that messages not be less than a minimum length, which is a function of the transmission speed and the length of the medium. Thus, this relationship places practical limits on the packet size and the medium length. Another problem in CSMA/CD is that the amount of time required to gain access to the medium is highly variable; in fact, there is theoretically no guarantee that a node will ever get a chance to transmit. This problem is generally overcome by not trying to carry more than about 40 percent of the theoretically possible traffic.

The preceding discussion of local area network applications, topologies, and control systems is intended only as an outline. The references listed below and the proceedings of recent conferences should be consulted for a complete and up-to-date view of progress in local area networks. Also note that local area networks are not the solution to all data communication problems. The direct connection of terminals to large computer systems, particularly for news services, stock exchanges, and other users of data communication over long distances, will be an important part of data communication in the future.

## References

1. Thurber, Kenneth J., and Harvey A. Freeman. *Tutorial—Local Computer Networks*, (IEEE Catalog No. EHO 163-6). New York: IEEE Computer Society, 1980. This publication contains reprints of the following references 2–8, in addition to others not listed here.
2. Clark, David D., Kenneth T. Pogran, and David P. Reed. "An Introduction to

Local Area Networks." In *Proceedings of the IEEE*, November 1978, pp. 1497–1517.

3. Fraser, A.G. "Spider—An Experimental Data Communications System." In *Conference Record*, International Conference on Communications, 1974, pp. 21F1–21F10.

4. Rawson, Eric G., and Robert M. Metcalfe. "Fibernet: Multimode Optical Fibers for Local Computer Networks." *IEEE Transactions on Communications*, July 1978, pp. 983–990.

5. Farber, David J. "A Ring Network." *Datamation*, February 1975, pp. 44–46.

6. Binder, R. et al. "ALOHA Packet Broadcasting—A Retrospect." In *Proceedings, National Computer Conference*, 1975, pp. 203–215.

7. Metcalfe, Robert M., and David R. Boggs. "ETHERNET: Distributed Packet Switching for Local Computer Networks." *Communications of the ACM*, July 1976, pp. 395–404.

8. Gordon, R.L., W. W. Farr, and P. Levine. "Ringnet: A Packet Switched Local Network with Decentralized Control." In *Proceedings, 4th Conference on Local Computer Networks*, 1979, pp. 13–19.

9. McNamara, John E. *Local Area Networks—An Introduction to the Technology.* Bedford, MA: Digital Press, 1985.

# RPPENDIX R

## How Far—How Fast?

"How far—how fast?" is one of the most difficult questions to answer in data communication. Intuition suggests that it would be possible to draw a curve similar to that in Figure A–1 and from it tell anyone who asked how far they could transmit a data signal at a particular signaling rate.

In practice, such a curve can be drawn, but the position of the curve is different for each hardware configuration. The use of various line driver circuits and various line receiver circuits will influence the position of the curve, as will extetnal influences such as noise. When signaling that relies on various voltage levels representing "1" and "0" states (such as EIA-232-D) is used, differences in ground potential between the transmitting and receiving stations become important. For example, if the transmitting station applies +5 volts to a line to represent a "0," but the receiving station measures the voltage on the line relative to a ground that is 10 volts higher than the ground at the transmitting station, the voltage on the line will

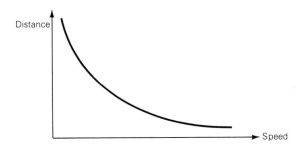

Figure A–1 Idealized Speed Versus Distance Performance Curve

appear to be −5 volts. The receiving station will interpret that as a "1." This problem is partially alleviated by running a Signal Ground lead between the transmitting and receiving stations to provide a common ground reference. This solution is not entirely adequate, however, because if current flows in the Signal Ground wire, the resistance of the wire will permit a voltage difference between the two ends of the wire.

While the most common cause of ground potential differences is imbalances in the power distribution systems supplying the transmitting and receiving stations, the use of voltage interfaces between different buildings brings special problems during lightning storms. At those times, entire buildings will assume varying potentials, even if lightning does not strike the buildings.

The best way to avoid ground potential problems is to make sure the equipment at the transmitting station and the equipment at the receiving station are powered from the same power distribution system. Using the same outlet box is ideal; using the same circuit breaker panel is almost as good; using the same step-down transformer/voltage distribution panel is quite good; using the same building distribution system is fair; using any other arrangement is risky but may work.

A more satisfactory method of transmitting information than the voltage-relative-to-ground method described above is differential transmission. In this type of transmission, two conductors are used for each data path, and the information to be conveyed is expressed as the difference in voltage between the two conductors. It does not matter what the ground potential difference is as long as it is not so high as to cause electrical breakdown in the receiver circuitry. The receiver needs only to determine whether the relative voltage between the two conductors is that appropriate to a "0" or that appropriate to a "1." Interfering signals are generally voltages relative to ground and will affect both conductors equally. Assume that a noise voltage $V_n$ is applied to two conductors, one carrying a voltage $+V$ and the other carrying a voltage $-V$. The resultant voltages will be $+V + V_n$ and $-V + V_n$. The receiver will take the difference between the two voltages, however, which is $2V$, just as it was before the noise was added. Noise of this kind is called "common mode" noise, and the differential properties of the receiver produce what is called "common mode rejection." EIA Standard EIA-422-A is an excellent example of a differential transmission system.

Chapter 3 mentions that the EIA-232-D specification places a limit of 2500 picofarads on the capacitance of the receiving station's receiver system, including the capacitance of the cable from the transmitting station to the receiving station. The consequence of violating this specification is that the amount of time needed to accomplish a transition from the MARK state to the SPACE state and vice versa will be increased from the 4 percent of a bit time allowed by the EIA-232-D standard. Since it is also likely that the resistance of the driver and receiver circuitry is different for the MARK–SPACE transition than for the SPACE–MARK transition, there will be a different amount of time required to charge the cable capacitance in the two transitions; the increased capacitance created by going beyond 2500 picofarads of cable capacitance will make that difference more dramatic. The result will be that the receiver circuits will produce MARK bits that are longer than SPACE bits ("marking distortion") or SPACE bits that are longer than MARK bits ("spacing distortion"). This type of distortion, called "bias distortion," can cause characters to be received incorrectly, especially if clock speed distortion, noise, or other effects are present.

While this effect is discussed here and in Chapter 3 with respect to EIA-232-D interfaces, cable capacitance and the differing resistances of cable drivers in the "1" and "0" states will cause bias distortion in 20 milliampere and other information transmission systems. Differential transmission systems are much less inclined toward this type of distortion.

To complicate the speed versus distance problem further, circuit design practices that improve noise immunity may contribute to distortion. For example, the use of shielded cable is highly recommended in noisy environments, but it has a higher capacitance per foot than unshielded cable, hence the operating speed may have to be reduced. This effect is shown in the speed versus distance charts in this appendix, as curves are plotted for both shielded and unshielded cables.

A second circuit design practice that is a mixed blessing is the use of "hysteresis." Consider the pulse shown in Figure A–2. The resistance, capacitance, and inductance of the transmission facility have "smeared" the square pulse that entered the transmission facility into a barely discernible hump. A receiver circuit can recover the pulse by asserting a high level whenever the hump exceeds a certain voltage and asserting a low level at all other times. This is demonstrated in Figure A–3.

There is a good possibility, however, that there will be noise on the

Figure A–2   Effect of Cable Capacitance on Transmitted Signal

Figure A–3   Reception of Signal Distorted by Cable Capacitance

Figure A–4   Reception of Signal Distorted by Cable Capacitance and Noise

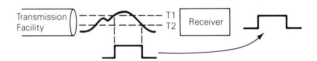

Figure A–5   Use of Hysteresis in Reception of Signal Distorted by Cable Capacitance

transmission facility. If the noise occurs just as the output voltage from the transmission facility is reaching the decision threshold of the receiver circuit, the receiver output will produce extraneous pulses. This is shown in Figure A–4. A common way to solve this problem is to add hysteresis to the receiver circuit. With hysteresis, as illustrated in Figure A–5, the receiver circuit will not recognize an input as being high until it passes threshold T1 and will not recognize it as being low until it passes threshold T2. This prevents noise near a single threshold point from producing extraneous pulses unless that noise is of quite substantial magnitude. Since T1 is higher than the old threshold point by the same amount that T2 is lower than the old threshold point, the length of the pulse coming from the receiver output is unchanged from that shown in Figure A–3, *provided that the waveform coming from the transmission facility has equal rise and fall times.*

Assume, however, that the output of the transmission facility has unequal rise and fall times. This is usually caused by driver circuits that do not have equal resistance in the ON and OFF states. As a result of the unequal resistances, the "time constant" of the signal differs for the rise time and the fall time, as the time constant is the product of the driver/line resistance and the driver/line capacitance. The effect on a nonhysteresis receiver is shown in Figure A–6 and on a hysteresis receiver in Figure A–7. Note that the pulse at the receiver output has been lengthened, causing bias distortion.

This example is not intended to imply that hysteresis is undesirable. On the contrary, it is a very useful technique for rejecting noise. The objective of this example is to indicate that, as cable length increases, the capacitance of the cable also increases, which accentuates distortion-causing phenomena.

So far, distortion has been assumed to be evil, but no proof of this has been provided. Chapter 1 describes the sampling process by which an asynchronous receiver detects the 1-to-0 transition signifying the arrival of a START bit. That discussion notes that typical receiver circuits sample the communication line at a rate 16 times the bit arrival rate. Thus, it is possible that a START bit that arrived just after a sample point would not

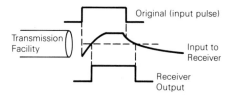

Figure A–6   Effect of Unequal Rise and
Fall Times of Signal at Ordinary
Receiver

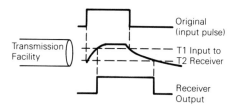

Figure A–7   Effect of Unequal Rise and
Fall Times of Signal at Hysteresis
Receiver

be detected until the next sample point, $\frac{1}{16}$ of a bit time later. This would introduce a $\frac{1}{16}$ of a bit time (6.25 percent) error in the subsequent sampling times—i.e., they would all be 6.25 percent of a bit time past the center of the bit being sampled. In theory, the sampling of a bit can be off by 50 percent of a bit time before an error occurs. That is because there is half a bit time between the sampling point at the center of a bit and the "edge" of the bit time, where the line changes state to the appropriate value for the next bit. Thus, distortion of $50 - 6.25$, or 43.75, percent can be accommodated by a receiver sampling at 16 times the bit rate. This is shown in Figure A–8.

The use of a 16X clock in receivers using UART chips is the reason such receivers often contain the phrase "Receiver Distortion Tolerance: 43.75 percent" in their specifications.

Assuming no noise effects, error-free reception requires that the sampling of the STOP element to check for a Framing Error not occur too early (so that it happens in part of the last data bit) or too late (so that it happens in part of the next START element). The time at which the sampling occurs is based on the detection of the 1-to-0 transition of the START element that began the character. That transition occurred $9\frac{1}{2}$ bit times before the sampling of the STOP bit, so any clock speed distortion must be multiplied by $9\frac{1}{2}$ and deducted from the 43.75 percent distortion tolerance described above. For example, a 2 percent clock distortion would cut the distortion tolerance to 24.75 percent.

The other distortion left to be tolerated is bias distortion. Figure A–8 assumes that the transition point between the two bits shown occurs where

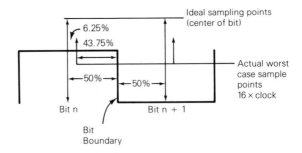

Figure A–8   Calculation of Distortion Tolerance of Receiver Using 16X Clock

it should. Marking distortion will cause bit *n* to last longer, moving the bit boundary to the right; spacing distortion will move the bit boundary to the left, as bit *n* + 1 will be lasting longer (both beginning earlier and terminating later). In this way, the bias distortion caused by the various cable capacitance effects discussed previously will add to the other distortions and possibly produce errors. In the example just cited, a 6.25 percent sampling error combined with 2 percent clock distortion (2 percent times 9½ equals 19 percent) and 24.75 percent bias distortion would produce marginal results, as the sampling of the STOP element would occur on the edge of that STOP element.

NOTE: Percent distortion is the difference between the time an event occurs and the time it should occur, expressed as a percentage of a bit time.

The preceding discussion is an introduction to the data presented in Figures A–9 through A–14. Figures A–9, A–10, and A–11 were developed on the basis of experiments performed by the Data Communication Engineering Group at Digital Equipment Corporation. The experiments were conducted using the wire types indicated, which were strung about a building rather than being kept on a reel. Noise effects were not measured

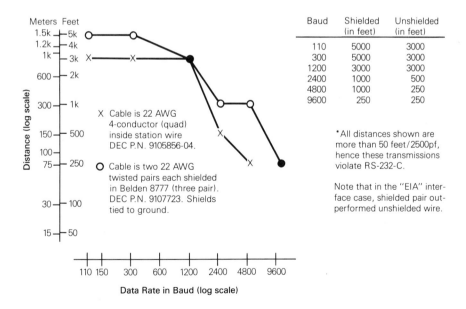

| Baud | Shielded (in feet) | Unshielded (in feet) |
|------|--------------------|-----------------------|
| 110  | 5000               | 3000                  |
| 300  | 5000               | 3000                  |
| 1200 | 3000               | 3000                  |
| 2400 | 1000               | 500                   |
| 4800 | 1000               | 250                   |
| 9600 | 250                | 250                   |

X Cable is 22 AWG 4-conductor (quad) inside station wire DEC P.N. 9105856-04.

O Cable is two 22 AWG twisted pairs each shielded in Belden 8777 (three pair). DEC P.N. 9107723. Shields tied to ground.

*All distances shown are more than 50 feet/2500pf, hence these transmissions violate RS-232-C.

Note that in the "EIA" interface case, shielded pair outperformed unshielded wire.

Figure A–9   EIA Interface

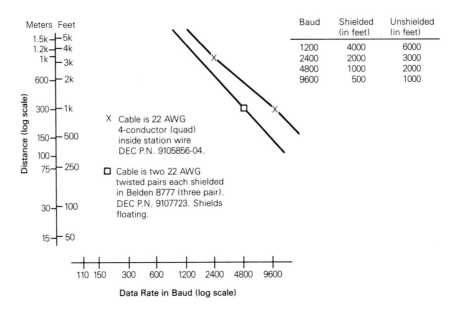

Figure A–10   20 ma Interface

quantitatively, but it was noted that signals within the same cable were a far more important noise source than any noise picked up from electrical machinery or fluorescent lighting. The building in which the wire was strung was used for office space and light manufacturing, although a medium-size machine shop was included in the cable route.

The transmitter and receiver units used were UART chips that tolerate 43.75 percent distortion. On the assumption that user applications might not have such a good distortion tolerance, or that user applications might involve a clock speed error of greater than 2 percent, an arbitrary limit of 10 percent was chosen for bias distortion. This limit determined the position of the curves in Figures A–9 and A–10. The curve in Figure A–11 was positioned based on crosstalk considerations.

For the EIA-232-D interface tests (Figure A–9) 1488 drivers and 1489 receivers (not 1489A) were used, with a ground potential difference of less than 2 volts between the transmitting and receiving stations. Since the 1488 and 1489 are widely used in the electronics industry, and the electrical properties of the EIA-232-D drivers and receivers are quite closely controlled by the specification, the curve given is probably also applicable for products made by companies other than Digital Equipment Corporation.

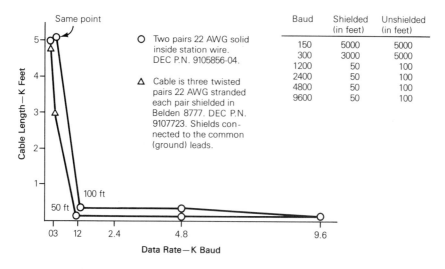

| Baud | Shielded (in feet) | Unshielded (in feet) |
|------|--------------------|----------------------|
| 150  | 5000 | 5000 |
| 300  | 3000 | 5000 |
| 1200 | 50   | 100  |
| 2400 | 50   | 100  |
| 4800 | 50   | 100  |
| 9600 | 50   | 100  |

○ Two pairs 22 AWG solid inside station wire. DEC P.N. 9105856-04.

△ Cable is three twisted pairs 22 AWG stranded each pair shielded in Belden 8777. DEC P.N. 9107723. Shields connected to the common (ground) leads.

Figure A–11    20 ma Interface Without Current Limiting Feature

The curves for 20 milliampere transmission (Figure A–10) are based on a circuit that limits line charging current and thus reduces crosstalk from transmitter units to their associated receiver units ("near-end crosstalk"). A more primitive circuit, without limitations on line charging current, was used to obtain the results plotted in Figure A–11. Here, crosstalk introduced errors before the 10 percent distortion limit was reached.

The curves given in these figures are very conservative, as no errors were permitted. In contrast, on standard switched telephone network lines, an error rate of one bit in $10^5$ is tolerable. Furthermore, the arbitrary limit of

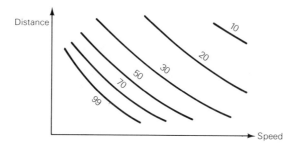

Figure A–12    Idealized Speed Versus Distance Performance Curves for Various Percentages of Satisfied Users

10 percent on bias distortion is fairly conservative. The reason for the conservative approach is best demonstrated by consulting Figure A–12, which is very similar in concept to Figure A–1.

The outermost curve in Figure A–12 shows outstanding speed versus distance performance, but only 10 percent of all system builders have conditions (ground potential difference, noise, etc.) ideal enough to obtain this performance. The innermost curve shows the speeds and distances that will yield satisfactory results for 99 percent of the systems built, assuming conditions similar to the test conditions in terms of noise environment and grounding conditions. Figures A–9, A–10, and A–11 are 99 percent curves.

Figures A–13 and A–14 are speed versus distance curves from EIA-422-A and EIA-423-A, respectively, and are reproduced with permission of the EIA. The Figure A–13 curve is based on empirical data using a 24-gauge twisted-pair telephone cable terminated in a 100 ohm resistive load. The signal quality requirements for determining the position of the curve were that the rise and fall times should not exceed half a bit time and that the

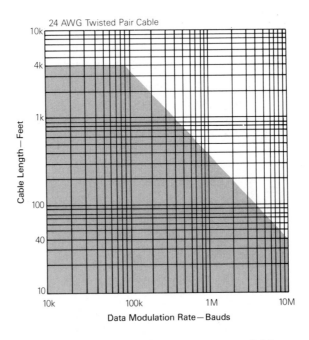

Figure A–13   Data Modulation Rate Versus Cable Length for Balanced Interface, RS-422

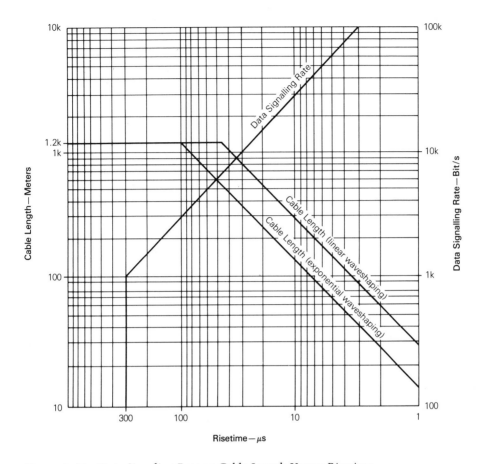

Figure A–14   Data Signaling Rate or Cable Length Versus Risetime

amplitude of the signal at the load should be no more than 6 dBV (a factor of two) below the voltage at the generator. The signal amplitude requirement is the limiting factor below 90,000 baud and accounts for the flat section at the left of the figure. Above 90,000 baud, the rise time requirement is the limiting factor, and the curve then begins to decline toward the lower part of the figure, reaching 40 feet at 10 megabaud. The figure does not account for cable imbalance or common mode noise beyond 7 volts (sum of ground potential difference, generator offset voltage, and externally introduced noise) that may be introduced between the generator and the load by exceptionally long cables, but it is nonetheless quite conservative, especially at low baud rates.

Figure A–14 is based on calculations and empirical data using twisted-pair telephone cable with a shunt capacitance of 16 picofarads per foot, a 50 ohm source impedance, and a 12 volt peak-to-peak source signal and allowing a maximum near-end crosstalk of 1 volt peak. The rise time of the signal at the generator from 10 to 90 percent of the voltage excursion (excluding ringing) is shown on the abscissa. Curves for both exponential and linear rise times are given (for details on the differences between these two kinds of waveshaping, see EIA-423-A). The maximum cable length can be determined by choosing a rise time, reading up to the intersection of the cable length curve, then reading the left-hand scale. The maximum signaling rate can be determined by reading up to the data signaling rate curve and reading the right-hand scale. The figure does not account for common mode noise, but that effect is usually minor compared with the near-end crosstalk sensitivity reflected in the figure.

While connection of EIA-422-A circuits yields fairly predictable results, some additional factors in EIA-423-A configurations should be discussed. Available EIA-423-A receivers can tolerate substantially more crosstalk than the 1 volt peak limit used to draw the curves in Figure A–14. Thus, experimental results with modern receivers may be better (a factor of two or three) than the results anticipated from Figure A–14. On the other hand, EIA-423-A circuits are susceptible to differential noise resulting from any imbalance between the signal conductor and the signal return. The sharing of a single signal return among several signal conductors will increase this problem. A far worse problem is the use of EIA-423-A receivers in an "EIA-232-D compatible" configuration where the B' input of the receiver is referenced to local ground rather than to ground at the generator. Noise picked up relative to ground at the receiving station will appear across the inputs of the EIA-423-A receiver. Hysteresis in EIA-423-A receivers is modest compared to that of EIA-232-D receivers, as EIA-423-A receivers are designed to operate differentially without requiring substantial hysteresis. Unfortunately, connecting the B' input to local ground defeats the differential feature and can lead to noise sensitivity, especially when the received signal is at or near the zero-crossing threshold. This is very troublesome when this configuration is used for clock circuits.

NOTE: Other high baud rate, short distance line drivers besides those described here are commercially available.

# APPENDIX B

## Modem Options

The information that follows lists many of the options found in Bell System modems. Many manufacturers make equivalent modems with similar options.

### Modem Options Concerned with Line Control (Call Answering and Call Disconnection)

*Send Disconnect (Choices: Yes/No)*

When this option has been installed, the modem, upon receiving a negation of DTE Ready, sends a $3 \pm 1$ second SPACE signal and then disconnects. Without this option, the modem, upon receiving a negation of DTE Ready, disconnects immediately.

*Yes* is the preferable choice. This permits the modem at the other end of the connection to disconnect from the line without special action by the modem control. It ensures that the distant modem will be available for future calls and will not appear off-hook to the telephone switching equipment.

*Response to Space Disconnect (Choices: Long/Short/None)*

With the Long option in place, the modem disconnects in response to receipt of 1.5 seconds of SPACE signal from the remote station. The Short option is similar to the Long option, but only 0.4 second of SPACE is required before disconnect occurs. With None, the modem takes no action upon receipt of the SPACE signal.

*Long* is the preferable choice.

### Loss of Carrier Disconnect (Choices: Yes/No)

When this option is provided, the modem disconnects when the incoming carrier is lost for more than 100 to 350 milliseconds.

*Yes* is the preferable choice, except that some operating systems prefer to do their own timing. In those cases, *No* may be preferred.

### Automatic Answer (Choices: Yes/No)

When this option is provided, the modem will answer all calls received while DTE Ready is asserted.

*Yes* is the preferable choice.

## Modem Options Concerned with Interface Lead Timing and Utilization

### CB and CF Indications (Choices: Separate/Common)

When the CB/CF Separate option is provided, Clear to Send remains ON despite loss of carrier. With CB/CF Common, performance mimics the earlier models of the Bell System 103, such as the 103A2, and Clear to Send turns OFF if Carrier Detect turns OFF. On the other hand, when the call is being established, the CB/CF Common option will not allow either to turn ON until the carrier has been received *and* the Clear to Send timer has run out.

*CB/CF Common* is preferred only if software compatibility requirements make it necessary to have new modems appear the same as old modems. Most operating systems prefer the added flexibility of *CB/CF Separate*.

### Request to Send, Clear to Send Delay (Choices, depending on modem: 150 msec/7 msec/0 msec or 180 msec/ 60 msec/30 msec/8 msec or 150 msec/50 msec)

This option determines the delay between the time the DTE asserts Request to Send and the time the modem asserts Clear to Send. For switched network or two-wire private line use, the longest possible delay is necessary to permit the direction of transmission to be "turned around." In some cases, this involves echo suppressors; in all cases, it involves a time allowance for letting echoes decay on two-wire lines. Many modems have a Squelch feature and a soft carrier turn-off feature for dealing with line echoes. The Clear to Send delay option must be chosen to be compatible with the remote modem's Squelch and Receive Line Signal Detect acquisition timing and for soft carrier turn-off options in two-wire applications.

The *180 millisecond delay* is required in applications where the remote modem has a 156 millisecond Squelch installed and is recommended for four-wire private lines equipped for "talkback." (Talkback is an arrangement available in four-wire multipoint configurations. When this feature is installed, the bridge circuit associated with each modem's connection to the transmission facility that constitutes the backbone of the multipoint line is arranged to repeat what the modem transmits back to the modem.) If the *150 millisecond delay* is not an available option, the 180 millisecond delay is recommended for all switched network applications and two-wire private lines.

The *150 millisecond delay* is recommended for all switched network applications and two-wire private lines.

Some modems offer a *50 millisecond delay* option. This will provide satisfactory service on most switched network connections, except those where the route of the call exceeds 2000 miles. The 2000 miles may be the length of the direct route from the calling place to the called place or may be accumulated if the call is alternately routed by the telephone system during periods of heavy traffic. In the case of long connections, echoes may cause received data errors at the beginning of a data reception due to an echo returning from the previous transmission. In this case, the *150 millisecond delay* should be used, although system throughput will be reduced as a result.

The *60, 30, 8, and 7 millisecond delay* options are preferred for four-wire point-to-point and multipoint lines requiring fast start-up. The *60 millisecond* option is compatible with the Received Line Signal Detector turn-on time of Bell System 202C, 202D3, and 202D4 and the 40 millisecond Receive Line Signal Detector option of Bell System 202D5, 202D6, and 202R. The *30 millisecond* option is compatible with the 20 millisecond Receive Line Signal Detector option of Bell System 202D5, 202D6, and 202R and with the Fast Carrier Detection OUT mode of 202S and 202T. The *8 millisecond* option is preferred for use in the 202T for duplex multipoint systems requiring fast start-up. This option is usable only when there is a 202S or 202T at the other end with Fast Carrier Detection IN. When this option is used, the DTE must maintain a MARK on the Transmitted Data circuit when Request to Send is ON and until the Clear to Send indication is given. For other modems on four-wire lines operated in switched carrier mode, the *7 millisecond delay* is sufficient to allow the distant modem (if equipped with Fast Carrier Detection) to synchronize with the carrier after it is switched on.

For four-wire lines operated in continuous carrier mode, either the 7 *millisecond* or the *0 millisecond* delay may be used. The *0 millisecond* option may be used for the master station in a polling system only if a "split bridge" configuration is used.

### *Fast Carrier Detection (Choices: In/Out)*

This option provides either a normal or a fast response time for the Received Line Signal Detector. When In, the Signal Detector turns ON in approximately 7 milliseconds when a MARK signal is received and OFF in approximately 5 milliseconds when it detects soft carrier turn-off. If turn-on is done with other than MARK and turn-off is done with other than soft carrier turn-off, the normal response times occur. The normal response times are ON in approximately 23 milliseconds when data signals are received and OFF in approximately 10 milliseconds when data signals are no longer received. These are the times used when the Fast Carrier Detection option is Out.

*Out* is preferred, except for use on duplex multipoint systems requiring fast start-up and using the 8 millisecond Clear to Send delay, in which case *In* is required.

### *Soft Carrier Turn-Off (Choices: In(8)/In(24)/Out)*

When In, this option causes the modem to transmit 8 or 24 milliseconds of a soft carrier frequency (typically 900 Hz) after the Request to Send lead has been turned OFF. This prevents the distant modem from seeing possible spurious SPACE signals as the carrier turns off. When this option is Out, the carrier is turned off within 1 millisecond after Request to Send is turned OFF.

*In (24)* is preferred, except that *In (8)* should be used when the distant modem has Fast Carrier Detect. In two-wire applications, use of this option influences the Clear to Send delay option needed at the distant modem. In all applications, this option should be used with the Received Data Clamp option (to produce a steady MARK on the Received Data lead of the distant modem when the local modem turns off its carrier). *Out* is preferred only when the Carrier Detector Reset option is used in the distant modem in applications requiring fast start-up.

### *Received Data Clamp (Choices: In/Out)*

When In, this option causes Received Data to be clamped to a MARK state when Carrier Detect is off.

*In* is preferred.

### Answer Mode Indication (Choices: On/Off)

With this option installed, the Calling/Ring Indicator (CCITT 125, EIA CE) circuit remains asserted after an incoming call has been answered and drops only when the connection has been broken.

*Off* is preferred, allowing the circuit to return to the OFF state after the call has been answered.

### Common Grounds (Choices: Yes/No)

When the Common option is provided, Protective Ground (Circuit AA, pin 1) is connected to Signal Ground (Circuit AB, pin 7)

AB Not Connected to AA (*No*) is the preferred arrangement in modern installations unless local regulations or conditions dictate otherwise. EIA-232-D recommends that Frame Ground references of the DCE and DTE be connected via the power cord grounding leads in accordance with recognized national electrical codes.

## Modem Options Unique to Private Line Modems

### Frequency Choices for Low-Speed Asynchronous Modems Operating on a Two-Wire Private Line (Choices: Originate/Answer)

This option determines whether the modem transmits on 2025/2225 Hz and receives on 1070/1270 Hz or vice versa.

Choose one modem to be *Originate* and the other(s) to be *Answer*, or choose one to be *Answer* and the other(s) to be *Originate*.

### Circuit Type (Choices: Half Duplex/Full Duplex)

Used on the switched network or on two-wire private lines, some modems are half duplex. Used on four-wire private lines, almost all modems are full duplex.

If at all possible, *four-wire private* line service is recommended.

### Carrier Control (Choices: Continuous/Request to Send Controlled)

This option determines whether the modem transmitter operates all the time (Continuous) or whether it is under the control of the Request to Send lead.

For four-wire point-to-point circuits, choose *Continuous*. For multipoint configurations or half-duplex service, use *Request to Send Controlled*.

### Alternate Voice (Choices: Yes/No)

Sometimes it is desirable to use the same private line for both voice and data communication. Some modems on the market achieve this by frequency separation techniques and allow simultaneous use, but with Bell System modems, alternate use is provided.

*Yes* is preferable because it could be of assistance to maintenance personnel. This is not a strong preference, and many users may prefer *No.*

### Switched Network Backup (Choices: Yes/No)

Switched Network Backup provides some additional hardware to permit use of the modem to be transferred from the private line to the public switched telephone network in the case of a private line failure. One call is made to back up a two-wire private line; two calls are required to back up a four-wire private line.

*Yes* is preferable if the importance of the application and the anticipated failure rate of the private line overcome the additional costs.

### Received Data Squelch
### (Choices: 156 msec /9 msec /0 msec)

The Squelch option prevents the demodulator (receiver) of a station that has been transmitting from delivering spurious data on the Received Data circuit when the Request to Send lead is turned off. Spurious data is a possibility because in half-duplex operation on two-wire facilities, the telephone line may reflect echoes back to the transmitting station for as long as 100 milliseconds after the Request to Send lead has been turned off.

The *156 millisecond* option is recommended for switched network service, two-wire private lines, and four-wire private lines that have been arranged for "talkback."

The *9 millisecond* option may be used on two-wire private lines less than 50 miles in length at the customer's risk.

The *0 millisecond* option is recommended for four-wire private lines.

The *9 or 0 millisecond* options can be used on two-wire private line facilities over any distance if the system software uses Start of Message codes or some other method of ignoring echo-induced spurious data. Use of these options in switched network service is not recommended because the varying call routing produces varying propagation delays and because of the possible existence of echo suppressors (which require 100 milliseconds to "turn around"). Use of these options may, however, be attempted at the customer's risk if the system software can ignore the echo-induced spurious data and can use the reverse channel to keep the echo suppressors disabled, and if modems at each end of the line have compatible options.

### *Carrier Detector Reset (Choices: In/Out)*

This option is intended to be used in a modem receiver at a master station of a four-wire multipoint system to permit rapid acquisition of incoming signals from different remote transmitters. An assertion of 0.2 milliseconds or more should be applied to the Carrier Detector Reset lead from the DTE to the modem after the End of Message has been detected. This circuit should be held off at all other times.

*Out* is preferable unless the modem control implements an interface to this lead, the system software supports control of the lead, and the application demands use of the lead. If all these conditions are satisfied, then *In* is preferred.

### *Request to Send Operation in Continuous Carrier Mode (Choices: Continuous/Switched)*

This option permits a master station in a multipoint network to appear to be operating in switched carrier mode when in fact it is operating in continuous carrier mode. With the Continuous option, Clear to Send is returned to the DTE 8 ± 0.5 milliseconds after the DTE asserts Request to Send.

When the Carrier Control option is *Switched*, the Request to Send Operation option also must be *Switched*. When the Carrier Control option is *Continuous*, either Request to Send Operation option may be chosen. *Switched* is preferable if the software is going to control Request to Send; otherwise, *Continuous* is preferable.

### *Multiplex (Choices: 1, 2, 3, 4, 5)*

Some 9600 bps modems offer a customer accessible switch that provides five different arrangements:

1. 9600 baud on Connector 1.
2. 7200 baud on Connector 1, 2400 on Connector 2.
3. 4800 baud on Connector 1, 4800 on Connector 2.
4. 4800 baud on Connector 1, 2400 on Connectors 2 and 3.
5. 2400 baud on Connectors 1, 2, 3, and 4.

Caution: If any connector is arranged for DTE-supplied timing ("External Clock"), that connector will have to be equipped with an "Elastic Store." This will not be necessary if all connectors operate on a modem-supplied "Internal" clock.

## Modem Options Unique to Synchronous Modems

### New Sync (Choices: With/Without)

This option may be used on four-wire private multipoint lines at the master station of a polling network to ensure rapid resynchronization of the receiver on a sequence of messages from several different remote transmitters. This feature is necessary because the receiver clock maintains the timing information of the previous message for some time interval (no more than 10 milliseconds) after it has ended; this may interfere with resynchronization on receipt of the next message. An ON condition should be applied to this lead for a millisecond or more after detection of End of Message and after Received Line Signal Detect (Carrier Detect) has gone OFF. At all other times the DTE must hold New Sync OFF.

CAUTION: Data terminal equipment that uses FIFO buffers or similar systems where characters are processed substantially after they are received must use New Sync cautiously, as leaving it ON too long will damage the next data message, which may arrive within 7 milliseconds of the previous message.

*Without* is the preferred choice, unless the user has both the exact application described above and a DTE that can control this lead. In the application described, this option is required where intermessage intervals of incoming messages at the master station are 10 milliseconds or less. The intermessage interval consists of the time from the end of one message to the beginning of the next. It is the sum of the Request to Send/Clear to Send delay of the master station as it prepares its next poll, the length of time required to transmit that poll, and the Request to Send/Clear to Send delay of the remote station as it begins its reply to the poll. If the Request to Send/Clear to Send delay in the master station is 7 milliseconds and the delay used in the remote station is also 7 milliseconds, the master station will not require the New Sync option, as the intermessage interval will be at least 14 milliseconds. If the master station uses a 0 millisecond Request to Send/Clear to Send delay, New Sync will be required.

### Clock Source (Choices: Internal/External)

When Internal clocking is selected, the modem supplies the clocking for data transfer between the DTE and the modem. When External clocking is selected, the DTE provides the clocking and the clock in the DTE must conform to the distortion accuracy of EIA-334, which requires peak individual distortion of no greater than 0.5 percent. Frequency accuracy must be ±0.005 percent.

*Internal* clocking is preferred for convenience.

### Slaved Transmitter Timing by Receiver (Choices: In/Out)

This option allows a modem transmitter to be timed by its receiver based on signals from a far-end modem that serves as a master timing source for the system. It is used in one modem in many multipoint or one-to-many multiplexing configurations involving extension service on either modem.

*Out* is preferred for simple point-to-point applications.

### One Second Holdover at Receiver on Line Dropout (Choices: Provided/Not Provided)

With this option, the Received Line Signal Detector circuit is kept ON up to 1 second beyond the time that carrier signal is lost, permitting the receiving modem to maintain timing synchronization during momentary line dropouts. The loss of carrier will be indicated by the Signal Quality Detector circuit's turning OFF after a carrier loss of greater than 2 milliseconds and back ON after return of the carrier for more than 4 milliseconds. Without this option, negation of Received Line Signal Detector and clamping of the Received Data lead to MARK occurs after 2 milliseconds.

This option is recommended for use in modems receiving a continuous carrier from a distant transmitter. *Provided* is preferred in that case. *Not Provided* is preferred when the distant transmitter uses switched carrier operation.

## Modem Options Concerned with Maintenance Tests

### CC Indication for Analog Loop (Choices: On/Off)

This option determines whether the DCE Ready lead is asserted or negated when the modem is in analog loop test mode. Some software systems require that DCE Ready be asserted before data can be sent, and some hardware also has this requirement.

*On* is the preferred option because it most closely obeys CCITT and EIA requirements and may be required by hardware and software, as indicated above.

### Response to Digital Loop (Choices: In/Out)

When this option is installed and the modem is in high-speed mode, another compatible modem can send signals to this modem, which will put it in loop (test) mode.

If an automatic remote test system is to be used, *In* would be preferred. If manual operation of the test capabilities is preferred to guard against false operation, select *Out*. Some modems include a user accessible button or switch that is operative regardless of which option is selected.

### Interface Controlled Remote Digital Loop (Choices: In/Out)

This option allows assertion of pin 21 (CCITT 140, EIA RL) to cause the modem to initiate the remote digital loop feature, placing the remote modem in digital loop mode.

If the DTE can control pin 21 and the appropriate software exists, *In* would provide a valuable maintenance aid. Otherwise, select *Out*.

## Modem Options Unique to Dual-Speed Modems

### Speed Control (Choices: Interface/Button)

When a dual-speed modem is used to originate calls, it is necessary to specify whether the modem should operate in the high-speed mode or in the low-speed mode. The speed may be selected by means of an interface pin (CCITT Circuit 111, EIA CH, pin 23) or, in some modems, by means of a user accessible push button or switch. This option selects the control method used.

If the DTE hardware and software support control of the 111/CH leads, *Interface* is the preferred choice. Otherwise, *Button* must be selected.

### Speed Mode (Choices: High/Dual)

With the High option installed, the modem passes data only on calls from similar dual-speed modems operating at high speed. In the Dual mode, data also is passed on calls from low-speed modems. Calls from both types of modems are answered regardless of option choice. The option determines from which calling modems data is passed.

*Dual* provides more functionality, unless there is a specific desire to exclude calls from low-speed modems.

### Interface Speed Indication (Choices: In/Out)

If this option is installed, the Speed Mode Indicator (CCITT 112, EIA CI) circuit is connected to pin 12.

If the DTE can monitor pin 12, that pin is not being used for another purpose, and appropriate software exists, select *In*. Otherwise, select *Out*.

## Modem Options Unique to Asynchronous/Synchronous Modems

### *Operation (Choices: Asynchronous/Synchronous)*

Some modems offer a choice of asynchronous or synchronous operation. The signal placed on the line is that of a synchronous modem, but the modem contains async/sync conversion logic. This option allows the conversion logic to be enabled or disabled depending on the type of DTE the customer wishes to use.

The preferred choice depends on the type of DTE being used.

### *Character Length (Choices: 9 bits/10 bits)*

Some modems offer a choice of asynchronous or synchronous operation. The signal placed on the line is that of a synchronous modem, but the modem contains async/sync conversion logic. This option determines the character length in asynchronous operation. The number of bits includes the START bit and the first STOP bit.

For eight-bit characters with a START bit and one or two STOP bits, *10 bits* is the preferred choice.

## Modem Options Concerned with the "Make Busy" Feature

Make Busy was a feature offered for use with time-sharing installations where dozens of lines went to the same computer. By means of a special feature in the telephone company's central office and the Make Busy lead (EIA designation CN) on the modem, calls to a malfunctioning line or malfunctioning computer could be blocked at the central office by returning a busy signal to the caller or advancing the call to another line that was in service. The Make Busy lead is not defined in CCITT Recommendation V.24 or in EIA-232-D and is rarely used today. Options associated with it are discussed here for the benefit of anyone who might have an older modem with this feature.

### *Make Busy (Choices: In/Out)*

When this option is installed and the DTE asserts lead 25 (CN), the line appears busy to incoming calls. A change in the telephone company's central office is required to make the feature functional.

*Out* is preferred unless the DTE and operating system are specifically designed to handle this feature and the local telephone company offers the central office change that is part of this service.

### Fail-Safe State of CN Circuit (Choices: On/Off)

In some older modems, notably the Bell System 113B and 103J, the Make Busy circuit (CN) was arranged so that if no lead was attached, the modem assumed that the cable was disconnected or that the DTE had somehow failed. The modem then went into the Make Busy state, busying out the associated telephone line.

*Off* is the preferred option.

## Other Modem Options

### Reverse Channel (Choices: In/Out)

When In, the reverse channel provides a five baud channel for circuit assurance and an error detection request for retransmission.

*In* is preferred. The reverse channel may be used to provide a break feature or circuit assurance or as part of an error detection and request for retransmission system. It also can be used to hold echo suppressors disabled in switched network applications.

### Local Copy Primary Channel (Choices: In/Out)

When this option is In and the modem is being used on two-wire facilities, the receiver section of the modem monitors the line signals at all times and thus reproduces the transmitted data on the Received Data lead.

*Out* is preferable, unless the system software wants it otherwise.

# APPENDIX C

## Codes

Tables C–1 through C–6 on the following pages are taken from information provided by Allan R. Kent of Digital Equipment Corporation. They are arranged in order by the number of bits used in the individual codes. In five-bit ("five-unit") codes and some six-bit codes, the meaning of a particular bit combination is dependent on whether the transmitting and receiving stations are operating in the "figures" shift mode or the "letters" shift mode, sometimes referred to as "shift" and "unshift," respectively. The shifting operation would be analogous to the shifting operation in a conventional office typewriter if the typewriter had only a "shift lock" facility. In other words, one depresses a key (shift lock on a typewriter, FIGS on a teleprinter) to enter the shifted state. From then on all characters typed are "upper-case" on a typewriter or "figures" on a teleprinter. To leave the shifted state, one depresses another key: shift on a typewriter, LTRS on a teleprinter.

To facilitate comparison of the various five-unit codes, the first section of the five-unit code charts (Tables C–1, C–2, C–3) presents the "letters" shift characters common to all the codes listed, showing those characters along the left hand edge of the chart. The next column in the charts shows the CCITT Alphabet #2 standard for the "figures" shift characters corresponding to the bit combinations. The remaining columns of the charts show the "figures" shift characters and symbols used in the various codes enumerated along the top of the charts.

In the seven-unit code example (Table C–6), there are sufficient bits to represent various characters and symbols without shifting.

Table C–1   Five-Unit Codes

| Octal | Letters (common to all codes on this page) | CCITT Alphabet #2 | American Communications Variant of CCITT #2 | Western Union "A" Keyboard | Western Union Telex | Western Union Telegraph | United Press International |
|-------|------|------|------|------|------|------|------|
| 00 | Blank | Blank | Blank | Blank | Blank | Blank | Blank |
| 01 | E | 3 | 3 | 3 | 3 | 3 | 3 |
| 02 | LF | LF | LF | LF | LF | LF | LF |
| 03 | A | — | — | — | — | — | — |
| 04 | Space | Space | Space | Space | Space | Space | Space |
| 05 | S | ' | BELL | ' | ' | THRU | BELL |
| 06 | I | 8 | 8 | 8 | 8 | 8 | 8 |
| 07 | U | 7 | 7 | 7 | 7 | 7 | 7 |
| 10 | CR | CR | CR | CR | CR | CR | CR |
| 11 | D | WRU | $ | $ | WRU | $ | $ |
| 12 | R | 4 | 4 | 4 | 4 | 4 | 4 |
| 13 | J | BELL | ' | BELL | BELL | BELL | ' |
| 14 | N | , | , | , | , | , | , |
| 15 | F |  | ! |  | $ | CITY | ! |
| 16 | C | : | : | : | : | : | : |
| 17 | K | ( | ( | ( | ( | ( | ( |
| 20 | T | 5 | 5 | 5 | 5 | 5 | 5 |
| 21 | Z | + | " | " | " | " | " |
| 22 | L | ) | ) | ) | ) | ) | ) |
| 23 | W | 2 | 2 | 2 | 2 | 2 | 2 |
| 24 | H |  | STOP# | # | # | £ | £ |
| 25 | Y | 6 | 6 | 6 | 6 | 6 | 6 |
| 26 | P | O | O | O | O | O | O |
| 27 | Q | 1 | 1 | 1 | 1 | 1 | 1 |
| 30 | O | 9 | 9 | 9 | 9 | 9 | 9 |
| 31 | B | ? | ? | ? | ? | ? | ? |
| 32 | G |  | & | & | & | & | & |
| 33 | FIGS | FIGS | FIGS | FIGS | FIGS | FIGS | FIGS |
| 34 | M | . | . | . | . | . | . |
| 35 | X | / | / | / | / | / | / |
| 36 | V | = | ; | ; | ; | ; | ; |
| 37 | LTRS | LTRS | LTRS | LTRS | LTRS | LTRS | LTRS |

Note: The symbols shown for codes 05 and 13 are apostrophes; those for code 14 are commas.

Table C–2   Five-Unit Codes

| Octal | Letters (common to all codes on this page) | CCITT Alphabet #2 | Australian Post Office Telex | American Weather Variant of CCITT #2 | Danish Weather Bureau | American 60 wpm TWX |
|---|---|---|---|---|---|---|
| 00 | Blank | Blank | Blank | — | Blank | Blank |
| 01 | E | 3 | 3 | 3 | 3 | 3 |
| 02 | LF | LF | LF | LF | LF | LF |
| 03 | A | — | — | ↑ | — | — |
| 04 | Space | Space | Space | Space | Space | Space |
| 05 | S | ' | ' | BELL | ' | BELL |
| 06 | I | 8 | 8 | 8 | 8 | 8 |
| 07 | U | 7 | 7 | 7 | 7 | 7 |
| 10 | CR | CR | CR | CR | CR | CR |
| 11 | D | WRU | WRU | ↗ | " | $ |
| 12 | R | 4 | 4 | 4 | 4 | 4 |
| 13 | J | BELL | BELL | ↙ | | |
| 14 | N | , | , | ⏸ | ' | ' |
| 15 | F | | % | → | F | ¼ |
| 16 | C | : | : | ○ | : | WRU |
| 17 | K | ( | ( | ← | ( | ½ |
| 20 | T | 5 | 5 | 5 | 5 | 5 |
| 21 | Z | + | + | + | + | " |
| 22 | L | ) | ) | ↖ | ) | ¾ |
| 23 | W | 2 | 2 | 2 | 2 | 2 |
| 24 | H | | £ | ↓ | H | # |
| 25 | Y | 6 | 6 | 6 | 6 | 6 |
| 26 | P | 0 | 0 | 0 | 0 | 0 |
| 27 | Q | 1 | 1 | 1 | 1 | 1 |
| 30 | O | 9 | 9 | 9 | 9 | 9 |
| 31 | B | ? | ? | ⊕ | ? | ⅝ |
| 32 | G | | $ | ↘ | % | & |
| 33 | FIGS | FIGS | FIGS | FIGS | FIGS | FIGS |
| 34 | M | . | . | . | . | . |
| 35 | X | / | / | / | / | / |
| 36 | V | = | = | ⏸ | = | ⅜ |
| 37 | LTRS | LTRS | LTRS | LTRS | LTRS | LTRS |

Note: The symbols shown for codes 05 and 13 are apostrophes; those for code 14 are commas.

*The Danish Weather Bureau uses number groups in a specified format to identify locations in a symbol containing meteorological symbols.

Table C–3   Five-Unit Codes, Elliot 803
Telecode

| Octal | Letters (Unshift) | Figures (Shift) |
|-------|-------------------|-----------------|
| 00 | Blank | Blank |
| 01 | A | 1 |
| 02 | B | 2 |
| 03 | C | 8 |
| 04 | D | 4 |
| 05 | E | & |
| 06 | F | = |
| 07 | G | 7 |
| 10 | H | 8 |
| 11 | I | ' |
| 12 | J | , |
| 13 | K | + |
| 14 | L | : |
| 15 | M | — |
| 16 | N | . |
| 17 | O | % |
| 20 | P | 0 |
| 21 | Q | ( |
| 22 | R | ) |
| 23 | S | 3 |
| 24 | T | ? |
| 25 | U | 5 |
| 26 | V | 6 |
| 27 | W | / |
| 30 | X | @ |
| 31 | Y | 9 |
| 32 | Z | £ |
| 33 | FIGS | FIGS |
| 34 | Space | Space |
| 35 | Return | Return |
| 36 | Line Feed | Line Feed |
| 37 | LETTERS | LETTERS |

Table C–4   Six-Unit Codes, PDP-8$^R$ Typesetting

| Octal | (Unshift) | (Shift) | Octal | (Unshift) | (Shift) |
|-------|-----------|---------|-------|-----------|---------|
| 00 | Tape Feed | | 40 | t | T |
| 01 | Thin Space | | 41 | 5 | 5/8 |
| 02 | e | E | 42 | z | Z |
| 03 | 3 | 3/8 | 43 | ) | ( |
| 04 | Word Delete | | 44 | l | L |
| 05 | With Leaders | WX | 45 | Tab Left | |
| 06 | a | A | 46 | w | W |
| 07 | $ | ! | 47 | 2 | 1/4 |
| 10 | Space Bar | | 50 | h | H |
| 11 | Justify | TA | 51 | Em Leader | |
| 12 | s | S | 52 | y | Y |
| 13 | Quad Middle | | 53 | 6 | 3/4 |
| 14 | i | I | 54 | p | P |
| 15 | 8 | —(Dash) | 55 | 0 | ? |
| 16 | u | U | 56 | q | Q |
| 17 | 7 | 7/8 | 57 | En Leader | |
| 20 | Return | | 60 | o | O |
| 21 | '(Quote) | '(Quote) | 61 | 9 | fi |
| 22 | d | D | 62 | b | B |
| 23 | -(Hyphen) | @ | 63 | Tab Right | |
| 24 | r | R | 64 | g | G |
| 25 | 4 | 1/2 | 65 | ; | : |
| 26 | j | J | 66 | Shift | |
| 27 | Call | | 67 | Tab Center | |
| 30 | n | N | 70 | m | M |
| 31 | ,(Comma) | ,(Comma) | 71 | .(Period) | .(Period) |
| 32 | f | F | 72 | x | X |
| 33 | Quad Left | | 73 | 1 | 1/8 |
| 34 | c | C | 74 | v | V |
| 35 | En Space | | 75 | Quad Center | |
| 36 | k | K | 76 | Unshift | |
| 37 | Quad Right | | 77 | Rubout | |

Table C–5   Six-Unit Codes, New York Stock Exchange

| Octal | | Octal | |
|-------|------|-------|------------|
| 00 | Null | 40 | ■ |
| 01 | E | 41 | 5 |
| 02 | ■ | 42 | c |
| 03 | A | 43 | l |
| 04 | Pr | 44 | ■ |
| 05 | S | 45 | s |
| 06 | I | 46 | q |
| 07 | U | 47 | Spare #4 |
| 10 | W | 50 | 0 |
| | I | 51 | 4 |
| 11 | D | 52 | ■ End Ann |
| 12 | R | 53 | ■ Beg Ann |
| 13 | J | 54 | Space |
| 14 | N | 55 | 6 |
| 15 | F | 56 | 3 |
| 16 | C | 57 | Spare #3 |
| 17 | K | 60 | 1/8 |
| 20 | T | 61 | 7/8 |
| 21 | Z | 62 | S |
| 22 | L | | S |
| 23 | W | 63 | 1/2 |
| 24 | H | 64 | 8 |
| 25 | Y | 65 | 3/4 |
| 26 | P | 66 | S |
| 27 | Q | | T |
| 30 | O | 67 | 1/4 |
| 31 | B | 70 | Spare #2 |
| 32 | G | 71 | 2 |
| 33 | & | 72 | 7 |
| 34 | M | 73 | b |
| 35 | X | 74 | $ |
| 36 | V | 75 | 5/8 |
| 37 | R | 76 | 3/8 |
| | T | 77 | Rubout |

Table C–6   Seven-Unit Codes, ASCII—1968*

| *Octal* | | | | *Octal* | | |
|---|---|---|---|---|---|---|
| 000 | NUL | (Blank) | | 035 | GS | (Group Separator) |
| 001 | SOH | (Start of Header) | | 036 | RS | (Record Separator) |
| 002 | STX | (Start of Text) | | 037 | US | (Unit Separator) |
| 003 | ETX | (End of Text) | | 040 | SP | (Space) |
| 004 | EOT | (End of | | 041 | ! | |
| | | Transmission) | | 042 | " | |
| 005 | ENQ | (Enquiry) | | 043 | # | |
| 006 | ACK | (Acknowledge | | 044 | $ | |
| | | (Positive)) | | 045 | % | |
| 007 | BEL | (Bell) | | 046 | & | |
| 010 | BS | (Backspace) | | 047 | ' | (Closing Single |
| 011 | HT | (Horizontal | | | | Quote) |
| | | Tabulation) | | 050 | ( | |
| 012 | LF | (Line Feed) | | 051 | ) | |
| 013 | VT | (Vertical | | 052 | * | |
| | | Tabulation) | | 053 | + | |
| 014 | FF | (Form Feed) | | 054 | , | (Comma) |
| 015 | CR | (Carriage Return) | | 055 | - | (Hyphen) |
| 016 | SO | (Shift Out) | | 056 | . | (Period) |
| 017 | SI | (Shift In) | | 057 | / | |
| 020 | DLE | (Data Link Escape) | | 060 | 0 | |
| 021 | DCI | (Device Control 1) | | 061 | 1 | |
| 022 | DC2 | (Device Control 2) | | 062 | 2 | |
| 023 | DC3 | (Device Control 3) | | 063 | 3 | |
| 024 | DC4 | (Device Control | | 064 | 4 | |
| | | 4—Stop) | | 065 | 5 | |
| 025 | NAK | (Negative | | 066 | 6 | |
| | | Acknowledge) | | 067 | 7 | |
| 026 | SYN | (Synchronization) | | 070 | 8 | |
| 027 | ETB | (End of Text Block) | | 071 | 9 | |
| 030 | CAN | (Cancel) | | 072 | : | |
| 031 | EM | (End of Medium) | | 073 | ; | |
| 032 | SUB | (Substitute) | | 074 | < | (Less Than) |
| 033 | ESC | (Escape) | | 075 | = | |
| 034 | FS | (File Separator) | | 076 | > | (Greater Than) |

*This code is often sent with parity and is thus often referred to as an eight-bit code.

*continues*

*Table C–6 (Cont.)*

| Octal | | | Octal | | |
|---|---|---|---|---|---|
| 077 | ? | | 140 | ´ | (Opening Single |
| 100 | @ | | | | Quote) |
| 101 | A | | 141 | a | |
| 102 | B | | 142 | b | |
| 103 | C | | 143 | c | |
| 104 | D | | 144 | d | |
| 105 | E | | 145 | e | |
| 106 | F | | 146 | f | |
| 107 | G | | 147 | g | |
| 110 | H | | 150 | h | |
| 111 | I | | 151 | i | |
| 112 | J | | 152 | j | |
| 113 | K | | 153 | k | |
| 114 | L | | 154 | l | |
| 115 | M | | 155 | m | |
| 116 | N | | 156 | n | |
| 117 | O | | 157 | o | |
| 120 | P | | 160 | p | |
| 121 | Q | | 161 | q | |
| 122 | R | | 162 | r | |
| 123 | S | | 163 | s | |
| 124 | T | | 164 | t | |
| 125 | U | | 165 | u | |
| 126 | V | | 166 | v | |
| 127 | W | | 167 | w | |
| 130 | X | | 170 | x | |
| 131 | Y | | 171 | y | |
| 132 | Z | | 172 | z | |
| 133 | [ | (Opening Bracket) | 173 | { | (Opening Brace) |
| 134 | \ | (Reverse Slant) | 174 | \| | (Vertical Line) |
| 135 | ] | (Closing Bracket) | 175 | } | (Closing Brace) |
| 136 | ^ | (Circumflex) | 176 | ~ | (Overline (Tilde)) |
| 137 | _ | (Underline) | 177 | DEL | (Delete/Rubout) |

# APPENDIX D

## Universal Synchronous Asynchronous Receiver Transmitter (USART)

This appendix provides an introduction to a commercially available USART, the Zilog Z8530 SCC Serial Communications Controller. This USART, like several others on the market, interfaces two serial communications lines to a microprocessor bus. The two lines share the bus interface, timing, interrupt, and control logic. In a way, this USART is a "two-line multiplexer." The manufacturer could have extended the design to more lines, but the pin count and resultant expense would have risen sharply, as each line has ten leads associated with it for data, clocks, and modem control.

The Z8530 USART is an MOS/LSI device packaged in a 40-pin DIP (or in a 44-pin surface mount package). It is a complete subsystem that transmits and receives synchronous or asynchronous data in full-duplex or half-duplex operation. The transmitter, which is double buffered, accepts parallel binary characters and converts them to a serial synchronous or asynchronous output. The receiver, quadruply buffered, accepts serial synchronous or asynchronous binary characters and converts them to a parallel output.

When operated in asynchronous mode, this USART provides a choice of 5, 6, 7, or 8 bits per character; 1, 1½, or 2 stop bits; odd or even parity; clocking (data sampling) at 1, 16, 32, or 64 times the bit rate; break generation and detection; and parity, overrun, and framing error detection. A baud rate generator is provided for each channel.

When operated in character-oriented synchronous mode, the Z8530 provides internal or external character synchronization and use of 1 or 2 sync

307

characters (6 or 8 bits per character). In bit-oriented synchronous mode, abort sequence generation and checking is provided, along with automatic zero insertion/deletion, automatic flag insertion, address field recognition, i-field residue handling, and SDLC loop mode.

In all synchronous operating modes, automatic CRC generation and checking is provided. A wide range of clocking options is offered, including a digital phase-locked loop connected to the incoming data stream. In addition, a wide range of output data encoding is offered, including NRZ, NRZI, Biphase Mark, and Biphase Space. These are summarized in Table D–1.

The pin functions of the Z8530 are shown in Figure D–1, and the pinning assignment for the 40-pin DIP version of the chip is shown in Figure D–2. The following brief presentation of the pin descriptions provides an introduction to the chip's features. The reader is cautioned that these definitions are not exact copies of the manufacturer's pin descriptions and that in a few cases the pin names have been changed slightly for clarity. Therefore, this appendix should not be used as a design guide.

## Bus Interface Pins

### A/$\overline{B}$: Channel A/Channel B Select (input)

As indicated above, this USART serves two lines, so it may be thought of as two separate interfaces. When data or modem control information is

Table D–1   Data Encoding

| Encoding | Bit | How Represented |
|----------|-----|-----------------|
| NRZ | 1 | High state on line for one bit |
| | 0 | Low state on line for one bit |
| NRZI | 1 | Previous state maintained for one bit |
| | 0 | Inverse of previous state for one bit |
| Biphase Mark | x | Transition on all bit boundaries, plus |
| | 1 | Transition in middle of bit |
| | 0 | No transition in middle of bit |
| Biphase Space | x | Transition on all bit boundaries, plus |
| | 1 | No transition in middle of bit |
| | 0 | Transition in middle of bit |

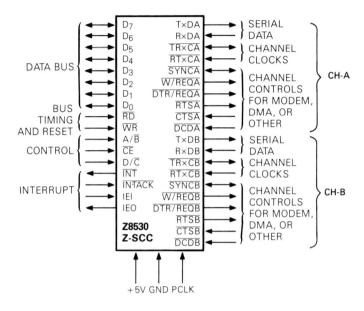

Figure D–1    Pin Functions SCC/AmZ-SCC

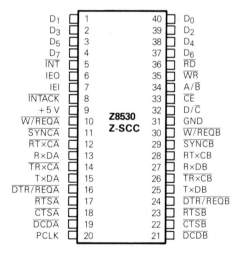

Figure D–2    Pin Designation for
AmZ8530 SCC

read or written, this bit selects to which line interface (channel) the read or write applies. A HIGH condition on this pin selects Channel A.

### $\overline{CE}$: Chip Enable (input)

This pin enables transactions on the microprocessor bus interface to read or write the USART. It must remain asserted (LOW) throughout any bus transaction involving this chip.

### D0–D7: Data Leads (input/output)

These lines are bidirectional and carry data or control information to and from the USART during transactions over the microprocessor bus.

### D/$\overline{C}$: Data/Control (input)

This pin determines whether the information being carried over the Data Leads is to or from the data section of the USART or to or from the control section of the USART. If this pin is HIGH, information is being transferred to or from the data section.

### $\overline{RD}$: Read (input)

When this pin is asserted (LOW), the bus drivers in the bus interface portion of the USART will be enabled. This occurs when the microprocessor bus is reading from the USART (Chip Enable also asserted). This pin also is used during an interrupt acknowledge cycle to gate the interrupt vector onto the bus (if the USART is the highest priority device requesting an interrupt).

### $\overline{WR}$: Write (input)

When this pin is asserted (LOW) and Chip Enable also is asserted, the information on the Data Leads will be written into the USART. If this pin and the Read pin are asserted simultaneously, the USART interprets this as a Reset.

## Interrupt Logic Pins

### IEI: Interrupt Enable In (input)

This pin is part of a daisy chain (along with Interrupt Enable Out). If this pin is asserted (HIGH), there are no higher priority devices requesting an interrupt or having an interrupt in the process of being serviced.

### IEO: Interrupt Enable Out (output)

If Interrupt Enable In is asserted and the USART has no interrupts pending or being serviced, this pin also will be asserted (HIGH). This pin is typically wired to the IEI pin of the next lowest priority device.

### $\overline{INT}$: *Interrupt Request (output)*

This signal is asserted (LOW) whenever the USART is requesting an interrupt. It is an open-collector pin, so multiple USARTs may be attached to the same INT line in a wired-OR arrangement. The IEI/IEO daisy chain will ensure that the highest priority USART gets its interrupt request serviced first.

### $\overline{INTACK}$: *Interrupt Acknowledge (input)*

This signal is asserted (LOW) during an active interrupt acknowledge cycle. During such a cycle, the interrupt daisy chain (mentioned above) settles, and when either $\overline{RD}$ or $\overline{DS}$ becomes asserted, the USART places an interrupt vector on the data bus if IEI is high (indicating that no higher priority device is requesting an interrupt). The $\overline{INTACK}$ signal is latched by the rising edge of PCLK or $\overline{AS}$.

### $\overline{WA}$, $\overline{WB}$: *WAIT*

These two pins allow the use of block moves to transfer data to the transmitter by asserting WAIT if an attempt is made to load a transmitter that is already full. They also permit the use of block moves to transfer data from the receiver by asserting WAIT if an attempt is made to read a receiver buffer that does not yet have a character. One Wait pin is provided for each channel, and its use is programmable. These pins also have an alternate use; see "Alternate Uses for Pins" below.

## Modem Control Pins

Note: The EIA-232-D standard says that a positive voltage is an ON condition for a control lead. Typical level converters convert this to a TTL level that is LOW. This is why the modem control signals discussed below are "LOW = true" signals. A positive voltage at the EIA-232-D interface is a SPACE or "0" condition for a data lead. As with control signals, typical level converters convert this to a TTL level that is LOW. "LOW = 0" is the normal TTL convention, so that data inputs and outputs of the USART are shown as normal "HIGH = true" pins.

### $\overline{CTSA}$, $\overline{CTSB}$: *Clear to Send (inputs)*

These pins are normally connected to level converters associated with the Clear to Send leads for the two channels being served by the USART. Both inputs are equipped with Schmitt-trigger circuits to improve performance with slow rise time inputs. The state of these leads can be read via registers within the USART, and circuitry within the USART can be programmed to detect transitions on these circuits and to generate an interrupt request. In addition, these inputs can be programmed as "auto-enables," such that the transmitters for each channel are enabled by the asserted state (LOW) of the corresponding Clear to Send inputs.

### $\overline{DCDA}$, $\overline{DCDB}$: *Data Carrier Detect (inputs)*

These pins are typically connected to level converters associated with the Data Channel Received Line Signal Detector (Carrier Detect) leads for the two channels being served by the USART. Both inputs are equipped with Schmitt-trigger circuits to improve performance with slow rise time inputs. The state of these leads can be read via registers within the USART, and circuitry within the USART can be programmed to detect transitions on these circuits and to generate an interrupt request. In addition, these inputs can be programmed as "auto-enables," such that the receivers for each channel are enabled by the asserted state (LOW) of the corresponding Carrier Detect inputs.

### $\overline{DTRA}$, $\overline{DTRB}$: *Data Terminal Ready (outputs)*

These pins are usually connected to level converters associated with the Data Terminal Ready leads for the two channels being served by the USART. The state of each pin is controlled by a bit in a register for each channel. These pins also have an alternate use; see "Alternate Uses for Pins" below.

### $\overline{RTSA}$, $\overline{RTSB}$: *Request to Send (outputs)*

These pins are normally connected to level converters associated with the Request to Send leads for the two channels being served by the USART. The state of each pin is controlled by a bit in a register for each channel. If asynchronous operation and auto-enable operation is selected, clearing the controlling bit will not immediately deassert this signal; deassertion will be delayed until the transmitter has emptied.

### $\overline{RTxCA}$, $\overline{RTxCB}$: *Receive Clocks (inputs)*

In most installations, these pins are connected to the level converters that receive the Receiver Signal Element Timing signal from the modem. The Z8530 samples received data on the rising edge of a signal connected to these pins.

Programming options within the USART also allow the Receive Clock function to come from the transmit clock, the baud rate generator, or the digital phase-locked loop connected to the Received Data pin. In these cases, no external connection to this pin is required. The RTxC pins also have an alternate use; see "Alternate Uses for Pins" below.

### $\overline{TRxCA}$, $\overline{TRxCB}$: Transmit Clocks (inputs)

In most installations, these pins are connected to the level converters that receive the Transmitter Signal Element Timing signal from the modem. The Z8530 generates a new bit of transmitted data on the falling edge of a signal connected to these pins.

Programming options within the USART also allow the Transmit Clock function to come from the receive clock, the baud rate generator, or the digital phase-locked loop connected to the Received Data pin. In these cases, no external connection to this pin is required.

### $\overline{SYNCA}$, $\overline{SYNCB}$: Synchronization (inputs or outputs, see below)

When a USART channel is programmed for asynchronous operation, these pins function as inputs. As such, they are similar to the CTS and DCD pins, except that they do not have Schmitt-trigger circuits, change detection circuits, or interrupt generation capabilities.

When a USART channel is programmed for synchronous operation, these pins may be used as inputs (External Synchronization mode) or as outputs (Internal Synchronization mode). In the former case, external logic can force the USART to begin character assembly at a particular time by driving a pin at an appropriate moment. In the latter case, logic within the USART asserts a pin when a SYNC character is recognized in character-oriented protocols or when a flag is received in a bit-oriented protocol (SDLC mode).

### RxDA, RxDB: Receive Data (inputs)

These pins are usually connected to the level converters associated with the Received Data leads from the modem.

### TxDA, TxDB: Transmit Data (outputs)

These pins are normally connected to the level converters associated with the Transmitted Data leads to the modem.

## Alternate Uses for Pins

### $\overline{TRQA}$, $\overline{TRQB}$: Transmit DMA Request (outputs)

This is an alternate use for the $\overline{DTRA}$ and $\overline{DTRB}$ pins. When this use is selected, these pins will be asserted (LOW) whenever the transmit buffer becomes empty and, in any of the synchronous operating modes, when the CRC has been sent at the end of a message.

Table D–2   Z8530 SCC Register Set

| | |
|---|---|
| | *Read Register Functions* |
| RR0 | Transmit/Receiver buffer status, and External status |
| RR1 | Special Receive Condition status, residue codes, error conditions |
| RR2 | Modified (Channel B only) interrupt vector and Unmodified Interrupt Vector (Channel A only) |
| RR3 | Interrupt Pending bits (Channel A only) |
| RR8 | Receiver Buffer |
| RR10 | Miscellaneous XMTR, RCVR status parameters |
| RR12 | Lower byte of baud rate generator time constant |
| RR13 | Upper byte of baud rate generator time constant |
| RR15 | External/Status interrupt control information |
| | *Write Register Functions* |
| WR0 | Command Register (Register Pointers, Z8530 only), CRC initialization, resets for various modes |
| WR1 | Interrupt conditions, Wait/DMA request control |
| WR2 | Interrupt vector (access through either channel) |
| WR3 | Receive/Control parameters, number of bits per character, Rx CRC enable |
| WR4 | Transmit/Receive miscellaneous parameters and codes, clock rate, number of sync characters, stop bits, parity |
| WR5 | Transmit parameters and control, number of Tx bits per character, Tx CRC enable |
| WR6 | Sync character (1st byte) or SDLC flag |
| WR8 | Transmit buffer |
| WR9 | Master interrupt control and reset (accessed through either channel), reset bits, control interrupt daisy chain |
| WR10 | Miscellaneous transmitter/receiver control bits, NRZI, NRZ, FM encoding, CRC reset |
| WR11 | Clock mode control, source of Rx and Tx clocks |
| WR12 | Lower byte of baud rate generator time constant |
| WR13 | Upper byte of baud rate generator time constant |
| WR14 | Miscellaneous control bits: baud rate generator, Phase-Locked Loop control, auto echo, local loopback |
| WR15 | External/Status interrupt control information—control external conditions causing interrupts |

### $\overline{REQA}$, $\overline{REQB}$: *Transmit/Receive DMA Request (outputs)*

This is an alternate use for the $\overline{WA}$ and $\overline{WB}$ pins. In addition to the WAIT function previously described, these pins may be used as either Transmit DMA Request pins or as Receive DMA Request pins. When Transmit DMA use is selected, these pins will be asserted (LOW) whenever the transmit buffer becomes empty and, in any of the synchronous operating modes, when the CRC has been sent at the end of a message. When Receive DMA use is selected, these pins will be asserted (LOW) whenever the receive buffer has a character available.

### $\overline{XTLA}$, $\overline{XTLB}$: *Crystal Oscillator*

This is an alternate use for the $\overline{SYNCA}$, $\overline{SYNCB}$, $\overline{RTxCA}$, and $\overline{RTxCB}$ pins. When this use is selected, these pins will be part of the crystal oscillator circuit. See the Z8530 manual for further details.

The pin descriptions given above refer in several instances to programmable registers that alter the "personality" of the USART by changing the definitions and functions of some of the pins. There are fourteen write registers and seven read registers for each of the two channels served by the chip. In addition, there are two write registers (WR2, WR9), which are shared by both channels. Table D–2, reproduced with the permission of Zilog Incorporated, lists the assigned functions for each read and write register.

## Reference

Zilog, Inc. *Z8030 Z-Bus SCC/Z8530 SCC Serial Communications Controller, Technical Manual*, September 1986.

# APPENDIX E

## Format and Speed Table
## for Asynchronous Communications

Tables E–1 through E–4 are arranged so that there is one table each for codes with five, six, seven, and eight information bits. For the purposes of these tables, a parity bit is considered to be an information bit.

In each of the codes, a single start bit is followed by the designated number of information bits. The information bits are followed by a stop time equivalent to the number of bit times shown in the "Stop Units" column.

Within each table, entries are arranged according to baud rate, in ascending order. Where there are several entries for the same baud rate, those entries are arranged in ascending order by character rate.

Other information can be derived from each table entry. For example, to derive the total number of bits per character, take the number of information bits specified for that table (e.g., 5), add 1 for the start bit, and add the designated number of stop bits (e.g., 1.42). The answer obtained in this example would be 7.42-bit characters. To obtain the bit length in milliseconds, divide 1 by the baud rate and multiply the answer by 1000. For example, for 45.45 baud, divide 1 by 45.45 to get 0.0220022. Multiplying that by 1000 produces the correct answer, which is that each bit is 22 milliseconds long.

To obtain the character length in milliseconds, take the result obtained in the bit time calculation and multiply that by the number of bits per complete character. Using the results of the previous two examples, one

316

Table E–1  Five-Unit Codes

| Baud Rate | Stop Units | Six-Character Words Per Minute | Usage |
|---|---|---|---|
| 45.45 | 1.5 | 60.6 | CCITT 60 wpm |
| 45.45 | 1.42 | 61.3 | U.S. government and Bell System 60 wpm |
| 45.45 | 1.0 | 64.8 | U.S. (obsolete), Western Union |
| 50 | 1.5 | 66.67 | CCITT #2, Western Union Telex |
| 50 | 1.42 | 67.3 | Some Western Union Telex |
| 50 | 1.0 | 71.4 | CCITT #1 (obsolete) |
| 56.86 | 1.42 | 76.6 | U.S. standard 75 wpm |
| 74.2 | 1.5 | 99 | |
| 74.2 | 1.42 | 100 | U.S. standard 100 wpm |
| 74.2 | 1.0 | 107 | U.S. military |
| 75 | 1.5 | 101 | CCITT Standard 100 wpm |
| 91 | 1.42 | 122.7 | Teleprinter duplex |

Table E–2  Six-Unit Codes

| Baud Rate | Stop Units | Six-Character Words Per Minute | Usage |
|---|---|---|---|
| 45.45 | 1.42 | 54 | Friden Teledata System 60 wpm |
| 48.0 | 1.0 | 60 | IBM 60 wpm |
| 49.1 | 1.0 | 61.3 | Teletypesetter |
| 55.21 | 2.0 | 61.35 | U.S. M35 Teletype[R] (optional) |
| 56.86 | 1.5 | 66.9 | U.S. Teletypesetter |
| 60.6 | 2.0 | 67.3 | |
| 56.75 | 1.42 | 68.1 | Friden Teledata System 75 wpm |
| 69.25 | 2.0 | 76.6 | U.S. M35 Teletype (optional) |
| 66.67 | 1.0 | 83.3 | Western Union #5A Stock Ticker |
| 74.2 | 1.42 | 88.2 | Friden Teledata System 100 wpm |
| 80.0 | 1.5 | 100 | NYSE Stock Ticker (obsolete) |
| 135.0 | 2.0 | 150 | NYSE 900 Stock Ticker |

## Table E–3   Seven-Unit Codes

| Baud Rate | Stop Units | Six-Character Words Per Minute | Usage |
|---|---|---|---|
| 45.45 | 1.42 | 48.2 | Friden Teledata System 60 wpm |
| 56.75 | 1.42 | 60.2 | Friden Teledata System 75 wpm |
| 61.35 | 2.0 | 61.35 | U.S. M35 Teletype[R] (optional) and Teletypesetter |
| 67.34 | 2.0 | 67.3 | |
| 76.92 | 2.0 | 76.6 | U.S. M35 Teletype (optional) |
| 74.2 | 1.42 | 78.8 | Friden Teledata System 100 wpm |
| 75 | 1.0 | 83.3 | IBM Model 1050 (optional) |
| 100 | 2.0 | 100 | IBM and U.S. M35 Teletype (optional) |
| 134.5 | 1.0 | 148 | IBM models 2740, 2741, 1050 standard speed |
| 600 | 1.0 | 666.67 | IBM System 1030 |

## Table E–4   Eight-Unit Codes

| Baud Rate | Stop Units | Six-Character Words Per Minute | Usage |
|---|---|---|---|
| 45.45 | 1.5 | 43.3 | IBM Transceiver 60 wpm |
| 45.45 | 1.42 | 43.6 | Friden Teledata System 60 wpm |
| 56.75 | 1.5 | 54.0 | IBM Transceiver 75 wpm |
| 56.75 | 1.42 | 54.5 | Friden Teledata System 75 wpm |
| 67.58 | 2.0 | 61.35 | U.S. M35 Teletype[R] (optional) |
| 73.33 | 2.0 | 66.7 | U.S. M35 Teletype (optional) |
| 74.07 | 2.0 | 67.3 | U.S. M35 Teletype (optional) |
| 74.1 | 1.5 | 70.4 | IBM Transceiver 100 wpm |
| 74.2 | 1.42 | 71.3 | Friden Teledata System 100 wpm |
| 84.61 | 2.0 | 76.6 | U.S. M35 Teletype (optional) |
| 100 | 1.0 | 100 | U.S. M37 Teletype (optional) |
| 110 | 2.0 | 100 | U.S. M35 Teletype (optional) |
| 135.0 | 2.0 | 122.5 | |
| 150 | 2.0 | 136.4 | |
| 150 | 1.0 | 150 | Standard computer terminal speed |
| 165 | 2.0 | 150 | U.S. M37 Teletype, Western Union |
| 300 | 1.0 | 300 | Standard computer terminal speed |
| 600 | 1.0 | 600 | Standard computer terminal speed |
| 1200 | 1.0 | 1200 | Standard computer terminal speed |
| 2400 | 1.0 | 2400 | Standard computer terminal speed |
| 4800 | 1.0 | 4800 | Standard computer terminal speed |
| 9600 | 1.0 | 9600 | Standard computer terminal speed |

would multiply 22 milliseconds by 7.42 bits per character and obtain 163.24 milliseconds per character. Dividing 1 second by that number produces the character rate in characters per second, which in this case would be 6.126. In the chart for five-unit codes, this entry has been rounded off to give 60 × 6.13, or 367.8 characters per minute (61.3 words per minute, assuming an average word has six characters).

# RPPENDIX F

## Channel Conditioning

As indicated in the main text of this book, data communication can take place over the public switched telephone network (PSTN) or over private lines. While the PSTN has cost benefits in low utilization situations and provides great flexibility, there are several circumstances in which private lines are attractive. Principal among these are cases in which a great deal of data traffic is passed between a limited number of points.

Private lines may be provided on either an analog or a digital basis. Most low-speed operation (9600 bps or less) currently takes place over analog facilities. Analog facilities require the use of modems, and the performance of modems can be increased at a modest cost by conditioning the channel to correct for various impairments.

This appendix discusses the analog private line services of AT&T and the application of channel conditioning to some of those services. For a more in-depth treatment, see AT&T Technical Reference PUB 43202. Other long-distance carriers have similar product offerings, and both AT&T and the other carriers offer a growing array of digital services.

Table F–1 lists ten analog private line services offered by AT&T. For the services listed, five types of conditioning are available: C-Conditioning, D-Conditioning, International, Tone Control, and Special Telephoto. Not all types of conditioning are available for each service. In particular, Tone Control conditioning is included only in Service Type 3, and Special Telephoto is an option only in Service Type 9. Further, some services do not have any conditioning options available.

The service with the greatest range of conditioning options available, and the one probably of greatest interest to readers of a data communication

Table F–1   AT&T Analog Private Line Service Offerings

| Service Type | Offerings |
|---|---|
| 1 | Basic voice applications |
| 2 | Voice applications with more stringent requirements, such as trunks that will access the PSTN, private switched network trunks, or tie trunks |
| 3 | Voice radio land lines for the FAA |
| 4 | Data applications requiring less than 1200 bps |
| 5 | Basic data applications |
| 6 | Voice and data applications on tie trunks or on trunks that will access the PSTN |
| 7 | Voice and data applications on access lines to a private switched network |
| 8 | Voice and data applications on private switched network trunks |
| 9 | Telephotographic or alternate voice/telephotographic |
| 10 | Tone transmission for electric utility system control |

book, is Service Type 5. Four types of C-Conditioning, two types of D-Conditioning, and two types of International Conditioning are available for this service.

C-Conditioning is useful for data applications and controls attenuation distortion and envelope delay distortion. Attenuation distortion specifications for a private line are similar to frequency response specifications for home audio equipment (20 to 20,000 Hz ±1 db). One difference is that in attenuation distortion specifications, "+" means loss relative to 1004 Hz, and "−" means gain relative to 1004 Hz.

Table F–2 lists the attenuation distortion limits for a basic (unconditioned) Service Type 5 line. It also lists the limits for lines having the four types of C-Conditioning available for Service Type 5: C-1, C-2, C-4, and C-5. For convenience in comparison, the frequency limits are listed in order of increasing frequency range.

While attenuation distortion can be compared to audio system frequency response, envelope delay distortion requires a bit more explanation. Telephone transmission facilities propagate signals of various frequencies at different rates. For example, signals at 1800 Hz propagate through such facilities faster than those at 600 Hz. If data transmission involved signaling that contained both these frequencies, the 1800 Hz signal would reach the

Table F–2   Effect of C-Conditioning on Attenuation Distortion

| Frequencies | Basic | Conditioning C-1 | C-2 |
|---|---|---|---|
| 1004–2404 Hz | | −1.0 to +3.0 | |
| 504–2504 Hz | −2.0 to +8.0 | | |
| 504–2804 Hz | | | −1.0 to +3.0 |
| 404–2804 Hz | −2.0 to +10.0 | | |
| 304–2704 Hz | | −2.0 to +6.0 | |
| 304–3004 Hz | −3.0 to +12.0 | −3.0 to +12.0 | −2.0 to +6.0 |

| Frequencies | Conditioning C-4 | C-5 |
|---|---|---|
| 504–2804 Hz | | −0.5 to +1.5 |
| 504–3004 Hz | −2.0 to +3.0 | |
| 304–3004 Hz | | −1.0 to +3.0 |
| 304–3204 Hz | −2.0 to +6.0 | |

Note: All attenuation variation values are given in decibels (db). The symbol "+" means loss and "−" means gain, relative to performance at 1004 Hz.

receiving station before the 600 Hz signal, possibly causing some confusion at the receiver. This frequency dependent property of the propagation delay is called "envelope delay distortion."

Table F–3 lists the envelope delay distortion limits for the same types of C-Conditioning compared in Table F–2. Again, the frequency limits are listed in order of increasing frequency range.

Reference to Tables F–2 and F–3 will reveal that increased amounts of conditioning generally broaden the frequency range over which a given performance is offered, then improve the performance over the original frequency range, then broaden the range, and so on.

D-Conditioning can also be applied to an analog private line circuit. This type of conditioning is particularly useful at speeds of 9600 bps and above, where a single noise "hit" can destroy a great deal of data. D-Conditioning provides control of the Signal-to-C-Notched-Noise Ratio and intermodulation distortion, two terms that require explanation.

All channels have a certain amount of noise, and some of that noise may increase when there is a signal present. Thus, to obtain a more accurate

Table F–3   Effect of C-Conditioning on Envelope Delay
Distortion

| Frequencies | Basic | C-1 | C-2 | C-4 | C-5 |
|---|---|---|---|---|---|
| | | | *Conditioning* | | |
| 1004–2404 Hz | | 1000 | | | |
| 1004–2604 Hz | | | 500 | 300 | 100 |
| 804–2604 Hz | 1750 | 1750 | | | |
| 604–2604 Hz | | | 1500 | | 300 |
| 804–2804 Hz | | | | 500 | |
| 504–2804 Hz | | | 3000 | | 600 |
| 604–3004 Hz | | | | 1500 | |
| 504–3004 Hz | | | | 3000 | |

Note: All delay values are given in microseconds.

signal-to-noise ratio, a 1004 Hz signal is placed on the line when the noise is to be measured, and the 1004 Hz is filtered out at the receiver while the noise around it is measured. The ratio of the signal received to the noise measured is the Signal-to-C-Notched-Noise Ratio.

Intermodulation distortion refers to the tendency of certain types of telephone equipment to generate harmonics (multiples) of the frequencies being transmitted through them.

Table F–4 compares signal-to-noise ratios and signal-to-spurious-modulation-product ratios for basic circuits and those with D-Conditioning. Unlike the previous tables, entries are "signal-to-evil" ratios, so high numbers are better than low numbers. While two types of D-Conditioning are offered for Service Type 5 circuits, AT&T PUB 43202 does not differentiate between them in a numerical fashion, hence the single entry in Table F–4.

Table F–4   Effect of D-Conditioning on Noise and
Intermodulation Distortion

| | Basic | D-Conditioned |
|---|---|---|
| Signal-to-C-notched-noise ratio | ≥24 db | ≥28 db |
| Intermodulation distortion | | |
| Signal to 2nd order modulation products | ≥27 db | ≥35 db |
| Signal to 3rd order modulation products | ≥32 db | ≥40 db |

International conditioning is used on two-point (as opposed to multipoint) overseas circuits. Like C-Conditioning, the attenuation distortion and envelope delay distortion are controlled to meet certain specifications. In this case, the specifications are those of CCITT Recommendations M.1020 and M.1025. Tables F–5 and F–6 show the attenuation distortion and envelope delay distortion, respectively, for a basic (unconditioned) Service Type 5 circuit and for a similar circuit conditioned with M.1020 and M.1025 International conditioning. For more details on this and other types of conditioning, see AT&T PUB 43202.

Table F–5    Effect of International Conditioning on Attenuation Distortion

| | | Conditioning | |
|---|---|---|---|
| *Frequencies* | *Basic* | *M.1025* | *M.1020* |
| 500–2500 Hz | | −2.0 to +8.0 | |
| 504–2504 Hz | −2.0 to +8.0 | | |
| 500–2800 Hz | | | −1.0 to +3.0 |
| 404–2804 Hz | −2.0 to +10.0 | | |
| 300–3000 Hz | | −2.0 to +12.0 | −2.0 to +6.0 |
| 304–3004 Hz | −3.0 to +12.0 | | |

Note: All attenuation variation values are given in decibels (db). The symbol "+" means loss and "−" means gain, relative to performance at 1004 Hz.

Table F–6    Effect of International Conditioning on Envelope Delay Distortion

| | | Conditioning | |
|---|---|---|---|
| *Frequencies* | *Basic* | *M.1025* | *M.1020* |
| 1000–2600 Hz | | 1500 | 500 |
| 804–2604 Hz | 1750 | | |
| 600–2600 Hz | | | 1500 |
| 600–2800 Hz | | 3000 | |
| 500–2800 Hz | | | 3000 |

Note: All delay values are given in microseconds.

# APPENDIX G

## Interface Connector Pinning

A 25-pin connector with pins arranged as shown in Figure G–1 is the most widely used connector for EIA-232-D and Recommendation V.28 interfaces. A male connector is used on the DTE and a female connector is used on the DCE.

For about half the pins there is an internationally accepted circuit assignment used by all modems implementing that circuit. These assignments are shown in Table G–1 and discussed in Reference 1.

Pins that do not have an internationally accepted circuit assignment (no asterisk) vary among different modems. Some variations are described in Reference 1. Most modems in the United States follow the pinning assignment given in EIA-232-D, which was used to assign the pins in Table G–1. Note that even in EIA-232-D, several pins have multiple assignments.

No one should use the unassigned pins unless doing so is for a purpose described in the reference. Many manufacturers have put 20 milliampere interfaces on the "unused" pins of acoustic couplers (DCE). Many manufacturers of terminal (DTE) have put TTL-level test points on the "unused" pins. Each manufacturer has them supplied cables that are appropriately

Figure G–1  View of Face Connector on Data Terminal Equipment

Table G–1   Circuit Assignments fo DTE/DCE Interface Using a 25-Pin Connector (EIA-232-D/CCITT V.24)

| Pin | CCITT | EIA | Circuit Name |
|-----|-------|-----|--------------|
| 1 | | | Sometimes used for Protective Ground (Frame Ground), a use no longer recognized by either EIA-232-D or CCITT V.24. Sometimes used for a connection to shield to provide shield continuity in cases where several cables are connected end-to-end, a use recognized in EIA-232-D. |
| 2* | 103 | BA | Transmitted Data |
| 3* | 104 | BB | Received Data |
| 4* | 105 | CA | Request to Send |
| 5* | 106 | CB | Clear to Send |
| 6* | 107 | CC | Data Set Ready |
| 7* | 102 | AB | Signal Ground |
| 8* | 109 | CF | Received Line Signal (Carrier) Detector |
| 9* | | | Often used for modem power test point. Do not connect. |
| 10* | | | Often used for modem power test point. Do not connect. |
| 11 | | | |
| 12 | 122/112 | SCF/CI | Secondary Received Line Signal Detector Data Signaling Rate Select (DCE Source) |
| 13 | 121 | SCB | Secondary Clear to Send |
| 14 | 118 | SBA | Secondary Transmitted Data |
| 15* | 114 | DB | Transmit Signal Element Timing—DCE Source (Synchronous Modems Only) |
| 16 | 119 | SBB | Secondary Received Data |
| 17* | 115 | DD | Received Signal Element Timing—DCE Source (Synchronous Modems Only) |
| 18 | 141 | LL | Local Loopback |
| 19 | 120 | SCA | Secondary Request to Send |
| 20* | 108/2 | CD | Data Terminal Ready |
| 21 | 140/110 | RL/CG | Remote Loopback/Signal Quality Detector |
| 22* | 125 | CE | Ring/Calling Indicator |
| 23 | 11/112 | CH/CI | Data Signal Rate Select (DTE/DCE Source) |
| 24 | 113 | DA | Transmit Signal Element Timing (DTE Source) |
| 25 | 142 | TM | Test Mode |

*Internationally accepted circuit assignment used in all modems with this circuit.

wired for these compromised purposes. When the customer buys a cable from a third party, a cable with all 25 conductors wired, the 20 milliampere interface in the acoustic coupler will blow up the TTL logic in the terminal.

Another standard that uses the 25-pin connector is EIA-530, "High Speed 25-Position Interface for Data Terminal Equipment and Data Circuit-Terminating Equipment." That standard uses EIA-422-A circuits for all circuits except Local Loopback, Remote Loopback, and Test Mode, which are EIA-423-A. There are two leads for each EIA-422-A circuit (see Chapter 5), the A-A' lead and the B-B' lead. In Table G-2, the A-A' leads use the same pins as their EIA-232-D counterparts in Table G-1.

Table G-2   Circuit Assignments for DTE/DCE Interface Using a 25-Pin Connector (EIA-530)

| Pin | EIA | Circuit Name |
|-----|-----|--------------|
| 1 | | Shield |
| 2 | BA | Transmitted Data (A-A') |
| 3 | BB | Received Data (A-A') |
| 4 | CA | Request to Send (A-A') |
| 5 | CB | Clear to Send (A-A') |
| 6 | CC | Data Set Ready (A-A') |
| 7 | AB | Signal Ground (C-C') |
| 8 | CF | Received Line Signal Detector (A-A') |
| 9 | DD | B-B' (A-A' is on 17) |
| 10 | CF | B-B' (A-A' is on 8) |
| 11 | DA | B-B' (A-A' is on 24) |
| 12 | DB | B-B' (A-A' is on 15) |
| 13 | CB | B-B' (A-A' is on 5) |
| 14 | BA | B-B' (A-A' is on 2) |
| 15 | DB | Transmit Signal Element Timing—DCE (A-A') |
| 16 | BB | B-B' (A-A' is on 3) |
| 17 | DD | Received Signal Element Timing—DCE (A-A') |
| 18 | LL | Local Loopback (EIA-423-A) |
| 19 | CA | B-B' (A-A' is on 4) |
| 20 | CD | Data Terminal Ready (A-A') |
| 21 | RL | Remote Loopback (EIA-423-A) |
| 22 | CC | B-B' (A-A' is on 6) |
| 23 | CD | B-B' (A-A' is on 20) |
| 24 | DA | Transmit Signal Element Timing—DTE (A-A') |
| 25 | TM | Test Mode (EIA-423-A) |

For those using the 37-pin and 9-pin connectors associated with RS-449 and the 15-pin connector associated with CCITT Recommendations X.20 and X.21, References 2 and 3 will be of assistance.

## References

1. International Organization for Standardization (ISO). "Data Communication—25-pin DTE/DCE Interface Connector and Pin Assignments" (ISO/DIS 2110).
2. ISO. "Data Communication—37-pin and 9-pin DTE/DCE Interface Connectors and Pin Assignments" (ISO/DIS 4902).
3. ISO. "Data Communication—15-pin DTE/DCE Interface Connector and Pin Assignments" (ISO/DIS 4903).
4. Electronics Industries Association (EIA). "Interface between Data Terminal Equipment and Data Circuit-Terminating Equipment Employing Serial Binary Data Interchange" (EIA-232-D).
5. EIA. "High Speed 25-Position Interface for Data Terminal Equipment and Data Circuit-Terminating Equipment" (EIA-530).

# RPPENDIX H

## Hayes Smartmodem 1200 and Hayes Smartmodem 2400 Dialing Commands and Responses

Tables H–1 through H–4 are reproduced by permission of Hayes Microcomputer Products, Inc. Table H–1 lists the dialing commands for a Hayes Smartmodem 1200; Table H–2 lists the result codes received in response to those commands; Table H–3 lists the dialing commands for a Hayes Smartmodem 2400; and Table H–4 lists the result codes received in response to those commands.

Table H–1   Hayes Smartmodem 1200™ Dialing Commands†

| Command | Description |
|---------|-------------|
|         | Prefix, Repeat and Escape Commands |
| AT | Attention prefix: precedes all command lines except + + + (escape) and A/ (repeat) commands |
| A/ | Repeat last command line (A/ is not followed by a carriage return) |
| + + +· | Escape code: go from on-line state to command state (one second pause before and after escape code entry; + + + is not followed by carriage return) |

*continues*

†Note: Commands entered with null parameters assume the parameter 0. For example, **M** is the same as **M0**. Defaults are in **bold**.

*Table H–1 (Cont.)*

| Command | Description |
|---------|-------------|
| | Dialing Commands |
| D | Dial |
| **P** | **Pulse** |
| T | Touch-tone |
| , | Pause |
| ! | Flash |
| / | Wait for 1/8 second |
| @ | Wait for silence |
| W | Wait for second dial tone |
| ; | Return to command state after dialing |
| R | Reverse mode (to call originate-only modem) |

Table H–2   Hayes Smartmodem 1200 Result Codes

| Digit Code | Word Code | Description |
|------------|-----------|-------------|
| 0 | OK | Command executed |
| 1 | CONNECT | Connected at 300 or 1200 bps.<br>Connected at 300 bps., if result of X1, X2, X3, or X4 command |
| 2 | RING | Ringing signal detected* |
| 3 | NO CARRIER | Carrier signal not detected or lost |
| 4 | ERROR | Illegal command<br>Error in command line<br>Command line exceeds buffer (40 characters, including punctuation)<br>Cannot operate at 300 bps. in CCITT V.22 mode<br>Invalid character format at 1200 bps.<br>Invalid checksum |
| 5 | CONNECT 1200 | Connected at 1200 bps. Results from X1, X2, X3, or X4 commands only. |
| 6 | NO DIALTONE | Dial tone not detected and subsequent commands not processed. Results from X2 or X4 commands only. |
| 7 | BUSY | Busy signal detected and subsequent commands not processed. Results from X3 or X4 commands only. |
| 8 | NO ANSWER | Silence not detected and subsequent commands not processed. Results from @ command only. |

* Note: When the Smartmodem 1200 detects a ringing on the telephone line, it sends a RING result code. However, the Smartmodem 1200 will answer the call only if it is in auto-answer mode or is given an A command.

Table H–3   Hayes Smartmodem 2400™ Dialing Commands and Modifiers

| Command | Description |
|---------|-------------|
| AT | Command line prefix (ATtention code); precedes command lines except + + + (escape) and A/ (repeat) commands |
| A/ | Re-execute last command line (A/ is not followed by a carriage return) |
| A | Off-hook in answer mode |
| B | Selects CCITT V.22 operation when communicating at 1200 bps |
| **B1** | **Selects Bell 212A operation when communicating at 1200 bps** |
| D | Dial number which follows D in the command line |
| E | Modem does not "echo" commands back to terminal |
| **E1** | **Modem "echoes" commands back to terminal** |
| H | On Hook (hang up) |
| H1 | Operates switch-hook and auxiliary relay |
| I | Request product identification Code |
| I1 | Performs checksum on firmware ROM; returns checksum |
| I2 | Performs checksum on firmware ROM; returns OK or ERROR |
| L,L1 | Low speaker volume |
| **L2** | **Medium speaker volume** |
| L3 | High speaker volume |
| M | Speaker off |
| **M1** | **Speaker on until carrier detected** |
| M2 | Speaker always on |
| M3 | Speaker on until carrier detected except during dialing |
| O | Return to on-line state |
| O1 | Return to on-line state and initiate equalizer retrain |
| **Q** | **Modem returns result codes** |
| Q1 | Modem does not return result codes |
| Sr = n | Set register r to value n |
| Sr? | Request contents of register r |
| V | Short form numeric result codes |
| **V1** | **Full word result codes** |
| V | Smartmodem 300 compatibility mode; **CONNECT** result code enabled |
| X1 | Modem blind dials; all **CONNECT XXXX** result codes enabled; busy signal not detected |
| X2 | Modem waits for dialtone before dialing; All **CONNECT XXXX** result codes enabled; busy signal not detected |

*continues*

*Table H–3 (Cont.)*

| Command | Description |
|---------|-------------|
| X3 | Modem blind dials; all **CONNECT XXXX** result codes enabled; modem sends **BUSY** result code if busy signal detected |
| **X4** | **Modem waits for dialtone before dialing; all CONNECT XXXX result codes enabled; modem sends BUSY result code if busy signal detected** |
| **Y** | **Long space disconnect disabled** |
| Y1 | Long space disconnect enabled |
| Z | Load stored configuration profile |
| **&C** | **DCD always ON** |
| &C1 | DCD ON indicates presence of data carrier |
| **&D** | **Modem ignores DTR** |
| &D1 | Modem assumes command state when ON-to-OFF transition detected on DTR |
| &D2 | Modem hangs up, assumes command state and disables auto answer upon detecting ON-to-OFF transition on DTR |
| &D3 | Modem assumes initialization state upon detecting an ON-to-OFF transition on DTR |
| &F | Load factory configuration profile |
| **&G** | **No guard tone** |
| &G1 | 550 Hz guard tone |
| &G2 | 1800 Hz guard tone |
| **&J** | **RJ-11/RJ-41S/RJ-45S telco jack** |
| &J1 | RJ-12/RJ-13 telco jack type |
| **&M** | **Asynchronous mode** |
| &M1 | Synchronous mode 1 (Sync/Async mode) |
| &M2 | Synchronous mode 2 (Dial Stored Number mode) |
| &M3 | Synchronous mode 3 (DTR control of Data/Talk) |
| **&P** | **Pulse dial make/break ratio = 39/61 (USA/Canada)** |
| &P1 | Pulse dial make/break ratio = 33/67 (UK/HK) |
| **&R** | **CTS follows RTS** |
| &R1 | Modem ignores RTS; CTS always ON |
| **&S** | **DSR always ON** |
| &S1 | DSR operates in accordance with EIA RS-232C specification |
| &T | Terminate test in progress |

*Table H–3 (Cont.)*

| Command | Description |
|---------|-------------|
| &T1 | Initiate Local Analog Loopback test |
| &T3 | Initiate digital loopback |
| &T4 | Modem grants request from remote modem for RDL |
| &T5 | Modem denies request from remote modem for RDL |
| &T6 | Initiate Remote Digital Loopback test |
| &T7 | Initiate Remote Digital Loopback with self test |
| &T8 | Initiate Local Analog Loopback with self test |
| &W | Write active configuration profile to nonvolatile memory |
| **&X** | **Modem sources transmit clock for synchronous modes** |
| &X1 | Data terminal sources transmit clock for synchronous modes |
| &X2 | Modem derives transmit clock for synchronous operation from receive carrier (slave operation) |
| &Z | Store telephone number |
| | Dial Modifiers |
| P | Pulse dial |
| T | Tone dial |
| , | Pause |
| ! | Flash |
| @ | Wait for silence |
| W | Wait for second dial tone |
| ; | Return to command state after dialing |
| R | Originate call in answer mode |
| S | Dial stored number |
| | Other Commands |
| A | Answer call without waiting for ring |
| B | CCITT V.22 mode |
| **B1** | **Bell 103 and 212A mode** |
| C | Transmit carrier off |
| **C1** | **Carrier on** |
| E | Characters not echoed |
| **E1** | **Characters echoed** |
| F | Half duplex |
| **F1** | **Full duplex** |

*continues*

*Table H–3 (Cont.)*

| Command | Description |
|---------|-------------|
| H | On Hook (hang up) |
| H1 | Off hook, line and auxiliary relay |
| H2 | Off hook, line relay only |
| I | Request Smartmodem product ID code |
| I1 | Manufacturing test |
| I2 | Test internal memory |
| L1 | Low speaker volume |
| **L2** | **Medium speaker volume** |
| L3 | High speaker volume |
| M | Speaker always off |
| **M1** | **Speaker on until carrier detected** |
| M2 | Speaker always on |
| O | Go to on-line state |
| **O1** | **Remote digital loopback off** |
| O2 | Remote digital loopback request |
| **Q** | **Result codes displayed** |
| Q1 | Result codes not displayed |
| S$r$? | Request current value of register $r$ |
| S$r = n$ | Sets register $r$ to value of $n$ |
| V | Digit result codes |
| **V1** | **Word result codes** |
| **X** | **Compatible with Smartmodem 300** |
| X1 | Result code CONNECT 1200 enabled |
| X2 | Enables dial tone detection |
| X3 | Enables busy signal detection |
| X4 | Enables dial tone and busy signal detection |
| **Y** | **Long space disconnect disabled** |
| Y1 | Long space disconnect enabled |
| Z | Software reset: restores all default settings |

Table H–4   Hayes Smartmodem 2400™ Result Codes

| Result Code | Short Form | Description |
|---|---|---|
| OK | 0 | Acknowledges execution of a command line |
| CONNECT | 1 | A connection has been established at 300 bps |
| RING | 2 | Ring detected |
| NO CARRIER | 3 | Failure to connect or loss of carrier |
| ERROR | 4 | Command not recognized<br>Command too long<br>Response to 1 command—incorrect checksum<br>Command issued at 110 or 300 bps and synchronous mode selected |
| CONNECT 1200 | 5 | A connection has been established at 1200 bps |
| NO DIALTONE | 6 | The **W** dial modifier is issued and a dial tone is not detected within the period specified by **S7**. The **X2** or **X4** result code option is selected and a dial tone is not detected within 5 seconds of going off-hook |
| BUSY | 7 | Modem detects busy signal |
| NO ANSWER | 8 | The "Wait for Quiet Answer" dial modifier, @, was issued, and five seconds of silence was not detected |
| CONNECT 2400 | 10 | A connection has been established at 2400 bps |

# APPENDIX I

## Where to Get More Information

**ANSI**
ANSI Sales Department
1430 Broadway
New York, NY 10018
(212) 642-4900

Handles U.S. distribution of ISO documents. Catalog of publications available ($10). Prepaid mail orders only.

**AT&T**
AT&T Customer Information Center
Commercial Sales Representative
P.O. Box 19901
Indianapolis, IN 46219
(800) 432-6600 (within continental United States)
(317) 352-8557 (outside continental United States)

Free *Catalog of Communications Technical Publications* available. Prepaid mail orders and credit card telephone orders accepted.

**Bell Communications Research**
Bell Communications Research
Attn: Documentation Coordinator
60 New England Avenue
Piscataway, NJ 08854
(201) 699-5800

Free catalog, *Bell Communications Technical References*, available. Prepaid mail orders and credit card telephone orders accepted.

### CCITT

United Nations Bookstore
Room GA 32B
United Nations General Assembly Building
New York, NY 10017
(212) 963-7680

Free catalog of CCITT books available. Prepaid mail orders and credit card telephone orders accepted. Prepaid mail orders preferred.

### EIA

Electronics Industries Association
Standards Office
2001 Eye Street, NW
Washington, DC 20006
(202) 457-4966

Catalog of publications available ($5). Prepaid mail orders and credit card telephone orders accepted. Prepaid mail orders preferred (substantial charge for credit card).

### IEEE

IEEE Service Center
445 Hoes Lane
P.O. Box 1331
Piscataway, NJ 08855-1331
(201) 562-5346 (credit card orders)
(201) 562-5420 or (201) 981-1393 (questions)
(201) 981-0060 (main switchboard for IEEE Service Center)
(212) 705-7900 (main switchboard for IEEE Headquarters, New York City)

Free catalog of publications available. Prepaid mail orders and credit card telephone orders accepted.

**ITU**
International Telecommunications Union
General Secretariat
Sales Service
Place de Nation, CH 1211
Geneva 20, Switzerland
0-22-99-5111 (National)
41-22-99-5111 (International)

# Glossary

**Access Methods**   Techniques for determining which of several stations that wish to transmit will be the next to use a shared transmission medium.

**Access Network**   A local area network, generally very limited in geographical coverage, that allows users to communicate among each other and also permits access to a spine network that covers a larger distance and connects several access networks.

**ACK0, ACK1 (Affirmative Acknowledgment)**   These replies (DLE sequences in binary synchronous communications) indicate that the previous transmission block was accepted by the receiver and that it is ready to accept the next block of the transmission. Use of ACK0 and ACK1 alternately provides sequential checking control for a series of replies. ACK0 is also an affirmative (ready to receive) reply to a station selection (multipoint) or to an initialization sequence (line bid) in point-to-point operation.

**Acoustic Coupler**   A device that converts electrical signals into audio signals, enabling data to be transmitted over the public telephone network via a conventional telephone handset.

**Active Interface**   In data transmission systems utilizing 20 milliampere current loops, there are three elements to the loop: a current source, a switch, and a current detector. The station containing the current source is referred to as having an active interface. Contrast with *Passive Interface*.

**Address**   A grouping of numbers that uniquely identifies a station in a network, a location in computer memory, a house on a street, etc.

**Address Field**   A section of a message, generally at the beginning, in which the address of the intended receiving station is found.

**Algorithm**   A set of rules for accomplishing a task. A repeated sequence of steps that a device or program executes to accomplish the task for which it was designed.

**Alternate Route**   A secondary path used to reach a destination if the primary path is unavailable.

**Amplitude Modulation (AM)**   A method of transmission whereby the amplitude of the carrier wave is modified in accordance with the amplitude of the signal wave.

**Analog Signal**   An electrical signal that can assume any of an infinite number of voltage or current values, in contrast to a *digital signal*, which can assume only one of a finite number of values.

**Application Level**   The highest protocol level in the ISO layered model of data communication protocols. This is the level that actually performs a service for the user—for example, a mail service.

**ASCII**   American Standard Code for Information Interchange. This is a seven-bit-plus-primary code established by the American National Standards Institute (formerly American Standards Association) to achieve compatibility between data services. Also called *USASCII*.

**Asynchronous Transmission**   Transmission in which time intervals between transmitted characters may be of unequal length. Transmission is controlled by start and stop elements at the beginning and end of each character. Also called *start-stop transmission*.

**Audio Frequencies**   Frequencies that can be heard by the human ear (usually between 15 and 20,000 Hz).

**Automatic Calling Unit (ACU)**   A device that permits a computer to dial calls automatically over the communications network.

**Bandwidth**   The measure of a transmission facility's ability to transmit signals that span a range of frequencies without degrading the amount of power in the signal more than some percentage (usually 50 percent). For example, if measurements are performed on a transmission line and it is found that all signals of frequency below 300 Hz and above 3000 Hz lose half their power traversing the line, while signals between 300 and 3000 Hz retain at least 50 percent of their power, the line is said to have a bandwidth of 2700 Hz (3000 − 300).

**Baseband Signaling**   Transmission of a signal at its original frequencies—i.e., unmodulated.

**Baud**   A unit of signaling speed equal to the number of discrete conditions or signal events per second. In asynchronous transmission, the unit of signaling speed corresponding to one unit interval per second; that is, if the duration of the unit interval is 20 milliseconds, the signaling speed is 50 baud. Baud is the same as "bits per second" only if each signal event represents exactly one bit. A baud is the reciprocal of the unit interval.

**Baudot Code**   A code for the transmission of data in which five bits represent one character. It is named for Emile Baudot, a pioneer in printing telegraphy. The name is usually applied to the code used in many teleprinter systems, which was first used by Murray, a contemporary of Baudot.

**Binary**    Relating to a number system that allows only two values, zero and one. Also related to a numeric quantity expressed solely in zeros and ones.

**Binary Digit**    In binary notation, either the character zero or one.

**Binary Synchronous Communications (BSC or BISYNC)**    A system that IBM developed in the early 1960s for transmitting data over synchronous data communication facilities. It utilizes special characters and special character sequences to indicate the beginning and end of a frame and to indicate which portions of the frame are the header, the data, and the frame check sequence. Special character sequences are also used to indicate the beginning and end of messages, "turnaround" half-duplex lines, and recovery from error situations.

**Bit**    Abbreviation for binary digit.

**Bit Transfer Rate**    The number of bits transferred per unit time, usually expressed in bits per second (bps).

**Block**    A group of digits transmitted as a unit, over which a coding procedure is usually applied for synchronization or error control purposes.

**Block Check Character (BCC)**    The result of a transmission verification algorithm accumulated over a transmission block and normally appended at the end (e.g., CRC, LRC). Also called *frame check sequence.*

**Blocking**    A condition in a switching system in which a call or message cannot be processed because control equipment, transmission paths, or storage is not available.

**Broadband**    A transmission system in which signals are applied to the transmission medium after being translated in frequency. For example, human voice signals in the 300 to 3000 Hz range might occur on the transmission facility in the 2,000,000 to 2,003,000 Hz range. In a broadband system, there are typically many different sets of signals on the transmission medium at one time, each set of signals having been translated to other noninterfering frequencies. In local area network usage, "broadband" refers to systems that handle many simultaneous signals and use cable television hardware to distribute the signals.

**Buffer**    A storage device used to compensate for a difference in the rate of data flow when transmitting data from one device to another.

**Bus**    The local area network topology in which all stations attach to a single transmission medium so that all stations are equal and all stations hear all transmissions on the medium. "Bus" is also used as an abbreviation for backplane bus, a collection of electrical wiring that interconnects the slots where printed circuit cards in a computer system are inserted.

**Busy Hour**    A peak 60-minute period during a business day when the largest volume of communications traffic is handled.

**Byte**    A binary element string operated on as a unit and usually shorter than a computer word—e.g., six-bit, eight-bit, or nine-bit bytes. Most commonly, an eight-bit quantity.

**Byte Count**    The number of eight-bit quantities in a message. Since ASCII characters can be encoded in eight bits, the byte count is also called the "character count." "Byte count" also is used to describe the set of protocols that use character counting to designate which portions of a frame are the header, data, and frame check sequence.

**Carrier**    A (usually) continuous sinusoidal signal, applied to a communications medium, which does not convey information until altered in some fashion, such as having its amplitude changed (amplitude modulation), its frequency changed (frequency modulation), or its phase changed (phase modulation). These changes convey the information.

**Carrier System**    A means of obtaining a number of channels over a single path by modulating each channel on a different carrier frequency and demodulating at the receiving point to restore the signals to their original form.

**CCITT**    Comite Consultatif Internationale de Telegraphie et Telephonie. An international consultative committee that sets international communications usage standards.

**Central Office**    The place where communications common carriers terminate customer lines and locate the equipment that interconnects those lines.

**Channel**    That part of a communications system that connects a message source to a message sink. A path for electrical transmission between two or more points. Also called a *circuit, facility, line, link,* or *path.*

**Channel Capacity**    A term that expresses the maximum baud rate that can be handled by the channel.

**Character Count**    See *Byte Count.*

**Circuit**    In communications, the complete electrical path providing one- or two-way communication between two points comprising associated go and return channels.

**Circuit Switching**    A method of allowing telephones or data stations to establish a connection on a temporary basis. When the connection has been established, the two stations appear to be connected by a piece of wire, as the full bandwidth of the wire used to reach the switching system is available between the stations and there is no noticeable delay in the transmission of voice or data between the stations.

**Coaxial Cable**    A type of electrical cable in which a piece of wire is surrounded by insulation and then surrounded by a tubular piece of metal whose axis of curvature coincides with the center of the piece of wire, hence the term coaxial.

**Code**    1) In data communication, a system of rules and conventions according to which the signals representing data can be formed, transmitted, received, and processed. 2) In data processing, the representation of data or a computer program in a symbolic form that can be accepted by a computer.

**Collision**    Simultaneous transmission over a transmission medium in a way that produces unusable data.

**Common Carrier**    An organization licensed to provide a specific set of services for a specific set of rates, as delineated in an agreed-upon document called a tariff. Generally, the organization will be using a resource such as highways, airways, or rights of way in which the public interest is best served by limiting access to the resource by means of the licensing process. In exchange for receiving the license, the organization agrees to serve all customers fairly and to charge only the designated rates.

**Computer Network**    An interconnection of assemblies of computer systems, terminals, and communications facilities.

**Concentrator**    A communications device that provides communications capability between many low-speed, usually asynchronous channels and one or more high-speed, usually synchronous channels. Usually different speeds, codes, and protocols can be accommodated on the low-speed side.

**Conditioning**    The addition of equipment to leased voice-grade lines to provide specific minimum values of line characteristics required for data transmission.

**Contention**    A method of having multiple stations access a transmission medium by having each station decide, on an equal basis with other stations, when it will transmit. This method is in contrast with methods in which a master station tells other stations when they may transmit and methods in which a permit-to-transmit token is passed from station to station.

**Control Character**    1) A character whose occurrence in a particular context initiates, modifies, or stops a control function. 2) In the ASCII code, any of the 32 characters in the first two columns of the standard code table.

**Control Procedure**    The means used to control the orderly communication of information between stations on a data link. Also called *line discipline* or *protocol*.

**Control Station**    In some forms of computer network, the station on a network that supervises the network control procedures, such as polling, selecting, and recovery. It is also responsible for establishing order on the line in the event of any abnormal situation arising between any stations on the network.

**CRC**    See *Cyclic Redundancy Check*.

**Crosstalk**    The unwanted transfer of energy from one circuit, called the disturbing circuit, to another circuit, called the disturbed circuit.

**CSMA/CD**    Carrier Sense Multiple Access with Collision Detection, a method of having multiple stations access a transmission medium (multiple access) by listening until no signals are detected (carrier sense), then transmitting and checking to see whether more than one signal is present (collision detection).

**Cyclic Redundancy Check (CRC)**    A method of detecting errors in a message by performing an involved mathematical calculation on the bits in the message and then sending the results of the calculation at the end of the message. The receiving station performs the same calculation on the message data as it is being received and then checks its results against those transmitted at the end of the message.

**DARPA**    Defense Advanced Research Projects Agency, a funding agency for the computer networking experiments performed over the ARPANET.

**Data Access Arrangement (DAA)**    Data communication equipment furnished or approved by a common carrier for attaching non–FCC-registered data terminal and data communication equipment to the common carrier network.

**Data Circuit-Terminating Equipment (DCE)**    See *Data Communication Equipment*.

**Data Communication**    The interchange of data messages from one point to another over communications channels.

**Data Communication Equipment (DCE)**    The equipment that provides the functions required to establish, maintain, and terminate a connection, the signal conversion, and coding required for communications between data terminal equipment and the data circuit. The data communication equipment may or may not be an integral part of a computer (e.g., a modem).

**Data Concentration**    Collection of data at an intermediate point from several low- and medium-speed lines for retransmission across high-speed lines.

**Data Integrity**    A performance measure based on the rate of undetected errors.

**Data Link Level**    The second level of the ISO layered model of communications protocols. The first level (physical level) performs the service of delivering data to this level, and this level performs the service of collecting data into frames, for the benefit of higher levels.

**Data Set**    1) A modem. 2) A collection of data records, with a logical relation of one to another.

**Data Terminal Equipment (DTE)**    1) The equipment comprising the data source, the data sink, or both. 2) Equipment usually comprising the following functional units: control logic, buffer store, and one or more input or output devices or computers. It may also contain error control, synchronization, and station identification capability.

**Data Transmission**    The sending of data from one place for reception elsewhere.

**Datagram**    A method of transmitting messages in which sections of the message are allowed to be transmitted through the transmission system in scattered order and the correct order is reestablished by the receiving station. Contrast with *Virtual Circuit*.

**DDCMP (Digital Data Communication Message Protocol)**    In this data link layer protocol, message headers contain a character count indicating the size of the message. This permits the transmission of arbitrary character sequences in the message without concern that some may be interpreted as control characters. The protocol may be used in serial or parallel, asynchronous or synchronous transmission.

**Decoding**     In digital telephony, the process of converting digital signals to analog signals, especially the process of converting digitized speech to recognizable speech.

**Delay Distortion**     Distortion resulting from nonuniform speed of transmission of the various frequency components of a signal through a transmission medium.

**Delimiter**     A character that separates and organizes elements of data.

**Demodulation**     The process of separating a data signal from a carrier signal. A carrier signal is a continuous sinusoidal signal, applied to a communications medium, that does not convey information until altered in some fashion, such as having its amplitude, frequency, or phase changed. The changes convey the information, and the demodulation process detects what those changes were.

**Destination Address**     The part of a message that indicates for whom the message is intended.

**Diagnostic**     A program for operating an electronic device over a range of operating conditions and input data patterns similar to (or more extreme than) those the device is likely to encounter in normal use. The program compares the results obtained with the known correct answers and reports discrepancies. The diagnostic also can be arranged to repeat a particular test until failure occurs or repeat a failing test so that measurement apparatus can be attached to various portions of the failing device.

**Dial-up Line**     A communications circuit established by a switched circuit connection.

**Differential Transmission**     A method of transmitting data in which a signal is sent on two wires in such a fashion that the information conveyed is the difference in voltage between the two wires. The two wires are run twisted about each other, so each wire is equally subject to interference. If the interference occurs on each wire equally, the effects of the interference will be canceled when the receiver subtracts one wire's voltage from the other's, yet the information (the difference between the voltages) will be revealed in the subtraction process.

**Digital Data**     Information transmitted as discrete electrical quantities—for example, as signals representing zeros and ones rather than as a continuum of voltages.

**Digital Switching**     In telephony, the practice of encoding analog voice samples into digital data and routing the data through logic circuitry in much the same fashion as a computer. Like a computer, digital switching systems are fast, compact, and economical, and they require less maintenance than comparable electromechanical systems.

**Digital Transmission**     In telephony, the practice of encoding analog voice samples into digital data, transmitting that data, and reconstructing (decoding) the analog voice samples at the receiving end. Digital transmission has the benefit of being less sensitive to noise than analog transmission, since only two states of information, zero and one, need to be sent. In addition, digital data can be regenerated rather than amplified, preventing noise from being amplified along with the signal, as it would be in analog transmission.

**Direct Memory Access (DMA)**   A facility that permits I/O transfers directly into or out of memory without passing through the processor's general registers; performed either independently of the processor or on a cycle-stealing basis.

**DLE (Data Link Escape)**   A control character used exclusively to provide supplementary line-control signals (control character sequences or DLE sequences). These are two-character sequences in which the first character is DLE. The second character varies according to the function desired and the code used.

**DMA**   See *Direct Memory Access.*

**Duplex**   Simultaneous two-way independent transmission in both directions. Also referred to as *full duplex.*

**EBCDIC (Extended Binary Coded Decimal Interchange Code)**   An eight-bit character code used primarily in IBM equipment. The code provides for 256 different bit patterns.

**Echo**   A portion of the transmitted signal returned from the distant point to the source with sufficient magnitude and delay to cause interference.

**Echo Check**   A method of checking the accuracy of transmission of data in which the received data is returned to the sending end for comparison with the original data.

**Echo Suppressor**   A device used to suppress the effects of an echo. The device usually functions by comparing signal levels for two directions of transmission and inserting substantial attenuation into the path of the weaker signal, believing it to be the echo.

**EIA (Electronic Industries Association)**   A standards organization specializing in the electrical and functional characteristics of interface equipment.

**Encoding**   In telephony, the practice of encoding analog signals into digital data. This is typically done by picking 255 voltage levels, assigning each an eight-bit binary number. The voltage level of a sample is compared with the 255 voltage levels, and the nearest level is chosen. The eight-bit number for that level is then sent.

**ENQ (Enquiry)**   Used as a request for response to obtain identification and/or an indication of station status. In binary synchronous (BSC) transmission, ENQ is transmitted as part of initialization sequence (line bid) in point-to-point operation and as the final character of a selection or polling sequence in multipoint operation.

**EOT (End of Transmission)**     Indicates the end of a transmission, which may include one or more messages, and resets all stations on the line to control mode (unless it erroneously occurs within a transmission block).

**Equalization**     Compensation for the increase in attenuation with frequency. Its purpose is to produce a flat frequency response.

**Error**     Any discrepancy between a computed, observed, or measured quantity and the true, specified, or theoretically correct value or condition. See *Systematic Error* and *Random Error*.

**Error Detection**     The process of performing a mathematical operation on the data sent and sending the results of that operation along with the data. The receiving station performs the same operation and compares the results with those sent. The operation may be a simple indication of whether the number of ones in some part of the message is even or odd; the operation may also be much more complicated.

**Ethernet**     A CSMA/CD system, utilizing coaxial cable, developed at Xerox Corporation's Palo Alto Research Center. The system is described in an article by R.M. Metcalfe and D.R. Boggs in the *Communications of the ACM*, July 1976. The initial system ran at 3 MHz; the system commercialized by Xerox, Intel, and Digital Equipment Corporation runs at 10 MHz.

**ETX (End of Text)**     Indicates the end of a message. If multiple transmission blocks are contained in a message in BSC systems, ETX terminates the last block of the message. (ETB is used to terminate preceding blocks.) The block check character is sent immediately following ETX. ETX requires a reply indicating the receiving station's status.

**Exchange**     A defined area, served by a communications common carrier, within which the carrier furnishes service at the exchange rate and under the regulations applicable in that area as prescribed in the carrier's filed tariffs.

**Facility**     See *Channel*.

**Facsimile (FAX)**     Transmission of pictures, maps, diagrams, and so on. The image is scanned at the transmitter, reconstructed at the receiving station, and duplicated on some form of paper.

**FDM (Frequency Division Multiplexing)**     Dividing the available transmission frequency range into narrower bands, each of which is used for a separate channel.

**Fiber Optics**     A data transmission medium consisting of fine glass or plastic fibers. Light emitting diodes or small lasers introduce light into one end of the fiber, and it bounces off the inside of the surface of the fiber until it reaches the other end, where a detector converts the light back into an electrical signal. There are also varieties of fiber, called graded index fibers, in which the light is bent back toward the center when it gets near the surface of the fiber, rather than actually bouncing off the inside of the surface.

**FIFO**   A first-in, first-out buffer. Such buffers are useful for handling data that arrives in bursts, as they allow a computer to process the data at an average rate rather than at intermittent peak rates.

**File**   An ordered collection of data, usually stored on a disk or tape and associated with or created by a particular person.

**Filter**   An electronic circuit that allows signals within a given frequency range to pass through the circuit without loss, while suppressing signals outside that range.

**Firmware**   Programs kept in semipermanent storage, such as various types of read-only memory; such programs can be altered, but with difficulty. Contrast with *Hardware* and *Software*.

**Flag**   A program-readable indicator signifying that data is available, that space is available to store data, or that some operation has been completed. Also, in HDLC and SDLC data link protocols, a distinctive bit pattern (01111110) that indicates the beginning and end of a frame.

**Flow Control**   Hardware or software mechanisms employed in data communication to turn off transmission when the receiving station is unable to store the data it is receiving.

**FM (Frequency Modulation)**   A method of transmission whereby the frequency of the carrier wave is changed to correspond to changes in the information signal wave.

**Foreign Exchange Line**   A line offered by a common carrier in which a termination in one central office is assigned a number belonging to a remote central office.

**Formats**   Ways of arranging data in a message in prescribed order so that a receiving station knows where to find specific information within the message.

**Forward Channel**   A data transmission channel in which the direction of transmission coincides with that in which information is being transferred. Constant with *Reverse Channel*.

**Frame**   A group of bits, the first several bits being a header containing address and other control information, the next bits being the data being conveyed, and the last bits being a frame check sequence for error detection.

**Frame Check Sequence**   Another name for *cyclic redundancy check*.

**Front End Processor**   A communications computer associated with a larger computer. It may perform line control, message handling, code conversion, error control, and applications functions such as control and operation of special purpose terminals.

**FSK (Frequency Shift Keying)**   Also called frequency shift signaling. A method of frequency modulation in which frequency is made to vary at significant instants by smooth as well as abrupt transitions. Typically a data "1" bit is represented as one frequency and a data "0" as another frequency.

**Full Duplex**    The capability of transmitting in both directions simultaneously.

**Fully Connected Network**    A network in which each node is directly connected with every other node.

**Half Duplex**    A circuit designed for transmission in either direction but not both directions simultaneously.

**Hardware**    Computers, printers, disks, or other devices whose fundamental characteristics were determined at the time of manufacture. Changes in such devices require the use of tools. Contrast with *Firmware* and *Software*.

**HDLC (Hierarchical Data Link Control)**    An international data link layer protocol in which data is transmitted with a zero inserted after each consecutive group of five ones, except for a distinctive flag pattern (01111110), which delineates the beginning and end of a frame. This protocol is very similar to SDLC, but the header provides a greater range of addressing and message numbering.

**Header**    The beginning portion of a message that contains destination address, source address, message numbering, and other control information.

**Hertz (Hz)**    A unit of frequency equal to one cycle per second. Cycles are referred to as Hertz in honor of the experimenter Heinrich Hertz.

**Holding Time**    The length of time a communications channel is in use for each transmission. Includes both message time and operating time.

**Host Computer**    A computer attached to a network, primarily providing services such as computation, data base access, or special programs.

**Host Interface**    The interface between a communications processor and a host computer.

**Hunt Group**    An arrangement of a group of telephone lines such that a single telephone number is listed in the directory. A person dialing that listed number is automatically connected by the telephone switching equipment to an available line in that group. Only if all lines in the group are busy does the caller get a busy signal.

**Hybrid Network**    A local area network employing a mixture of topologies and access methods. For example, a network that includes both a token ring and a CSMA/CD bus.

**Idling Signal**    Any signal applied to a communications line that indicates that no data is being sent. Such a signal is often used to reassure receiving stations that the line is still electrically intact and, in systems that recover clocking information from data, to keep clock recovery circuits prepared for the arrival of data.

**IEEE**    The Institute of Electrical and Electronic Engineers, an information exchange, publishing, and standards body responsible for many standards used in local area networks, notably the 802 series.

**Impedance**    An electrical property similar to resistance but varying with frequency.

**Impedance Discontinuity**    A point at which the electrical properties of a transmission medium change, either because the medium itself has changed (different type of cable, for example) or because additional devices or sections of cable have been joined to the medium at that point. A change of impedance is important because when an electrical signal arrives at the point where the change occurs, a portion of that signal's energy will be reflected back in the direction from which the signal arrived, possibly causing a malfunction.

**Information Bit**    A bit that is generated by the data source and is not used for error control by the data transmission system. Contrast with *Overhead Bit.*

**Interchange Point**    A location where interface signals are transmitted between pieces of equipment by means of electrical interconnections. See *Interface.*

**Interface**    (1) A shared boundary defined by common physical interconnection characteristics, signal characteristics, and meanings of interchanged signals. (2) A device or piece of equipment making possible interoperation between two systems—e.g., a hardware component or a common storage register. (3) A shared logical boundary between two software components.

**Interrupt**    A signal given to a computer that, when acknowledged, causes the computer to stop what it is doing (storing the details thereof) and turn its attention to the device asserting the signal. After the device has been serviced, the computer will recover the status information concerning the previous task and will resume its execution.

**IP**    Internetwork Protocol, a network layer protocol used on the ARPANET.

**ISDN**    The Integrated Services Digital Network, a network (generally evolving from a telephony network) that provides end-to-end digital connectivity to support a wide range of services, including both voice and nonvoice services. Users can access these services by means of a limited set of standard interfaces.

**ISO**    The International Organization for Standardization, a standards body. This organization has developed standards for pin assignments in data communication plugs, has promulgated the layered model of communications protocols, and has specified and approved protocols for many of the layers in the model.

**ISO Layered Model (or ISO Reference Model)**    A way of thinking about communications protocols that models them as existing in even layers, each layer performing services for the layers above it. The seven layers (from lowest to highest) are physical, data link, network, transport, session, presentation, and application. This model is sometimes also called the OSI (Open Systems Interconnect) Layered Model.

**ITB (Intermediate Text Block)**    In binary synchronous communications, a control character used to terminate an intermediate block of characters. The block check character is sent immediately following ITB, but no line turnaround occurs. The response following ETB or ETX also applies to all the ITB checks immediately preceding the block terminated by ETB or ETX.

**Layered Protocols**    Protocols designed to obtain services from, and deliver services to, other protocols in the fashion described in *ISO Layered Model*.

**Leased Line**    A line reserved for the exclusive use of a leasing customer without interexchange switching arrangements. Also called *private line*.

**Line**    (1) The portion of a circuit external to the apparatus consisting of the conductors connecting a telegraph or telephone set to the exchange or the conductors connecting two exchanges. (2) The group of conductors on the same overhead route in the same cable.

**Line Driver**    A circuit designed to transmit data outside the enclosure of a computer systems, but not more than a few hundred feet. The data is not modulated or changed in any fashion, but higher voltage and current levels are used than would be used within a computer system.

**Link**    (1) Any specified relationship between two nodes in a network. (2) A communications path between two nodes. (3) A data link.

**Linked List**    A system of organizing data within a computer memory; it is often used for the storage of data communication messages and is characterized by the storage of both data and the address of the next block of data.

**Linked List Header**    A block of information indicating (1) the address of the next linked list header, (2) the address of the message text buffer, (3) the size of the message text buffer, and (4) control bits indicating special actions to be taken before or during the transmission of the text.

**Load Sharing**    The distribution of a given load among several computers on a network.

**Local Area Network**    A data communication network that spans a physically limited area (generally less than a mile or two), provides high-bandwidth communication over inexpensive media (generally coaxial cable or twisted pair), provides a switching capability, and is usually owned by the user (i.e., not provided by a common carrier).

**Local Exchange**    An exchange in which subscribers' lines terminate. Also called an *end office*.

**Logic Levels**    The voltages used within computers to convey digital information, usually between 0.4 and 3.0 volts DC.

**Logical Address**    A grouping of numbers that identifies one or more stations in a local area network that can accomplish the same class of tasks or are in some other way similar.

**Long Line Driver**    A circuit designed to transmit data outside the enclosure of a computer system, but not more than a few thousand feet.

**Longitudinal Redundancy Check (LRC)**    An error checking technique based on an accumulated exclusive-OR of transmitted characters. An LRC character is accumulated at both the sending and receiving stations during the transmission of a block. This accumulation is called the block check character (BCC) and is transmitted as the last character in the block. The transmitted BCC is compared with the accumulated BCC character at the receiving station for an equal condition. An equal comparison indicates a good transmission of the previous block.

**LSI**   Large-scale integration, the art of putting tens of thousands of transistors into a single integrated circuit, typically a quarter inch square.

**MARK**   Presence of a signal. In telegraphy, MARK represents the closed condition or current flowing. Equivalent to a binary "1" condition.

**Master Station**   See *Primary Station*.

**Medium**   A person, mechanism, electronic pathway, or other means of conveying information from one point to another.

**Megabit per Second**   One million bits per second.

**Message**   An ordered collection of data that is intelligible to the sender and to the recipient.

**Message Numbering**   A method of ensuring that messages are in the correct order at the receiving station, detecting lost messages, acknowledging the receipt of correct messages (see *Cyclic Redundancy Check*), and requesting the retransmission of specific messages that were damaged in transit or lost.

**Message Switching**   A method of handling messages over communications networks. The entire message is transmitted to an intermediate point (i.e., a switching computer), stored for a period of time, perhaps very short, and then transmitted again toward its destination. The destination of each message is indicated by an address integral to the message. Contrast with *Circuit Switching*.

**Metropolitan Area Network**   A data communication network that spans the area of a township, provides high-bandwidth communications over relatively inexpensive media (generally an installed cable television system), may provide a switching capability, and is usually provided to all users for a subscription fee by a cable television company or a communications common carrier.

**Microsecond**   One-millionth of a second.

**Millisecond**   One-thousandth of a second.

**Modem**   An acronym made from the words modulator and demodulator. A device that uses digital data to alter the signal that can be transmitted over an analog transmission facility (modulator) and can also receive an altered signal from an analog transmission facility and determine what digital signal the alterations in the received signal represent (demodulator).

**Multicast**   A message intended for a subset of the stations on a network rather than for an individual station or for all the stations.

**Multiplexer**   A device used for multiplexing. It may or may not contain a computer or microprocessor. Also, a device for connecting a number of communications lines to a computer.

**Multiplexing** The process of sending several signals over a single transmission medium and separating them at the other end.

**Multipoint Line** A single communications line to which more than one terminal is attached. Use of this type of line normally requires some kind of polling mechanism, addressing each terminal with a unique ID. Also called *multidrop*.

**Nanosecond** One-billionth of a second.

**Narrowband Channels** Sub–voice-grade channels characterized by a speed range of 100 to 200 bps.

**Negative Acknowledgment (NAK)** Indicates that the previous transmission block was in error and that the receiver is ready to accept a retransmission of the erroneous block. NAK is also the "not ready" reply to a station selection (multipoint) or to an initialization sequence (line bid) in point-to-point operation.

**Network Access Control** Electronic circuitry that determines which station may transmit next or when a particular station may transmit. This circuitry may be centrally located or located in each of the network interface controllers.

**Network Interface Controllers** Electronic circuitry that connects a station to a network. The circuitry determines when the station may transmit, detects arriving messages, indicates error conditions, and may include buffers for storing transmitted and received messages.

**Network Layer** The third layer of the ISO layered model of communications protocols. It receives data that has been formatted by the data link layer below it, performs additional services, and passes the results up to the transport layer above it.

**Network Topology** The pattern of connection between points in a network. Examples include a mesh (all points connected to all other points), a star, a bus, or a ring.

**Nodes** Points in a network where service is provided, service is used, or communications channels are interconnected.

**Noise** Undesirable disturbances in a communications system. Noise can generate errors in transmission.

**Nonswitched Line** A communications link that is permanently installed between two points. Also called a *leased line* or a *private line*.

**Nontransparent Mode** Transmission of characters in a defined character format (e.g., ASCII or EBCDIC), in which all defined control characters and control character sequences are recognized and treated as such.

**Null Modem** A device that interfaces between a local peripheral that normally requires a modem and the computer near it that expects to drive a modem to interface to that device; an imitation modem in both directions.

**Off-hook** In telephony, the state of a station requesting service from a switching system or the state of a station that has been connected to another station and desires to maintain that connection.

**One-Way Only Operation**   A mode of operation of a data link in which data is transmitted in a preassigned direction over one channel. Also called *simplex operation*.

**Open Circuit**   An arrangement of electrical components through which no current flows because the wiring is disconnected at some point or because an electrical component has failed.

**Operating System**   Software that controls the execution of computer programs and that may provide scheduling, debugging, input and output control, accounting, storage assignment, data management, and related services. Sometimes called *supervisor, executive, monitor,* or *master control program,* depending on the computer manufacturer.

**Optical Fibers**   See *Fiber Optics.*

**Overhead Bit**   A bit other than an information bit—e.g., a check bit or framing bit.

**Packet**   A group of bits, including data and control elements, that is switched and transmitted together. The control elements include a source address and a destination address. The data and control elements, and possibly error control information, are arranged in a specified format.

**Packet Switching**   A data transmission method utilizing packets, whereby a channel is occupied only for the duration of the transmission of the packet. By limiting the length of the packets, the system limits the amount of time other users will have to wait. Depending on the length of the message and the system being used, the data may be formatted into a packet or divided and then formatted into a number of packets for transmission and multiplexing purposes. Contrast with *Circuit Switching.*

**Parallel Transmission**   Method of data transfer in which all bits of a character or byte are transmitted simultaneously, either over separate communications lines or on different carrier frequencies on the same communications line.

**Parity Check**   Addition of noninformation bits to data, making the number of ones in each grouping of bits either always odd for odd parity or always even for even parity. This permits single error detection in each group.

**Passive Interface**   In data transmission systems utilizing 20 milliampere current loops, there are three elements to the loop: a current source, a switch, and a current detector. The station without the current source is referred to as having a passive interface. Contrast with *Active Interface.*

**PBX**   Private branch exchange, a telephone switching system that serves one company (usually), is located on the company's premises, and connects to the national telephone network.

**Personal Computer**   A computer (including elements such as a keyboard, a display, memory, and computational elements) provided for the use of one person and remaining idle when that person is not using it.

**Phase Modulation (PM)**   A method of transmission whereby the angle of phase of the carrier wave is varied in accordance with the signal.

**Physical Address**   A grouping of numbers that identifies a particular piece of computer hardware connected to a local area network or other data communication system. Contrast with *Logical Address*.

**Physical Level**   The bottom-most layer of the ISO layered model of protocols. The physical layer involves the electrical process of getting data from one point to another.

**Point-to-Point**   (1) A network configuration in which a connection is established between two, and only two, points. The connection may include switching facilities. (2) A circuit connecting two points without the use of any intermediate terminal or computer. Contrast with *Multipoint Line*.

**Polling**   A method of controlling access to a shared communications facility by sending messages, addressed to each station sharing access to the facility, inquiring whether that station has any data to send.

**Presentation Level**   The sixth level of the ISO layered model of protocols. This level and those below it perform services for the top level, the applications level.

**Primary Station**   (1) The station that at any given instant has the right to select and transmit information to a secondary station and the responsibility to ensure information transfer. There should be only one primary station on a data link at one time. (2) A station that controls a data link at a given instant. The assignment of primary status to a given station is temporary and is governed by standardized control procedures. Primary status is normally conferred upon a station so that it may transmit a message, but a station need not have a message to be nominated primary station.

**Protocol**   A formal set of conventions governing the format and relative timing of message exchange between two communicating processes.

**PTT (Post, Telephone, and Telegraph Authority)**   The governmental agency that functions as the communications common carrier in most areas of the world except North America.

**Quantization Error**   In the process of converting an analog signal into digital data, the difference between the signal level as expressed by the digital value and the actual analog value. Since an analog signal can have an infinite number of values, it cannot be expressed absolutely accurately without an infinite number of bits. Since that is impractical, some round-off error must occur in choosing the digital value nearest the analog value.

**Radial Wiring**   Wiring in which all wire runs from a common point to the point requiring service by the most direct means possible.

**Random Error**   An error that varies in a random fashion (e.g., an error resulting from radio static).

**Redundancy**   In a protocol, the portion of the total characters or bits that can be eliminated without any loss of information.

**Redundant Circuits**   Two (or more) circuits designed to perform the same task: one used to perform the task and the other standing by to take over performance of the task should the first one fail.

**Regulatory Agency**   In data communication, an agency controlling common and specialized carrier tariffs. In the United States, the Federal Communications Commission (FCC) and the state public utility commissions.

**Relay**   An electromechanical device consisting of an electromagnet whose magnetic field operates a set of contacts that establish and interrupt electrical circuits. Also, an electronic system that receives information and passes it on.

**Remote Station**   In a multipoint system, this is synonymous with *tributary station*. In a point-to-point switched network, a station that can be called by the central station or can call the central station if it has a message to send.

**Repeater**   A device used at the physical level of the ISO layered model of communications protocols that amplifies or otherwise conditions signals received from one piece of a transmission medium and passes them on to another similar piece of a transmission medium without reading the addresses or the data content. Also called a *level 1 relay* or *physical level relay*.

**Response Time**   The elapsed time between the generation of the last character of a message at a terminal and the receipt of the first character of the reply. It includes terminal delay, network delay, and service node delay.

**Retransmission**   A method of error control in which stations receiving messages acknowledge the receipt of correct messages and either do not acknowledge or acknowledge in the negative for the receipt of incorrect messages. The lack of acknowledgment or receipt of negative acknowledgment is an indication to the sending station that it should transmit the failed message again. Retransmission is preferable to methods that repair a few damaged bits by sending special codes because typical communications lines have bursts of errors that severely damage an occasional message rather than slightly damage many messages.

**Reverse Channel**   A channel used for transmission of supervisory or error-control signals. The direction of flow of these signals is in the direction opposite that in which information is being transferred. The bandwidth of this channel is usually less than that of the forward channel (i.e., the information channel).

**Reverse Interrupt (RVI)**   In binary synchronous communications, a control character sequence (DLE sequence) sent by a receiving station instead of ACK1 or ACK0 to request premature termination of the transmission in progress.

**Ring**   A local area network topology in which each station is connected to two other stations, with this process repeated until a loop is formed. Data is transmitted from station to station around the loop, always in the same direction.

**Ring Buffers**   A method of storing data in memory such that the same locations in memory are being constantly reused. A "write pointer" specifies where new data is to be written, and a "read pointer" specifies the next location to be read. When all locations have been read or written, the process resumes ("wraps around") and starts at the beginning of the block of memory being used. Obviously, the write pointer must not be allowed to write over data not yet written, and the read pointer must not point to locations not yet rewritten since the last read. This system is also used with linked list headers arranged as ring buffers, in which case the write and read pointers complement a single bit in the header indicating whether the data buffer pointed to by the header has been read or written.

**Routing**    The process of determining how to forward a packet toward its destination, based on tables that indicate costs, congestion status, and other factors associated with possible routes.

**SDLC (Synchronous Data Link Control)**    Synchronous Data Link Control, an IBM data link layer protocol in which data is transmitted with a zero inserted after each consecutive group of five ones, except for a distinctive flag pattern (01111110), which delineates the beginning and end of a frame. This protocol is very similar to HDLC, but the header limits the addressing and message numbering to fewer bits.

**Secondary Station**    A station that has been selected to receive a transmission from the primary station. The assignment of secondary status is temporary, under control of the primary station, and continues for the duration of a transmission.

**Serial Transmission**    A method of transmission in which each bit of information is sent sequentially on a single channel rather than simultaneously as in parallel transmission.

**Server**    A program, and possibly a dedicated computer system, that provides a service to local area network users, such as shared access to a file system, control of a printer, or the storage of messages in a mail system.

**Short Circuit**    An electrical system in which current flows directly from one conductor to the other without passing through the device(s) that are supposed to receive the current.

**Signal Conversion Device**    An electrical circuit that changes electrical signals from one form to another. For example, from TTL levels to light for transmission through a fiber-optic system.

**Signal Element**    Each part of a digital signal, distinguished from others by its duration, position, and/or sense. In start-stop operation, a signal element has a minimum duration of one unit interval. If several unit intervals of the same sense run together, a signal element of duration of more than one unit element may be formed. Signal elements may be start elements, information elements, or stop elements.

**Signal-to-Noise Ratio (SNR)**    Relative power of the signal to the noise in a channel, usually measured in decibels.

**Silo**   A first-in/first-out (FIFO) buffer.

**Simplex Mode**   Operation of a channel in one direction only with no capability of reversing.

**Slave**   A remote system or terminal whose functions are controlled by a central "master" system.

**SNA**   Systems Network Architecture, IBM's layered communications protocols.

**Software**   A set of computer programs, procedures, rules, and associated documentation concerned with the operation of computers—e.g., compilers, monitors, editors, utility programs. Contrast with *Hardware*.

**SOH (Start of Header)**   A communications control character used at the beginning of a sequence of characters that constitutes a machine-sensible address or routine information. Such a sequence is referred to as the *header*.

**Source Address**   That part of a message that indicates from whom the message originated.

**Space Division Switch**   In telephone switching, a system in which each conversation takes a physically identifiable path that is not shared by any other conversation. Contrast with *Time Division Switching*.

**Spine Network**   In local area networks, a network to which users' computers and network servers do not connect directly. Instead, users' computers and network servers connect to access networks, and the access networks are connected via gateways to the spine, thus providing interconnection of the access networks.

**Standards**   Documents that describe an agreed-upon way of doing things such that independent groups or companies can design and build hardware, firmware, software, or combinations thereof and have them work with similar products built by others.

**Star**   A local area network topology in which all stations are wired to a central station that establishes, maintains, and breaks connections between the stations. Also descriptive of wiring systems in which radial wiring is used, although the control of connections is established in some other fashion.

**Start Element**   In start-stop transmission, the first element in each character, which serves to prepare the receiving equipment for the reception and registration of the character.

**Start-Stop Transmission**   Asynchronous transmission in which a group of code elements corresponding to a character signal is preceded by a start element and is followed by a stop element.

**Station**   That independently controllable configuration of data terminal equipment from or to which messages are transmitted on a data link. It includes those elements that serve as sources or sinks for the messages, as well as those elements that control the message flow on the link by means of data communication control procedures. See also *Terminal*.

**Stop Element**    In start-stop transmission, the last element in each character, to which is assigned a minimum duration, during which the receiving equipment is reset in preparation for the reception of the next character.

**STX (Start of Text)**    A communications control character preceding a sequence of characters that is to be treated as an entity and entirely transmitted through to the ultimate destination. Such a sequence is referred to as *text*. STX may be used to terminate a sequence of characters (heading) started by SOH.

**Switched Line**    A communications link for which the physical path may vary with each usage—e.g., the dial-up telephone network.

**SYN (Synchronous Idle)**    Character used as a time fill in the absence of any data or control character to maintain synchronization. The sequence of two continuous SYNs is used to establish synchronization (character phase) following each line turnaround.

**Synchronous Transmission**    Transmission in which the data characters and bits are transmitted at a fixed rate with the transmitter and receiver synchronized. This eliminates the need for start-stop elements, thus providing greater efficiency. Compare *Asynchronous Transmission*.

**Systematic Error**    A constant error or one that varies in a systematic manner (e.g., equipment misalignment).

**T1 Carrier**    A time division multiplex transmission system introduced by the Bell System in 1962. Eight thousand times per second, an 8-bit sample from each of 24 voice channels is transmitted, along with a framing bit whose binary sense varies in a prescribed fashion. The transmission of 193 bits 8,000 times per second produces a 1.544-megabit transmission rate.

**Tandem Exchange**    A telephone switching office that handles traffic between local exchanges.

**Tariff**    1) A published rate for services provided by a common or specialized carrier. 2) The means by which regulatory agencies approve such services. The tariff is part of a contract between customer and carrier.

**Teletype**    Trademark of Teletype Corporation. Usually refers to one of their series of teleprinters.

**Telex Service**    A worldwide teletypewriter exchange service.

**Terminal**    An input/output device consisting of at least a keyboard and a display (paper or video), intended for human interaction with a computer. A "dumb terminal" consists only of the parts mentioned above, while a "smart terminal" contains some computer functions, such as editing and message formatting.

**Terminator**    An electrical device that can be attached to the end of a cable to simulate the attachment of an infinite amount of additional cable. If this device has the same impedance as the cable, signals arriving at the end of the cable will not experience an impedance discontinuity, and signal reflections will not be created.

**Text**    (1) A sequence of characters forming part of a transmission that is sent from the data source to the data sink and contains the information to be conveyed. It may be preceded by a header and followed by an "End of Text" signal. (2) In ASCII as well as in general communications usage, a sequence of characters treated as an entity if preceded by a "Start of Text" and followed by an "End of Text" control character.

**Tie Line**    A private line communications channel of the type provided by common carriers for linking two or more points together.

**Time Division Multiplexing**    A method of sharing a transmission facility among many users by allocating short periods of time for each pair of transmitting and receiving stations using the facility.

**Time Division Switching**    A method of switching data or voice that has been encoded (see *Encoding*) into the form of data. Buses within the switch are shared by time division multiplexing. Logic circuits sample data from one bus, store it, and deposit it on another bus (or on the same bus at a different time) to achieve the switching function.

**Time-Sharing**    A method of operation in which a computer facility is shared by several users for different purposes at (apparently) the same time. Although the computer actually services each user in sequence, the high speed of the computer makes it appear that users are all handled simultaneously.

**Token**    In a local area network, a unique combination of bits, the receipt of which indicates permission to transmit.

**Token Bus**    The use of a token to control access to a bus. A station receiving the token transmits if desired and then forwards the token to a specified next address.

**Token Ring**    The use of a token to control access to a ring. A station receives all messages currently circulating on the ring, followed by the token. The station may allow everything to pass (copying messages addressed to it and removing any messages it sent), append a message to those circulating, then reinsert the token.

**Touch Tone**    AT&T registered trademark for push-button dialing. The signaling form is multiple tones.

**Transit Exchange**    European version of *tandem exchange*.

**Transmission Medium**    Anything, such as wire, coaxial cable, fiber optics, air, or a vacuum, that is being used to propagate an electrical signal and thus is propagating electrically represented information.

**Transparent Mode**    Transmission of binary data with the recognition of most control characters suppressed. In binary synchronous communications, entry to and exit from the transparent mode is indicated by a sequence beginning with a special Data Link Escape (DLE) character.

**Transport Level**    The fourth layer of the ISO layered model. The transport layer receives the services of protocols located in the network level and below and performs services for the session, presentation, and application levels above.

**Tributary Station**  A station, other than the control station, on a centralized multipoint data communication system that can communicate only with the control station when polled or selected by the control station.

**Trunk**  A single circuit between two points, both of which are switching centers or individual distribution points.

**TTD (Temporary Text Delay)**  In binary synchronous communications, a control character sequence (STX . . . ENQ) sent by a transmitting station either to indicate a delay in transmission or to initiate an abort of the transmission in progress.

**TTL**  Transistor–transistor logic, descriptive of the electronic circuits used in typical computers.

**Turnaround Time**  In communications, the time required to reverse the direction of transmission from sender to receiver or vice versa when using a two-way alternate circuit. Time is required by line propagation effects, modem timing, and computer response.

**Twisted Pair**  Two insulated wires wrapped one about the other in a uniform fashion so that each is equally exposed to electrical signals impinging upon the wires from their environment. The pair may be surrounded by a shield, a jacket of additional insulation, or similar pairs of wires.

**Two-Way Alternate Operation**  A mode of operation of a data link in which data may be transmitted in both directions, one way at a time. Also called *half-duplex operation* (U.S.).

**Two-Way Simultaneous Operation**  A mode of operation of a data link in which data may be transmitted simultaneously in both directions over two channels. Note: One of the channels is equipped for transmission in one direction, while the other is equipped for transmission in the opposite direction. Also called *full duplex* or *duplex*.

**Unit Interval**  A unit interval is the duration of the shortest nominal signal element, the minimum period between two significant instants (i.e., the minimum time between changes of signal state). It may also be thought of as the longest interval of time such that the nominal durations of the signal elements in a synchronous system or the start and information elements in a start-stop system are whole multiples of this interval. The duration of the unit interval (in seconds) is the reciprocal of the transmission speed, expressed in baud.

**USASCII**  See *ASCII*.

**Value Added Service**  A communications service utilizing common carrier networks for transmission and providing added data services with separate additional equipment. Such added service features may be store and forward message switching, terminal interfacing, and host interfacing.

**Virtual Circuit** A system that delivers packets in guaranteed sequential order, just as they would arrive over a real point-to-point electrical circuit.

**VLSI** Very large scale integration, the art of putting hundreds of thousands of transistors into a single integrated circuit, typically a quarter inch square.

**Voice-Grade Channel** A channel used for speech transmission, usually with an audio frequency range of 300 to 3400 Hz. It is also used for transmission of analog and digital data. Up to 18,000 bps can be transmitted on a voice-grade channel.

**Voltage** A measure of electrical potential, expressed in volts, named after Count Alessandro Volta.

**VRC (Vertical Redundancy Check)** A check or parity bit added to each character in a message such that the number of bits in each character, including the parity bit, is odd (odd parity) or even (even parity).

**WACK (Wait Before Transmitting Positive Acknowledgment)** In binary synchronous communications, this sequence is sent by a receiving station to indicate that it is temporarily not ready to receive.

**WATS (Wide Area Telephone Service)** A service provided by telephone companies in the United States that permits a customer to make calls to or from telephones in specific zones for a flat monthly charge. The monthly charge is based on size of the zone instead of number of calls. WATS may be used on a measured-time or full-time basis.

**Waveform** The pattern made on a piece of paper or other display when the voltage of a signal is plotted as a function of time.

**Wideband** Communications channel having a bandwidth greater than a voice-grade channel.

**Windows** A method of displaying information on a screen in which the viewer sees what appears to be several sheets of paper much as they would appear on a desktop. The viewer can shift the positions of the sheets on the screen. The system is particularly attractive for working on several related tasks, or portions of the same task, simultaneously.

**Word** (1) In telegraphy, six characters (five characters plus one space). (2) In computing, an ordered set of characters that is the normal unit in which information may be stored, transmitted, or operated on within a computer.

**Word Processing** The use of a computer, especially a personal computer, to assist in composing, editing, formatting, and printing memorandums, letters, books, or other text material.

*Index*

# Index

Abandon Call (ACR), 104
Abandon call timer, 104
Abort, 199, 204–205
Access methods, defined, 339
Access network, defined, 339
ACK, 188, 189, 192
  packets, 191
ACK0, ACK1 (Affirmative
  Acknowledgment), 179, 180
  defined, 339
Acoustic coupler, defined, 339
Active interface, defined, 339
Adaptive packet assembly, 225
Address, defined, 339
Addressed call mode, 105–111
Address fields, defined, 339
Address leads
  in UART, 12
  in USRT, 157
Algorithm, defined, 339
ALOHA network, 271–272
Alternate buffer, 217
Alternate Mark Inversion (AMI), 231
Alternate route, defined, 340
Alternate Voice, 291–292
Amplifiers
  digital vs. analog, 232
  four-wire, 39–40
Amplitude modulation (AM), 146–147
  defined, 340
Analog amplifiers, 232

Analog/digital conversion, 226
Analog samples, 227–228
Analog signals, defined, 340
Analog transmission, 39
  vs. digital transmission, 232
ANSI, 336
Answer Mode, 44, 291
Answer mode modems, 95, 97
Application layer, 173, 340
ARPANET, 236
ASCII, 4, 176, 177, 179
  defined, 340
  sync character, 143
Associate memory, 211
Asymmetrical full duplex operation, 92
Asynchronous communications, 1–10
  codes for, 3–4
  defined, 1, 3, 340
  DMA reception in, 210–211
  format and speed table for, 316–319
  history of, 2–3
  use of, 2
Asynchronous modems
  chip circuitry, 4–10
  error-correcting, 223
  low-speed full-duplex switched network
    modems, 86–87
  private lines and, 43–44
  for switched network use, 94–100
  vs. synchronous modems, 145–146
  *See also* Modems